The New Sadlier Geography Series

SOUTHERN
NEIGHBORS

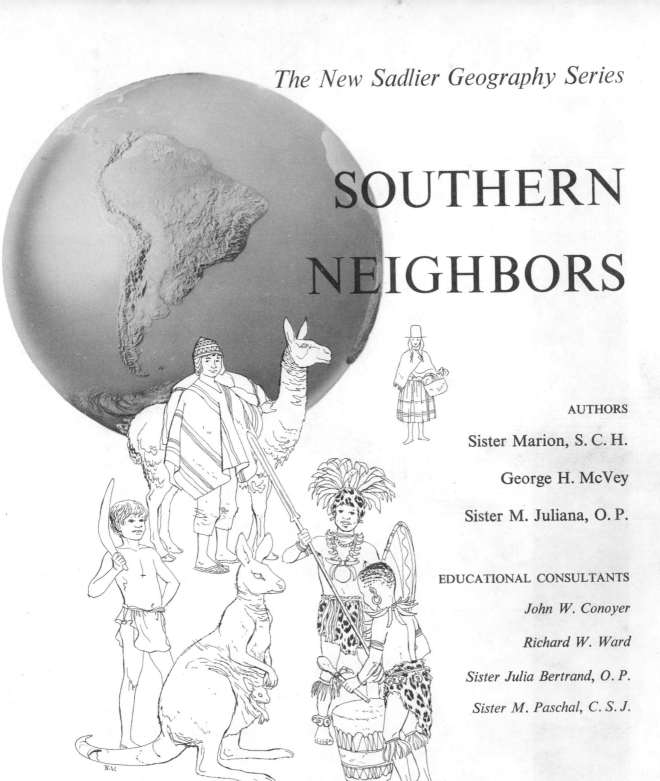

AUTHORS

Sister Marion, S. C. H.

George H. McVey

Sister M. Juliana, O. P.

EDUCATIONAL CONSULTANTS

John W. Conoyer

Richard W. Ward

Sister Julia Bertrand, O. P.

Sister M. Paschal, C. S. J.

W. H. Sadlier, Inc.

New York, Chicago

CONTENTS

P R 7—8-67 VB CU
AUGUST PRINTING 1967

MAPS

Product Maps

Global Maps

Comparative Area Maps

Political Maps (atlas)

Physical-Political Maps Page

Other Maps

FEATURES

Page

At exactly twelve noon, on the deck of a ship sailing across the wide Pacific Ocean, a strange ceremony takes place. The "court of Davy Jones" is in session. An old sailor is dressed as Davy Jones, the legendary king of the ocean. He is assigning harsh "punishments" to younger members of the crew. Other sailors are joining in the fun, teasing the victims of Davy Jones' strange justice.

The victims are called "pollywogs." They have to scrub decks, shave their heads, and perform all sorts of silly tasks. This is an initiation ceremony, and it has long been a tradition among seafaring men. The ship has just crossed the equator. All those men who have never crossed the equator—the "pollywogs"—are now becoming "shellbacks." This means that they have now had the experience of crossing the equator. From now on, they will be proud to be shellbacks, and will tease other pollywogs on future voyages.

Crossing the equator has a special meaning for sailors. It has a special meaning for us, too. We who have lived all our lives in the Northern Hemisphere will find in the pages of this book some of the attraction and excitement that people have always found in Southern Seas and Southern Lands.

Thinking About Geography. *Geography* means the study of the earth and its people. Last year you studied the geography of Eurasia. You learned that most of the lands of Eurasia are in the Northern Hemisphere. This year, you will study the geography of the Southern Hemisphere. In order to study geography correctly, you must follow certain principles, or guides. Plan to use these principles as you study.

Location. By location, we mean the position occupied by a continent, a country, a region, or a city—where it is situated, or placed. The location of a region tells much about the region. Look for details such as nearness to the equator, boundaries, and trade routes. For each region you study, make yourself familiar with its location by using your classroom globe, the maps in this book, and other aids.

Climate. Climate is the kind of weather a place has over a long period of time. In the same way that the weather affects you, climate affects people all over the world. It has an influence on people's choice of a place to live, how they make their living, and how they clothe and house themselves and their families. You can learn a great deal about people by studying the ways in which they adjust to different, and sometimes unpleasant, climate conditions.

Surface Features. A very important principle to keep in mind as you study each new country is the appearance of its surface. Mountains, hills, plains, valleys, grasslands, and plateaus are some of the kinds of surface features you will find. Notice the way in which each of these has a strong effect on the way people live and work, and on the climate which they enjoy.

Natural Resources. By natural resources we mean anything of use or value placed within a region by God. Wherever these gifts are plentiful, and man uses them wisely, people are better off. Not all countries, however, have equal amounts of these blessings. The United States has been generously supplied with these gifts; other countries are not so fortunate.

Trade and Transportation. In many places, people have learned to make up for a lack of resources by trading with other countries. In this way, the family of men around the world share the blessings of God upon the earth. Transportation includes all the means which people have for moving goods back and forth in trade, and for moving themselves from place to place. You will learn, for example, that the airplane is fast becoming important in the transportation of goods and people throughout the Southern Hemisphere.

Occupations and Cities. The work which men choose often depends upon the natural resources, transportation, location, and climate of their region. Knowing the occupations of people in other lands helps us understand them. Many people are occupied in farming. They grow the food which people need to live. More and more, however, people's work is bringing them together in cities. You will be interested to see the kinds of cities in which your Southern neighbors live.

The People. You must always keep in mind that your study of geography is a study of people in different parts of the world. Understanding the geography of a country is only important when it helps us understand the people. How the people govern themselves, how they worship God, how they educate their children, how they amuse themselves and express themselves in literature and art are also important. Your study of geography this year will be successful if you have learned more about the people who are your neighbors to the South.

LET'S LEARN ABOUT SOUTH AMERICA

When we say, "I am an American," we mean, "I am a citizen of the United States of America." We often use the word America to mean our country, the United States. North America really is a continent which includes many countries besides the United States. South America is another continent to the southeast, which is joined to North America by a narrow strip of land.

Our neighbors in South America can also say, "I am an American." Like us, they live and work in America. As we study the fascinating continent of South America, we shall be learning more and more about these people. We shall learn that their lives and our lives are closely tied. We trade valuable goods and services with them and we share with them a deep interest in world peace. In addition, we send them, from our established schools and parishes, priests, Brothers, and Sisters to strengthen the Church where conditions in South America have slowed its growth.

We shall find also that South Americans, like people everywhere, enjoy their share of God's blessings on this earth. South America is a continent of vast resources. Minerals, petroleum, rubber, coffee, wheat, corn, and meat are some of the many products which South Americans enjoy, and which they share with us and others in the family of neighbors throughout the world.

At first glance, our neighbors of South America seem different from our neighbors at home. Indians and descendants of Indians live in many South American lands, in some places outnumbering the white population. There are Negroes in different parts of South America, as well as recent immigrants from Europe and Asia, and descendants of the original Spanish and Portuguese settlers. Many of these different peoples live and work in close harmony, showing a truly Christian respect for each other.

1

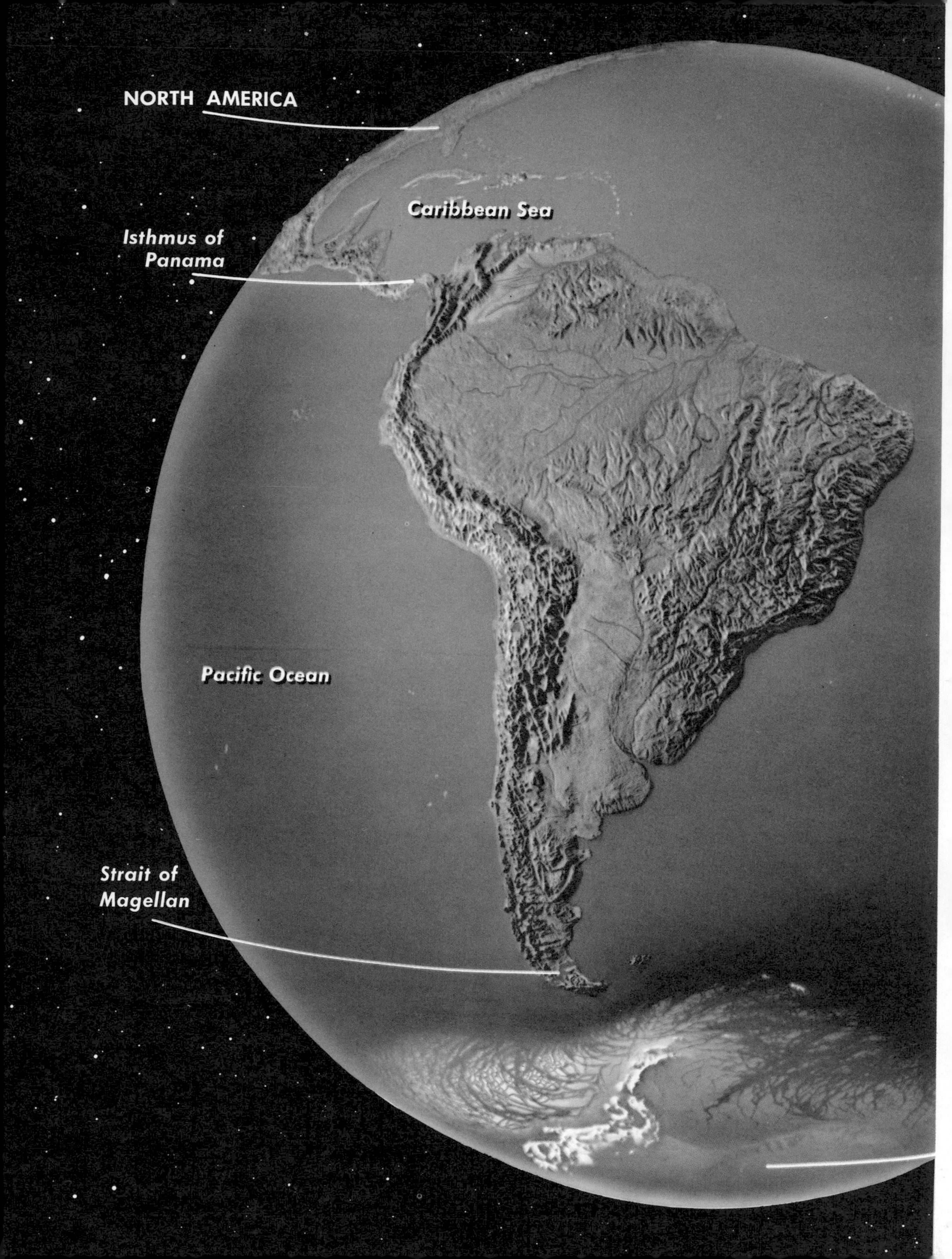

NORTH AMERICA

Caribbean Sea

Isthmus of
Panama

Pacific Ocean

Strait of
Magellan

AFRICA

Atlantic Ocean

ANTARCTICA

SOUTH AMERICA

Here you see all the land and water features of South America, and some other parts of the Western Hemisphere as well. South America is linked in the north by the Isthmus of Panama to North America. Also to the north are the Caribbean Sea, the West Indies, Central America, and the United States.

The Atlantic Ocean washes the entire eastern coast of South America. 1600 miles to the east is the western coast of Africa. The Pacific Ocean is west of South America. It joins with the Atlantic at the Strait of Magellan in the south, and with the Caribbean at the Panama Canal. In the extreme south you see the icy wastes of Antarctica.

A spiny chain of mountains can be traced, running from North America down the western coast of South America, where it becomes the Andes Mountains. Two other groups of lower mountains can also be seen—the Guiana Highlands in the north and the Brazilian Highlands in the east.

A green area extends almost the entire width of the northern section. It is a vast rain forest, drained by the mighty Amazon River flowing eastward to the Atlantic. Another large river system, the Paraguay-Paraná, flows southward toward the Atlantic.

Surface Features. Look at a globe, and locate the continent of South America. It is to the south and east of the continent of North America. Now refer to the map of the world in your atlas. You will discover that the shape and surface of South America resemble those of North America in many ways. Both continents are shaped like a triangle—wide toward the north and very narrow in the south. Both continents have old, worn-down mountains in the east and young, high mountains in the west.

World's Largest Mountain Lake. These Indian girls, wearing hats like derbies, walk along the shore of Lake Titicaca high in the Andes Mountains.

The Brazilian Highlands are the low mountains in eastern South America. They are like the Appalachians in the eastern part of the United States.

Rugged mountains extend all the way from Alaska in North America to the southern tip of South America. They are known as the Rocky Mountains in North America and the Andes Mountains in South America. The towering, snow-capped peaks of the Andes lie close to the Pacific Ocean. Though narrower than the Rockies, the Andes are even higher and harder to cross. They form a western barrier to inland travel that is more than 4000 miles long, from the Caribbean coast to Cape Horn.

East of the Andes lies a vast central lowland region. The northern part of these plains is drained by the Amazon River, just as our great central lowland is drained by the mighty Mississippi. Each of these two great rivers has built up a large delta at its mouth. They differ in some respects, however. The Amazon is the longer of the two; in fact, it is one of the longest rivers in the world. It flows through a countryside of sparsely populated tropical forest, while the Mississippi flows through rich and well-populated plains. In addition, the Amazon flows east and empties directly into the Atlantic Ocean, whereas the Mississippi flows south into the Gulf of Mexico.

South America has no deep coastal gulfs or bays like the Gulf of Mexico or Hudson Bay in North America. The coast of South America is quite regular. This means that South America has fewer natural harbors than North America.

Beautiful Lake Titicaca, in the central part of the continent, is the world's largest mountain lake. There is, however, no chain of large lakes in South America to compare with our Great Lakes.

The Climate. The climate over much of South America differs greatly from ours. That part of the earth's surface which lies roughly between the Tropic of Cancer and the Tropic of Capricorn is known as the Tropical Zone, or the low latitudes. In lands of the Tropical Zone, the sun is directly overhead at some time of the year and almost directly overhead at all other times of the year.

Now look at the map of South America on page 6. You will see that more than two thirds of its total area lies in the low latitudes. In most of this section it is hot all year round. The mountainous areas and the Pacific coast areas, however, have a cooler climate than the lowland areas.

Between the Tropical Zone and the two Polar Zones are the two Intermediate Zones, or the middle latitudes. About one third of South America lies in the middle latitudes. Here there is a climate with hot or warm summers and cool or cold winters. This is something like the climate found in North America.

The northern part of the continent of South America has no winter. This is true, of course, of tropical lands in other parts of the world as well. Only in the great heights of the Andean mountains and valleys is there ever any cool weather in this part of South America. The reason is that the thinner air at these heights does not absorb so much of the sun's heat.

In southern South America, the temperatures vary from warm to cool. There are four distinct seasons each year, as in the United States. However, when we have summer, the lands in southern South America have winter. In southern South America, July is a winter month, and January is the warmest month of the year. Try to imagine how it would feel celebrating Christmas in the summertime!

Tropical Rain Forest. After the daily downpour, the blazing sun filters through a heavy cover of leaves onto this quiet stream near the equator.

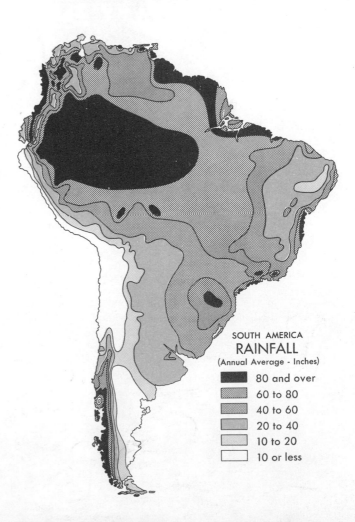

SOUTH AMERICA
RAINFALL
(Annual Average - Inches)

■	80 and over
	60 to 80
	40 to 60
	20 to 40
	10 to 20
□	10 or less

SOUTH AMERICA

Capital Cities .... ◎

	over 10,000
	5,000 to 10,000
	2,000 to 5,000
	1,000 to 2,000
	0 to 1,000
	Below Sea Level

ELEVATIONS IN FEET

International Boundaries ▬▬▬

Scale of Miles

0   200   400   600

CARIBBEAN SEA

NETH. ANTILLES

ATLANTIC

MIDDLE AMERICA

Barranquilla
Santa Marta
Cartagena
Maracaibo
Valencia
La Guaira
Caracas
Barquisimeto
Ciudad Bolívar
Port of Spain
TRINIDAD (British)
Delta of the Orinoco

Panamá Canal
Colón
Panamá
Gulf of Panamá
Medellín
Bucaramanga
Buenaventura
Bogotá
COLOMBIA
Cali

VENEZUELA
GUIANA HIGHLANDS
Orinoco R.
Georgetown
Paramaribo
BRITISH GUIANA
SURINAM (Neth.)
FRENCH GUIANA
Cayenne

EQUATOR

Mt. Cotopaxi
Mt. Chimborazo
Quito
Guayaquil
ECUADOR
Cuenca
Gulf of Guayaquil
Talara
Iquitos
Napo R.
Marañón
Japurá R.
Rio Negro
Manaus
Delta of the Amazon
Pará R.
MARAJÓ I.
Belém
São Luíz
Fortaleza
Natal

Amazon R.
Juruá R.
Purús R.
Madeira R.
Tapajóz R.
Xingú R.
Tocantins R.
BRAZILIAN HIGHLANDS
Recife
Maceió

Cerro de Pasco
Callao
Lima
Cuzco
PERU
Mamoré R.
Guaporé R.
BRAZIL
São Francisco R.
Salvador

Arequipa
Matarani
Mollendo
Puno
L. Titicaca
La Paz
Guaqui
Oruro
Mt. Illimani
Cochabamba
BOLIVIA
Sucre
Poopó
Potosí
Brasília
Diamantina
Belo Horizonte
Arica
Iquique
ALTIPLANO
Chuquicamata

TROPIC OF CAPRICORN

Antofagasta
ATACAMA DESERT
Salta
Bermejo R.
Pilcomayo R.
Salado R.
CHACO
PARAGUAY
Asunción
Villarrica
Paraguay R.
Paraná R.
Tieté R.
Mt. Itatiaia
Volta Redonda
Petrópolis
Rio de Janeiro
Niterói
São Paulo
Santos
Curitiba
Iguassú Falls

Tucumán
Corrientes
Posadas
Uruguay R.
Pôrto Alegre
Lagoa dos Patos

El Tofo
Cruz Grande
Córdoba
Santa Fe
Paraná
Valparaíso
San Juan
Mt. Aconcagua
Mendoza
Rosario
Fray Bentos
Salto
Paysandú
URUGUAY
Mercedes
Montevideo
Buenos Aires
Avellaneda
La Plata
Rio de la Plata

JUAN FERNÁNDEZ IS. (Chile)
Chillán
Concepción
Bío-Bío R.
Santiago
ARGENTINA
PAMPAS
Bahía Blanca
Colorado R.
Negro R.
Gulf of San Matías

Valdivia
Puerto Montt
CHILOE I.
Chubut R.
ANDES
Puerto Aysén

WELLINGTON I.

Punta Arenas
Strait of Magellan
TIERRA DEL FUEGO
Ushuaia
Cape Horn
Port Stanley
FALKLAND IS. (British)

LONGITUDE WEST FROM GREENWICH

SOUTH GEORGIA I. (British)

PACIFIC OCEAN

ATLANTIC OCEAN

Studying the Map

A. 1. Is any part of South America directly south of any part of North America? (See the world map, Plate 1, in the Atlas at the back of this book.) **2.** What large sea lies north of South America? **3.** Which ocean borders eastern and northeastern South America? western South America? **4.** Both the equator and the Tropic of Capricorn cross South America. In what climatic zone is the northern part of the continent? the southern part? **5.** Use the scale of miles to measure the distance across South America along the equator. **6.** How far is it from the Caribbean coast to the southern tip of South America? **7.** Name the famous strait which separates Tierra del Fuego from South America.

B. 1. How does the surface of eastern South America compare with that of the western part of the continent? **2.** Name the mountain chain running the entire length of South America. Through which countries does this mountain chain extend? **3.** Use the map key to compare elevations in the Andes. In which countries are the elevations the highest? **4.** Use the map key to locate the principal lowland areas of South America. Name the river or rivers which drain each of these lowlands. **5.** Name the desert area along the western coast of South America.

C. 1. Name the important South American river located near the equator. Compare it with the Mississippi in length, direction of flow, and number of tributaries. **2.** Find the Orinoco River in northern South America. In which direction does it flow? Into which body of water does it empty? **3.** In which direction does the Magdalena River flow? Into which body of water does it empty? **4.** Find the Paraná and Uruguay Rivers. Into which body of water do they flow? **5.** The largest lake in South America lies high in the Andes, on the border between Peru and Bolivia. What is the name of this lake? How high is it above sea level?

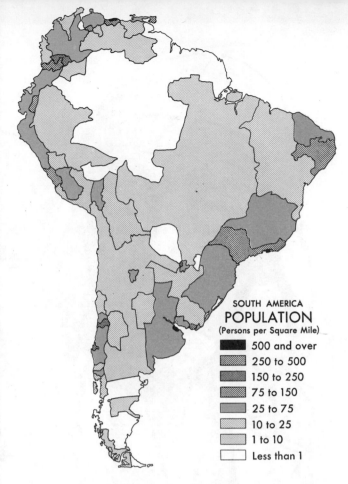

SOUTH AMERICA
POPULATION
(Persons per Square Mile)

- 500 and over
- 250 to 500
- 150 to 250
- 75 to 150
- 25 to 75
- 10 to 25
- 1 to 10
- Less than 1

Where the People Live. The population map on this page shows that most South Americans live near the coast. Few live in the interior. Colors are used on the map to show the number of people living in a certain area. This is called the *density of population*.

The solid black area represents 500 people per square mile. Where this color appears, many people are living close together. This usually occurs in towns and cities, or on large plantations. Where the shades of blue appear, there are fewer people. Notice that there are few people in the lowlands of northern South America.

In tropical South America more people live in the highlands than on the lowland plains because the highland climate is cooler. Part of the Andes and the Brazilian Highlands have larger populations than the nearby coastal plains.

THE PEOPLE OF
SOUTH AMERICA

The Way the People Look. In South America, as in all places, the people are of different appearances — rich and poor, young and old, gay and sad.

Thousands of years ago, many small groups of people from Asia and the islands of the western Pacific crossed the ocean. After many months, they reached the shores of North America and South America. In South America, as in North America, some became highly civilized and built peaceful nations. Others remained wandering savages, war-like and cruel. Columbus, thinking he had sailed around the world to India, called these people "Indians" when he first saw them. That is the name we know them by.

Most of the people who followed Columbus to South America were from Spain. Some were from Portugal. Spain and Portugal are "Latin" countries, and today we call South America and part of North America by the name, "Latin America." This is because the Spanish and Portuguese left such a strong impression upon the lands in which they settled throughout the New World.

The Spanish and Portuguese wanted the Indians to work for them on farms and plantations. When the Indians refused, Negroes were brought by force from Africa and used as slaves. Of course, slavery has long been abandoned; the Negroes in South America now live in freedom together with the Indians, the Spanish, and the Portuguese.

Not very long ago, a fourth group arrived. When the countries of South America declared their independence, immigrant families from many different countries of Europe came to settle in the new free lands, just as they did in our country. They helped build the railroads and the modern cities, settle the farms, and work in the growing industries.

Today in South America descendants of

all of these groups live together. Because the early Spanish and Portuguese settlers often married Indian women, there are many people in South America with both Indian and European ancestors. Look at the pictures of the different kinds of people you see in these pages. Their features, clothes, and activities demonstrate a varied background of Indian, Latin, Negro, and European influence. This is what makes them very colorful, handsome, and interesting people.

One thing the varied people of South America have in common. In most of the countries a very large number of people are Roman Catholics. In some countries the Catholics among the population outnumber the members of all other religious groups.

This is mostly due to the tremendous influence of Spain and Portugal, two Catholic countries. When explorers, settlers, and soldiers came from these two countries, they were accompanied by many missionaries. The priests devoted their lives to converting the Indians and establishing a strong Church

The Past and the Present. The young Indian (above) celebrates a holiday of his ancestors. The two boys (right) are looking toward the future.

in the New World. Several saints of the Church came from lands you are soon going to study.

During the last 150 years, however, many changes have occurred. The countries of South America achieved their independence from Spain and Portugal—some violently and some peacefully. When they did, Spanish priests either left or were driven out. The result was that the Church in South America was left without priests. Many churches, and most schools were abandoned. Many people did their best to continue the practice of their Faith. However, without priests to say Mass and administer the sacraments, the faith of the people was often weakened. Superstition often took the place of Faith.

Many missionary priests from the United States and other countries are busy in South America today, helping to restore the Church. Native South American priests are badly needed. We should pray that the true Faith will be restored in all its glory throughout South America.

At Work and at Play. The young men (above) are not fishing, but helping build a drainage canal. The Peruvian girl (left) laughs during a game.

Powerful Invaders. Here a group of invading Conquistadors approach an Incan village. The Indians, fearing the armed soldiers, have fled.

Early Settlers. Spanish and Portuguese explorers began to arrive in South America soon after the first voyage of Columbus in 1492. Crossing the Atlantic Ocean in those days was an adventure for bold and daring men. The ocean voyage was long and dangerous. The American continents were still an unmapped wilderness. Only a few brave people were willing to risk their lives in such a dangerous enterprise.

Among the first to come were the soldier-adventurers in search of gold. These men had heard stories, from Columbus and other explorers, about the riches of the New World. There have always been men who would risk their lives crossing deserts or oceans, wage war, lie, steal, cheat, or even murder for gold. Many good men were among the gold-seekers who arrived early in South America. In spite of their efforts, others treated the native Indians cruelly, cheated them, and stole their gold.

Another class of men were just as bold and daring as the gold-seekers. They were the missionary priests who came with every fleet that reached South America. They came seeking souls for God's kingdom. Often the missioners used their influence to save the Indians from slavery or death at the hands of the rough soldiers and pioneers. The missioners helped to civilize and educate everywhere on the continent. The conversion of South America's Indians was one of the great missionary achievements of all time.

The Incas. The Spaniards who arrived in Panama with Balboa heard of a nation of civilized Indian people called the Incas. The Incas lived in the highland areas of western South America. Tales of their wealth aroused interest and ambition among the Spanish adventurers.

In 1531, almost forty years after the first voyage of Columbus, Francisco Pizarro led a small army of Spanish soldiers through the jungle areas of northern South America, into the mountainous Incan territory.

Pizarro was one of the most famous *conquistadors,* or Spanish soldier-adventurers, ever to come to the New World.

High in the mountains of Peru lay the Indian city of Cuzco. Here the Indian emperor, called the *Inca,* ruled his people. These people were pagans who worshiped the sun as though it were God. They looked upon the Inca as a god-child of the sun.

The Inca with his soldiers, his nobles, and his pagan priests kept the common people in bondage. In the Incan civilization, each man was given a definite job to do. Some tended herds or built roads; others made pottery, mined silver, wove wool, or raised crops. In return for his labor, each man received food and clothing for his family. People had to do as they were told, or starve. No one but the emperor, the nobles, and the pagan priests had any voice in the government. It was really an ancient dictatorship. There was no democracy among the Incas.

When Pizarro reached the lands of the Incas, his soldiers were helped by the fine roads that the Incan laborers had built. With less than 200 men and twenty-five horses, Pizarro made a surprise attack. His men were clever, veteran soldiers, well-trained in the use of their weapons. Steel

Building the New Upon the Old. A Catholic Church was built up from the original stones of the ancient Incan temple which are underneath it.

armor, horses, and guns were new to the Incan Indians. In a short time Pizarro's small army had captured the Inca and defeated six thousand of his Indian warriors. Without its leaders the empire of the Incas fell apart. Pizarro missed a golden opportunity, however. He overthrew the Incan civilization but neglected to replace it with a good Christian society.

The Incan Civilization. In this picture you can see what the villages of the Incas looked like before the Europeans arrived in South America.

A Spanish Church in the New World. Spanish builders showed their preference for square towers and arched doorways in churches like this.

The Spanish in Peru. Spain became master of Peru. A Spanish colony sprang up in the land of the Incas. Pizarro built a new capital city called Lima where the Spanish governor would live. There the settlers

A Portuguese Church in the New World. Contrast this picture with the one at the top of the page. They show two varieties of the Latin culture.

built fine houses as well as churches and government buildings. By 1551 the University of San Marco, the first in the New World, had opened in Lima.

In the colony lived the Spanish masters and their Indian subjects. Soldiers, gold-seekers, and others who came hoping to make their fortune in this part of the New World soon took up residence there, too. The Spanish colony also had many who lived good Christian lives; some were saints. St. Rose of Lima lived there and spent her days talking to God and doing penance for sinners. The heroic archbishop, St. Turibius de Mogrovejo, and the Dominican brother, St. Martin de Porres, accomplished great things for God in Lima. The Spanish Franciscan priest, St. Francis Solano, set out from Lima to preach the word of God to the natives. He journeyed over mountains and deserts, through jungles and swamps. He spent years with savage Indian tribes, learned their languages, and converted them to Christ. The Indians loved to hear St. Francis play his violin. He was safe where no other white man dared to go.

The Portuguese in Brazil. Explorers and sailors from Portugal arrived in South America shortly after the first voyage of Columbus. They landed in what is now called Brazil and claimed it for Portugal. Colonists soon began to settle on the low, level coastal plain along the northeast shore.

When the Portuguese were first arriving in South America, sugar was in great demand in Europe, and it was selling at a high price. The Portuguese settled mostly in a tropical lowland area. They found that the climate there favored the growth of sugar cane. Soon they had started large plantations to raise sugar for the markets of Europe.

Slavery in the New World. The Portuguese planters found difficulty in persuading the native Indians to work on their sugar plantations. To fill the need for laborers, they started to bring in slaves from Africa, and the Spaniards likewise followed this practice. When these slaves began to be sold in South America, a Jesuit missioner, Father Peter Claver, arrived in the New World. The slave ships deposited their human cargo at the city of Cartagena, on the coast of Colombia. Father Claver made that city his headquarters, and spent many years working among the unfortunate captives. He made many converts.

The Indians of South America. Pizarro and his soldiers conquered the Incas of Peru. Warfare between the native Indians and the newly-arrived Europeans broke out in other parts of South America as well. In time, however, this warfare ceased, and the Spaniards and Portuguese learned to live peacefully with the Indians. This is in contrast with the experience of the English settlers in North America. In our country, peace between whites and Indians was rare; whites and Indians seldom lived or worked together. In many parts of South America the Indians had achieved a high degree of civilization. Unlike many of the fierce and primitive tribes of North America, these peaceful people found it possible to live in harmony with the European newcomers.

Spanish missionaries were concerned for the souls of the Indians in South America. They worked among the natives, sharing their homes, their food, and their labor. Young Spanish men often chose Indian girls for their wives because few Spanish women came to the New World. Today, many people in South America are partly Spanish or Portuguese, and partly Indian. They are called *mestizos,* from a Spanish word meaning "mixed."

GOVERNMENT IN SOUTH AMERICA

Most countries of South America have good governments. Their citizens live in peace, and take part in the democratic election of their leaders. This has not always been the case, however.

Just as we in the United States have had our share of dishonest and cheating leaders, crooked or weak governments have risen from time to time in various parts of South America as well. Often it is only by revolution that wicked governments can be overthrown. Only watchful exercise of civic duty on the part of educated people can prevent the evil from happening again. This kind of civic duty is being shown throughout most of South America today.

Pan-American Neighbors. *Pan* means all. When we use the word Pan-American we are talking about all the countries of North America and South America except Canada. A union of these countries was started in 1890. In 1910 the name Pan-American Union became official, but in 1948 it was changed to the Organization of American States. Twenty-one republics of North and South America are its members. The purpose of the Pan-American movement is to promote international peace, friendship, and trade.

For a long period South American merchants traded mostly with Western Europe. During World War II a change was noted. Most of the European markets were closed during the war, and much business was lost. More than ever before, South Americans started trading among themselves and with the United States. The Pan-American Union Building in Washington, D. C., stands as a symbol of the close ties which should bind all of the American nations.

The Airplane and the Americas. In addition to the many shipping lanes, the use of the airplane as a popular means of transportation has hastened progress in South America. The cost and difficulty of highway and railroad construction, especially through high mountains, explains why so many small airlines have sprung up throughout Latin America. Natural barriers like mountains present no difficulty to airplane travel.

The airline map to the left shows the direct flying routes from any of the large cities of the United States to the islands of the Caribbean Sea, to Middle America, and down either coast of South America. For example, it takes nearly three weeks to go by sea from New York City to Buenos Aires in Argentina. The same trip takes only 24 hours by airplane, and even less by jet.

Until recently, the airlines carried only passengers and mail. Today cargo planes are even transporting large amounts of freight back and forth among the countries of both continents.

South America Today. There are eleven independent nations and two European colonies in South America. Guyana, formerly British Guiana, became independent in 1966. It is the first South American country to achieve its independence from a colonial power in this century. Argentina, Brazil, Chile, Colombia, and Uruguay are the most progressive countries. Peru, Bolivia, Venezuela, Ecuador, and Paraguay are the other South American republics.

The two small European colonies are on the north coast of the continent, near Guyana. They are Dutch Guiana, or Surinam, and French Guiana. These colonies have very small populations because of their very hot and moist climate. Their great mineral wealth makes them valuable, however.

In recent years, Communists have appeared in Latin America. They have taken advantage of some governments whose leaders were weak in order to stir up trouble. Today, it is very necessary for the United States to understand its southern neighbors.

We must be willing to offer material help and guidance to overcome the threat of communism south of our border. More than that, we have a Christian duty to help our neighbors in whatever way we can. Charity in this case will have worldly benefits also—we will gain the goodwill of the people of South America, raw materials for our factories, and a vast market for our manufactured goods.

Even more important than material goods, however, is the respect and friendship we can offer to our good neighbors in South America. They want this from us more than anything else.

Neighbors in Northwestern South America

VENEZUELA   COLOMBIA

ECUADOR   PERU

BOLIVIA

**In this Unit
you will learn that:**

1 The Caribbean countries are Venezuela and Colombia. Most of the people in Venezuela and Colombia live in the mountain valleys or the coastal lowlands.

2 Air travel is common because the Andes Mountains present a barrier to land travel. The Orinoco River in Venezuela and the Magdalena River in Colombia are the major inland water routes.

3 Oil, iron, and cattle are the chief products of Venezuela. Gold, platinum, bananas and coffee are the chief products of Colombia.

4 The Andes form a large part of the surface of Ecuador, Peru, and Bolivia. Ecuador and Peru border the Pacific, and Bolivia is an inland country.

5 Ecuador, Peru, and Bolivia also have lowland areas where tropical crops are grown.

6 Most of the population of the Andean countries lives in the highlands.

7 The chief exports of Ecuador are cacao and bananas, while cotton and sugar cane are exports of Peru. Peru also has a great wealth of minerals including copper, vanadium and petroleum. Bolivia exports tin.

8 In all three of the Andean countries, most traveling is done by foot or by pack animal.

The northwest part of South America can be divided into two general areas, the Caribbean region and the northern Andean region. Venezuela and Colombia are located on the Caribbean coast. These two countries will be studied in the first chapter as the Caribbean Countries.

Ecuador and Peru on the Pacific coast and Bolivia, which lies inland, make up the remaining area in the northwest part of the continent. These three countries will be studied in the second chapter under the title Northern Andean Countries. They are called Andean because the Andes Mountains occupy so much of their land area.

A global view of northwestern South America appears on the next page.

17

NORTHWESTERN SOUTH AMERICA

The outstanding physical feature of this area, as you can see, is the towering Andes Mountain Range. It curves south along the western edge of the continent, crossing each of the countries you will learn about in this unit.

In the southern part of this map you can see Lake Titicaca, high in the Andes Mountain region. It is the largest inland lake in South America. To the north, west, and south of it is the highland area called the *Altiplano*.

Along the Pacific coast there is a long, narrow coastal plain. In the north, this plain is a hot, wet, tropical lowland. Farther south, it is a barren coastal desert. The Andes Mountains rise to the east of this low plain.

The green area to the east of the Andes marks the Amazon Valley, a wide stretch of tropical rain forest. The Amazon and its tributaries have their sources on the eastern slopes of the Andes, and flow east to the Atlantic. The Orinoco River flows around the Guiana Highlands toward the Atlantic, where it has built up a large delta at its mouth.

Also drained by the Orinoco is a wide grassy plain in the north called the *llanos*. It appears yellowish-green on this map. Across a spur of the Andes from the llanos, along the northern coast, there is a low, hot coastal plain.

Pacific Ocean

NORTH
AMERICA

Caribbean Sea

Llanos   River

Orinoco

Andes

Lake Titicaca

Mountains

1

The Caribbean Countries

Gateway to South America. Caracas, Venezuela, is often the first stop of visitors entering the continent by airplane from the United States.

Our nearest neighbors in South America are Venezuela and Colombia, the Caribbean countries. These two independent republics on the Caribbean Sea are located in the Tropical Zone. There is a good reason for beginning our study of South America with them. Because of their location, they are in an ideal position for trade with the United States. Both countries have therefore, become very closely associated with our country. Venezuela, in particular, is one of the most important suppliers of raw materials to the United States.

VENEZUELA

Lake Maracaibo. A small boat is chugging across this wide lake. Perhaps it is bringing farm products to the people living along the shores.

Whene the Spaniards were exploring the northern coast of South America, they found native Indians living along the shores of a lake near the Caribbean Sea. Look at the map on page 22. You will find an inlet into Lake Maracaibo. The Indians' huts were built on wooden piles driven into the bed of the lake at the water's edge. Boats and rafts were used to travel from place to place, reminding the explorers of the city of Venice in Italy. That is why they called the land around the lake *Venezuela,* which is the Spanish way of saying "Little Venice."

Venezuela is the northernmost country of South America. It has a coast line stretching about 1700 miles along the Caribbean Sea and the Atlantic Ocean. The area is about the size of three of our large southern states — Louisiana, Mississippi, and Texas — taken together.

The Venezuelan People. The population of nearly 6,000,000 is composed mostly of people of mixed races. As you know, the name for these people is mestizos. The rest of the population is made up of Indians, Negroes, and a small number of white people, mostly of Spanish descent.

Most Venezuelans are Catholics. Unfortunately, not all of them practice their religion faithfully. There is a serious shortage of vocations, and not enough priests, Brothers, or Sisters, to do all the work of the Church.

Spanish is the national language of Venezuela, spoken by most of the people. There is a law that all Venezuelans must attend school at least through the elementary grades. This is not strictly enforced, however, and there are still many who cannot read or write. Other Venezuelans take advantage of the free education that is offered them right through college.

Although Venezuela has been a republic since 1830, it has not always had a free and democratic government. At times, the people have been ruled by dictators. Often, violent revolutions took place and these dictators were overthrown, only to have other strong men become dictators in their place. Perhaps, as the Venezuelan people become better educated, they will become more aware of the need to choose their leaders wisely, through fair and democratic elections.

Studying the Map

A. 1. The five countries of northwestern South America are crossed by the Andes. Name the countries, going from north to south. **2.** Which countries of northwestern South America border on the Caribbean Sea? Which border on the Pacific Ocean? Name the country which borders on both the Caribbean and the Pacific. Name the country with no seacoast. **3.** Name three countries which touch the equator or are crossed by it. **4.** What route would a traveler take in going by sea from Barranquilla on the Caribbean coast of Colombia to Buenaventura on the Pacific coast? **5.** In northwestern South America, are the areas of lowland greater on the eastern or the western side of the Andes?

B. 1. Name the mountains which extend into western Venezuela. How do they compare in elevation with the Guiana Highlands in the eastern part of country? **2.** Name the river which crosses Venezuela and flows into the Caribbean Sea. What physical feature has this river formed at its mouth? **3.** Name the lowland area extending from Venezuela into Colombia. **4.** Find Lake Maracaibo in Venezuela. How would ships from the Caribbean get into Lake Maracaibo? **5.** La Guaira and Caracas in Venezuela are less than eight miles apart. Use the map key to figure out why it is difficult to travel overland between the two cities. **6.** Name the river flowing in a valley between two prongs of the Andes Mountains in Colombia.

C. 1. Which Andean country takes its name from the equator? **2.** Comparing Ecuador, Peru, and Bolivia, which has the largest area? the smallest area? **3.** Use the scale of miles to estimate the width of the coastal lowland in Ecuador and Peru. In which country is it narrower? **4.** Guayaquil in Ecuador and Callao in Peru are seaports. Which one do you think has a natural harbor? Why was it necessary to build a man-made harbor at the other city? **5.** Name the country of northwestern South America in which each of the following cities is located: Lima, La Paz, Valencia, Medellin, Cali.

Four Natural Regions. Venezuela is divided by nature into four regions. Since each has its own distinct surface and climate, we will study each of them separately. As in many countries of South America, the different regions of Venezuela are noted for their different products, different occupations, and different ways of living.

The Caribbean Lowland. In the northwestern part of the country there is a swampy lowland region surrounding Lake Maracaibo. Here the temperature is always hot, and the air moist. Millions of small insects thrive in this area, making living conditions for humans uncomfortable and unhealthy. Farther east along the coast, it is hot but not so rainy.

The Andes Mountains Region. East of the Maracaibo lowland, yet also in the northwest area, lies a long spur, or extension, of the Andes Mountain Range. The climate in this mountainous area is cooler than in the lowland. Most Venezuelans live here in the high valleys and on the Andean slopes. As in many parts of South America, the mountainous area is the only section of the country which provides a pleasant and healthy climate in which to live.

The Llanos. The central interior of Venezuela is part of the large grassy plain called the *llanos*. The llanos extends far inland along the Orinoco River and its tributaries. Much of the land in this region is low and nearly level.

Between the streams which flow across the llanos into the Orinoco River are some higher flat areas called *mesas*. The mesas have some trees and tall grass. Since the llanos and mesas are near the equator, their climate is hot. During the rainy season the streams overflow. At other times very little rain falls on the llanos, and many small streams even dry up completely.

Laundry Time at the River Bank. These women from a small village of Venezuela have come to the shores of the Orinoco to do the family wash.

The Guiana Highlands.

The Guiana Highlands in eastern and southern Venezuela occupy about one half of the country. These low mountains have no high peaks. The climate here is hot and moist. Forests and dense vegetation cover much of the

"Little Venice." Indian villages built on stilts in Maracaibo's waters gave Venezuela its name. Indian children are playing a game on the pier.

surface. Transportation is hampered by the rapids which interrupt travel and shipping along the streams.

The few people in this region live in villages along the streams. The population is smaller than in the Andean highlands because the area is not at a high enough altitude to provide relief from the heat.

The Orinoco River. About four fifths of the surface of Venezuela is drained by the Orinoco and its tributaries. The Orinoco is the second longest river in South America. Its branches rise in the Andes, and from there the Orinoco flows 1600 miles to its mouth in the Atlantic Ocean. Boats can make their way up the Orinoco from the ocean for 700 miles. Even large vessels can travel far up the river because its channels have been deepened by recent dredging.

Over the centuries, layers of soil have been deposited by this river at its mouth. These deposits form a fertile piece of land called a *delta*. The land here is low and swampy, and the weather is hot. The few Indians who inhabit the Orinoco delta live chiefly on fruit, nuts, fish, and large turtles. Crocodiles are often seen sunning themselves on the river banks.

Black Gold. Venezuela has more oil than any other country in South America. In fact, some of the richest oil fields in the world are located in the region around Lake Maracaibo. Oil wells have been drilled several thousand feet into the rock layers beneath the lake. Hundreds of steel derricks used in drilling for the oil crowd the lakeshores and even reach far out into the water.

Recently the Caribbean entrance to Lake Maracaibo was deepened. Now huge oil tankers can be loaded right near the wells. Oil is also shipped by barge and pipe line to two small offshore islands. These islands belonging to the Netherlands are known as Curaçao and Aruba. In refineries on the islands gasoline and other products are derived from the crude oil. Large ocean tankers carry Venezuelan petroleum products to the United States and many other parts of the world.

The oil business brings so much money into the country that oil is sometimes called Venezuela's "black gold." The government of Venezuela has given American, British, and Dutch companies the rights to drill wells and pump oil. These foreign countries pay the government of Venezuela a percentage of the money they make from the oil. The government of Venezuela uses this money to build and to maintain schools, hospitals, and roads, and for other public needs.

Iron Ore. Important deposits of high grade iron ore are found in the low mountains along the northern edge of the Guiana Highlands. The iron region is near the Orinoco River, about 50 miles southeast of the city of Ciudad Bolívar. Here iron ore lies close to the surface and can be scooped up by huge steam shovels.

Large steel companies from the United States built a railroad to transport the ore

Oil Derricks in the Waters of Lake Maracaibo. Today Venezuela ranks first as a world exporter of oil, and second only to the USA as a producer.

from the open-pit mines to the docks on the Orinoco River. At the docks the ore is loaded on ocean-going freighters which carry some of it to blast furnaces in the Chesapeake Bay-Delaware River area of the United States. Iron from Venezuela helps to supply the steel mills around Baltimore and Philadelphia which can no longer be fully supplied by the Mesabi Range in Minnesota.

Iron Mine at Cerro Bolivar. In 1954 U. S. companies developed this open-pit mine, and built a railroad to carry the ore to Ciudad Bolivar.

Venezuelan Cowboys. Modern means of refrigerating meat have helped the cattle industry. These men tend the herds on Venezuela's wide plain.

Venezuelan Cowboys. On the llanos live daring and skillful cowboys known as the *llaneros*. These herders, who are expert horsemen, work on the large cattle ranches located on the grassy plains of the interior.

During the rainy season when the rivers flood, the llaneros drive the herds of cattle to the high mesas to feed on the tall grass. In the dry season, the animals are driven back down to the lower grazing lands along the streams and rivers, where they feed on the more tender grass. The wet and dry seasons keep the Venezuelan cowboys constantly on the move.

The cattle industry in Venezuela has been improved recently by introducing special breeds. For example, animals with tough hides that resist mosquitoes and other insects were brought in from the hot, wet lands of southern Asia. The quality of the beef and dairy products has been improved as a result. The use of refrigeration and the building of freezing plants for meat products have also helped to build up Venezuela's cattle industry.

Farming. Some large tropical plantations which produce sugar cane, cacao, and coconuts are found near Lake Maracaibo. In a few other places small areas have been cleared in the tropical rain forests. Here farmers raise oranges, bananas, breadfruit, rice, manioc, corn, beans, tobacco, and cotton.

Where the climate is cooler in the high Andean valleys, farmers raise food crops, including fruits, vegetables, grain, and potatoes. With these they supply Caracas and other highland cities and towns. Because of the cool climate, most of the population of Venezuela is located in the highlands.

Higher up in the mountains, between Caracas and Valencia, coffee is grown. Valuable as an export, coffee is Venezuela's most important money crop. On the lower slopes of the mountains around Caracas sugar cane and cacao are raised on plantations.

More farmers are needed in this country because not enough food crops are now grown to feed the large population. When more Venezuelans turn to raising crops, the standard of living in Venezuela should become much higher.

Caracas, La Guaira, and Valencia. Caracas is the capital and largest city of Venezuela. It is set in a beautiful valley of the Andes, 3020 feet above sea level. The altitude gives Caracas a delightfully mild climate.

Caracas is one of the fastest growing cities of South America. To take care of the needs of its increasing population, business, and industry, many new avenues, subways, housing developments, and schools are now being built.

Despite its mountainous location, transportation is good between Caracas and other cities of North and South America. Many foreign visitors reach Venezuela and other parts of South America by way of the large international airport at Caracas.

Venezuela has about 12,000 miles of modern roads. A section of the Pan-American Highway crosses the Andes in this country and connects Caracas with Bogotá in Colombia. Automobiles and motor buses already use this part of the highway, which passes through several mountain tunnels and over three high bridges.

A good highway and a railroad both connect Caracas with the nearby seaport of La Guaira. Caracas and this seaport are only eight miles apart, yet the railroad must travel 23 miles as it winds its way up the mountainside.

La Guaira is Venezuela's most important commercial seaport. This tiny town with only one main street is on a narrow strip of coastal lowland between Caracas and the Caribbean Sea. It has an excellent harbor. The weather in La Guaira is uncomfortably hot and dry most of the time.

Valencia is the largest manufacturing city in Venezuela. It is about a hundred miles west of Caracas in a fertile mountain valley. Cacao, sugar cane, cotton, tobacco, and other crops grow on farms nearby.

Mountain Capital. Caracas, Venezuela, perches high in the Andes. Although one of the oldest cities in the New World, it is growing rapidly today.

Ciudad Bolívar. *Ciudad* is the Spanish word meaning city. Ciudad Bolívar is the only important city on the llanos of Venezuela, and is located on the Orinoco River about 260 miles upstream from its mouth. Because the city is built on land a little higher than the surrounding plain, it keeps dry during the annual flood season when the Orinoco overflows its banks.

Ciudad Bolívar is an important river port and trading center. Ships bring manufactured goods and other products needed by the people of this region. When they sail away these ships carry cattle and hides from the nearby ranches as well as gold and other products from the Guiana Highlands.

Since the discovery of valuable iron ore deposits nearby, several steel companies have built a bridge across the Orinoco River near Ciudad Bolívar. The railroad and highway connections which this has made possible have caused Ciudad Bolívar to become a center of transportation.

COLOMBIA

Caribbean City. Built in 1533, Cartagena is even older than Caracas. This city of many races has a spacious harbor through which oil is shipped.

A glance at the map on page 22 will show you that a narrow neck of land called the Isthmus of Panama joins the American continents. East of the Isthmus is the Caribbean Sea; west of it is the Pacific Ocean. The southern part of the Isthmus of Panama lies partly in Colombia. This South American country has a coast on the Pacific Ocean and one on the Caribbean Sea.

The Andes Mountains form a large part of the surface of Colombia. The mountains present a barrier to easy travel and transportation between the country's Pacific coast and its populous interior mountain valleys where the cities and industries are located. This busy area is far more easily reached from the Caribbean Sea, because rivers flow from the mountain valleys into the Caribbean. Most of Colombia's foreign trade moves toward and across the Caribbean Sea rather than the Pacific Ocean.

The Colombian People. This country has a population of nearly 13,000,000 people, and ranks third in population among South American countries. Only Brazil and Argentina have larger populations. A little more than half the Colombians are mestizos, and most of the remainder are white people of European descent. There are also some Indians and some Negroes among the population.

As in Venezuela, the language spoken by most Colombians is Spanish, and the great majority of the people are Catholics. Colombia was ruled by Spain until the beginning of the nineteenth century when the people, under the leadership of Simon Bolívar, won their freedom. At first, the republic of Colombia was much larger than it is today, and included what is now Venezuela, Ecuador, and Panama. These three countries later became independent republics themselves.

In certain rural and coastal areas of Colombia progress has been slow, hampered by poor communications and unfortunate civil conflicts. In the western part of the country, where most of the people live, the standard of living is one of the highest in South America. There are excellent daily newspapers, many schools and universities, and a very high level of culture.

Education is free throughout Colombia, but it has not yet been made compulsory. The Catholic school system is the largest in South America; of the 600 secondary schools in Colombia, 400 are Catholic. Unlike other countries of South America, there is not a serious shortage of priests, Brothers, and Sisters here. In fact, the Church is stronger in Colombia by far than in most of the neighboring countries.

Four Natural Regions. Colombia may be divided into four regions which differ from each other in many ways. They are: the northern lowlands near the Caribbean coast; the western highlands near the Pacific Ocean; the western lowland strip on the shores of the Pacific; and the eastern plains. The southeastern corner of Colombia is crossed by the equator. The Magdalena River and its long tributary, the Cauca River, rise in the high Andes and flow north toward the Caribbean. The Magdalena crosses the northern lowlands and is navigable for over 800 miles.

The Northern Lowlands. The northern lowlands along the Caribbean are hot and sunny. They receive plenty of moisture during the rainy season. During the dry season streams furnish water for irrigation. This region has a rich soil composed of mixed sand and clay. Much of its surface is covered with tropical forests which have been cleared in some places to make room for banana plantations.

The Western Highlands. The most important region of Colombia is the western highlands. Here the high Andean peaks rise more than 18,000 feet above sea level, and the valleys lie at elevations of 5000 to 10,000 feet. As far up as 6000 feet, the slopes of the mountains have a hot or very warm climate.

From about 6000 to 10,000 feet, the climate of the western highlands area is mild. Here conditions are ideal for growing coffee and food crops. It is here, in the long fertile valleys between the ranges, that most of the Colombian people live. Most of the railroads and highways of Colombia have been built in this region. Above 10,000 feet it becomes too cold for comfortable living, and the high peaks are covered with snow.

Pleasant Highlands. This is near Bogotá, capital of Colombia. Most Colombians live in the high Andean valleys where the climate is cooler and drier.

The Pacific Lowland. To the west of the Andes, along the Pacific Ocean, is a narrow strip of coastal lowland where few people live. Here the rainfall is heavy, and the climate extremely hot. Dense tropical forests grow everywhere, and insects make life unhealthy and unpleasant.

The Eastern Plains. More than half the area of Colombia is included in the eastern plains region. The northern part of this area, east of the Andes, is a continuation of the llanos of Venezuela. Branches of the Orinoco River cross this area.

Few people live on these grassy plains. There are some herders who raise cattle and drive them west over the mountains to markets in the highlands. Cattle hides are also shipped from this region.

The southern part of the eastern plains region is covered by tropical forests and is crossed by a number of tributaries of the Amazon River. The population here, too, is very small. It is composed mostly of Indians who live close to the rivers, their chief means of transportation. The natives send rubber and other forest products to ports on the Amazon. Missionaries labor here among the settlers and Indians.

The Important Banana Crop. Bananas are an important crop in Colombia. This fruit does well in the hot lowlands near the Caribbean coast. As in Middle America, most of the work on the banana plantations is done by Negroes.

Before starting a banana plantation, the land must first be cleared of trees. Often the trees are burned off. Next, ditches are dug for drainage and irrigation. Finally the stalks are planted.

Because weeds and other vegetation grow rapidly in this tropical climate, the plantation must be frequently weeded while the banana plants are growing. When it is time for the harvest, the bunches of bananas are cut down with long sharp knives. It is not necessary to plant new stalks in the ground each year, because new plants spring up from the old ones.

Colombia exports bananas to the United States through the ports of Santa Marta and Barranquilla on the Caribbean coast.

Banana Port. Buyers' agents at Barranquilla are examining green bananas. Their choices will be loaded on ships and sent to markets abroad.

Coffee From the Highlands. Colombian coffee, famous for its fine flavor, is the country's most valuable crop and its chief export. The coffee plantations are located in the western highlands, far inland from the Caribbean coast. The trees are planted on the mountain slopes, because coffee thrives best in well-drained soil.

There are three main centers of Colombia's coffee industry. They are located near three cities in different parts of the Andean highland region. One good coffee region is located on the warm, lower mountain slopes below the city of Bogotá. Another fine coffee district is farther north near the new city of Bucaramanga. The third famous coffee district lies near Medellin.

The coffee plantations in the Bogotá and Bucaramanga sections are very large. The rich coffee planters usually hire people to work their plantations. The owners live in beautiful homes in the capital, spending only a small part of the year on the plantations which bring them their wealth. In the Medellin area the plantations are small. Here the farmers and their families live and work on their own land instead of hiring workers to raise the crops.

Coffee from the three sections is blended. Combining their different flavors in this

Top Quality Coffee. The superior flavor of coffee from Colombia is well-known. Here the hand-picked berries are spread to dry in the sun.

way produces the most delicious beverage. Most of Colombia's high-quality coffee crop is exported to the United States. There it is again blended with the less expensive Brazilian coffee, which is of more ordinary quality.

Bogotá, Bucaramanga, and Medellin each have large warehouses where the beans are stored until shipping time. Then railroads transport the still unroasted coffee in burlap bags over the Andes to the Magdalena River. It is transferred to large river boats which carry it to the seaports of Barranquilla and Santa Marta on the Caribbean coast.

Coffee is not the only crop raised in the Colombian highlands. Food crops, including corn, wheat, potatoes, and other vegetables, are raised in the cool, high valleys. In the lower, warmer valleys sugar, cacao, tobacco, and cotton are grown.

Cattle, sheep, and mules graze in the highland valleys where insects do not annoy and weaken them as much as they would in the hot, wet lowlands. Near Bogotá and other large cities, farmers keep dairy herds to supply milk.

Precious Stones. These hands hold a fortune in raw emeralds. One large stone sells for $50,000. Colombia produces the world's finest emeralds.

Mineral Resources. Colombia's highlands are rich in many minerals, and mining is a very important industry. Most of the world's emeralds, for example, come from the mountains of Colombia. Emeralds are beautiful green stones highly prized as jewels. The emerald mines around Bogotá have been operated for centuries, even before the Europeans came.

In the past, gold and platinum were mined in the mountain valleys near the Pacific coast. Miners with picks, shovels, and pans found these minerals mixed with gravel in the river valleys. Large mechanical dredges are now used to mine the platinum, and Colombia is one of the world's chief producers of this precious metal. Gold and platinum are both exported, mostly to the United States, through the Pacific port of Buenaventura.

Colombia has oil fields, too, but its oil supply is small compared with that of Venezuela. A pipe line has been constructed through jungle and swamps to Cartagena on the Caribbean coast, where oil refineries have been built. The refineries not only supply Colombia with gasoline and petroleum products, but export some as well. The petroleum industry is not a major one in Colombia, however.

Other mineral resources of Colombia include silver, copper, lead, manganese, coal, and iron.

Bogotá, the Capital. The chief city is Bogotá, which is located high in a beautiful valley of the Andes. Although situated only 5 degrees north of the equator, the city has a comfortable climate. Bogotá is warm in the daytime and cool at night throughout the year, because its altitude is nearly 9000 feet above sea level.

The capital city has wide streets, fine government buildings, and modern apartment houses. Good schools and colleges make it a center of learning and culture. Many artists, writers, and scholars live in Bogotá. Visitors to South America usually plan to see this beautiful city.

A fine section of the Pan-American Highway connects Bogotá with cities in Venezuela and Ecuador. Transportation between the capital and the Caribbean, however, is still slow. Few long railroads have been built in Colombia because of the rugged mountains and dense tropical forests to be crossed.

A railroad winds up the mountains to Bogotá, but it does not directly connect the city with Caribbean ports. Passengers and freight must transfer to busses or trucks for part of the trip, or to steamers on the Magdalena River. It takes ten days to make the trip between Bogotá and Barranquilla on the coast by this combination of rail and bus, truck or steamer. However, it takes only 2½ hours by air to make the same journey, so it is easy to understand why so many travelers choose the airlines. Today more and more of Colombia's freight is also being carried by transport planes over the rugged mountains.

Barranquilla, Caribbean Port. Barranquilla, the chief seaport, is on the Caribbean Sea near the mouth of the Magdalena River. The river mouth has been deepened to permit ocean-going ships to reach this city. Barranquilla has a big airport where connections can be made for Bogotá, Medellin, and other cities in the interior.

Most of Colombia's exports and imports enter and leave the country by way of Barranquilla. Manufactured goods, including textiles, machinery, and chemicals, are the chief imports. The leading exports are coffee, bananas, and emeralds.

Some manufacturing is done in Barranquilla. Its factories turn out cotton goods, hats, shoes, flour, soap, and other products. These goods are used in Colombia.

Other Cities. Cartagena, where St. Peter Claver labored among the Negro slaves, is a city of historic importance on the Caribbean. During colonial times it was an even more important port than it is today. The Spanish once had to build a large wall around Cartagena to protect it from pirate raids. On a number of occasions the city was attacked and captured by pirates. Today, it is still used as a port, but it is not nearly so busy as Barranquilla. Coffee and petroleum are exported from Cartagena.

Medellin is Colombia's most important manufacturing center. It is located in a fertile valley near the northern edge of the highland region. Cotton textiles are the leading product of its factories. Medellin, like Bogotá, is in a coffee-growing region and is an important coffee-shipping city. In addition, the recent discovery of coal and iron deposits near this city indicate that it may become an important steel center.

Cali is the largest city in the Cauca River valley. It is the inland trading center for the surrounding area which produces sugar cane, cacao, and tobacco. Cattle-raising has

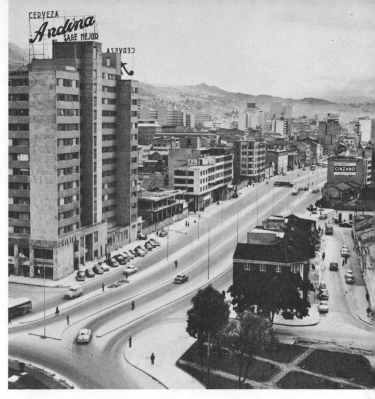

Colombia's Beautiful Capital. This scene shows why the people of Colombia are proud of their capital. Here is one of Bogotá's wide boulevards.

also become important here.

Buenaventura is a seaport on the southern part of Colombia's Pacific coast. It has a good harbor and is connected by railroad with Cali.

Cartagena. Very old buildings and streets with few cars are typical of this ancient city. Notice the balconies overhanging the narrow street.

Facts *to remember*

1. Venezuela and Colombia border on the Caribbean Sea. Colombia has a Pacific seacoast as well. The Orinoco River drains much of Venezuela; the Magdalena River with its long tributary, the Cauca, drains much of Colombia.
2. Nearly six million people live in Venezuela. Most are mestizos, with some Indians, Negroes, and white people.
3. The principal regions of Venezuela are the Andes mountains and valleys, the Guiana highlands, the Caribbean lowlands around Lake Maracaibo, and the grassy plains called llanos.
4. The oil wells of the Lake Maracaibo region bring much money to Venezuela. They have been developed by U. S., British, and Dutch companies.
5. The Guiana Highlands have rich deposits of high grade iron ore. Ocean freighters carry this ore to the steel mills of the United States.
6. Large cattle ranges are located on the grassy plains (llanos) of the interior of Venezuela.
7. On the lowlands of Venezuela tropical fruits, cotton, sugar cane, cacao, and coconuts thrive. On the lower slopes of the highlands coffee, a valuable export, is grown. In the high cool valleys fruits, grains, potatoes, and vegetables are grown to supply the people of the larger cities.
8. Caracas is the capital and largest city of Venezuela. A highway and a railroad connect Caracas with its seaport, La Guaira, but air transportation to the city is more important. Valencia is noted for manufacturing, and Ciudad Bolívar is an important trading port.
9. The Andes Mountains form a barrier between the interior valleys of Colombia and the coast. However, water transportation between the Caribbean and Pacific coasts can be accomplished through the Panama Canal.
10. Colombia has nearly thirteen million people. Over half are mestizos; most of the remainder are whites.
11. In the hot, wet lowlands of Colombia bananas are an important crop. In the western highland area coffee is raised for export. Other crops raised in the cool highlands are corn, wheat, potatoes, and vegetables. Cattle, sheep, mules, and dairy cows also do well here.
12. Colombia is rich in minerals. Emeralds, gold, and platinum as well as oil, silver, copper, lead, manganese, coal, and iron are plentiful.
13. Bogotá is the capital and cultural center of the nation. Barranquilla, the chief Caribbean port, and Cartagena handle the exports and imports. Medellin is the chief manufacturing center. Cali is a fast-growing city in the Cauca Valley. It is connected by railroad with Buenaventura, Colombia's Pacific coast port.

What *have I learned?*

Write the answers on your paper.
Name the . . .
1. inlet of the Caribbean Sea in Venezuela.
2. term given to people of mixed races.
3. highlands in eastern and southern Venezuela.
4. large grassy plains in central Venezuela.
5. two islands on which the oil refineries of Venezuela are located.
6. city near the iron ore mines of Venezuela.
7. capital city of Venezuela.
8. two important plantation crops of Venezuela.
9. two important rivers of Colombia.
10. two important cities of Colombia that are located in its river valleys.
11. city in Colombia which is called a "center of learning."
12. five important minerals of Colombia.
13. inland trading center in the Cauca River Valley.
14. three agricultural products from Colombia's lowlands.
15. three agricultural products from Colombia's highlands.

Facts *to understand*

Answer each of the questions in a sentence or two.
1. Of the countries of northwestern South America, why has Colombia the best location for trade?
2. Why do more people live in the highlands of northwestern South America than in the lowlands?
3. Why is the Magdalena River of such great importance to Colombia?
4. Why is the airplane such an important means of transportation in Colombia and Venezuela?
5. Why is oil sometimes called Venezuela's "black gold"?

2
Northern Andean Countries

The Andean countries of northwestern South America are Ecuador, Peru, and Bolivia. Ecuador and Peru border on the Pacific Ocean, but Bolivia is an inland nation. The Andes Mountains cover a large area of each of these three countries.

Most of the people live in the high mountain valleys, or on the plateaus which lie between or at the edge of the mountains. In no other part of the world does such a large proportion of the population live in the highlands.

ECUADOR

The name Ecuador, a Spanish word meaning "land of the equator," is a reminder that the equator crosses this country. Ecuador is on the Pacific coast of South America, just south of Colombia. Two of the highest Andean peaks are in Ecuador. Mount Chimborazo, a volcanic peak, rises to a height of 20,577 feet above sea level. Another volcanic peak, Mount Cotopaxi, is 19,344 feet high.

The People. Although Ecuador is twice as large as New York State, it has only 3½ million people, less than one fourth the population of New York State. About one half of Ecuador's population is made up of

INDIANS OF THE ANDES

The Indians still live in much the same way as they did when the Spaniards first came to the country many years ago. Their homes are mud-walled houses, and they work on small farm plots. Some tend their flocks on the grassy slopes of the mountains. Indian women spin and weave wool into a cloth which is used to make warm clothing for their families. This work is done mostly by hand.

A few Indians live in the tropical forests of Ecuador, east of the Andes. They are often hostile to strangers and prefer not to see any outsiders enter their domain. They live in small houses built on poles near the rivers. They travel mostly by boat or canoe. These forest Indians live on nuts, wild fruits and berries, roots of certain plants, and the meat of wild animals which they hunt with blowguns.

The *blowgun* is a long, hollow tube of bamboo in which a small pointed dart is placed. To fire it, the Indian places the gun in his mouth, and shoots the dart out by blowing into the tube. He creeps up very quietly on his prey, and kills it suddenly with the small darts which have been dipped in poison.

Marker Stone. This monument is on the equator near Quito. It says that the latitude is 0 degrees, reminding visitors that Ecuador means *equator*.

Indians who live mostly in the high valleys of the Andes where they farm and tend their flocks.

The other half of the population is made up of mestizos, some Negroes, and whites. Many of the mestizos, and practically all the Negroes, live in the coastal lowlands. There they work on the plantations or in the forests, or carry on trade in the towns.

The official language of Ecuador is Spanish, although the Indians speak their own tongue. The chief religion is the Roman

Children of Ecuador. These are Indian and mestizo boys, pictured outside their school waiting for the bell which will summon them to class.

Catholic. Education is free, but many children complete only the first three grades of the elementary schools. Unfortunately, many never learn to read and write. Ecuador has been an independent republic since 1830, when it separated from Colombia.

Highlands and Lowlands. Ecuador has three regions. There are lowlands along the Pacific coast in the west. There is another lowland region in the eastern part of the country. Separating the two lowland areas are the Andes with their high valleys and towering peaks.

The narrow coastal plain along the Pacific Ocean is very hot. Around the Gulf of Guayaquil, and to the north of it, the rainfall is abundant. Tropical forests cover most of the Pacific lowland. Short, swift-flowing rivers flow from the mountains across the plain. When they overflow, they flood the fertile lowlands. Plants grow rapidly here because of the high temperatures and plentiful moisture. South of the Gulf of Guayaquil the rainfall is lighter and this is an area of tropical grasslands.

Inland from the coastal plain are the densely forested western slopes of the Andes. Because of the higher altitude, the climate in the valleys is mild, with warm days and cool nights. From the valleys can be seen snow-covered peaks which stretch high into the clouds and make the scenery very beautiful. In this land of the equator it seems strange to see the snow, until we remember how high these peaks are, and how cold it always is in very high places.

The lowlands of eastern Ecuador are hot and rainy. They are cut off from the rest of the country by the Andes Mountains. Only a few steep and dangerous trails cross the mountains. The eastern lowlands are drained by many streams that belong to the Amazon River system. The thick tropical forests are full of wild animals and birds.

Lowland Plantations and Farms. Great areas of tropical forest have been cleared on Ecuador's coastal lowlands, and large cacao plantations have been established. The beans which grow on the cacao tree are used to make chocolate and cocoa.

Cacao trees require well-drained soil, hot rainy weather, and shelter from winds. These conditions are found on the coastal lowlands. Cacao is harvested two or three times a year because all the pods on the tree do not ripen at the same time. Sharp knives, fastened to the ends of long poles, are used to cut the pods down.

The pods are placed in piles on the ground and left to dry for two or three days. Then they are split open and the seeds are removed. The cacao seeds, or beans, are next put into pans where they remain for several days until they lose their bitter taste.

Finally the beans are removed from the pans and dried in the sun for several more days. The cacao beans are now ready to be packed into sacks for shipping. They are transported on rivers by boats and barges to the markets in Guayaquil. Cacao is one of Ecuador's chief exports. It is shipped to the United States and other countries.

In addition to the cacao plantations in this part of Ecuador, there are large banana plantations. These have increased in number during recent years. Bananas, too, are exported to the United States. In fact, in recent years Ecuador has become the largest exporter in South America.

People living on the coastal lowland have cleared small areas of forest where they raise the food for their families. The principal crops are rice, beans, sweet potatos, and bananas. Good farm methods have been recently introduced and thus the crop production of the small farmer has steadily increased.

Cacao Pods. These pods contain the seeds which go to make chocolate and cocoa. When dried, the valuable seeds are exported to many countries.

Forest Products. The forests of Ecuador are sources of tree products which make valuable exports.

A palm tree which grows on the Pacific lowland yields tagua nuts. They are not used for food. Buttons, umbrella handles, chessmen, and various kinds of ornaments resembling ivory are made from the hard, white kernels of tagua nuts. Recently, however, the increasing use of plastics in the United States and elsewhere has caused the market for these nuts to decline.

The nuts ripen at different times during the year. Men gather them in baskets, load them in small boats and take them to Guayaquil. From there they are shipped to the United States and other countries. Tagua nuts are sometimes called "vegetable ivory."

Another important palm tree grows wild in Ecuador. Its leaves yield a straw-like fiber popular for making light-weight summer hats. These are usually hand-woven with marvelous skill by Indian workers. Long before these hats became popular outside of South America, tourists shopping

Panama Hats. An Indian worker puts the final touches on this hat. After women have woven them by hand, men scrub them to bleach the straw fiber.

in Panama purchased some which had been sent there from Ecuador. Since the hats were purchased in Panama rather than in Ecuador, however, the shoppers understandably called them Panama hats. This name for Ecuador's straw hats has stuck.

Forest Industry. Balsa trees grow wild in the tropical lowlands between Guayquil and the Pacific. This worker strips the bark from a balsa log.

The balsa tree grows wild in the tropical forests along the coast of Ecuador. Many boys have built model airplanes of balsa wood, which is the lightest wood known. Only half as heavy as cork, balsa is twice as strong.

The natives use the balsa wood to make small boats for carrying tagua nuts and other forest products to market. Some balsa wood is exported. It is used in making life rafts and airplanes, and for insulation and sound-proofing.

At Work in the Highlands. Family farming is the chief occupation of the people in the mountain valleys of Ecuador. Though efforts are being made to change their ways, the farmers still use primitive methods. They often work with homemade wooden tools to plow their fields and turn the soil. Oxen are still used to thresh the grain. The stalks are laid on a stone floor, and the animals trample out the seeds. You have read about this way of threshing grain in Bible stories.

Barley, potatoes, beans, peas, corn, and alfalfa are the chief crops raised in the highlands. Each family grows just enough to supply its own needs. This is unfortunate, because it means they have no surplus with which to trade. They are therefore unable to obtain other goods which would help to improve their way of living.

Some cattle and other animals are raised. Sheep, alpacas, and llamas graze on the higher slopes of the mountains. The highland people are clever with their hands and make fine woolen cloth from the fleece of these animals.

The highlands are known to be rich in mineral resources including silver, copper, iron, lead, coal, and sulphur. Mining on a large scale is not done in Ecuador, however. There is no money for machinery, and few means of transportation are available.

Guayaquil. Guayaquil is now Ecuador's largest city and chief seaport. It has a good harbor and handles most of the country's trade. Guayaquil is located about 40 miles from the mouth of the Guayas River. This is a small but navigable river that flows into the Gulf of Guayaquil on the Pacific coast.

Guayaquil has a hot, moist climate. Until recent years, it was a very unhealthy place. Living conditions improved greatly, however when sewers were installed, and the water supply was made safe.

Quito. The Capital of Ecuador is Quito, a very old city high in the Andes. When the Spanish arrived more than 400 years ago, it was already an important city. Quito is about 300 miles inland from Guayaquil. It is reached by a sharply-climbing railroad.

Quito, a lovely place in which to live, is practically on the equator, located in a valley about 9000 feet above sea level. It is surrounded by beautiful snow-covered peaks. The city has a very pleasant climate throughout the year because of its high elevation. People who live and work in Guayaquil often go to Quito for vacations to escape the heat of the coastal lowland. The capital of Ecuador is noted as a great center of culture. It has many art galleries, beautifully designed churches, and the nation's best schools and colleges.

The Galápagos Islands. A group of twelve large volcanic islands and dozens of small ones straddle the equator 500 miles off the coast of Ecuador in the Pacific Ocean. Tomas de Berlanga, Bishop of Panama, discovered these islands in 1535. He was astonished at the enormous turtles he saw there, and the islands were named *galápagos,* which is the Spanish word for turtles.

English pirates once hid among the islands as they preyed upon Spanish gold ships. Later, American whalers found them

Quito, Ecuador. This inland capital is surrounded by snow-capped peaks. Many years ago, a volcano erupted and buried the city in hot lava.

a convenient stopping place. During World Wars I and II, the United States made use of them as a naval and air base to protect the Panama Canal.

Nowadays scientists visit the Galápagos Islands to study the different varieties of plants and animals. Many kinds of cold-water fish and birds are to be found here. They migrate from Antarctic waters, following the path of the cold Peruvian Current which passes close by. The islands belong to Ecuador, and tourists must obtain permission from the government of Ecuador to visit them.

Land of Giant Turtles. This ugly monster is one of the *galapagos,* or turtles, which live in the Galápagos Islands. He is over 100 years old.

PERU

Making Friends. A young missionary priest from North America chats with Indian llama herders in an Andean village. These llamas are pack animals.

The center of the ancient empire of the Incas which the Spaniards found when they first came to South America lay within the land now called Peru. Peru is one of the larger countries of South America. It stretches along the Pacific coast south of Ecuador for nearly 1500 miles. It is about the same area as our new state of Alaska.

The People. Peru has a population of nearly ten million people. More than half of them are Indians. Those of Spanish descent make up about one tenth of the population. Of the remainder, most are mestizos. There are also small numbers of Negroes and Orientals.

The people of Peru gained their independence from Spain early in the 19th century. The country is now a republic with a government like that of the United States. The official language is Spanish, although many of the Indians still use their ancient languages. Most Peruvians are Roman Catholics, but the practice of the Faith is not strong among the people.

Children between the ages of seven and fourteen are supposed to go to school in Peru. Although education is free, there are still not enough schools for all.

Surface and Climate. This country, like Ecuador, has three distinct regions. The way the people work and live in each region differs greatly. Peru has a coastal desert along the Pacific, plateaus and the highlands of the Andes Mountains in the interior, and lowlands in the northeast on the rim of the Amazon Valley. The coastal desert and the northeastern lowlands are almost completely cut off from each other by the Andes Mountains.

A narrow desert less than 100 miles wide runs along the entire Peruvian coast. It is broken by mountain ridges which reach down from the Andes to meet the Pacific Ocean. The prevailing winds over this desert strip are land winds from the east. They lose their moisture on the eastern slopes and thus are dry by the time they reach this region. Sometimes breezes will blow in from the Pacific. These, too, are dry, because they are warmed by the land as they blow across it. They absorb moisture instead of dropping it.

Although Peru is in the Tropical Zone, the coastal area is not so hot as we might expect. The Pacific winds help to lower the temperature. In winter mists form, and fog settles over the desert.

Mountain ranges and plateaus of the Andes cover almost half of Peru. More than two thirds of the people of Peru live in the cooler highlands.

The northeast lowlands east of the Andes occupy an area about equal to that of the highlands. These lowlands are covered by dense tropical rain forests. Their small population is composed mostly of tribal Indians. Only a small portion of them have been converted to Christianity.

The Irrigated Lowland. Although the coastal lowlands of Peru are a desert, farming is the chief occupation. Most of the farms are near rivers, which flow down from the Andes.

The warm climate and fertile soil along the coast make large crops possible through the use of irrigation. More than fifty short mountain streams flow across the dry lowland on their way to the sea. These streams furnish water for irrigating the land along their banks, making strips of green farmland in the desert.

This region is Peru's chief farming area. Cotton is the most important crop. The yield of cotton per acre in Peru is much greater than in the United States. Peruvian cotton is of very high quality, and is in great demand. It is mixed with wool to make fine cloth.

The type of cotton plant which grows in Peru is different from the kind raised in our country. After this Peruvian cotton is

Fertile River Valley. Near the city of Arequipa, Peru, there are miles of rich, fertile farmland irrigated by clear streams from the Andes.

picked, the bushes are cut back, and the same plant grows again the following year. Cotton does not have to be replanted each year, because in tropical countries there are no killing frosts.

Sugar cane is the second most valuable farm crop of this irrigated lowland. Both cotton and sugar cane are important exports from Peru.

Guano, a Fertilizer. Millions of sea birds have been flying to the islands off the coast of Peru for centuries, seeking fish for food. Many small animals and plants live in the cool waters of the Peruvian Current which flows past the islands. These animals and plants draw large schools of fish, which feed on them. The fish attract the sea birds.

Bird manure, called *guano,* has been collecting on Peru's offshore islands for ages. The dry climate has kept it from being washed away by rain water. Guano is gathered and sold as fertilizer in Peru. It is excellent for the "robber crops," like cotton, which destroy the soil when grown year after year. The use of guano accounts partly for the large Peruvian crops.

Mountainside Terraces. Indian farmers in the highlands of Peru cut these step-like terraces. They help to keep the rain water from running off.

Highland Farmers. Most of the Indians in the central highlands are farmers. Their small farms lie in the mountain valleys and on the lower slopes. Since Inca days the Indian farmers have planted in terraces which resemble broad steps on the mountainsides. These narrow but level fields hold the rain water. The Indians still use handmade tools, since modern farm machines would be useless on these mountain farms.

Corn is the principal food of the Peruvian Indians. These highland farmers raise the crops needed to feed their families, and sell their surplus to the mine workers. They also raise wheat, fruits, and potatoes.

Llamas and sheep. Highly prized for their wool, and helpful as beasts of burden, these llamas are tended by Indian herders. Notice the sheep also.

It was in the mountains of Peru that the white potato was first grown. When the Spanish explorers arrived in the country, they found the Indians raising this crop. The Spaniards later took the Peruvian white potato to Europe. As time went by, these potatoes were sent to Ireland, where they became an important food crop. Today, many people call them "Irish potatoes," although "Peruvian potatoes" might be a better name.

Andean Animals. Some of the Indians who live in the lower Andean valleys raise cattle, sheep, and mules. The cattle are raised for meat and hides. Sheep are raised for meat and wool. The mules are raised as work animals.

Llamas and alpacas graze on the higher slopes of the mountains. These hardy animals are able to live on stony land which cannot support cattle or even sheep. Centuries ago the Incas tamed the llamas and alpacas which ran wild in these highlands. Today the llama is the chief beast of burden on the high, rugged mountain trails of Peru and Bolivia. Automobiles and trucks are of little use in this region of steep slopes and few roads.

The llama resembles both a sheep and a camel. Its hair is like that of a sheep, and it has a long neck like a camel. This hardy animal is the Indians' friend, because it carries packs, furnishes wool for clothing, and provides meat.

The alpaca is a little larger than a sheep, but smaller and less hardy than a llama. Alpacas are raised for their wool and skins. In some regions the Indians shear them once a year. Elsewhere, the wool is clipped every two to four years.

A third distinctly Andean animal is the vicuña, a small, shy creature of the upper mountains. The vicuña grows a soft, fleecy coat which provides a beautiful wool.

Mineral Riches. Most Peruvians are engaged in farming and raising animals. Mining, however, remains the more important industry, because of the value of the minerals which this country produces. The great mining center of Peru is high in the Andes near the city of Cerro de Pasco. The mines of this region have been a source of gold and silver for centuries.

Today, other minerals are more important than gold or silver. Copper from Peru is in great demand. Lead, zinc, tin, bismuth, and vanadium are also mined. *Vanadium* is a metal which is blended with iron to make the kind of steel needed in automobile and airplane engines. Today Peru is the world's largest producer of vanadium ore. Nearly all of this mineral is exported to the United States.

A great amount of money had to be invested to build railroads and highways to Peru's Andean mines. The rich minerals which have been mined there have made the investment worthwhile.

Near the northern end of Peru's dry coastal lowland lies a productive petroleum field. The oil is pumped through pipelines to the refineries at Talara, a port on the coast. Tankers carry petroleum products from there to Callao and Mollendo to be used by Peruvian industry and railroads. Some petroleum is also being exported.

Difficult Climate and Conditions. The lowlands of northeastern Peru are mostly an unexplored tropical wilderness crossed by streams that feed the Amazon River. Until recently, few people have been able to live in this hot, moist region.

People who live in tropical lands anywhere in the world are exposed to a disease called *malaria*. It is spread by germs carried by a certain kind of mosquito. *Quinine* is the medicine commonly used to cure or prevent malaria.

Copper from the High Andes. This copper mine near Cerro de Pasco is more than 14,000 feet above sea level. Most of the copper ore is exported.

Quinine is obtained from the bark of the cinchona tree which was first discovered in Peru, growing wild on the eastern slopes of the Andes. Cinchona bark at first was called Jesuits' bark because the Jesuit missioners taught Europeans how to use it.

At one time Peru, Ecuador, and Bolivia produced all of the world's quinine from bark which was gathered in the forests by native Indians. Today, however, these countries produce only a small amount, just enough for their own use. Most of the world's supply of quinine now comes from Indonesia. There cinchona plantations have been established, and quinine is mass-produced efficiently and cheaply.

Through the use of quinine and other drugs, we are learning more and more about the control of tropical diseases. It is now becoming possible for people to work and live in such areas as the eastern lowlands of Peru. Here, in recent years, large sections of tropical forests have been cleared, and banana plantations are now being operated successfully.

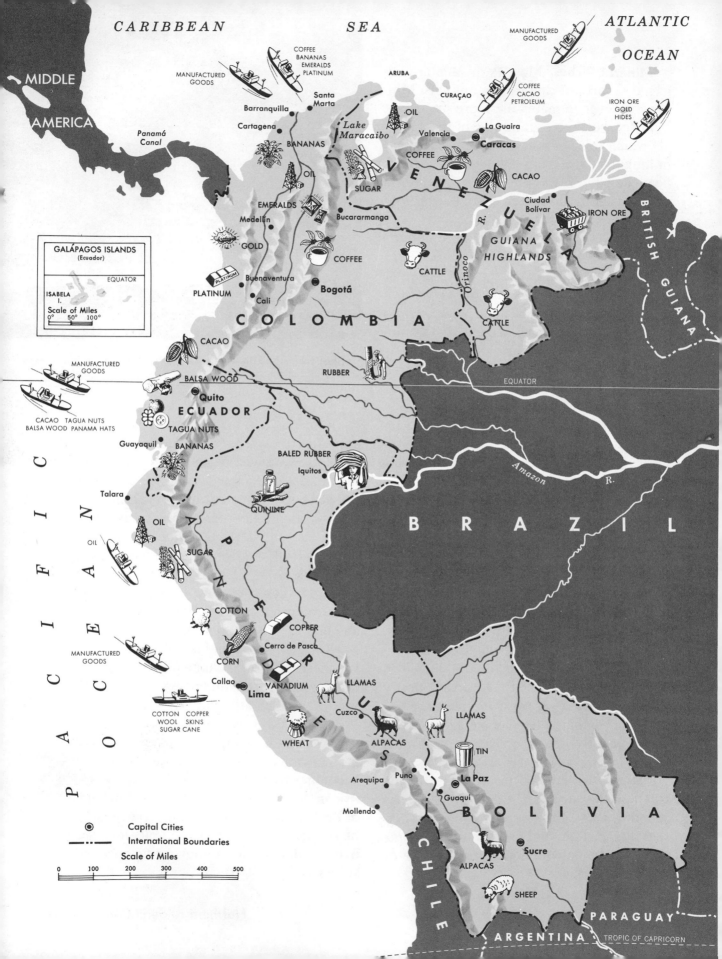

Lima, Beautiful Capital of Peru. This modern city, with its "twin city" of Callao, is the industrial and cultural capital of the country.

Lima, the Capital. Lima is the capital of Peru as well as the largest city and commercial center. This city was built about eight miles inland in a low valley. Pizarro, the Spanish conquistador, chose this site for the capital because he thought the inland location would protect the city from pirate sea raiders. Today Lima has outgrown its inland location and reaches to the coast.

Since Lima is situated in the lowlands of the tropics, you might expect it to have an unpleasantly hot climate. It is surprisingly cool, however, because of its slight elevation above the surrounding countryside and the cool breezes from the Pacific Ocean.

Manufacturing is an important industry in Lima. Its factories turn out cotton and woolen textiles, cottonseed oil, alcohol, tobacco products, and leather goods. Food products are processed in the city and there are several large meat-packing plants.

In 1940, an earthquake destroyed much of the city. Since then, many modern buildings have been erected. Green parks and wide boulevards beautify the newer parts of Lima. An ancient Spanish cathedral, a palace, and the University of San Marcos are in the older part of Lima. This university is the oldest one in America. It was founded by the Spanish in 1551, eighty-five years before Harvard University opened.

Lima has good railroad connections with the other cities on the coastal lowland. A railroad that climbs more than 14,000 feet connects the city with Cerro de Pasco, Peru's mining center. Lima has a large modern international airport. As in other South American countries, air travel between cities is part of the modern scene.

Building a New Freighter. Commerce and shipbuilding are key industries in Callao, "twin city" of Lima, and Peru's chief seaport on the Pacific.

Callao. The seaport, or "twin city" of Lima is Callao. It handles most of the country's trade. A railroad and several highways connect Callao with Lima.

Ancient City of the Incas. High in the Andes Mountains, northwest of Cuzco, lie these ruins of temples and gardens which the Incas once used.

The city is located on the mainland behind a small off-shore island. This protects the port from gales while ships are loading and unloading. The coast of Peru is too regular to provide any good natural harbors. Callao has a man-made harbor formed by stone breakwaters. Manufactured goods are imported, and cotton, sugar cane, wool, skins, and copper are exported through this port.

Other Peruvian Cities. Arequipa is the second city in size. It is located in a mountain valley in the southern part of the country, about 20 miles inland. Arequipa is the center of a rich irrigated farm area where food crops and livestock are produced. The city has direct railroad and highway connections with the seaport of Mollendo. Mollendo, like Callao, has a good man-made harbor on the Pacific coast, and handles much foreign trade.

The principal cities of the Andean region of Peru are Cerro de Pasco and Cuzco, the mining center. Cuzco was the capital of the ancient Inca Empire. Here ruins of Inca forts and other buildings still attract visitors. The Indians who live near this city go there on market day to sell or exchange their surplus farm crops and handmade blankets, rugs, baskets, and pottery for the items they need.

Iquitos is a port on the Ucayali River, a tributary of the Amazon. It is the only important city in Peru's northeast lowlands. This city serves as an inland trading center where quantities of wild rubber from the nearby Amazon region are collected and shipped down the river by steamboat.

Until recently it was very difficult to reach Lima and the west side of the Andes from Iquitos. Now a 500-mile span of modern highway crosses the Andes and connects with a branch of the Amazon River leading to this inland port.

BOLIVIA

Bolivia is a completely land-locked country east of Peru and northern Chile. Its inland location high in the Andes makes Bolivia a difficult land to reach, except by air. This country is smaller than Peru, and has only one third as many people.

Before the arrival of the Spaniards, Bolivia had been part of the Inca Empire. Then it became a Spanish colony. In 1825, after almost three centuries of Spanish rule, Bolivia won its independence. The name of this country honors Simon Bolívar, the famous South American freedom fighter.

Surface and Climate. The Andes are widest where they cross Bolivia. In Bolivia, mountains occupy one third of the land area, and most of the people live in the highlands, as they do in other Andean lands.

Two high ranges of mountains, which are really separate parts of the Andes, cover the western part of the country. Between these ranges lies the high Bolivian plateau called the *Altiplano,* meaning high plain.

The Altiplano in Bolivia reaches an elevation of 12,000 feet above sea level. Although it lies in the Tropical Zone, winters on the Altiplano are very cold because of the great height, and nights are frosty even in summer. Dry, cold winds sweep over the Altiplano, and the rainfall is always light. High mountains on all sides shut out the moisture-bearing winds. During the summer months, from October to April, the rainfall increases slightly.

Lake Titicaca is located on the Altiplano more than two miles above sea level. This body of water, on the border between Peru and Bolivia, is the largest in South America and one of the highest lakes in the world. Its surface is sometimes disturbed by furious gales. The water is usually warmer than the land, and the air over the lake is warmer, too. Soft breezes from the lake help to keep the climate nearby mild.

Indian Boats on Lake Titicaca. These fishing boats are made of reeds which grow on the lakeshore. Titicaca is on the border of Bolivia and Peru.

Northern Bolivia is part of the Amazon lowland and is covered by tropical forests. Here the climate is hot with heavy rainfall. Rubber, cacao, and other tropical products come from northern Bolivia. Few people live there.

Another hot lowland area of Bolivia lies to the southeast and is a tropical grassland. It is part of a larger region known as the Gran Chaco, which extends into Paraguay and northern Argentina, two countries south of Bolivia. Much of this area is flat, and some of it is swampy. Rain falls only during part of the year, and the region becomes increasingly more dry toward the border of Argentina.

The quebracho tree which grows in the Gran Chaco is used not only for lumber but also for producing the tannin which is extracted from its bark. The tannin extract is used to harden cowhides in finishing leather. The tree is named quebracho, or ax-breaker, because of its hard wood.

Transportation. Bolivia's location in the Andes without any coastal area makes transportation unusually difficult. Railroads from the west coast must cross Peru or Chile before reaching Bolivia. The railroads start at the Pacific ports of Mollendo in Peru and Arica and Antofagasta in Chile. They proceed cross-country to the end of the line at Puno, a small port on the Peruvian shore of Lake Titicaca. Here travelers board a steamer to cross the wide lake, which finally brings them to the Bolivian border. Another railroad line links Santa Cruz in eastern Bolivia with the Atlantic coast by crossing Brazil to the great city of Sao Paulo.

Although some modern highways have been built through the interior in recent years, most parts of this country can be reached only by way of Indian trails. The Bolivians, like their Indian neighbors in Peru, still travel mostly by foot or on horseback. Llamas are still the most common means of transporting freight.

The airplane has become an increasingly important means of transportation inside the country, as well as in connecting Bolivia with other countries on this very air-minded southern continent. The chief cities of Bolivia are linked with each other by air.

Land of Tin. Bolivia's most important industry is mining. The country has large deposits of tin, gold, silver, copper, lead, zinc, antimony, tungsten, and other minerals. Some oil fields have been located, and the petroleum industry is growing.

Tin is the most important resource of Bolivia, and the most valuable export of the country. This mineral is found only in a few other widely scattered parts of the world. About one fifth of the world's supply of tin comes from Bolivia. The mines are high up on the slopes of the Andes and are hard to reach. The tin ore is carried down to the railroad by pack animals.

Most of the mine workers are native Indians who are accustomed to the thin mountain air. Here breathing is very difficult. For people from the lower regions who are unaccustomed to the altitude, the lightest work is wearying. The Indians, however, can climb and carry burdens as at lower levels.

The ore is sent to a mill in the mountains where it is broken and washed and the waste rock removed. Tin is extracted from the ore by smelting. This is not done in Bolivia because the country lacks sufficient fuel to operate large smelters. The tin ore

Tin Mining. This mine, high in the Andes Mountains, at one time produced silver; now it yields tin. Bolivia today ranks high as a source of tin.

is shipped to the United States and Great Britain where it is prepared for use. Neither of these lands has any tin of its own, so they must import large amounts of this mineral for use in their industries. Difficulties in transportation, however, are seriously affecting the tin industry in Bolivia. More and more the tin-importing nations are turning to other countries, where the tin is more easily and more cheaply mined and transported.

Sorting Tin Ore. Most of the tin mines in Bolivia are more than 15,000 feet above sea level. Only Indians can work at such high altitudes.

A Shepherd and his Flock. The Indian wearing a large hat and cloak leads his sheep to pasture. Notice that the house behind him has no windows.

The Bolivian People.
More than half of the population is pure Indian, and one third is mestizo. The remainder of the people are mostly of Spanish descent. A smaller number of North Americans who have business interests in the country live there.

Despite the short growing season in the mountains, the light rainfall, and the stony soil, most Bolivians are farmers. They raise corn, potatoes, barley, and garden vegetables on the Altiplano. Indian herders watch over small flocks of sheep, alpacas, or llamas that graze in the hilly highlands, moving from place to place in search of grass and water.

La Paz, Bolivia. This high Andean capital is situated 12,000 feet above sea level. It lies in the shadow of Mount Illimani in the background.

All over the world people build their houses from the materials which they can obtain most easily. Since trees for lumber are scarce on the dry plateau where most of the Bolivians live, the Indians use sun-dried mud or bricks to build their homes. They construct thick walls and thick roofs to shelter their families from the cold. Many of these houses have no windows, because glass is hard to obtain.

Few of the people heat their houses because wood and other fuels are also scarce. It is even hard to obtain enough firewood to cook their meals. Bushes, moss, and dried manure have to be used for fuel.

Bolivia has elementary schools which provide free education. All children are expected to attend school today, but seven out of ten adults are still unable to read or write. Spanish is the official language, but many of the Indians speak in native dialects. Although most of the people are Roman Catholics, religious training and Catholic life suffer because of the great scarcity of clergy and religious teachers.

The Two Capitals.
Bolivia has two capitals. The old capital, Sucre, was named after a general who helped free the country from Spanish rule. This city was so hard to reach that the people made La Paz, near Lake Titicaca and the Peruvian border, the working capital. Sucre, however, still retains the title.

La Paz is on the Altiplano in a beautiful, sheltered valley about 12,000 feet above sea level, with snow-covered peaks of the Andes for a background. The city is a great trading center. Sunday is market day in La Paz and the day on which the Indians come to the city to sell and exchange grain, dried potatoes, vegetables, and other products. They attend Mass and then go to the market to buy and sell their surplus products and visit with their friends.

Facts *to remember*

1. Ecuador, Peru, and Bolivia lie entirely in the tropics. Their eastern lowland areas are jungles.
2. Most of the people of Ecuador, Peru, and Bolivia live in the high valleys of the Andes Mountains where it is cooler. The native Indians in these countries live in much the same way as they did in the days of Columbus.
3. Quito is the capital of Ecuador, but Guayaquil on the lowland coast is the largest city.
4. The principal products of Ecuador are bananas, cacao, tagua nuts, and balsa wood.
5. More than half of Peru's 9 million people are Indians descended from the Incas.
6. Peru's narrow dry coastal area must be irrigated to produce crops of cotton and sugar cane.
7. Lima is the capital and most important manufacturing city of Peru. It is noted for its universities and as a center of learning.
8. Bolivia is an inland country and has no seacoast.
9. Between two ranges of the Andes lies the high Bolivian plateau, called the Altiplano.
10. Lake Titicaca and the capital city, La Paz, are located on the Altiplano. The people of Bolivia are mostly Indians and mestizos. They raise corn, potatoes, vegetables, and small flocks of sheep, alpacas, and llamas.

What *have I learned?*

Answer each question in a complete sentence.
1. Which city is the chief seaport of Ecuador?
2. Name the largest lake in South America.
3. Which race of people is native to the Andes?
4. Name the capital of Peru.
5. What kind of plantations thrive on Ecuador's coastal lowlands?
6. What use is made of tagua nuts?
7. Why is balsa wood valuable?
8. How do most of the people in the Andean countries earn their living?
9. Which city lies almost on the equator?
10. How would you describe the climate of the coastal lowland of Peru?
11. What use is made of guano?
12. What animals graze in the Andes?
13. What city serves as a port for Lima?
14. After what great general was Bolivia named?
15. What name is given to the high plateau of Bolivia?

Facts *to understand*

In a complete sentence, give a reason for each of the statements.
1. Most of the people of the Andean countries live in the highlands.
2. The mining of tin is now less important in Bolivia than it was in the past.
3. Irrigation is necessary for farming on the coastal lowland of Peru.
4. Population is sparse on the Altiplano of Bolivia.
5. The llama is used as a beast of burden in the Andes.

Unit One Review

Questions for Discussion and Review

1. Give two reasons why transportation and communication are difficult in the Andean countries. **2.** How does the coast of South America compare with that of North America in the number of coastal bays and harbors? **3.** What modern means of transportation has helped South America? **4.** Why is the cost of building roads and railroads high in South America? **5.** Describe the production of cacao beans and their use. **6.** Where can snow be found at the equator? Why? **7.** How do the cotton plants grown in Peru differ from those grown in the southern United States? **8.** Describe the life of the highland Indian in Bolivia. **9.** What obstacles must be overcome before men can live comfortably in the Amazon lowlands? **10.** Why is South America chiefly a producer of raw materials rather than of manufactured goods? **11.** Why is the interior of South America sparsely populated? **12.** Why are llamas and alpacas raised on the higher slopes of the Andes while cattle and sheep are raised in the lower valleys? **13.** What difficulties are encountered in mining tin in Bolivia? **14.** Where are the Galápagos Islands and for what are they known? **15.** What conditions favor the growth of coffee in the highlands of Colombia?

Using the Maps and Globe

1. In what zone is northern South America?

2. How close does the southern tip of South America come to Antarctica?

3. Name the countries crossed by the equator.

4. What is the latitude and longitude of Mt. Cotopaxi? What is its height?

5. In what country is the source of the Amazon River?

6. What Indian city lies directly south of Pittsburgh, Pennsylvania?

7. Through which South American countries does the Tropic of Capricorn pass?

8. In what direction does the Magdalena River flow?

9. Name the countries that border on Colombia.

10. Using your scale of miles, figure out how far it is from Talara in Peru to Natal in Brazil.

Using Geography Words

Here is a list of special words that have been used in this unit. Write a sentence using each to show that you know its geographic meaning.

Tropical Zone	"black gold"	mesa
mestizo	llanos	quinine
guano	vanadium	Intermediate Zone
Altiplano	cacao	balsa

Getting Information from Books

Use reference books, such as *Compton's Pictured Encyclopedia,* for information on these topics. Prepare to give a report on one of them.

1. Inca Civilization
2. Pan-American Highway
3. Making Panama Hats
4. Animals of the Tropical Rainforests
5. The Galápagos Islands

Final Test

Choose the correct word or words from the parenthesis to complete each sentence. Write the complete sentence correctly on your answer paper.

1. The early settlers of the Andean countries were from (Portugal, Spain, England). 2. These early settlers were seeking (new homes, religious freedom, gold). 3. A person who cannot read or write any language is called (an illiterate, a mestizo, a llanero). 4. The river that drains most of Venezuela is the (Amazon, Magdalena, Orinoco).

5. La Guaira is the seaport for (Lima, Caracas, Bogotá). 6. Large grassy plains in Venezuela are called (llanos, mesas, jungles). 7. The (Tropic of Capricorn, equator, Tropic of Cancer) crosses Ecuador. 8. The chief mineral of Bolivia is (platinum, oil, tin). 9. The Portuguese settled in (Brazil, Venezuela, Bolivia). 10. A country that borders on the Pacific Ocean and the Caribbean Sea is (Ecuador, Colombia, Venezuela). 11. (Ecuador, Colombia, Venezuela) leads in the export of oil. 12. The capital of Bolivia is (Lima, Quito, La Paz). 13. The chief industry on the grassy plains of Venezuela is (herding, farming, mining). 14. Colombia's chief seaport is (Santa Marta, Barranquilla, Buenaventura). 15. By means of irrigation, Peru's coastal desert produces much (coffee, cacao, cotton). 16. Of the following, the country with the largest population is (Peru, Colombia, Venezuela). 17. The largest exporter of oil among the countries of South America is (Colombia, Peru, Venezuela). 18. Vanadium is an important mineral resource of (Peru, Ecuador, Bolivia). 19. Lake Maracaibo is in (Bolivia, Colombia, Venezuela). 20. Most of the world's emeralds come from (Venezuela, Peru, Colombia).

Applying Christian Principles

Choose the correct ending for each incomplete sentence. Then copy the sentences on your answer paper.

1. The early Spanish missioners in South America helped the Indians most when they a. saved them from slavery b. gave them some education c. shared with them the truths of the Christian religion.

2. The best reason for improving the transportation and communication in South America is that a. people may share ideas and resources with each other b. this continent may catch up with the progress of other continents. c. more wealth may be created on this continent.

3. The best use for the profits from the sale of oil in Venezuela is for the a. drilling of more oil wells b. welfare of uneducated and poverty-stricken people c. building of parks and tourist attractions.

4. The best reason for encouraging the Pan-American Union is that it may promote a. better trade agreements b. more highway projects to unite the countries c. better understanding of each other's problems.

Neighbors in Southern South America

CHILE   ARGENTINA

URUGUAY   PARAGUAY

**In this Unit
you will learn that:**

1 Chile and Argentina extend so far from north to south that they have a variety of climate, vegetation, and land use.

2 Chile, Argentina, and Uruguay are among the most progressive countries of South America.

3 The mineral resources of Chile and the farm products of its rich Central Valley have helped make it a modern progressive country.

4 Argentina, the second largest country in South America, makes excellent use of its agricultural resources and animal industries and has become one of the great food-producing regions of the world, as well as one of the world's great trading nations.

5 Argentina has a large trade with the nations of Western Europe to whom she sends wheat and grain.

6 The people of Uruguay have used their vast grassland area to develop animal industries which play a major part in supporting its small population.

7 Paraguay, with fewer people than the city of Detroit, has not been able to develop a high standard of living in spite of some rich natural resources.

The five South American countries that we have already studied are located in the Tropical Zone. Now we come to four countries which lie mostly in the Southern Intermediate Zone. A look at the map shows that Chile and Argentina have all but their northern tips in this zone. The greater part of Paraguay, also, and all of Uruguay, lie in the Southern Intermediate Zone.

Chile and Argentina both extend a long way from north to south. On page 56, a map of these countries has been placed over a map of North America. Notice that Chile and Argentina extend from the northern part of Ontario, in Canada, southward across the United States to southern Mexico. Therefore, the two countries have a climate which varies greatly from north to south.

Uruguay and Paraguay, much smaller countries, do not have the wide range of climate found in Chile and Argentina. Uruguay has a temperate, seacoast climate; Paraguay, an inland country, has a subtropical climate, where it is pleasantly warm most of the time.

Pacific Ocean

SOUTHERN
SOUTH AMERICA

The narrowing tip of southern South America displays many different surface features. Along the Pacific coast lies the bone-dry strip of the Atacama Desert. To the south, the barren desert gives way to the green valley of central Chile. Farther south still, the coast breaks up into a number of rocky, forested islands, reaching to Cape Horn.

In the center you can see the brownish area which is the wilderness of the Gran Chaco. South of it, extending inland from the mouth of the Paraguay-Paraná River, is the fertile grasslands area called the Pampa, the "breadbasket of South America." South of the Pampa is the desert-like plateau of Patagonia. The white area shows the frozen ice-packs of Antarctica.

ANTARCTICA

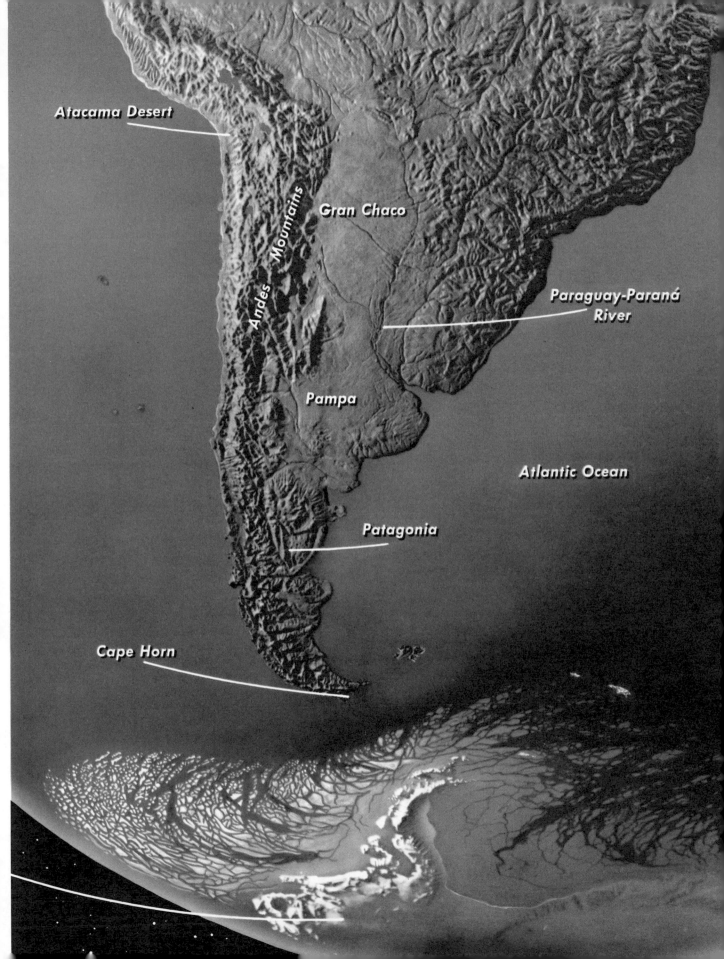

Atacama Desert

Andes Mountains

Gran Chaco

Paraguay-Paraná
River

Pampa

Atlantic Ocean

Patagonia

Cape Horn

Chile

Chile is sometimes called "the shoe-string country." A look at the map on page 58 will show that Chile does look somewhat like a shoestring lying along the southwestern coast of South America. Chile extends 2620 miles from north to south. Although it is about 250 miles from east to west at its widest point, most of the country is only about 100 miles in width.

Chile is wedged between the Pacific Ocean on the west and the snow-capped Andes Mountains which form its eastern boundary. Peru touches Chile's border in the north, Bolivia is located to the northeast, and Argentina lies along its eastern border, across the Andes. In area, Chile is about 20,000 square miles larger than the state of Texas, but its population numbers only four fifths the population of Texas.

The Chilean People. The Spaniards who came to Chile over 400 years ago settled in a long central valley. The climate found there by the early explorers was very much like the Mediterranean climate of Spain. As in other Latin American countries, the Spaniards married and settled down to live among the native Indians. Today, out of a population of more than seven million people, about two thirds are mestizos. About one tenth of the population is made up of Indians, and the remaining quarter consists of white Europeans and South Americans, mostly of Spanish, Italian, and German descent.

The language of Chile is Spanish. Most of the people are Roman Catholics by birth, but the shortage of priests, Brothers, and Sisters makes it difficult for some to learn and practice their religion. Educational opportunities are not complete, but they are better in Chile than in most South American countries.

The hard-working people of Chile strive to make it a modern, progressive country. In fact, Chile is often ranked with two other leading countries of South America—Argentina and Brazil. Together, these three prosperous leaders of South America are called the "ABC countries."

Chile and the United States have been friendly neighbors for many years. Recently, in 1960, a severe earthquake struck Chile, causing great damage and loss of life. The people of the United States, especially the Catholic people, contributed large amounts of food and clothing to their suffering neighbors in Chile.

Three Regions. Chile has three distinct climatic regions, each one sharply contrasting with the others. The dry northern desert, the pleasant central valley, and the rainy southern forest are different in many ways.

The Northern Desert Region. The narrow coastal region in the north is really a continuation of Peru's dry Pacific coastal area. In Chile it is called the Atacama Desert, and it is one of the driest areas in the world. The rainfall is extremely light. In some parts of the Atacama Desert, ten or fifteen years have been known to pass without any rainfall. One weather station here has never reported a single drop of rain.

A look at the map on page 58 will help to explain this unusually dry condition. The Andes Mountains tower to their greatest heights just east of the Atacama Desert. The trade winds which blow from the southeast are completely blocked by this high mountain wall. The air rises, is cooled, and loses all its moisture as it strikes the eastern slopes of the Andes. Thus the winds are dry by the time they reach the desert on the Pacific coast. Sometimes cool, moisture-bearing winds will blow toward the desert from the Pacific Ocean in the west. These winds are heated when they reach the land,

however, and so retain their moisture instead of releasing it.

Of course, the lack of rain seriously affects the vegetation in this area. People who cross this desert part of Chile often go for miles without seeing grass, shrubs, or trees. Even the usual desert plants like cactus are seldom seen in this dusty, arid land.

The Rainy Southern Region. Southern Chile, on the other hand, has a cool, wet climate. It is lashed by many storms, high winds, and heavy rain and snow. This hilly region, which includes thousands of islands lying along the irregular shore line, is mostly a wilderness of rain-swept forests and grassland.

A rocky coastal chain of islands forms the southern tip of Chile, ending with the island called Tierra del Fuego. The western part of Tierra del Fuego is Chilean territory, whereas the eastern part belongs to Argentina. Cape Horn, the southernmost tip of South America, is located on this island. Ushuaia, the capital of Tierra del Fuego, was for many years the world's most southern permanent settlement. Now there is a small town even farther south.

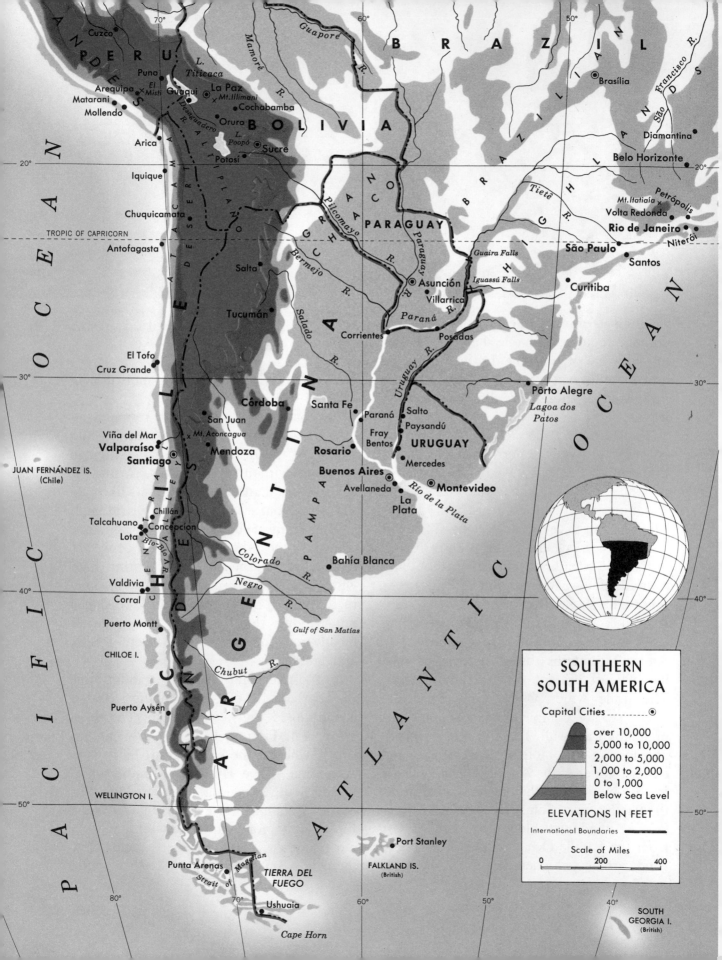

SOUTHERN
SOUTH AMERICA

Capital Cities .... ⊙

over 10,000
5,000 to 10,000
2,000 to 5,000
1,000 to 2,000
0 to 1,000
Below Sea Level

ELEVATIONS IN FEET

International Boundaries _____

Scale of Miles
0   200   400

Studying the Map

A. 1. To understand why Chile is called the "shoestring country," use the scale of miles on the map to measure the length and width of the country. How much greater is the length of Chile than its width? **2.** Name the large island south of the Strait of Magellan. What two countries share possession of this island? **3.** Where in Chile are the lowland areas located? the highlands? **4.** Why would you expect overland transportation between Chile and Argentina to be difficult? **5.** In what part of Chile is the climate very dry? How can you tell from the map? **6.** In what part of Chile do you suppose the greatest number of people live? How can you tell from the map? **7.** Find Valparaíso and Santiago, Chile's largest cities.

B. 1. How does the latitude of Argentina compare with that of Australia? (Check with the map of Australia on page 198.) Which extends farther north? farther south? **2.** What is the latitude of Buenos Aires? How does it compare with the latitude of New York City? Which city is farther from the equator? **3.** Where in Argentina are the lowland areas located? the highland areas? **4.** Why would you expect agriculture to be a more important industry in Argentina than in Chile? **5.** What name is given to the Argentine lowland inland from Buenos Aires? **6.** Buenos Aires is Argentina's chief city and port. On what body of water is it located?

C. 1. Compare Uruguay with Paraguay in area and location. **2.** How does the surface of these two countries compare with that of the countries in western South America? **3.** Name the countries which border Uruguay. Which countries border Paraguay? **4.** Name the river which forms the boundary between Uruguay and Argentina. **5.** On which rivers would one travel by boat to reach Asuncion, the capital of Paraguay? **6.** On which body of water is Montevideo, Uruguay's chief city and port? Name the southern country in which each of the following cities is located: Bahia Blanca, Antofagasta, La Plata, Cordoba, Concepcion, Tucuman, Villarica.

The Fertile Central Valley. Between the Atacama Desert in the dry north and the area of forests and grasslands in the rainy south lies Chile's Central Valley. The early explorers settled here, and most of the people live here today. This fertile central region is the heart of Chile.

The Central Valley is about 900 miles long. It lies sandwiched between the high Andes on the east, and a range of lower mountains along the west coast. The entire valley is criss-crossed by many streams, which are fed by the melting Andean snows. These streams provide an excellent source of water for irrigation, especially important in the drier northern part of the Central Valley. In the same way the central valley of California is irrigated by the streams flowing down from the Sierra Nevada Mountains.

The northern and southern parts of the Central Valley of Chile are considerably different. The northern two thirds is dry in summer. During this season it resembles the Atacama Desert farther north. In winter, however, moist winds blow in from the south, bringing abundant rainfall. The climate of this northern part of the Central Valley is very like that of California's central valley. It has a Mediterranean type of climate—warm, dry summers and cool, rainy winters.

The southern part of the Central Valley of Chile has rain all year round. Its climate somewhat resembles the rainy climate of the region of forests and grasslands in the south of Chile. The southern Central Valley, however, does not experience the extremes of cold, wind, and rain which are the rule farther south.

In addition to being an agricultural district, the Central Valley of Chile is fast becoming a center of industry, trade, and commerce.

Chilean Nitrate Mine. First, drills like these break up the ore. Then power shovels load it onto cars to be transported to the crushing mills.

The Chilean nitrate beds were probably formed millions of years ago by chemical deposits in streams that have long since dried up and disappeared. The extreme dryness of the desert has kept intact the mineral deposits in the dry creekbeds. The lack of rainfall prevents the nitrate from being dissolved and washed away.

Most of the deposits of nitrate are found within a few feet of the surface of the ground in Chile. In the mining operation, the top layer of earth is scraped away by bulldozers. Blasting powder is then used to break up the exposed nitrate rock. This is picked up by steam shovels, loaded on trucks or railway cars, and hauled to nearby processing plants. Railroads carry the nitrate to Pacific ports for export.

A number of towns in northern Chile

Nitrate From the Desert. Nitrate is a mineral widely used as a fertilizer because it contains *nitrogen,* a chemical very necessary to strong plant life. When spread on the ground, nitrate enriches the soil with nitrogen. Nitrate is also used in the manufacture of explosives and other useful chemical products. *Iodine,* for example, is a valuable substance obtained as a by-product in processing nitrate.

Years ago, the Atacama Desert was the world's principal source of nitrate, and nitrate was then Chile's leading export. During the first World War, however, scientists learned how to produce this mineral from the nitrogen in the air. Since then it has become cheaper to manufacture nitrate this way than to mine it. Nevertheless, two thirds of the iodine which the world uses still comes from Chile.

LIFE IN A COPPER CITY

Everybody who lives in Chuquicamata—"the copper city"—is involved in some part of the copper mining business. In fact, this city came into being for only one purpose. It serves the needs of the people who produce copper from the richest deposit of copper ore in the world.

Some of the people of Chuqui are from the United States—engineers and technicians who supervise the job of mining and smelting the ore. The largest number of people here are Chilean, however. These ambitious people — some Spanish, some Indian or mestizo — have become very skillful at their various jobs.

They are proud of their work, of the good wages they earn, and of their

still depend on the nitrate industry. Workers and their families live near the nitrate plants. Water from lakes and streams high in the Andes must be piped into the mining towns in the desert. Some of these water pipes extend for more than a hundred miles.

Copper Mining. Chile is one of the largest producers of copper in the world. It ranks second only to the United States in the production of this valuable metal. Most of the copper mined in Chile is exported.

Vast deposits of copper ore lie in the dry, mountainous Atacama Desert in northern Chile. The richest part of this copper region is located inland, near the town of Chuquicamata. Chuquicamata, or "Chuqui" as it is called for short, is about two miles above sea level. It is almost one hundred miles from the port city of Antofagasta. There are also a few smaller copper mines in other parts of northern Chile.

The copper ore around Chuqui lies near the surface. This means that all the work is done at the surface of the ground in an open-pit mine. With the help of modern machinery, the miners of Chuqui are actually cutting down a whole mountain to supply copper for the world's industry. The ore is hauled to a nearby smelting plant where the copper is removed. Since a ton of ore yields less than 50 pounds of pure copper, the smelting must be done near the mine. It would cost too much to ship the raw copper ore which contains so much heavy, waste rock.

The town of Chuqui was once only a

homes. The example shown by these ambitious copper workers does much to encourage the growth of industry in other parts of Chile.

small mining camp. It has grown year by year until today it is a city of 25,000 people. Most of the men work in the copper mine or smelter. Chuqui is situated in an arid, bleak desert region, where no trees, gardens, or vegetation can thrive. As in the case of the nitrate workers' settlements, food and water for the copper workers and their families must be brought in from the outside.

The mine and all the other facilities at Chuqui are owned and operated by an American company. This company has built houses for the Chilean workmen and their families. It also provides water by running pipelines great distances, and electricity by stringing high tension wires from power plants on the coast. Food, clothing, and other necessities are shipped into Chuqui and sold in company stores. Several large schools and churches have been built by the company, and hospitals have been installed to provide medical care. Even motion picture theatres have been built to bring entertainment to the people of Chuqui.

Iron and Coal Resources. High grade iron ore is plentiful in many parts of Chile, but so far only a small part of this natural resource has been put to use. In the northern region of the Atacama Desert, about 15 miles from the coast, an American company operates a large open-pit mine. The ore from this mine is very high in iron content; in fact, each ton of ore is almost one half pure iron.

The iron ore is hauled to the coast by railroads. There it is loaded on freighters which carry it through the Panama Canal to the company's steel mills near Baltimore, on Chesapeake Bay. This same company also operates the iron mines we read about when studying Venezuela. Since Venezuela is much closer to the United States steel mills, it is likely to produce more iron ore than Chile for some time. Chile's own rapidly growing industries, however, will soon require larger and larger amounts of iron ore to supply tools, machinery, railroad tracks, and structural steel. In the years ahead, Chile should become a major producer of iron ore for industries both at home and abroad.

More coal is mined in Chile than in all the other South American countries combined. From an area on the coast of central Chile, the coal fields extend out under the Pacific Ocean. The shafts leading to these deep mines have their entrances on the coast near Lota, south of Concepción, and reach out to the beds of coal under the ocean. Although Chilean coal does not make the best grade coke for blast furnaces, it costs much less to use than imported coke.

Chuquicamata. This large copper refining plant was built by a North American company. Notice the dry, barren landscape of the Atacama Desert.

Farming in the Central Valley. Most of Chile's farmland lies in the fertile Central Valley where the use of irrigation produces rich crops. Most of the land is divided into large estates. An estate owner hires workers, who bring their families to live with them. Each worker is paid a small salary and receives some of his food free. He is also given a small adobe house, and a piece of land for garden crops to feed his family. One-family farms, such as those in our country, are still rare in Chile, although the government is trying to encourage small farmers.

A traveler journeying southward in the Central Valley passes many vineyards. Some of the grapes are eaten fresh; others are dried for raisins. Most of the grape crop, however, is used to make the fine wines for which Chile is noted. Growing in the vineyard country are small orchards of orange, lemon, grapefruit, fig, peach, cherry, and olive trees. These are the crops which do well in this Mediterranean climate. Here and there are fields of wheat, corn, potatoes, beans, and peas. There are many large dairy farms, and cattle can be seen grazing in pastures by the roadsides.

Farther south in the Central Valley, the climate gradually becomes cooler with more rain. Here irrigation is not needed to grow wheat and other grains, potatoes, hay, and apples. There is plenty of good pasture land for cattle and sheep.

Forests and Forestry. There are many forests in the rainy southern section of Chile, but their wood is used mainly for fuel. Although some lumbering is done here, Chile can produce only a small part of the wood it requires. The dampness and the rain make lumbering difficult, because the wood must be shipped long distances to market, and it is hard to haul logs over muddy roads.

Vineyards in the Central Valley. Farmers, shielded from the sun by their wide-brimmed hats, stop for a chat. Note the rider's colorful costume.

There are some furniture factories around Valdivia, and boats are built of wood on the island of Chiloe. In general, however, Chilean timber is more suitable for fence posts and poles than for use in construction. Some wood for building purposes is imported from the United States.

Lumbering in Southern Chile. In the heavily forested southern section, the cold and the rain make it very difficult to produce much lumber.

Sheep Grazing near Punta Arenas. These mounted shepherds are herding their flocks along the level plains and good pastures of south Chile.

Ranchers and Ranching. The settlers in the southern section of Chile, especially on Tierra del Fuego, are mostly sheep ranchers. The ocean breezes help to keep the climate of the island moderate. They bring cooler weather in the summer and keep the winters from getting too cold. Even though some snow falls in winter, the sheep can still find enough food to eat. They usually remain outdoors throughout the year.

Many of the island ranches are a thousand acres or more in extent. They are far apart, and towns are few. Friendly Scottish herders and their dogs look after the herds.

Both sheep and wool are brought to the city of Punta Arenas. There are meatpacking plants in this city where the sheep are slaughtered, and the mutton is frozen. The meat is packed for shipment, along with large quantities of wool.

Punta Arenas is located in the middle of the Strait of Magellan. Ships passing through the strait usually stop at this port city and deliver manufactured goods needed by the people of the island. When leaving, they carry away wool and hides.

Chilean Industry. In recent times manufacturing has become very important in cities of the Central Valley. Chileans are now beginning to take advantage of their rich mineral resources and the products of their farms, forests, and ranches. More and more machines and other items which once had to be imported are now made in Chilean factories and mills.

Much money has been invested to spur the growth of Chilean industry and produce a large variety and quantity of manufactured products. Mills and factories have been modernized by the addition of new machinery, and many new plants have been built. Students from Chile have spent time in schools and factories of the United States and Europe, learning and observing modern industrial methods. They return to their country with valuable knowledge and experience. Chilean industry has also profited from advice received from the governments of the United States and other countries.

Factories and mills in Chile require electric power, of course, for their operation. Electricity is generated in plants which use coal from Chile's own mines, or water power provided by streams running down the slopes of the nearby Andes.

Santiago. The capital and largest city in Chile is Santiago, which has more than a million people. Located in the northern part of the Central Valley, in the heart of a farming region, the city serves as a great trading center. It has a delightful climate.

Mountains and hills surround Santiago on all sides. The city streets are lined with trees. Small parks, beautiful churches, and fine public buildings add to the charm of the city. Most of the houses are built in the Spanish style, with an open area in the center called a *patio*. Providing water is no problem here; a good supply is available from nearby mountain lakes and streams.

Santiago is Chile's leading manufacturing center. A great many items are made here, including iron and steel products, woolen textiles, shoes, furniture, clothing, paints, paper, glass, and food products.

Santiago has railroad connections with other parts of Chile and with Buenos Aires, Argentina, nearly one thousand miles to the east. It has a busy international airport with regular flights to and from North American and European countries as well as local flights to other South American cities. Transportation is excellent between Santiago and the port of Valparaíso on the coast. In addition to the railroad, a fine, 90-mile highway connects the two cities.

Valparaíso. Less than 100 miles northwest of Santiago is Valparaíso, the second largest city of Chile and the leading seaport on the entire Pacific coast of South America. Ocean travelers reach Chile through this port. It is also the gateway to the Central Valley, hence the name Valparaíso, which means "Valley of Paradise."

Valparaíso is the western terminal of the only transcontinental railroad in South America. In addition, it is linked by rail, highway, air, and sea with other cities on the continent and throughout the world.

Santiago in Chile. The Plaza Libertad, with its stately monument, is the heart of modern Santiago. Note the skyscrapers, automobiles, and trucks.

Valparaíso's natural harbor is deep and wide. It had no natural protection from storms, winds, and rough waves until the city constructed a breakwater, a protective barrier one half mile long. The port has very modern equipment for loading and unloading ships, and large warehouses for storage.

Manufacturing of the same type as in Santiago is carried on in Valparaíso. There are also many hotels, banks, stores, and other commercial buildings in this bustling port city.

The Harbor at Valparaíso. This is one of the busiest and biggest ports on the Pacific coast of South America. Notice the new cars on the dockside.

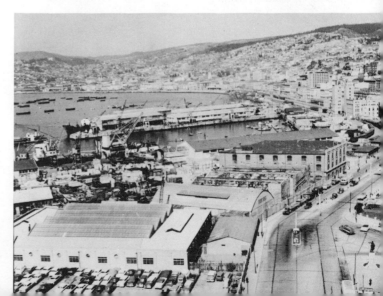

A Steel Mill at Concepción. Modern steel mills like this one, with its ovens, converters, and coal chutes, demonstrate Chile's growing industry.

Concepción. This is a coastal city on the estuary of the Bio-Bio River, several hundred miles south of Santiago and Valparaíso. It is Chile's third largest city and has 90,000 inhabitants. Large modern ships cannot reach Concepción, so the city is served by a small port on the coast.

Concepción owes its importance as a manufacturing city to the nearby coal fields. From them comes the fuel for the power plants which produce the electricity to run the textile mills. Both woolen and cotton goods are made in these large mills.

City of the North. Antofagasta, located in the north of Chile, handles the trade of the Atacama Desert region. Notice the warehouses and cranes.

Chile's largest steel mills are also located near Concepción. Some of the iron that was once exported from northern Chile is now brought here. Coal from the local mines is used to extract the iron and convert it into steel. Busy plants at Concepción are now turning out a great variety of heavy industrial products which once had to be imported.

Valdivia. On the Bio-Bio River in the southern part of the Central Valley is the small but lively city of Valdivia. Valdivia is growing by leaps and bounds, and now has a population of 40,000 people.

Two Northern Ports. The two most important cities in the northern part of the country are Iquique and Antofagasta.

Nitrate and nitrate products are shipped from both Iquique and Antofagasta. Antofagasta, the more important of the two, exports copper and iron as well. It serves as the port for Chuquicamata, to which it is connected by railroad. Another railroad runs inland to Bolivia.

Like many other west coast ports, Antofagasta lacks a good natural harbor. Since the water is not deep enough for large ocean ships to come right up to the docks, they are forced to drop anchor about a half mile from shore. Small boats called *lighters* transfer freight and passengers between the shore and the large ships.

"ROBINSON CRUSOE'S ISLAND"

Two small bits of land called the Juan Fernandez Islands lie about 500 miles off the coast of Chile. They are west of Valparaíso, and about thirty hours away by steamship. The islands have been set aside as national parks by the government of Chile.

A sailor named Alexander Selkirk was once shipwrecked near these islands. He spent four lonely years on one of them before being rescued. Daniel Defoe, the author of "Robinson Crusoe," based his famous story on Selkirk's true adventure. Ever since then, one of the Juan Fernandez Islands has been called "Robinson Crusoe's Island."

Facts to remember

1. Chile is a long, narrow, coastal country with three climatic regions: the dry northern desert, the fruitful, well-populated central valley, and the rainy southern forest.

2. The Atacama Desert region in northern Chile is rich in minerals, especially nitrate, copper, and iron ore.

3. Coal is mined in the coastal area of central Chile south of the city of Concepción. The coal is used in new iron and steel mills built near the mines.

4. Much of Chile's farming is carried on in the Central Valley on large estates. Vineyards and orchards produce Mediterranean type crops, such as grapes, citrus fruits, olives, and figs. Irrigation is necessary in the northern part of the valley.

5. Lumbering is difficult in the forests of the rainy southern section of Chile because of poor transportation. Some lumber is cut and is used for furniture, boats, posts, and poles.

6. The island of Tierra del Fuego is partly Chilean territory. Here the cool wet climate is ideal for sheep raising. Punta Arenas is a port for exporting frozen mutton, fine wool, and sheep skin.

7. Santiago, the capital city, has a population of more than one million people. It is located in the heart of the Central Valley farming section and leads in the manufacture of food products, iron and steel, textiles, furniture, and clothing.

8. Valparaíso, an excellent port city, has good rail, water, and air transportation. Farther south Concepción, Chile's third largest city, is noted for its manufactures of iron and steel products.

9. Iquique and Antofagasta are northern ports. Chile's nitrate, copper, and iron, as well as Bolivia's tin, are exported through these cities.

What have I learned?

Answer each of the following in a complete sentence.

1. Name the ABC countries of South America.
2. In which part of Chile is the Atacama Desert?
3. Name a valuable by-product of nitrate.
4. What is the capital and largest city of Chile?
5. What services must the mining company provide for the people who live in Chuquicamata?
6. Name a Chilean seaport on the Strait of Magellan.
7. Name three manufacturing cities of Chile.
8. Give two uses of central Chile's large grape crop.
9. What Pacific ports of Chile can be used by Bolivia?
10. Name two sources of electric power in Chile.

Facts to understand

Give a reason in a complete sentence for each of the following statements.

1. Most of Chile's people live in the Central Valley.
2. Chilean nitrate and copper is easy to mine.
3. Chile's largest steel mills are located near Concepción.
4. Nitrate is no longer Chile's leading export.
5. Chile is called "the shoestring country."

2

Argentina

Argentina's Capital. Buenos Aires is a world port, located on the Rio de la Plata. Channels had to be deepened to admit large ships like this.

Argentina, next-door neighbor of "the shoestring country," is the largest of the four countries in southern South America and somewhat resembles a triangle in shape. Look at the map on page 58. It shows that Argentina is widest in the north, and tapers gradually toward the south.

Argentina is about one third the size of the United States, and has a population one eighth as large as that of the United States. Among the countries of South America, Argentina ranks second in area and size of population. Only Brazil is larger.

Argentina ranks second among the countries of South America in one other very important respect—number of acres of fertile farm land. Again, only Brazil has more land suitable for raising crops. Argentina has made excellent use of its great agricultural resources. Today it is a world leader in the production and export of food products.

The People and the Government. Like other countries of South America, Argentina was originally settled by Spaniards. It remained a colony of Spain until 1810, when the Argentine people joined the general movement throughout South America and won their freedom. It did not develop into a modern country, however, until the beginning of widespread railroad building in 1860. Today, of all the countries originally colonized by Spain, Argentina is the most prosperous and successful.

Immigrants from Europe flocked to Argentina, just as they did to the United States. As in our country, they supplied the labor, imagination, and ambition which helped to build a growing nation. Argentina's waves of immigrants arrived at a slightly later date in history than ours, the largest numbers arriving between 1900 and 1914. The Argentine government has always encouraged immigration.

About four fifths of Argentina's twenty million people are of Spanish descent, and Spanish is the national language of Argentina. There are also many whose families came from Italy, France, and Germany. Unlike the other countries we have been studying, Argentina has only a small number of mestizos, and an even smaller number of Indians, among its population.

By far the largest part of the population of Argentina are Roman Catholics. However, as in other countries of South America, the Catholic Faith is not as strong among the people as it would be if there were more priests and more Catholic schools.

The constitution of Argentina is patterned after ours in the United States. For a time, Argentina was controlled by a dictator. After he had been in office for some years, he began to assume powers not granted him by the constitution. He persecuted the Church and closed some Catholic schools. In 1955, however, the Argentine people overthrew this dictator. An elected, constitutional government was put into office. It is still trying to solve many of the financial problems brought on during the rule of this wasteful dictator.

A Natural Boundary. The Andes Mountains form a clear, natural boundary between Chile and Argentina. The actual political boundary line is set along the Continental Divide at the top of the Andes. High crests and ridges here separate the rivers which flow east to the Atlantic from those which flow west to the Pacific.

Argentines and Chileans at one time bitterly disagreed about the exact location of their common boundary. When the disagreement threatened to break out into open warfare, the leaders of both countries wisely decided to find a Christian solution by meeting together to settle their dispute. As a result of their conference, the present line was agreed upon.

To seal the agreement, a pledge of everlasting peace was made between Argentina and Chile. As a reminder of this pledge, the nations erected a huge statue of Christ in a mountain pass on the border. *The Christ of the Andes,* as this statue has been named, is now world-famous.

"Sooner Shall These Mountains crumble into dust than the Argentines and Chileans break the peace sworn at the feet of Christ the Redeemer."

Highest Peak in the Americas. Mount Aconcagua, on the border of Argentina and Chile, is 2500 feet higher than Mount McKinley in North America.

Surface Features. The western border of Argentina, as you have seen, is formed by high, rugged mountains. In this section of the Andes, there are few passes through the mountains, and they are very high. For this reason, transportation by land between Argentina and Chile is difficult.

Resort City on Argentine Coast. This is a scene in Mar del Plata, on the Atlantic coast, known for its excellent swimming and fishing facilities.

Mt. Aconcagua in Argentina rises to a height of more than 23,000 feet. Not only is it the highest peak in South America, but it is the highest in the entire Western Hemisphere. A plateau, 200 miles wide in some places, lies along the eastern foothills of the Andes in western Argentina. East of this plateau is a region of broad plains called the Pampa. The level Pampa extends eastward to the Atlantic Ocean.

The Rivers. A great network of rivers drains the northern half of Argentina. The Uruguay and the Paraguay-Paraná rivers and their tributaries empty into the Rio de la Plata, forming one of the world's great river systems. Although the word *rio* is Spanish for river, the Rio de la Plata is not really a river. It is an *estuary*. This means that it is an arm of the Atlantic Ocean indenting the coast at the point where the Uruguay and Paraguay-Paraná rivers empty.

An early explorer entered the estuary from the ocean and sailed up its tidal waters for several miles. Soon he met some Indians wearing silver ornaments. Mistaking the estuary for a wide river, and believing it would lead him to regions where there were deposits of silver, the explorer called the body of water *rio de la plata*—river of silver. He was also mistaken about the silver. Very little has ever been found there.

The Rio de la Plata is deep enough for ocean-going ships to sail as far as the harbor of Buenos Aires. Passengers and cargo transfer there to other shallow-draft boats which take them to the northern interior of Argentina, to Uruguay, and to Paraguay.

Five Regions of Argentina. Argentina may be divided into five natural regions which differ in surface, in climate, and in other ways. They are: the Pampa, Argentine Mesopotamia, the Gran Chaco, Northwestern Argentina, and Patagonia.

Argentine Gauchos. Like cowboys in the United States, these herders of the Pampa are skillful horsemen. They take pride in their fancy clothing.

The Pampa. The Spanish word meaning a grassy, treeless plain is *pampa*. One of the world's great grassland areas occupies a large part of Argentina and is called the Pampa. Locate it on the map on page 58. The Pampa includes about 250,000 square miles of land, spread out like an open fan from its base at Buenos Aires. It takes in one fourth of the area of Argentina, extending 700 miles from north to south and 400 miles from east to west. Here a traveler can ride for miles without seeing a hill.

The Pampa extends inland from Buenos Aires, the capital of Argentina and chief city of the plain. Many villages and cities are scattered over the region, which in many respects resembles the Great Central Plains of the United States.

The soil of the Pampa is deep, fertile, and easily plowed. The temperate climate and the rainfall conditions favor many kinds of farming and the animal industries. Level land makes it easy to use farm machinery. About half of the region is farm land; the remainder is used to graze livestock. Summers on the Pampa are warm, and the winters tend to be cool rather than cold. Frosts rarely occur, but even when they do they are seldom severe enough to kill crops. Some snow falls in the interior parts of the region during the winter season.

Despite the fine soil and the fairly long growing season, farmers of the Pampa have their problems, just as farmers everywhere. Certain sections of the Pampa do not always get enough rainfall. Frosts have sometimes damaged the crops. Occasionally hot winds from the north or sudden summer hailstorms cause damage to the growing plants. During certain years great swarms of locusts have invaded the fields, eating every plant and seed in sight. The farmers try to keep these insects under control, but they never succeed in killing all of them.

A Gaucho at Work. Twirling his lasso, this cowboy of the Pampa goes into action on his herd of fine cattle. Notice the level land all around him.

The Livestock Industry. The early Spanish settlers brought horses, cattle, and sheep to the Argentine Pampa. The wide grassy plains were ideal for raising livestock. Vast cattle ranches were founded, similar to those in Texas and other parts of our Great Plains. Later, fine strains of cattle were imported from England and the Netherlands to improve the quality of the Argentine stock. Today, Argentine cattle are among the finest in the world.

Large Argentine ranches are called *estancias,* and the herders who work on them are called *gauchos.* An owner of an estancia hires many gauchos to care for his large herds of cattle. The cowboys and their families live on the estancia in quarters provided by the owner. The hard-riding gauchos work with the cattle in much the same way as cowboys do in the western part of our country. They drive the animals from pasture to pasture and brand the calves. They also keep in repair the miles and miles of barbed wire fencing which surround the grazing areas.

Beef cattle cannot be expected to produce the best quality of meat if fed only on native grass. On the estancias large areas are given over to growing alfalfa. This crop, when cut, provides hay which is used to fatten the animals before they are driven to market. At least three fourths of the beef cattle in Argentina are raised on the Pampa.

Ranchers on the Pampas drive or ship their cattle to the stockyards at the large meat-packing plants in the cities of Buenos Aires and La Plata. Argentina exports many meat products to Great Britain and Europe, especially frozen, chilled, and canned meats. Hides from the animals are also an important export.

Horses, hogs, and sheep are raised on the Pampa, in addition to beef cattle. Part of the sheep industry has moved westward to the drier parts of the Pampa region, where mutton sheep are raised. A major part of Argentina's woolen industry has moved southward to Patagonia.

GAUCHOS OF ARGENTINA

Cowboys in Argentina, once called *gauchos,* do the same work on the pampa that cowboys of America do on the western cattle ranges. Like the American cowboys also, the modern Argentine cowboys are no longer the lonely, reckless riders of the range they once were. Because of the improved methods of herding cattle, the colorful gauchos are being replaced by modern cowboys, using modern equipment.

At one time, the gauchos were hardy frontiersmen. They came to the pampa when it was unknown and unsettled. They took jobs for low wages, herding the wild range cattle to market. They wore colorful costumes, loved to dance and sing, and were proud of their skill at riding and throwing the *bola,* a kind of lasso. At times, they lived for weeks in rough camps along the trails.

Today, railroads carry the cattle to market, and a modern cowhand on a ranch can cover more miles in a jeep or a truck than the old-fashioned gaucho could on horseback. Still, the old-time gauchos and their modern descendants like to gather together and talk of past adventures.

They dress up for rodeos and special occasions, and are proud of their skill at dancing, singing, and horsemanship.

Harvest Time on the Pampa. The wheat crop is being brought in by means of a horse-drawn combine. Argentina ranks first in the export of wheat.

Cultivating Corn. These men are plowing along the rows, killing weeds. This corn belt produces more corn than any other part of South America.

A Great "Bread Basket." Argentina is South America's "bread basket." Wheat is the chief crop. It is raised along a 600-mile belt stretching across the Pampa from Santa Fe to Bahia Blanca on the coast. The wheat belt receives less rain than some other parts of the Pampa. This is ideal, since wheat requires less rain than other cereal crops.

Argentine wheat is planted between May and August. These are fall and winter months in the Southern Hemisphere. The wheat is harvested during the summer season which, on the Pampa, extends from November through January. Tractors are used on most of the large wheat farms to pull the plows that prepare the soil for planting. Horses and oxen are still used on the smaller farms. The wheat is harvested with combines and other types of farm machinery imported from the United States.

Some of the wheat crop goes to flour mills and to factories that make cereal products. Argentina raises much more wheat, however, than its people need. At Buenos Aires, La Plata, and Bahia Blanca, the surplus wheat is stored in grain elevators. When ready for export, it is poured into the holds of vessels and shipped to Great Britain and other countries of Western Europe.

Another Cereal Crop. Argentina's corn belt extends from an area of the Pampa just north of Buenos Aires westward to the foothills of the Andes. Corn is another cereal crop grown in surplus quantities in this country. Like its companion crop, wheat, most of the corn is exported to Britain and other countries of Western Europe. In fact, Argentina exports more corn than any other country in the world.

Some of the corn is ground into meal for table use. A small amount is also used as

feed for cattle, horses, hogs, and chickens, but corn is not used so widely here for animal feed as it is in the United States. The vast grasslands of the Pampa supply more than enough grazing for livestock.

Flax and Linseed Oil. Flax can be grown either for its fiber or for its seed. North of the corn belt lies an area where flax is raised for its seed, and the *linseed oil*, which is pressed from the seeds, is one of Argentina's leading exports. The oil is used in making paints, varnishes, linoleum, printer's ink, and rubber substitutes. What remains after the oil has been squeezed out is known as *linseed cake*. It is used as feed for animals or ground into fertilizer.

Other Grassland Crops. In the area near the city of Buenos Aires are numerous fruit orchards and truck and dairy farms. They supply vegetables, fruit, and fresh milk for Buenos Aires and other cities on the Pampa. Since this area has the same latitude as our states of Georgia and South Carolina, and is not far from the sea, the winter climate is mild. Vegetables can be raised throughout the year, and fruit-damaging frosts are rare.

Buenos Aires the Capital. The largest city in Argentina is the capital, Buenos Aires, which has more than three and one half million inhabitants. Buenos Aires is the third largest city in the Western Hemisphere. Only New York and Mexico City are larger. One fourth of the people of Argentina live in Buenos Aires and its suburbs. In fact, more Spanish-speaking people live in Buenos Aires than in Madrid, the capital of Spain.

Argentina has more miles of railroads than any other South American country. The life of the Pampa depends on the railroads which radiate like the spokes of a wheel from Buenos Aires, the railroad center for the country's most productive region. The level stretches of the Pampa make it ideal for building railroads and highways, and Buenos Aires has become the Argentine "hub city." This means that the railroads and highways connect the city with all parts of the Pampa and with the more remote parts of the country.

Argentina **75**

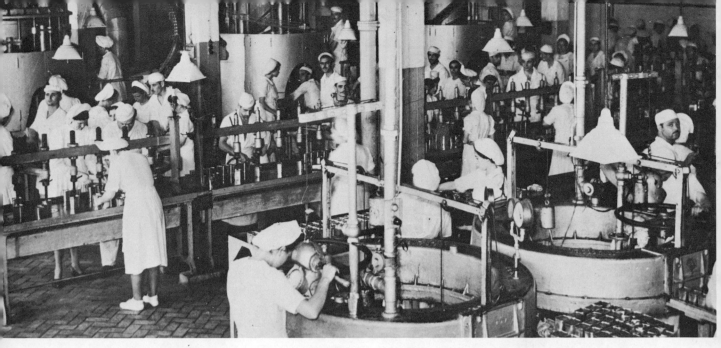

Meat Packing in Buenos Aires. Beef is cooked before being packed into cans in this large plant. White-clad workers fill and seal up the cans.

Automobiles and trucks use modern concrete highways which link Buenos Aires to other large Argentine cities. There is a large modern airport about 20 miles outside the city and an express super highway runs to the airport from the city. Planes fly from this airport to all parts of the world.

Buenos Aires is Argentina's chief seaport and one of the ten leading ports of the world. It is located on the wide Rio de la Plata, about 125 miles from the Atlantic Ocean. Its harbor is man-made. Mud and silt have been dredged away to create channels and basins large enough and deep enough to handle ocean steamers. The dredging still goes on almost continuously to keep the channel and basins open. A long breakwater has been built to protect the wharves and docks along the shore. Ships from many parts of the world load and unload throughout the year at this busy port. Smaller ships also sail between Buenos Aires and the upper-river ports on the Paraná, Paraguay, and Uruguay rivers.

Buenos Aires is the chief manufacturing city of Argentina. The busiest places are the slaughterhouses and refrigeration plants which prepare beef for shipment. Next in importance are the flour mills. Other important products made in the city include textiles, iron and steel goods, cement, ships, automobiles, and airplanes.

In general, Buenos Aires is somewhat like our large cities of New York and Chicago. Big office buildings line the streets in the business areas, and stores, cars, avenues and homes resemble those of other modern Western cities. The Argentine capital is a very attractive city with wide streets and boulevards, numerous parks, large plazas, fine public buildings, and beautiful churches. Wide use is made of electricity, telephone service, and other modern conveniences.

Other Cities on the Pampa. Two hundred miles north of Buenos Aires on the Paraná River is Rosario. It is Argentina's second city in size and importance, with a population of about half a million people. Farm products, chiefly grain and meat, are sent to Rosario for export. The Paraná River was deepened to make it an inland port. Rosario's factories turn out flour, furniture, bricks, and leather goods.

Only a few miles from Buenos Aires on the Rio de la Plata is the busy port of La Plata. Like its neighbor, Buenos Aires, it is a very beautiful city. Large ocean-going ships stop here to load grain, meats, hides, and other products.

Bahia Blanca serves the southern part of the Pampa. Strangely enough, Bahia is a port which is located four miles inland. A railroad connects the city with its well protected, man-made harbor on the coast. Bahia Blanca is most important as a wheat-shipping port.

Argentine Mesopotamia. Between the Paraná and Uruguay Rivers lies a fertile region called Mesopotamia. The word *mesopotamia* means "between rivers."

The Mesopotamia region of Argentina has heavy rainfall. The summers are hot and the winters warm. Few people live in the forested region of northern Mesopotamia. The chief occupation in the region is the gathering of yerba maté leaves from which a kind of tea is prepared. The southern part of Mesopotamia is gently rolling land, and makes excellent cattle country.

The Gran Chaco. Far northern and northeastern Argentina is part of a region which also extends into Paraguay and Bolivia. It is called the *Gran Chaco.* This Spanish name means "great hunting ground." It is a frontier land where the population is still very small. The people engage mostly in farming, cattle raising, or lumbering.

The Gran Chaco is a great lowland plain of scrub forest with patches of grass. The low, flat land is swampy in many places, and includes large stretches of unexplored wilderness.

The most important crop in this area is cotton. It does well because of the long growing season and the plentiful summer rain. Tobacco and oranges are other cash crops produced in this part of Argentina. Farmers also raise the rice, corn, and vegetables needed to feed their families.

As you remember from your study of Bolivia, forests of quebracho trees grow in the Gran Chaco. The hardwood quebracho trees are cut down with special axes. Oxen then drag the heavy logs to the railroads which transport them to a mill. Here the logs are cut into small pieces and boiled in water to extract a substance called *tannin.* The tannin boils down to a jellylike mass which is then dried and packed in bags for shipment. Tannin is used to process hides when making them into leather. Much of it is exported to the United States.

Quebracho wood has other uses. Its hardness and resistance to rot makes it most suitable for railroad ties, telegraph poles, and fence posts. There is a ready market for quebracho lumber on the Pampa.

Tannin Factory. Huge logs of quebracho wood are going to be cut up and then boiled to extract their tannin. Tannin is then used to cure leather.

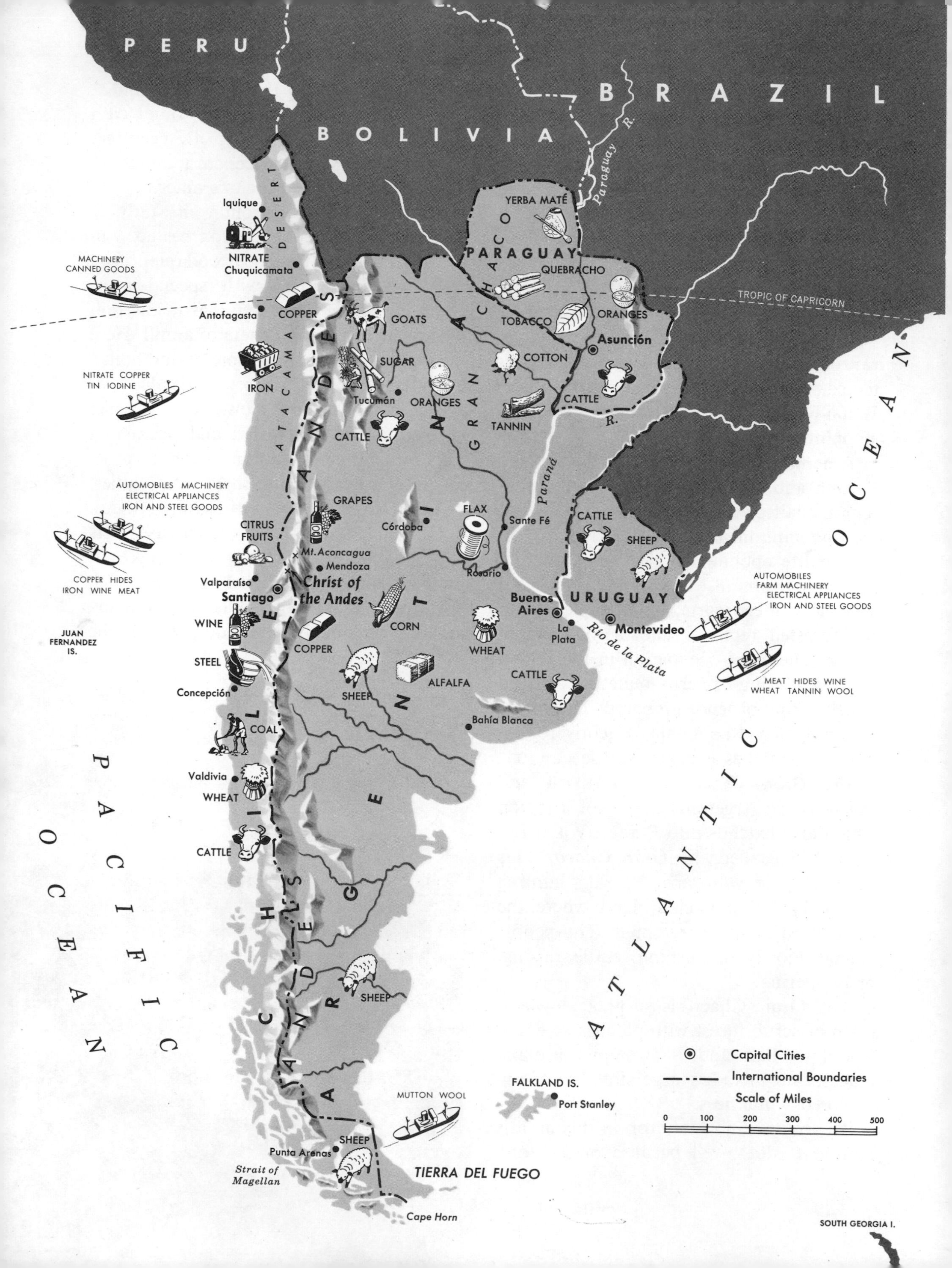
PERU
BRAZIL
BOLIVIA
Paraguay R.
YERBA MATÉ
PARAGUAY
GRAN CHACO
QUEBRACHO
TROPIC OF CAPRICORN
Iquique
ATACAMA DESERT
NITRATE
Chuquicamata
MACHINERY
CANNED GOODS
Antofagasta
COPPER
GOATS
TOBACCO
ORANGES
Asunción
COTTON
SUGAR
IRON
NITRATE COPPER
TIN IODINE
Tucumán
ORANGES
CATTLE
TANNIN
CATTLE
R.
Paraná
ANDES
ARGENTINA
AUTOMOBILES MACHINERY
ELECTRICAL APPLIANCES
IRON AND STEEL GOODS
GRAPES
FLAX
Córdoba
Sante Fé
CATTLE
SHEEP
CITRUS FRUITS
Mt. Aconcagua
Mendoza
Rosario
COPPER HIDES
IRON WINE MEAT
Valparaíso
Santiago
Christ of the Andes
Buenos Aires
URUGUAY
AUTOMOBILES
FARM MACHINERY
ELECTRICAL APPLIANCES
IRON AND STEEL GOODS
WINE
CORN
WHEAT
La Plata
Montevideo
Río de la Plata
JUAN FERNANDEZ IS.
STEEL
COPPER
SHEEP
ALFALFA
CATTLE
MEAT HIDES WINE
WHEAT TANNIN WOOL
Concepción
Bahía Blanca
COAL
CHILE
Valdivia
WHEAT
CATTLE
PACIFIC OCEAN
ATLANTIC OCEAN
SHEEP
Capital Cities
International Boundaries
Scale of Miles
0 100 200 300 400 500
FALKLAND IS.
Port Stanley
MUTTON WOOL
SHEEP
Punta Arenas
Strait of Magellan
TIERRA DEL FUEGO
Cape Horn
SOUTH GEORGIA I.

A Private Home in Córdoba. Lying between the Andes and the Pampa, this picturesque resort town has many fine residences like the one above.

Northwestern Argentina. On the eastern side of the Andes, in northwestern Argentina, the climate is quite dry and hot. Much of the land is covered with bushes and grass. Cattle graze on the better grasslands, and sheep are pastured in the cooler areas. Goats graze on the rocky slopes which cattle and sheep cannot reach.

Because of the light rainfall, the farmers here must irrigate their land. Their farms are in the lower valleys and along the lower slopes of the mountains. Water for irrigation is obtained from the many streams pouring down from the snow-capped Andes. In some places dams have been built across the streams to hold the water in basins or reservoirs until needed.

Tucumán and Córdoba. A farming center, called a garden spot, surrounds the city of Tucumán. Although this area receives more rainfall than others, irrigation is still needed. There are also many sugar cane plantations nearby which make Tucuman the center of Argentina's important sugar industry.

Southeast of Tucumán is Córdoba, a quaint old city nestled in the foothills of the Andes. The grassy plains of the Pampa roll gently eastward from this city, while the jagged snowcapped Andes tower on the west.

Córdoba is the largest city in this part of Argentina. Hydroelectric power from a great dam on a nearby river is now available. As a result, manufacturing of many kinds is being developed in Córdoba, in addition to its many flour mills and leather tanneries. Each year many visitors come to see the beautiful scenery around the city. Students come from all over Argentina to study at its famous university. Córdoba is regarded as a center of Argentine cultural and religious activity.

Southwest of Córdoba is Mendoza. It lies in the eastern foothills of the Andes, near a narrow pass which leads through the mountains into Chile. Through this pass lie the tracks of the only transcontinental railroad in South America. The weather in this region is clear and very dry during most of the year. Hundreds of vineyards cover the surrounding countryside.

The largest part of the grape crop from these vineyards is used to make the wine for which Mendoza is famous. Some of the grapes are also sent to the United States in refrigerator ships to provide fresh grapes when they are out of season in our own country.

Shepherd on Horseback. One mounted herder and his dog care for thousands of sheep in Patagonia. Wool and meat are the principal exports here.

Patagonia. The part of Argentina that lies south of the Pampa is called Patagonia. The early Spanish explorers who came to this region met giant-sized Indian natives wearing big leather moccasins. The Spaniards named the region Patagonia, which is the Spanish term for "big feet."

Most of Patagonia is a desert-like plateau, cut off from the moisture-bearing westerly winds by the high Andes Mountains to the west. Rivers flowing down from the Andes have cut deep valleys across this plateau. The rocky soil and light rainfall do not favor farming, and wild grass and shrubs are its only natural vegetation.

In the places where farming is carried on, irrigation is necessary. Only in the western part of Patagonia, on the highest mountain slopes, is there considerable rainfall, and forests of pine and cypress grow there. Some grains and fruits are raised in the river valleys, and alfalfa is grown for animal fodder.

The chief feature of Patagonia's climate is the stormy, constant wind which blows over most of the region winter and summer. The winters are cold with some light snow, but the summers are warm.

The population of Patagonia is quite small in proportion to its area. Only a quarter of a million people live in this region, which is almost as large as Texas and Illinois combined. The Patagonians are mostly immigrants of English, Scottish, Welsh, German, and Spanish ancestry. Sheep raising is the principal industry, and wool is the chief product.

Coastal Islands. The name of the large island at the southern tip of Argentina—Tierra del Fuego—means "land of fire." It is not certain how the island received that name, but it is believed that early explorers saw the native Indians carrying lighted torches while hunting birds at night.

Tierra del Fuego is separated from the continent by the Strait of Magellan. You will recall from your study of Chile that Argentina owns the eastern half of the island, and the other half belongs to Chile. As in Patagonia, sheep-raising is the chief industry of Tierra del Fuego.

About 350 miles to the east of southern South America are the Falkland Islands.

Although these islands are claimed by both Argentina and Chile, the British have held possession of them for many years.

The climate of the Falklands is cool and damp, ideal for sheep raising, which is carried on there extensively. In addition, the whaling boats which sail the Antarctic waters use Port Stanley in the Falklands as a center for supplies.

Facts *to remember*

1. Argentina, like most of the South American countries, claims the Spanish language and the Catholic religion. Twenty million people live in an area that is one third that of the United States.
2. Argentina has two natural boundaries: on the west the crest of the Andes Mountains, and on the east the Atlantic Ocean.
3. The five natural regions of Argentina are: the Pampa, Argentine Mesopotamia, the Gran Chaco, northwestern Argentina, and Patagonia.
4. Northern Argentina is drained by the Uruguay and the Paraguay-Paraná rivers and their tributaries. All finally empty into the Rio de la Plata estuary.
5. Extending for hundreds of miles around the capital of Buenos Aires is the Argentine Pampa. It is a grassy, treeless plain with deep, fertile soil. On the Pampa wheat is harvested during the summer season from November to January. Much corn is also grown. Both wheat and corn are exported. Truck and dairy farms surround Buenos Aires and other large cities on the Pampa.
6. Bccf cattle, hogs, sheep and other animals are raised on large Argentine ranches called estancias. Sheep are raised on the drier western part of the Pampa and also to the south in Patagonia.
7. Buenos Aires, the capital city, has more than 3½ million people. It is the largest city in South America, an important railroad center, and an international air terminal. It has a fine man-made harbor.
8. Rosario and La Plata are busy river ports for the grain and meat products of the northern Pampa. Bahia Blanca is the important wheat-shipping port for the southern Pampa.
9. Quebracho trees are found in the forests of the Gran Chaco. Their hard wood is used for railroad ties and posts. An extract from quebracho bark, called tannin, is used for tanning leather.
10. In northwestern Argentina sugar cane is raised in the irrigated area surrounding the old city of Tucumán. Farther south in this region is the city of Córdoba, with flour mills and leather tanneries. Córdoba is also noted for its university, famous wines, and natural beauty.
11. Patagonia is a cool, dry, wind-swept plateau of southern Argentina. It covers one fourth of Argentina and is sparsely populated. Sheep-raising is the principal industry.
12. Argentina claims two island territories: part of Tierra del Fuego and the Falkland Islands (also claimed by Great Britain). Both are noted for sheep raising.
13. Argentina is principally an agricultural country. Manufacturing grows slowly because of the lack of coal, oil, and available water power.

What *have I learned?*

Copy the names in the first column. Write opposite each name the description from the second column which best suits it.

	A	B
1.	Rosario	land between the Paraná and Uruguay Rivers
2.	Gran Chaco	center of the sugar industry
3.	Patagonia	pass city in Argentina
4.	Buenos Aires	highest peak in the Americas
5.	Mendoza	most productive region in Argentina
6.	Aconcagua	an arm of the sea
7.	Rio de la Plata	city on the Paraná River
8.	Pampa	dry southern region
9.	Mesopotamia	capital of Argentina
10.	Tucumán	a great scrub forest lowland

Facts *to understand*

Give a reason in a complete sentence for each of the following statements.

1. The Pampa has fine railroad transportation.
2. Argentina ships more meat and wheat to Great Britain than to the United States.
3. Much alfalfa is grown on the Pampa.
4. Refrigeration is of great importance to Argentina's meat-packing industries.
5. A man-made harbor is necessary at Buenos Aires.

3

Uruguay and Paraguay

A Rancher's Paradise. Two Uruguayan countrymen ride through the grassy Penitente Hills. The gently rolling countryside favors Uruguay's ranches.

URUGUAY

Uruguay and Paraguay are two small countries in southern South America, located near each other. It would be a mistake, however, to think that Uruguay and Paraguay are similar in every way. In fact, two more dissimilar countries, located close together, would be hard to find anywhere.

Uruguay is an Atlantic seacoast country. The people of this up-to-date, progressive land are well educated, prosperous, and energetic. They enjoy a delightful climate and their country attracts many visitors.

Paraguay is land-locked—it has no seacoast. Its people must struggle to make a bare living, and they have a long way to go to achieve the standard of living enjoyed by people in neighboring countries. In this chapter, we shall see some of the reasons for the differences in the way people work and live in the two countries.

Uruguay, the smallest republic in South America, is about the size of our state of North Dakota. Uruguay is bounded on the north and east by Brazil. The Atlantic Ocean washes the southeast shore, and the Rio de la Plata lies to the south of Uruguay. On the west is Argentina, across the Uruguay River which forms the boundary between the two countries.

A Rolling Grassy Land. Most of Uruguay is hilly, rolling land covered with grass. It is neither as flat as the Pampa nor as dry. Many streams flow across the country's wooded valleys, supplying plenty of water for the herds of animals which graze there. Conditions are ideal for raising cattle and sheep. The livestock industry is the most important in Uruguay.

The gently rolling grasslands have simplified the building of highways and railroads. Uruguay has excellent railroad connections with Argentina and Brazil, its western and northern neighbors.

Delightful Climate. Uruguay lies entirely in the southern intermediate zone. This country is located about the same distance south of the equator as our states of Georgia and South Carolina are north of it.

Uruguay's climate resembles the climate of Georgia and South Carolina, except in the summer. Unlike those states, Uruguay has warm, rather than hot summers. This is partly because refreshing breezes blow in from the oceans to temper the land heat in summer. Winters, too, are mild, and Uruguay has plenty of rainfall throughout the year.

Sheep and Cattle. Nearly four fifths of Uruguay is grassland. Large herds of sheep and cattle graze on these natural pastures. There are numerous lakes, streams, and springs. The livestock industry in Uruguay is also favored by the mild winter climate, which allows animals to graze on the open range all year long.

Sheep raising is more important than cattle raising in Uruguay. There are from two to three times as many sheep as cattle. Most of the sheep are of the Merino breed, noted for the high quality of its fleece. Fine Merino wool has always been Uruguay's principal export. It sells for a high price in the textile-making countries.

For a long time, sheep in Uruguay were raised almost entirely for their wool and skins. Recently, however, more and more sheep are being raised for meat. Modern methods of refrigeration and freezing now make it possible to ship mutton great distances without danger of its spoiling. Frozen mutton has become an important Uruguayan export.

Uruguayan Shepherds. The mild climate of Uruguay allows herds to graze outdoors all the year round. The streams supply water for the sheep.

Uruguay's second most valuable meat export is beef. Like mutton, most of the beef is frozen before being shipped out of the country. Uruguayan beef finds a ready market in Western Europe.

Cereals and Other Crops. Farming is seldom carried on as a separate occupation in Uruguay. Crops are usually grown in fields on the sheep and cattle ranches.

The principal crops are the grains—wheat, rice, oats, and barley. Most of the grain crops are used at home, but some wheat is exported. Other Uruguayan crops are flaxseed, alfalfa, sugar beets, potatoes, wine grapes, and fruits.

Round-up Time. Uruguayan cowboys, like cowboys everywhere, must spend long, weary hours in the saddle. They, too, have a special way to dress.

The Uruguayan People. Uruguay has more than two and a half million people. Almost all of them are of Euroepan descent. Some are descendants of the original Spanish settlers, while others descend from more recent immigrants from Spain, Italy, and Germany. Uruguay was originally a Spanish colony, but since 1825 it has been an independent country. The official language is Spanish, and most of the people are born into the Roman Catholic Church.

The people of Uruguay are among the most progressive in South America. Education, including college, is free. All children are expected to attend school, at least through the elementary grades.

The government of Uruguay has worked hard to provide good living conditions for the people. Workers have an eight-hour day and are protected by health and accident insurance as well as old-age pensions, just as in our country. Child labor is not allowed in Uruguay, although still practiced in some other South American countries.

The City of Roses. The capital and only large city of Uruguay is Montevideo. About one third of the country's population lives in this beautiful city, and the meat-packing plants are also located here.

Montevideo is situated near the mouth of the Rio de la Plata. The city extends along the shores of a large bay which provides a natural harbor. Like the harbor at Buenos Aires, it needs dredging to keep the channels deep enough for large ocean-going vessels to enter and dock.

Ships from all over the world stop at Montevideo. The port has numerous warehouses, docks, and modern machinery for loading and unloading. Manufactured goods are the chief imports at Montevideo. Wool, meat, hides, skins, linseed oil, and wheat are exported.

This southern capital is a charming city, with fine churches and public buildings, shops, theatres, and a large university. There are beautiful parks where great numbers of blooming plants are grown. Roses are so plentiful that Montevideo is often called "The City of Roses."

Its location on the Rio de la Plata and its pleasant climate combine to make Montevideo popular as a summer resort. Here vacationers can swim and relax on the sandy beaches. Fine hotels and homes line the shore. Visitors from other parts of South America, especially Argentina and Brazil, find Montevideo an attractive and pleasant summer resort.

Montivideo's Shady Boulevards. From the appearance of the clothing worn by the people in this picture, can you describe the climate in Uruguay?

PARAGUAY

A Land-locked Country. Eastern Paraguay is a region of sunshine, rain, and rich vegetation. Roads are so poor that travel by river is quicker.

Only two countries in South America do not touch the ocean, and Paraguay is one of them. Paraguay is located more than a thousand miles from the Atlantic Ocean by way of the Paraná and Paraguay rivers, and the Rio de la Plata.

The map on page 58 shows that Paraguay lies between the two largest countries on the continent. One of its giant neighbors, Brazil, lies to the north and east; Argentina lies to the south. Bolivia, South America's only other inland country, lies on the western and northern border.

Country of Few People. Paraguay has only about one and a half million people. This is the smallest population of the ten South American republics. Unlike most countries, Paraguay had a larger population a century ago than it has today.

Paraguay gained its independence from Spain in 1811. During the last century, the country lost many people and some of its land through a series of damaging wars with Brazil, Uruguay, Argentina, and Bolivia. The effect of these wars is still felt, and progress is slow in Paraguay.

Most Paraguayans are mestizos of Spanish and Guarani Indian blood. A few thousand tribal Indians still live in Paraguay. Two languages are commonly spoken— Spanish and Guarani, an Indian language.

Although many of the grownups in Paraguay have had little or no education, all Paraguayan children are now required by law to finish elementary school. This law is not always observed, however, and the number of people who complete their education is still small. Some high schools and even some colleges and universities have been opened in recent years in Paraguay. In the future, the people of Paraguay will be educated more and more completely. Progress and living standards may improve as a result.

Most of the people of Paraguay are Catholic. However, active participation in the religious life of the Church is generally found only among the people in the more heavily populated areas.

THE PEOPLE OF PARAGUAY

One very noticeable difference between Paraguay and other countries of South America is the people who make up its small population. Throughout the rest of South America, there is generally a varied background among the people. Negroes, Spanish, Portuguese, Indians, and mestizos mix with more recent arrivals from Germany, Italy, Scotland and many other countries of the world.

This woman walks to market with a chicken over her arm, and a basket of fruit on her head. The Indians (right and below) are Guaranis.

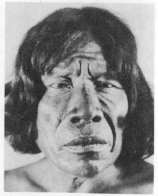

Practicing an Ancient Craft. Just as her ancestors did many years ago, this woman of Paraguay is weaving woolen textiles by hand on a frame.

This is not true of Paraguay. Almost all the people here are mestizos, descendants of the original Indians and early Spanish settlers. Hardly any other nationalities are represented, although there are some Indians, nearly uncivilized, living in the western part of the country, in the Gran Chaco. The people of Paraguay do not speak Spanish, except in Asunción, the capital. There the Spanish language is the language of business and government. Throughout the rest of the country, *Guarani* is spoken. Guarani is the native Indian language, and can truly be called Paraguay's native tongue.

The Guarani Indians of Paraguay, from whom many of the Paraguayans of today are descended, were once very famous. For a long time, they were the only native people in the New World to have a complete Christian civilization of their own. It came about in a very interesting way, and lasted for over one hundred years.

In the early days of the exploration and settlement of South America, certain Spanish plantation owners wanted to use native Indians as slaves to work in their fields. The missionaries who came to South America— the Franciscans, the Dominicans, and the Jesuits, mostly—resisted this evil plan and defended the Indians against their white oppressors.

In Paraguay, Jesuit missioners led their flocks of Indian Christians back into the forests. There they established settlements called *Reductions*. This name comes from a Latin word which means "to lead back." The Jesuit Reductions in Paraguay became famous as Catholic communities in which each individual lived and worked in peace and harmony with the others. The Jesuit padres administered to the spiritual needs of their people, and the Indians cultivated farms, made their own clothing and tools, and governed themselves.

As a result of the white plantation owners' greed and jealousy, however, the Reductions were smashed by the Spanish government, and the Jesuits were forced to leave. To this day, the Catholic people of Paraguay do not have the priests they need.

For other reasons also, the people of Paraguay have not yet been able to achieve the kind of happy civilization they enjoyed

A Family of Paraguay. This young couple and their baby are typical of many of the people of Paraguay — happy in the life God has given them.

Market Day in Asunción. The woman above prepares her stall of vegetables for sale. Below, the man wearing a *serape*, or cape, is buying bread.

in the days of the Reductions. Several very tragic wars came close to wiping out the entire population. The land-locked location of the country has discouraged trade and commerce, and several bad governments prevented the people from taking full advantage of the many natural resources which bless their land.

Today, most of the people make a bare living on their farms. They live a simple life, and do not seem to mind the poverty under which they live. As you can see by the pictures on these pages, the people of Paraguay are happy, energetic, and friendly. Perhaps, with better methods of farming, better roads, and the development of some industries, they will be able to improve their standard of living. We should pray also that native priests will soon take over the important task of educating the people in their Faith, making the Catholic Church once again a powerful force for good in Paraguay.

Loading Quebracho Wood. This truck is backed into the water of the Paraguay River to load quebracho logs. They make fences and railroad ties.

Two Regions. The Paraguay River divides the country roughly into two regions. The land west of the river is part of the Gran Chaco which you learned about when you studied Argentina and Bolivia. This region has few inhabitants because it is too hot and dry to support crops or animals without irrigation. The main resource of this region is the quebracho tree, which grows in forests along the streams.

Most of the people live in the region east of the Paraguay River. This part of the country has a subtropical climate somewhat like our state of Florida. There are about nine warm months and three hot months. Plenty of rain falls in the eastern region. The soil is fertile, and crops and grass can grow throughout the year.

Grazing and Farming. An important industry in Paraguay is cattle raising. Large areas of grassland are suited for grazing, and meat products and hides are among the chief exports.

Most of the farms are small. Farmers raise corn, rice, manioc, peanuts, and sugar cane for home use. Tobacco is the principal cash crop.

The farmers use crude tools and know very little about scientific farming. The government, with some assistance from the United States, is trying to help the farmers by making loans for equipment and by sending farm agents to teach them to raise larger and better crops. It is hoped that these measures will also help to raise the standard of living by providing varied crops at low cost.

Orange trees grow well in Paraguay. The Jesuits brought the first orange trees from Spain hundreds of years ago. Today, many grow wild; others are cultivated in groves. Oranges are shipped by boat down the Paraguay River to Argentina and Uruguay. Orange oil, an important product obtained from the leaves, is sent to other countries for use in making perfumes and flavoring extracts.

A Long Sip of Tea. This Paraguayan peasant, shaded from the sun by his straw hat, drinks some cool yerba maté from a cowhorn with a silver straw.

Paraguay Tea. A useful product obtained from the forests is *yerba maté,* which is sometimes called Paraguay tea. Yerba

Asunción. The main square of Paraguay's capital is this pleasant park. The office buildings and the cars are rare sights in a country so poor.

maté is made from the dried leaves of an evergreen tree which resembles holly. Early Spanish settlers found the native Indians of Paraguay drinking a beverage made from these leaves. The Spaniards tried it and liked it.

To make this tea, the Indians put dried leaves into a gourd hollowed out like a cup. Hot water is poured over the leaves just as in making our kind of tea. The gourd used as a tea cup is called a *maté* and *yerba* means herb, so you can see how this product received its name.

Yerba maté is gathered from both wild and cultivated trees. Branches are cut, and the leaves stripped. The leaves are set out to dry in the sun and then crushed. Bags of yerba maté are carried to warehouses where they are stored until shipping time. This kind of tea is used in other South American countries as well as Paraguay.

Asunción, the Capital. There are no very large cities in Paraguay. The largest is Asunción, a city which is more than four hundred years old. Asunción is a thriving river port on the Paraguay River.

A small amount of manufacturing is carried on in Asunción. Among the products are cotton and leather goods, furniture, refined sugar, and tobacco products.

Most travelers from Buenos Aires to Asunción go by boat. They must travel about a thousand miles by water, using the Rio de la Plata, the Paraná, and the Paraguay rivers to reach Asunción. The two cities are also linked by rail and air lines. However, transportation is generally poor in Paraguay. There are very few good roads, and scarcely any railroads.

Modernization of roads, railroads, farming, manufacturing, and education is the hope for the future of Paraguay. Only when these things are accomplished will Paraguay start to catch up with its neighbors.

Facts *to remember*

1. Uruguay, the smallest of the South American republics, lies between Brazil and Argentina with a coastline on the Atlantic Ocean. Its rolling grassy plains are well suited for grazing cattle and sheep, the principal occupation of the people.
2. Uruguay has mild snowless winters, and in the summer cool sea breezes keep it from becoming too warm.
3. One third of the country's population lives in Montevideo, the capital city. Its natural harbor is on the Rio de la Plata estuary. Many beautiful beaches extend along the shore line.
4. Frozen meats and fine wool are the chief exports of Uruguay. Machinery, motor vehicles, gasoline, textiles, and sugar are imported.
5. Paraguay has the smallest population of all the South American republics. The Paraguay River divides the country into two very different parts. West of the river is the Gran Chaco with a sparse population. Most of the people live east of the river where the capital city, Asunción, is located.
6. Paraguay is an inland country but it has water transportation to the Atlantic Ocean. The few exports of this country—cotton, tobacco, yerba maté, and forest products—go through Asunción, which is a river port.
7. The people of Paraguay are poor and illiterate. Wars and poor government have prevented them from raising their standard of living.

What *have I learned?*

Write the numbers 1 to 15 on your answer paper. After each number, tell which country is being described—Uruguay or Paraguay.

1. smallest South American republic in area
2. largely surrounded by water
3. capital is Asunción
4. lies entirely in the Intermediate Zone
5. smallest population of all South American republics
6. largely a great grazing area
7. exports forest products
8. has strong native Indian influence
9. government provides many services
10. has an international seaport
11. majority of people cannot read
12. separated into two parts by a river
13. exports fine quality wool
14. has a population of 2½ million people
15. exports considerable wheat

Facts *to understand*

Give a reason in a complete sentence for each of the following statements.

1. Paraguay is not a progressive country.
2. Grazing is the most important industry of Uruguay.
3. Paraguay has less trade than Uruguay.
4. Montevideo has a large tourist industry.
5. It is summer in Uruguay when it is winter in the United States.

Unit Two Review

Questions for Discussion and Review

1. Why is Chilean coal used in their blast furnaces, even though it is of poor quality? 2. Describe three different types of climate found in Chile. 3. Explain the way of living on the large farm estates of Chile. 4. How is copper mined in northern Chile? 5. Explain the value of the Pampa to the people of Argentina. 6. What dangers do farmers on the Pampa have to face? 7. Why is more farm machinery used in Argentina than in the Andean countries? 8. Why is the vast region of Patagonia so sparsely populated? 9. How does the region east of the Paraguay River differ from the region to the west of it? 10. How is "Paraguay tea" prepared? 11. Compare Uruguay with Paraguay as to standards of living. 12. Why has Montevideo grown more prosperous than the city of Asunción?

Using the Maps and Globe

1. Name the bodies of water a freighter would pass through carrying iron ore from Antofagasta, Chile, to Baltimore, Maryland.
2. Using the scale of miles on your map, measure the distance from Asunción in Paraguay to Santa Fe in Argentina.
3. Over how many degrees of latitude does Chile extend from Arica to Cape Horn?
4. Name the only South American country that lies entirely in the Intermediate Zone.
5. Name the countries that border Paraguay.

6. Locate Mount Aconcagua and read its height on the map.

7. What part of Chile's coast line is most regular?

8. In what general direction does the Paraná River flow?

9. Give the latitude and longitude of Antofagasta.

10. What city is located 35 degrees south latitude and 58 degrees west longitude?

Using Geography Words

Write a sentence using each of the following to show that you understand its geographic meaning.

lighters	pampa	estancia
nitrate	dredging	tannin
Mediterranean climate	Gran Chaco	Guarani
gauchos	yerba maté	estuary

Getting Information from Books

Use reference books, such as *Compton's Pictured Encyclopedia,* for information on these topics. Prepare to give a report on one of them.

Jesuit Reductions in Paraguay

Building of the Railroad through the Andes

Legend of El Dorado

Life of the Gauchos on the Pampa

The Customs of the Guarani in Paraguay

Final Test

Choose the correct word or words from the parenthesis to complete each sentence. Write the complete sentence correctly on your answer paper.

1. The northern part of the Central Valley of Chile has a (dry tropical, Mediterranean, continental) climate. **2.** The Tropic of Capricorn does not pass through (Argentina, Uruguay, Chile). **3.** The Andes Mountains form a natural boundary between Argentina and (Paraguay, Chile, Uruguay). **4.** The capital of Chile is (Santiago, Antofagasta, Valparaíso). **5.** Valuable forest products are obtained from a region known as (Patagonia, the Pampa, the Gran Chaco). **6.** The wettest section of Chile is the (central, southern, northern) part. **7.** Large nitrate deposits are found in (Chile, Argentina, Paraguay). **8.** Of the following, the driest area is (northern Chile, southern Argentina, Uruguay). **9.** A by-product of nitrate is (tannin, iodine, latex). **10.** Copper and iron ore are exports of (Argentina, Uruguay, Chile). **11.** Large estates in Argentina are called (fazendas, haciendas, estancias). **12.** A country which has sufficient minerals to develop its own manufacturing industry is (Argentina, Chile, Paraguay). **13.** The leading seaport on the Pacific coast of South America is (Antofagasta, Callao, Valparaíso). **14.** Robinson Crusoe has been associated with the (Falkland, Juan Fernandez, Galápagos) Islands. **15.** Among the countries of South America the chief producer of flaxseed is (Uruguay, Chile, Argentina). **16.** A corn-exporting country is (Chile, Argentina, Paraguay). **17.** Most of Argentina's food exports go to (the United States, Great Britain, Canada). **18.** A South American city with more than 3½ million people is the city of (Buenos Aires, Rio de Janeiro, Santiago). **19.** A city famous for its wine production is (Mendoza, Tucumán, Rosario). **20.** The center of Argentina's sugar industry is in (Tucumán, Rosario, Bahia Blanca).

Applying Christian Principles

Select the best ending for each sentence. Then write the sentences on your answer paper.

1. The people of Chile help their country best when they **a.** develop their natural resources for the good of the people **b.** import products made by foreign companies **c.** export their minerals.

2. The Chileans and the Argentines are most to be admired for **a.** building a transcontinental railroad **b.** settling a border dispute peacefully **c.** establishing their independence from Spain.

3. Progress in Paraguay has been held back most by **a.** a poor location **b.** wars and poor leaders **c.** the climate and soil.

4. Paraguay will be helped most when there are **a.** better means of transportation **b.** higher wages for workers **c.** more opportunities for education and practicing their religion.

5. The greatest evil resulting from bad leaders in a country is that **a.** most of the goods and money are held by a few people **b.** people are afraid to speak freely **c.** other countries fear to trade with them.

Neighbors in Northeastern South America

BRAZIL   THE GUIANAS

In this Unit
you will learn that:

1 Brazil is the largest country in South America. It comprises about half the area of the continent, and has about half the total population.

2 The Amazon Region of Brazil is in the low latitudes and has a wet tropical climate.

3 Most of the Brazilian people live near the coast between the border of Uruguay and the mouth of the Amazon River.

4 Brazil has rich minerals and agricultural products and many fine harbors.

5 The upland region of Southern Brazil produces more coffee than any other part of the world.

6 Brazil was once a colony of Portugal. Portuguese is the national language, and most Brazilians are Catholics.

7 British Guiana, French Guiana, and Surinam (Dutch Guiana) are the only colonies left on the South American continent. All three are tropical coastal lands where the climate is unhealthy.

8 The hot, wet lowlands of the Guianas are used to grow agricultural products to supply the small native populations. Some minerals have been located there, especially gold and aluminum.

In the northeastern section of South America there is not the same strong Spanish influence found in other parts of the continent. The reason for this dates back to the time of the first European explorations of South America.

At that time, Spain and Portugal were fierce rivals. They almost went to war over their conflicting claims to the same parts of the new continent. Instead, they called upon the Pope for a ruling in their dispute.

On the map of South America, the Pope drew a north-south line. All lands to the east of this line were to belong to Portugal; all lands to the west were to belong to Spain.

The northeastern section fell to Portugal. Today it is occupied mostly by one large independent country—Brazil. The language, customs, and national descent of the people of Brazil are Portuguese, not Spanish.

Also in Northeastern South America are three tiny European colonies, which were settled at a later date than Brazil. They are called British Guiana, French Guiana, and Surinam (Dutch Guiana).

Pacific Ocean

NORTHEASTERN SOUTH AMERICA

Northeastern South America is like a huge shoulder jutting out into the Atlantic Ocean. Its easternmost tip is only 1600 miles from Africa—the shortest distance separating the New World from the Old.

The rugged Brazilian Highlands occupy most of this eastern "shoulder" of South America. In the north are the Guiana Highlands. Between these two low mountain ranges stretches the wide green belt of the Amazon Valley rain forest.

The Amazon River pours across the continent all the way to the Atlantic Coast in the east. It is swelled by the many tributaries which join it. At the coast, this mighty river has deposited tons and tons of silt and mud over the years. You can see the huge delta which has been formed where the Amazon meets the Atlantic Ocean.

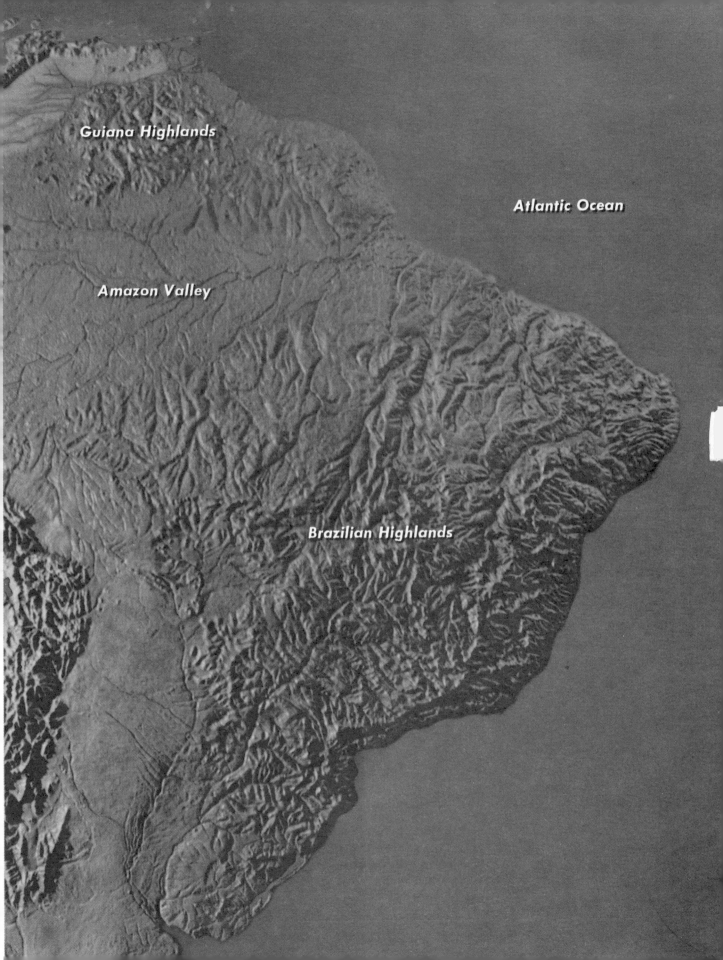

LET'S LEARN ABOUT BRAZIL

Rio de Janeiro. Some of the people of Rio de Janeiro live in these luxury apartments. Others, less fortunate, live in crowded areas of the city.

Brazil received its name in an interesting way. Portuguese explorers found a variety of redwood trees growing along the northeastern coast of South America. Because of its peculiar red color, the explorers named the tree, and the surrounding countryside, Brazil. The Portuguese word *brasil* means glowing coals or flaming red.

Location and Size. The country of Brazil has many neighbors. On its northern border lie Venezuela and the Guianas; on the southern border are Uruguay, Argentina, and Paraguay; on the western border are Bolivia, Peru, and Colombia. In fact, there are only two countries in South America which do not touch Brazil's borders—Chile and Ecuador. To the east, Brazil faces the Atlantic Ocean.

Brazil is by far the largest country in South America. It is almost as large as all the other countries of South America taken together. This huge land extends 2700 miles from approximately 5 degrees north latitude to 33 degrees south latitude. The northern part of the country stretches a similar distance east and west. Brazil's coast line on the Atlantic Ocean is long—almost 5000 miles.

The area of Brazil is more than 3 million square miles. This means that it ranks fifth in size among the countries of the world. Only the Soviet Union is much larger in area. China, the United States, and Canada are slightly larger.

The People of Brazil. Although Brazil is almost as great in area as the United States, it has only about one third as many people. Even so, Brazil's 63 million people represent half of the entire population of South America.

The people of Brazil are white, Indian and Negro. Many of its people are of mixed ancestry, representing various combinations of the races and nations. Although the first settlers of Brazil were Portuguese, people of many other nationalities have settled there, too. Immigrants came to Brazil from Spain, Italy, Germany, and Poland. There is also a good number of people who have come from oriental countries, especially Japan. Brazil is a country where many different races and nationalities live together in peace and harmony. Like the United States, it is a "melting pot."

Until recent years only a small proportion of the Brazilian people learned to read and write. Now, however, great steps are being taken to extend Brazilian education to the entire population. New schools are being built, and children are now required by law to go to school. Most Brazilians are happy, healthy and energetic people who value education and progress.

The Three Regions of Brazil. Because Brazil is so large, we will divide it for study into three sections or parts: southern Brazil, northeastern Brazil, and the Amazon region.

The southern region of Brazil is the area where most of the people live. Here the warm highland areas are covered by many large plantations raising the coffee for which Brazil is famous. Farther north and inland, but still in southern Brazil, is the section where most of the country's mineral wealth is found. In the extreme south of Brazil are farms, ranches, and lumber camps.

The People of Brazil. Portuguese, Indians, Negroes, and mestizos make up most of the population. People from many other countries also live here.

The northeastern region of Brazil includes the central interior as well as the northeastern corner, which extends farther to the east than any other part of South America. Along the Atlantic coast of this region there are hot, rainy lowlands. This is an area of plantations which produce tropical and sub-tropical crops.

Inland from the coast, and extending far into the interior, are hilly uplands where the rainfall is light and uncertain. This hilly interior of Brazil's northeastern region is the driest part of the country. It is still undeveloped, although pioneers are now moving into it.

The Amazon region, as the northern region of Brazil is known, is covered by tropical rainforests. In this area of dense vegetation, high temperatures and heavy rainfall, the population is understandably small, averaging only one person to every two square miles. The cities, towns, and villages of the settlers are concentrated on the Amazon River and its tributaries. The Indians who are native to this region make their living by selling products of the forest.

OCEAN (top left region)

40° · 30°

EQUATOR · 0°

Fortaleza

Natal

Recife

Maceió

Salvador

OCEAN

10°

20°

NORTHEASTERN SOUTH AMERICA

Capital Cities .... ⊙

over 10,000
5,000 to 10,000
2,000 to 5,000
1,000 to 2,000
0 to 1,000
Below Sea Level

ELEVATIONS IN FEET

International Boundaries ▬▬▬

Scale of Miles

0 — 200 — 400

30°

30°

Studying the Map

A. The lands of northeastern South America are Brazil, the largest country on the continent, and three small European colonies called the Guianas. **1.** Find Brazil on a globe. What other countries of the world are as large in area as Brazil? (Check your information with Table 1 in the Appendix.) **2.** Use the scale of miles on the map to find the east-west distance across Brazil at its widest point. How does this distance compare with the distance across the United States? **3.** In what climatic zone is most of Brazil located? **4.** Name the famous Brazilian river which roughly follows the equator. Where does it have its source? **5.** Locate the principal lowland area of Brazil. Name the highlands which lie to the north and south of this lowland. **6.** The Amazon carries more water to the sea than any other river. What does the map show that would help you to understand this?

B. 1. What does the map tell you about the surface of southern Brazil? **2.** Why do more people live in this part of the country than in any other? **3.** The two largest cities of Brazil are located in southern Brazil. Name them. **4.** In southern Brazil do more people live in the interior or near the coast? How can you tell? **5.** How far is it from Santos to São Paulo? What is the difference in elevation between the two cities? What effect do you think this difference has on transportation between the two cities? **6.** Find the coastal lowland of northeastern Brazil. From its location, what kind of climate would you expect to find there? **7.** Name the principal cities of this coastal lowland. **8.** About how much of the area of Brazil is drained by the Amazon and its tributaries? **9.** Why do few people live in the Amazon lowland? **10.** Locate the cities of Manaus and Belem on the Amazon River. How far is Manaus from the mouth of the river? Of what importance would the two cities be to the Amazon region?

C. 1. Locate the two colonies and the independent nation near Brazil's northern border. **2.** How do these countries compare in area with the other countries of South America? Which of them is the largest? **3.** Describe the surface of each nation. **4.** What kind of climate might you expect to find here? **5.** The most important city and port in each country is also its capital city. Name each of these capitals.

1

Southern Brazil

Look at the map on page 98. It shows that southern Brazil takes in only a small part of the total area of the country. Nevertheless, almost half the people of Brazil make their home in this region. Most of them live near the coast, in and around the great cities of Rio de Janeiro and São Paulo.

Because it is the richest and most progressive part of the country, southern Brazil is sometimes called "the heart of Brazil." There is a narrow coastal plain which gradually gives way inland to rolling mountains and plateaus. The climate in this hilly country is most pleasant. It is cooler than in the lowlands, and the people here can work and live in comfort.

Southern Brazil is the chief farming region of the country, and is particularly famous for the production of coffee. In fact, half of all the coffee grown in the world comes from Brazil. The southern region also has vast mineral wealth, much of it still undeveloped. There are fine railroads and highways crossing this region, and manufacturing has become an important industry in the larger cities.

There are few people living now in the interior and extreme southern parts of this region. These areas form, however, a kind of frontier. They will eventually provide living and working opportunities for large numbers of Brazil's rapidly growing population who find little room in the cities.

Soil and Climate. The first coffee trees probably grew in Africa and on the Arabian plateau in Asia. At some time, traders brought coffee beans to the tropical regions of the New World. In the highlands of Brazil's southern region, early settlers soon discovered the soil and climate which were ideal for growing coffee trees.

The major coffee region lies northwest of the city of São Paulo, in the southern Brazilian Highlands. Here the reddish purple soil, formed by decaying volcanic rock, is deep, fertile, and well-drained. The weather never becomes so hot as in the nearby coastal lowlands. This region has the kind of climate which coffee requires. Its climate is mild and sunny, neither too hot nor too cold, and free from frost.

About two thirds of the yearly rainfall in this part of Brazil comes between October and April. These are the warmest months in southern Brazil, when the coffee is growing. From April through September, the cooler months in southern Brazil, the weather is dry and cool, and there are bright sunny days. This is the best kind of weather for harvesting and drying the coffee.

Since the climate in this area is so favorable, it is easy to see why Brazil has become the world's leading coffee producer. Even so, there is occasionally a bad year when unusual weather conditions reduce the size of the harvest. After such a poor year, coffee-drinkers in the United States and elsewhere must pay higher prices for the beverage because of the shortened supply.

Harvesting Coffee. Coffee plants look more like evergreen bushes than trees. They seldom grow over 10 feet high. The trees blossom from August to October. After the blossoms have fallen from the branches, a green, cherry-like fruit appears. These berries turn red when ripe, and some of them drop onto canvas sheets that have been spread under each tree. The remaining berries are then picked from the lower branches by children, while the adult workers use ladders to reach the berries growing at the top.

Next the coffee berries are raked up and carried by truck or wagon to flat areas where they are spread out to dry in the sun. It takes about two months to dry coffee properly. The soft part of each berry is removed, usually by machine. This leaves only the raw seed, called the coffee bean. Another machine removes the skin which holds the two halves of the grey bean together. The split beans are then packed in bags ready to be shipped. Later they will have to be roasted and ground before being used to brew the beverage which everyone knows.

Cultivating Coffee. This lady with a sun hat is weeding the coffee field. Note the patterns of contour farming, a way of conserving the soil.

Classroom on a Fazenda. School is just about the same everywhere. In the picture above, boys and girls are writing compositions as you do.

The Costume of the Coffee Workers. In the pictures above and below, notice the wide hats worn by the workers in the fields to ward off the sun.

LIFE ON A COFFEE PLANTATION

A Brazilian coffee plantation is called a *fazenda*. A fazenda is usually several thousand acres or more in area. At least one third of the land is occupied by the coffee trees, which are planted in rows on the higher slopes. Here they can get the good drainage which they require.

Coffee, of course, is not the only crop grown on a fazenda. Food crops are raised for the workers and their families. Many families tend their own gardens. Orchards supply oranges, grapefruit, peaches, pears, and other fruits. Bananas and pineapples are also grown.

There are fields of corn and beans, and pasture land for animals. Some corn is ground into meal, and some is fed to hogs. Patches of trees are usually left standing to supply lumber and wood for fuel.

There are usually several hundred workers living on a large coffee fazenda. The plantation owner not only provides homes for these workers, but builds a church and a school as well. He operates a store where they can obtain groceries and meat, clothing, and other needs for themselves and their families. A coffee fazenda is really a community in itself. It supplies all a family needs—food, shelter, clothing, school, and church.

The average worker's home is a small, one-story house. It is built of brick, covered with whitewashed stucco. The furniture is simple and light in weight. Brazilian women are very skillful at sewing, embroidery, and crocheting. As a result, the average home on a fazenda displays many colorful examples of handwoven covers, sheets, tablecloths, and curtains.

Going to Mass. On Sunday morning, coffee workers, planters, and their families attend Mass in a beautiful chapel located on the plantation.

A Growing City. Another new building is going up on this busy boulevard in the heart of São Paulo. Note the contrast in old and new architecture.

São Paulo, the Coffee Center. One of the world's fastest growing cities today is São Paulo, the largest city in Brazil and the second largest in South America. São Paulo is a beautiful metropolis with art galleries and fine public buildings, tree-lined streets and shady parks, and an up-to-date shopping district. Despite its location near the Tropic of Capricorn, São Paulo enjoys a mild climate all year. This is because it is situated on a high plateau about 3000 feet above sea level.

In less than 100 years, this inland coffee center in southern Brazil changed from a small river port with a tiny population to a large city with more than 3 million people. The thriving coffee industry around São Paulo accounts mainly for the city's rapid growth. Many of the people work in some phase of the coffee industry.

São Paulo is also the chief manufacturing city of Brazil. There are thousands of factories, large and small, which have the advantage of inexpensive hydroelectric power. One of the largest power plants in the world is only 35 miles from São Paulo. It makes use of the stored up power in the waters of mountain rivers which have been dammed to form a large lake. Cotton textiles, clothing, shoes, furniture, electric appliances, machinery for coffee processing, automobile tires, chemicals, and building materials are some of the products of São Paulo's factories. The manufacture of cotton cloth is especially important in this city, and its mills supply most of Brazil's textile needs.

São Paulo is a great railroad center, and fine modern highways connect it with its port, Santos, as well as with Rio de Janeiro and other cities of southern Brazil.

Santos, Port of São Paulo. Santos is the coffee-shipping port for the entire São Paulo district. Its harbor is formed by a deep coastal bay, and the city is located on an island in the bay. Ships from many nations line the docks at Santos to take on cargoes of coffee. In fact, more coffee passes through Santos than through any other port in the world.

Almost everybody in Santos is engaged in some part of the coffee industry. Some are traders, buying and selling coffee beans. Others weigh, pack, and sort coffee, or load and unload it at warehouses and docks.

Santos is located at sea level on the hot coastal plain. It does not share the pleasant climate of São Paulo, which is 3000 feet above Santos on the inland plateau. Transporting the coffee down from the highland fazendas to Santos has always been a problem, since steep cliffs rise almost straight up from the coastal plain. At one time the bags of coffee beans were loaded on the backs of donkeys. These sure-footed animals carried the coffee down steep, narrow trails winding from the São Paulo district to Santos. Later, a railroad was built which used cables to raise and lower the cars in places that were too steep for locomotives. More recently, another railroad was built which makes use of a longer, more winding trail, and avoids the steepest slopes. It does the job with locomotives alone. A good modern highway also connects São Paulo and Santos.

Making Electricity. Near São Paulo, this power plant generates electricity from water flowing under high pressure through the tubes at the bottom.

Famous Beach. Rio de Janeiro lies on Guanabara Bay where the Brazilian Highlands meet the Atlantic. Copacabana Beach is nearby, edging the shore.

Rio de Janeiro. Approximately 450 years ago, on the first of January, two explorers sailing along the coast of southern Brazil entered a narrow opening and came upon a small bay. Thinking they had discovered the mouth of a great river, they named the bay Rio de Janeiro which means, in Portuguese, "River of January."

The city which now spreads out along the southern shore of this bay is called Rio de Janeiro. One of the world's largest cities, it is the third largest in South America. Only Buenos Aires and São Paulo are larger. Rio, as it is often called, has over 2½ million inhabitants.

Ships from ports all over the world dock in its fine natural harbor. Airlines, highways, and railroads connect Rio with other leading cities throughout Brazil, South America, and other parts of the world.

Manufacturing is an important industry in Rio de Janeiro. Its factories and mills turn out processed foods, boots and shoes, cotton textiles, clothing, rubber products, chemicals and furniture. Most of these items are made for use in Brazil, rather than for export. Although Brazil lacks a supply of high quality coal, hydroelectric power is easily available for use in factories and homes.

Many visitors come to this city, the center of Brazilian art, culture, and fashion. They also enjoy its attractive scenery and resort accommodations. Sugar Loaf Mountain and Copacabana Beach are world-famous.

Brasilia. 600 miles north of Rio de Janeiro, in the interior of Brazil, a new capital city has been planned and is now being built. It is called Brasilia. The government of Brazil hopes that this new city will attract more people to the interior of the country where the population is still sparse and land is available for farms and ranches.

Plans for the design of the new capital are very ambitious. This beautiful city, with its gleaming new government buildings, apartment houses, churches, and schools, rises out of a former wilderness. There are pictures of Brasilia on pages 110-111.

Mineral Resources. The Brazilian Highlands north of Rio de Janeiro contain valuable mineral resources. It is possible that Brazil may contain as much as one fifth of all the world's iron deposits. The iron ore deposits near the city of Belo Horizonte, for example, are generally considered to be the richest in the world. This Brazilian ore is very high in quality, and lies close enough to the surface to be mined easily from open pits.

Brazil has been slow to develop its great iron resources. Until recent years, there had been neither the capital to invest in equipment and mills, nor the good coal necessary for converting iron ore to steel. Now, however, a modern steel mill has been built at Volta Redonda, 100 miles from Rio. This mill was built with some aid from the United States, and is the largest in South America. It produces steel for Brazil's bridges, tracks, buildings, and machinery.

Looking for Diamonds. These miners, famous for their honesty, are panning gravel in search of precious stones near Diamantina in southern Brazil.

Gold was mined in Brazil's colonial days long before it was discovered in California, South Africa, and Australia. At one time Brazil mined half of the world's supply of the precious metal, but now its production is small. One gold mine in the Brazilian Highlands is more than 8000 feet deep. It is said to be one of the deepest mines in the world.

Forests of Pine. Camps like this one in the pine forests of southern Brazil supply construction lumber to the cities. Note the piles of logs.

Brazil also led the world in the production of diamonds until greater supplies of these precious stones were discovered in South Africa. Today some diamonds are still mined in Brazil. They are found in the region around Diamantina, a city which received its name from the gems it produced. Some clear gems are mined, and these can be cut and polished as jewels.

Most Brazilian diamonds are the type known as industrial diamonds. Since the diamond is the hardest natural substance known to man, industrial diamonds are used to make drilling, grinding, polishing, and cutting tools. Brazil is one of the leading producers of industrial diamonds and exports them to the United States and other industrial nations.

Brazil is also rich in other minerals, among them very large deposits of manganese, bauxite, asbestos, and quartz crystals.

The Southern Tip of Brazil. This part of the country lies about the same distance south of the equator as northern Florida and Georgia are north of it. The climate is sub-tropical; there are long, hot summers and rather mild winters.

Into this part of Brazil came settlers from Germany, Poland, and other countries of Middle Europe. These pioneers cleared the forested areas for farms. They raise corn, which they use mostly to fatten hogs. Other cereal crops raised in this part of Brazil include wheat, rice, and manioc. There are also numerous vineyards that produce wine grapes.

Inland there are grassy regions where stockmen raise cattle. Near the borders of Paraguay and Argentina, Brazilian workers gather yerba maté leaves. The pine forests in this area are especially valuable for construction lumber. Large modern sawmills cut up the trees and supply wood for the busy areas around São Paulo and Rio de Janeiro. Some lumber is also exported to Argentina and Uruguay.

The principal city of this part of Brazil is Porto Alegre. It has become an industrial center with meat-packing and freezing plants, food processing factories, leather tanneries, wineries, and textile mills.

Facts *to remember*

1. Brazil is the fifth largest country in the world. Its 63 million people are of white, Indian, Negro, and mixed ancestry. Brazil is a republic and Portuguese is the national language.
2. Most Brazilians live in the southern section of Brazil, in and around the great cities of Rio de Janeiro and São Paulo.
3. Great coffee plantations lie northwest of São Paulo where the soil and climate is just right for the coffee trees. Coffee plantations, called fazendas, are usually thousands of acres in area.
4. São Paulo, in the southern part of the Brazilian Highlands, is the coffee center and the chief manufacturing city of Brazil. It is the largest city of Brazil and the second largest in South America. Modern highways and railroads connect São Paulo with its port city, Santos, and with Rio de Janeiro and other cities.
5. The city of Rio de Janeiro is the third largest city in South America. Its 2½ million people are

engaged in the manufacture of processed foods, textiles, clothing and other articles. Rio is a beautiful city with excellent means of transportation to other parts of South America and the rest of the world. The new capital city is called Brasilia.
6. Pioneering immigrants in the extreme southern part of Brazil have been successful in raising corn, wheat, rice, grapes, and cattle. Porto Alegre is the industrial city for this section.
7. At Belo Horizonte, north of Rio de Janeiro, is one of the largest iron ore mines in the world. At Volta Redonda a modern steel mill produces heavy iron and steel goods.
8. In the Brazilian Highlands gold and industrial diamonds are mined. Other abundant minerals are iron ore, manganese, bauxite, asbestos, and quartz crystals.

What *have I learned?*

Answer each question in a complete sentence.
1. What is the national language of the people of Brazil?
2. Give the area and population of Brazil.
3. Name the three races of people who live together as members of the one human race in Brazil.
4. Give the names of three important minerals found in abundance in Brazil.
5. Which Brazilian city leads in manufacturing?
6. Name the coffee-shipping port of Brazil.
7. What is the common name for a coffee plantation in Brazil?
8. What industry accounts for the rapid growth of São Paulo?
9. Which city is the second largest in Brazil?
10. From what source do the factories of São Paulo draw their power?

Facts *to understand*

Give reasons for each of the following statements.
1. Coffee grows well in the region northwest of São Paulo.
2. Brazil has been slow to develop its iron ore resources.
3. Diamonds from Brazil are used to make cutting tools.
4. The capital of Brazil has been moved to the interior.
5. The São Paulo region enjoys a mild climate despite its location near the Tropic of Capricorn.

BRASILIA,
THE "DREAM CITY"

Unusual Building Design. In this brand-new city, a surprising sight is the modern architecture. Notice the sail-shaped supports and curved roofs on the buildings. Plans for the new city call for one chapel, like the one above, for every two streets. Below is "The Palace of the Dawn," the home of Brazil's president.

Chapel Interior. Notice, in the picture to the left, that modern ideas in design have been carried inside Brasilia's buildings as well. Here you see the altar in one of the many new chapels. Below, the framework of one of the modern government buildings is nearing completion. The tall building will contain the executive offices, and the saucer-shaped one the Senate.

In the spring of 1960, an important event took place in Brazil. The capital of the country was moved from Rio de Janeiro to another city. What made this event so important was that the other city did not even exist five years before!

Far in the interior of Brazil, 600 miles from the heavily populated seacoast, there is a wide tree-covered plateau. Until very recently, nobody lived in this wilderness at all. It has always been the aim of the government of Brazil to coax settlers into leaving the crowded coast and coming inland. Brazilian leaders felt that here many people would find room to live, to work, and to help their country prosper.

This was one important reason for establishing the new capital here in the interior. Another reason is that, in order to make their new capital beautiful, the Brazilians wanted to build an entirely new city where there was none before. In this way, every detail could be planned, from the ground up.

You can see some of the results of their planning in these pictures. Modern architecture, or building design, has been used everywhere. Each building has been especially designed to do its job efficiently.

In five years, the people of Brazil have made a breathtakingly beautiful capital in the wilderness. It took great courage and much hard work to make their dream come true. Roads had to be built, homes for workmen provided, and all tools and materials transported over 600 miles. Today, Brazilians are proud of Brasilia. They like to think of it as a symbol of the growing place of Brazil as a leader among the family of nations.

2 Northeastern Brazil

Sugar Industry. Nestling in the wooded hills near Salvador, there are sugar mills surrounded by plantations. The cane here has just been cut.

Look at the map on page 98. You will see that the continent of South America reaches its most eastern point in northeastern Brazil. In fact, this corner of Brazil bulges so far out into the Atlantic Ocean that the distance between South America and Africa at this point is only 1600 miles. Today, jet airplanes can cover this distance between the continents in a few hours. Regular air service is maintained between the cities of northeastern Brazil and Dakar on the west coast of Africa.

The area along the coast of northeastern Brazil is a hot, rainy lowland. Many of the settlements located near the coast are densely populated. The people here make their living mostly by working on sugar, cacao, and cotton plantations. The climate makes living conditions difficult.

Inland from the coast is an area where few people live. This is the driest section of the country. The surface is hilly, and it is difficult to make a living here. The government is trying to get more people to settle here.

Sugar Cane Plantations. Many of the Portuguese colonists who came to Brazil in the early years settled on the northeastern coast. They started sugar cane plantations, and began exporting sugar to the countries of Europe.

In colonial days Brazil was the largest sugar producer in the world, and sugar still is an important Brazilian crop. At first, native Indians were used as plantation workers. Since they did not like to do the hard work, however, Negro slaves were brought in from Africa. Negroes still work on the sugar plantations, but there are no longer any slaves.

The plantations extend along the coastal lowland between Fortaleza and Salvador. Conditions here are ideal for growing sugar cane. The soil is fertile and the growing season lasts all year. There is a long rainy season, and a shorter dry season during which the cane can be cut.

Today, sugar is not an important export of Brazil. Most of the crop is needed at home to sweeten the coffee of the large numbers of people who enjoy that beverage.

Cacao and Other Crops. Brazil produces about one fifth of the world's supply of cacao. Only the lands along the Guinea coast of western Africa produce more.

On the coastal lowland south of the city of Salvador there are many cacao plantations. Workers care for the cacao trees and gather the pods which grow on the trunk and lower branches. They break open the pods, remove the cacao beans, and dry them in the sun.

The beans are carried to Salvador and other markets for export. The United States, where cacao does not grow, buys most of Brazil's cacao. Cacao is made into chocolate and cocoa. Both of these products are in great demand in our country.

Harvesting the Sugar Cane. This plantation worker is using a long knife called a *machete* to cut the sugar cane. It grows to twice the man's height.

Other crops grown in the northeastern lowland of Brazil include tobacco, cotton, bananas, and manioc. The cotton produced on the wet lowland has short fibers and is of poor quality. The plants are small, and new seed must be planted every year.

Tall Tobacco Plants. The planter here is examining a tobacco plant. The leaves are nearly ready to be cut and then dried in the warm sunshine.

Northeastern Brazil **113**

Upland Cotton. The farmer sprays his cotton plants with poison to prevent insects from destroying his crop before it is ready to be harvested.

The Dry Uplands. The uplands of northeastern Brazil are rocky. The rainy season is short, and the climate is dry and hot

Carnauba Palm Trees. These strange-looking trees grow to a height of more than thirty feet in northeastern Brazil. They have very many uses.

during most of the year. As a result, not many people live in this part of Brazil. Most of the area is suitable only for grazing livestock. Goats especially thrive on the poor pasture. Some cattle are also raised, but they must be driven from place to place in search of pasture and water.

The upland farmers plant their crops during the rainy season on land along the San Francisco and other rivers. There water can be obtained for irrigation when necessary. Beans and corn are raised on these riverside farms.

The principal crop, however, is upland cotton. This does well in areas where the climate is dry during part of the year. It grows on a tree-like plant which continues to bear cotton for years. Upland cotton is of high grade with long, silky, strong fiber. It is in great demand because it can be woven into fine cloth. Some cotton is exported, but most of it is used to supply Brazil's growing textile industry.

A valuable tree, the carnauba palm, grows along the rivers in this dry part of Brazil. Wax is obtained from its leaves and used to make polish for furniture, automobiles, and floors. Carnauba wax is also used to make phonograph records and motion picture film. The ripe fruit of the carnauba palm can be eaten fresh or made into preserves. Medicine is obtained from the roots, the bark is ground into meal, and lumber is made from the trunk. The carnauba palm is a very useful tree for the people of the uplands of northeastern Brazil.

Some day more people may be able to make their living in this part of Brazil when the San Francisco River is developed for electric power and for irrigation. A start has already been made. The government of Brazil is planning a large power and irrigation project to increase the opportunities of this region.

Recife and Salvador. The two most important cities of northeastern Brazil are Recife and Salvador. Both are important seaports.

Recife means "reef." It is a good name for this city which has a fine harbor behind a rocky ridge or reef. The city has two parts, one on an island and the other on a narrow peninsula, with bridges connecting the two. Sugar, tobacco, coffee, and other products are shipped from Recife. Some of the people work in the cotton mills, tanneries, and sugar refineries.

Salvador, a few hundred miles southwest of Recife, has one of the best natural harbors in South America. Cacao, sugar, and tobacco are shipped from Salvador, and many goods come in through this port.

Salvador is a two-layer city like Quebec in Canada. The lower section is a narrow strip along the coast. The upper section spreads over a series of hills which tower several hundred feet over the lower city. Donkey carts and automobiles use the steep roads which connect the two sections of the city. In addition, there are elevators which carry people from one level to another. Hotels, shops, public buildings, and homes are in the upper city, while offices, warehouses, and banks can be found in the lower city.

Natal. The eastern bulge of Brazil stretches out into the Atlantic Ocean toward Africa. It is here that the city of Natal is located. The distance across the ocean from Natal to Dakar on the west coast of Africa is about only 1600 miles. Natal is in an excellent location for trans-Atlantic passenger and freight service.

Natal is an important air base with large air fields, hangars, and radio towers. Airlines link Natal with Africa, Western Europe, other parts of South America, and the United States.

The Harbor of Recife. Sugar and cotton have made this seaport Brazil's third largest city. The section on the peninsula has been modernized.

Salvador. The name of this seaport in the heart of the cacao country means *Saviour*. Notice the two different levels of the city in this photo.

Northeastern Brazil **115**

Facts *to remember*

1. Northeastern Brazil is only 1600 miles from western Africa. Air flights connect Natal with Dakar.
2. Some dense population centers lie on the hot wet lands of the northeastern coast with its sugar cane, cacao, and cotton plantations. Fertile soil and a long growing season favor these crops. Tobacco, bananas, and manioc are also grown.
3. Much of the dry interior uplands of northeastern Brazil is suitable for raising livestock, especially goats. Water from the San Francisco and other rivers in this region is used to irrigate land for raising long-fiber cotton, corn, and the carnauba palm tree which yields a valuable wax.
4. Three important coastal cities of northeastern Brazil are Recife, Salvador, and Natal. Recife and Salvador have good natural harbors.

What *have I learned?*

The word in capital letters in each sentence is wrong. Change it to the correct word and rewrite the complete sentence.

1. Northeastern Brazil is nearer EUROPE than any other continent.
2. Brazil produces MORE cacao than the lands along the Guinea coast of western Africa.
3. INDIANS work on Brazil's sugar plantations.
4. On the dry uplands of northeastern Brazil the animal that thrives best is the DAIRY COW.
5. Cacao beans are exported from SANTOS.
6. Wax is obtained from the QUEBRACHO tree.
7. An important international air base in Brazil is SALVADOR.
8. A high grade fiber plant grown on Brazil's eastern uplands is FLAX.
9. A city with a fine harbor behind a rocky ridge is SALVADOR.
10. A two-layer city like Quebec is RECIFE.

Facts *to understand*

Give a reason in a complete sentence for each.
1. Northeastern Brazil has a hot climate.
2. Upland cotton is more valuable than lowland cotton.
3. The carnauba palm is a useful tree.
4. Cotton can be grown in the dry uplands of northeastern Brazil.
5. More people live in the coastal lowlands of northeastern Brazil than in the uplands.

3 The Amazon Region

Trace the course of the Amazon River on the map on page 98. You will notice that it generally follows a line just south of the equator. It flows from the Andes in Peru to the Atlantic in the east, across the northern part of South America.

The region drained by this long river is vast. It extends several hundred miles north and south of the Amazon, and reaches into Venezuela, Colombia, Ecuador, Peru, and Bolivia. However, the greater part of the Amazon region, or basin, is in northern Brazil.

The Amazon region of Brazil is covered by the largest tropical rain forest in the

world. This jungle is almost completely impassable, except along the rivers and streams. In the dark forests there are beautifully colored parrots, noisily chattering monkeys, and many other strange animals and plants.

The Amazon River. The only highway across the northern part of Brazil is the Amazon River. It rises high in the Andes near the Pacific Ocean. As it flows eastward it is joined by many branches, and grows very deep and wide.

The lowland region drained by the Amazon and its tributaries is about twice the size of the area drained by the Mississippi River system. So much rain falls in the Amazon region that the mighty river carries five times as much water to the Atlantic Ocean as the Mississippi carries to the Gulf of Mexico. During the rainy season the level of water in the Amazon and its branches rises so high that it overflows its banks into the neighboring lowlands.

Rain Forests Along the Amazon. Most of the Amazon Basin is covered by dense tropical rain forests. Plants grow quickly in the hot, moist climate.

A Hot, Moist Region. The main stream of the Amazon River is located a short distance south of the equator. The climate in this lowland region is always hot or warm because the sun is directly or nearly directly overhead throughout the year. The weather from day to day is montonous and regular. The temperature, around 70 degrees at sunrise, rises to about 90 degrees in the shade soon after midday. Sunset brings relief, and during the night the temperature drops.

The climate is not only hot but very moist. There is usually much rainfall, especially during the months from December to May. Rarely a day passes without heavy afternoon showers during the most rainy months. Even during the drier months, rain falls very frequently. It is very difficult to work and live in such a hot, wet climate.

Wild Rubber. The Indians of Brazil were probably the first people to use rubber. They obtained it from trees which grew near the Amazon River. Early explorers saw the Indians bouncing large lumps of rubber, and were amazed at its springiness. Gradually, rubber was adopted by Europeans for one special use: it was good for rubbing out lead pencil marks. This is how it was named. When automobiles became popular in the 20th century, rubber took on a new importance. Great quantities were needed to make automobile tires. At that time, Brazil led the world in rubber production.

To satisfy the demand for rubber, manufacturers had to increase the amounts which were available from wild rubber trees. They found that it could be produced in greater quantities and more cheaply from trees grown on plantations. Scientists also found ways to make artificial rubber from chemicals. As a result, not much wild rubber is used today, although the production of some goods still requires wild rubber. Most of the wild, or natural, rubber which is in use comes from trees growing wild in the Amazon region.

The wild rubber trees are scattered throughout the dense Amazon forests, often two or three hundred feet apart. The rubber trees have a milky juice called *latex,* which is gathered by tapping the trees. This is done by Indians who usually work for a rubber trader. He supplies the Indians with knives, cups, food, clothing and other articles they need, and pays them for the rubber which they bring him.

Rubber Plantations. As you have learned, most of the world's rubber once was gathered from wild rubber trees which grew in the Amazon region. When the demand for rubber increased, rubber plantations were started in a number of places

GATHERING WILD RUBBER

A rubber worker travels in a small boat along the river to the district where he is to work for four months. When he arrives, he builds a small hut for himself, and hacks a series of paths through the jungle. These paths will enable him to travel from one rubber tree to another when he is gathering the latex. Since a worker taps several hundred trees, he may have to cut five or six miles of jungle paths for himself.

The rubber gatherer must get up early each morning to go to work because the milky latex flows best early in the day. The tapping process is similar to the process of tapping maple sugar trees in New England. The trunk of each tree is slashed, and a cup placed beneath the cuts catches the latex which oozes out. The latex begins to thicken as soon as it comes in contact with the air. From a clear liquid, it turns white.

In the afternoon, the worker collects the cups of latex, and empties them into a larger container. At his hut he builds a fire of palm nuts, which gives off a thick smoke. A stick is dipped in latex and held over the smoky fire. The latex dries and hardens. Every few seconds, more liquid latex is added, and soon a ball of rubber forms.

outside Brazil.

The plantations in southeastern Asia and in Indonesia are now producing most of the world's supply of rubber. There are more people to work on the plantations in that part of the world than there are in northern Brazil. In addition, most of the Brazilian wild rubber trees grow far from an ocean port, whereas the Asiatic rubber plantations are situated near the sea. This lowers

This is called *curing*. Day by day more latex is added, until the ball of cured rubber, called a ham or a biscuit, weighs many pounds.

At the end of the season, the worker takes the hams to a trader in a river village. The trader's boats carry the rubber down the Amazon to the coast. There, the hams are shipped to cities in Brazil and elsewhere to be made into various articles.

transportation costs. The cost of gathering rubber from trees which grow close together on a plantation is also lower than it is from trees widely scattered in the jungle. In addition, the trees on a plantation can be carefully cultivated and made to yield more latex than the wild rubber trees. For these reasons, the demand for plantation rubber now exceeds the demand for wild rubber.

Brazilian Rubber Plantations. In recent years, successful attempts have been made to start rubber plantations in Brazil. Near Belem, in the lower Amazon region, a huge plantation run by the Brazilian government has several million productive rubber trees. The best quality rubber, however, still comes from the trees which grow wild in the forests. The Amazon region remains the wild rubber center of the world.

Brazil Nuts. Inside the hard shells, the meat of the popular, three-sided nuts shown here is very delicious when eaten raw or made into a candy.

Jungle Doctor. In the tropical Amazon region, doctors wage constant war against disease and ignorance. This doctor administers first aid.

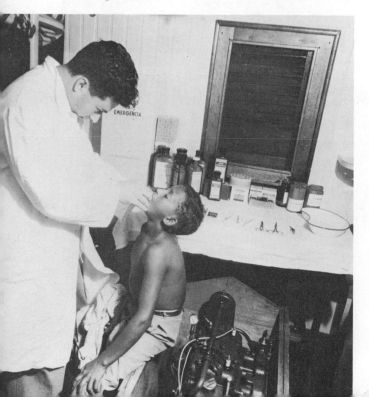

Other Forest Products. Brazil nuts are gathered from large trees that grow wild in the Amazon region. The trees grow as high as 150 feet. Twelve to thirty nuts grow together in a heavy ball-like pod with a hard shell. When the ripe pods fall to the ground, the natives gather them, break them open, and remove the nuts.

A single tree may yield as much as 1000 pounds of nuts. Large quantities of Brazil nuts are exported. Many of them are sold in the United States where they are a popular delicacy, especially at holiday meals and special occasions.

Babassu nuts are another product of the Amazon forests. They grow in clusters on a palm tree. When they are ripe the nuts are collected, and their oil is pressed out. The part that remains makes good food for livestock. Oil from babassu nuts is often sold as a substitute for olive oil. Soap, candles, and margarine are also made from it.

The Amazon Region is rich in many other forest products, including lumber, medicinal plants, and tanning extract. The great forests of tropical hardwoods produce valuable mahogany and rosewood. The lumber is difficult to ship out of the region, however, because transportation is still poor.

Disease-carrying insects thrive in these hot wet forests making it difficult and dangerous for people to live and work there. In recent years doctors and nurses have gone into Amazon villages and taught the inhabitants how to control insects and keep their water supply pure. Perhaps, in the future, with improved transportation and better living conditions, the vast plant resources of the Amazon region will be put to greater use. Many people might then come here to settle from more crowded regions of Brazil or other South American countries.

The People of the Amazon. The Amazon region is mostly uninhabited except for some tribes of Indians, most of whom are part Indian and part white. Years ago, their ancestors intermarried with Portuguese explorers and traders, and with settlers from other parts of Brazil.

These people live in the dense forests on the rivers and journey in small boats. Their homes are made of mud and poles, thatched on top with grass or large leaves. The home-made furniture is crude and rough. Instead of using beds, they sleep in hammocks, a comfortable Indian invention. A hammock insures a cool sleep in a hot land, and provides some protection against snakes and insects which creep along the ground.

The Indian families usually make a clearing where the women and children tend a small garden. Bananas, sugar cane, beans, corn, and yams are grown to feed the family. It does not take long for the thick tropical undergrowth to crowd its way

An Indian Family. Many tribes of Amazon Indians live just as their ancestors did before the discovery of America. They hunt, fish, and farm.

into these gardens, however; then the families must move on to a new clearing.

The Indian men help feed the family by hunting and fishing, or by catching edible turtles. They also gather nuts, rubber, fruits, and the roots of certain plants. They paddle downstream to exchange forest products for the things they need.

How to be Comfortable in the Tropics. These natives of the Amazon jungle demonstrate the advantages of resting in a hammock—comfort and safety.

Air View of Manaus. This inland port is a center of trade and travel along the Amazon River. Note the modern buildings, unexpected in this area.

Manaus, Amazon City. The chief city in the interior of the Amazon region is Manaus. Although it is located almost one thousand miles from the Atlantic Ocean, large ships sail up the Amazon to this city. Indeed, ocean vessels can journey up the

Boats on the Amazon. Small, brown-sailed trading boats carry mail, products, and traders up and down the river, two miles wide in some places.

Amazon 2400 miles to Iquitos in Peru. Manaus is on the Rio Negro, just a few miles north of the point where this tributary flows into the Amazon. Several other tributaries also join the Amazon River near Manaus, so the city is reached easily from many parts of the Amazon region.

Visitors to the Amazon region are surprised to find Manaus a bright modern city in the heart of the tropical rain forest. There are paved streets, trolley cars, electricity and modern buildings. The people who live here have a fine opera house, a beautiful cathedral, and many churches.

Manaus is a trading center for all the products of the Amazon region. Wild rubber, tropical hardwoods, Brazil nuts, and other forest products are carried to Manaus on rafts or small boats. Here they are loaded on ships that carry them down the river.

Belem, Amazon Port. Belem, the chief port of the Amazon region, is on the Para River about 100 miles from the Atlantic Ocean. Vessels from the Atlantic enter the Amazon by way of the Para River, which is really one of the two major mouths of the huge Amazon. It has calm, deep waters and is easily navigated.

The city of Belem is the gateway to the Amazon region. Rubber, nuts, tropical woods and cacao from the nearby plantations are all shipped to other countries through this port. Canned goods, clothing, knives, axes, and many other items needed by the people of the Amazon region come into Brazil through Belem. Ships also travel along the coast between this city and Rio de Janeiro. Belem has a busy airport. Regular flights connect Belem with Manaus and other South American cities. Planes from the United States often stop here.

Belem, like Manaus, is a modern tropical city with paved streets, electric lights, telephones, large modern buildings, shops, theaters, and street cars. Tropical shade trees line many of the streets. Visitors to Belem are always interested in the fine museum of natural history which contains all kinds of plants and animals native to the Amazon region.

Facts *to remember*

1. The Amazon region is drained by the mighty Amazon River and its many large tributaries. This region is the largest and densest tropical rain forest in the world. The Amazon flows from its source in the Andes eastward to the Atlantic Ocean.
2. The Amazon region is sparsely populated because of the hot, wet climate, frequent floods, tropical diseases, and poor transportation.
3. Wild natural rubber comes from the trees growing in the Amazon tropical forests. Indians gather the milky juice, called latex, by tapping the trees. This liquid latex is cured by heating and rolled into balls before it is shipped down the river.
4. At one time Brazil led the world in rubber production. Later, it was discovered that rubber could be produced more cheaply from trees grown on plantations. Wild rubber, which is better than plantation rubber for certain purposes, is still exported from Brazil.
5. Life is difficult for the Indians of the Amazon. Food is obtained by fishing and hunting.

Dense tropical vegetation is cleared away for small vegetable gardens. Transportation is by small boats on the rivers.
6. Manaus, the chief city and trading center in the interior of the Amazon region, is a very modern city built when rubber was bringing large sums of money in the world market. Today it is a trading center mostly for forest products such as nuts and hardwoods.
7. Belem, near the mouth of the Amazon River, is the gateway city to the Amazon region. Imports and exports pass through this busy port. It is a modern city in every way with excellent transportation by air and water.

What *have I learned?*

Write each answer in a complete sentence.
1. Give two reasons why so few people live in the Amazon region.
2. Why is plantation rubber easier to collect than wild rubber?
3. Name two valuable hardwoods of the tropical rainforests.
4. Give two good reasons why the native people sleep in hammocks rather than beds in the Amazon region.
5. What crops do Indian women and children plant in their clearings in the Amazon forest?
6. How do the Indian rubber workers "cure" latex?
7. What natural conditions hold back progress in the Amazon region?
8. Give two uses of the babassu nuts.
9. What is the chief port city of the Amazon region?
10. What city was built in the interior of the Amazon region when much Brazilian rubber was being sold on the world market?

Facts *to understand*

Give a reason in a complete sentence for each of the following statements.
1. The Amazon overflows its banks every year.
2. The demand for rubber increased greatly in the early part of the 20th century.
3. Little lumber is cut in the Amazon region.
4. Portuguese rather than Spanish is spoken in Brazil.
5. The interior of Brazil has a small population.

The Guianas

All-purpose Water Supply. In a village in Surinam, a stream is used for many purposes. This one is used for boating, bathing, laundry, and drinking.

Guyana (formerly British Guiana), French Guiana, and Surinam (formerly Dutch Guiana) are tropical lands lying along the Atlantic coast of northern South America. Venezuela lies to the west of these colonies, and Brazil lies to the east and south. The Atlantic Ocean is to the north.

Lowlands and Highlands. The coastal lowlands and the interior highlands are the two chief surface features of the Guianas. The lowland areas stretch some fifty miles inland from the coast. Despite the hot, wet, unhealthy climate, most of the people live in the lowlands because of the tropical plantations there which provide the chief occupation.

Few people live in the highlands of the Guianas. These jungle-covered highlands are generally less than two thousand feet above sea level. Unlike other tropical countries, there is not enough difference in altitude here from the highlands to the lowlands to make much difference in temperature. It is not very much cooler in the highlands than it is in the lowlands.

Transportation in the Guianas is made difficult by the dense tropical forests which cover much of the countryside. Traveling is done along the short swift-flowing rivers in small boats. Even river transportation is not easy because of the rapids and falls which interrupt travel wherever the streams flow from the highlands to the lowlands.

There are only a few miles of railroads in the Guianas, and good overland roads are scarce. People must get from place to place by walking along trails, since there are few rivers.

Farming. Most of the people of the Guianas earn their living as farmers or plantation workers on the coastal lowlands. The fertile soil of this area was brought down from the highlands by the swift streams. The lowland area is swampy, however, and must be drained before crops can be raised. Dikes have been built along the streams to control the flood waters, and a system of drainage ditches carries away excess water.

The chief plantation crop and most important export of Guyana is still sugar cane. Plantation farming is limited, however, because the population of the Guianas is too small to provide the needed workers. Many laborers are needed to cultivate and cut the cane, to keep the dikes in repair, and to pump water from the ditches.

Rice and cacao are other plantation crops grown in the Guiana lowlands. Manioc, maize, tobacco, vegetables, fruit, coffee, and bananas are raised for home use.

Forest Products. The tropical forests which cover a large area of the Guianas are an important natural resource of the colonies. Balata sap is the chief forest product. Because it is a poor conductor of

Jungle Home in Surinam. In a clearing in the jungle stands this native cottage. Its steep, sloping roof helps to shed the heavy tropical rainfall.

electricity, it is used to make insulation for wires. Balata sap is also used in place of rubber in making certain other products.

Lumbering is difficult in the dense forests because of the lack of transportation. The tropical hardwoods that grow in the Guianas are too heavy to be floated down the streams. Small amounts of hardwood lumber are cut and taken to sawmills on flat-bottomed boats called *punts*. The punts are moved along by long poles, a difficult task in the swift-flowing streams.

Sugar Plantations in Guyana. The workers are cutting the ripe sugar cane. Guyana received her independence on May 26, 1966.

Jewel Hunters. These Negro miners are washing gravel in pans. In this way, any diamonds which the gravel contains can be sorted out and kept.

Mineral Resources. Since the interior of the Guianas has not been carefully explored, no one really knows just how rich in minerals the region may be. Gold has

Catholic Schoolroom in Guyana. This teaching Sister has a very large class. The children display a wide variety of races and nationalities.

been panned for many years in the streams flowing down from the Guiana Highlands. Gold mining is the most important industry in French Guiana, and diamonds are mined in the highland areas of Guyana. Transportation to and from the mines is difficult, and workers do not want to labor in this hot, rainy, fever-infested region.

The chief mineral of this region is bauxite, the ore from which aluminum is obtained. It is mined in the highlands of both Guyana and Surinam. The bauxite is deposited near the surface and is mined by steam shovels. The ore is carried in small railroad cars to nearby mills, where some of the impurities are removed. Then the ore is shipped in more concentrated form to large aluminum plants in the United States and Canada. In recent years more than half the bauxite used in the United States came from Surinam.

The People of the Guianas. The population of the Guianas is very small. Less than three quarters of a million people occupy the three countries. Guyana includes the largest population—about 650,000 people. Surinam has only about half that number, and French Guiana has about 25,000. Negroes, Chinese, Hindus, and people of mixed races make up the largest part of the population. There are a small number of Europeans and some native Indians.

The Europeans who discovered and claimed the Guianas came from temperate lands. They started plantations to grow sugar cane and other tropical crops but found it difficult to live and work in these hot, wet lands. Workers were needed on the plantations. The native Indians would not do the work, so laborers had to be brought in.

Negro slaves were shipped in from Africa just as they were in southern United States. Later, Chinese were brought in to work on the plantations. They were good farmers, but the climate was difficult for them. Next, Hindus from India and the East Indies were brought in to work on the plantations. They came from lands where the climate was somewhat like that of the Guianas, so they were able to endure the heat and dampness better than the other groups. The plantation laborers work for low wages and live chiefly on rice.

The native Indians live in scattered villages along the streams. The Indian mother raises food for her family in a small garden. A few cotton plants supply enough fiber for clothing and for sleeping hammocks. The father and the older sons catch game and fish.

The Cities. Most of the people live on small plantations or in villages or towns near the rivers. There are few cities in the Guianas. The largest are Georgetown, capital city of Guyana, and also Paramaribo, capital of Surinam. Cayenne is the small capital of French Guiana. These cities, which are all on the coast, are the ports through which the trade of these colonial countries is conducted.

Facts *to remember*

1. Guyana is the first South American country to gain independence from a colonial power in this century. French Guiana and Surinam are the only colonies left in South America.
2. The sparse population lives mostly in the cities and on the plantations that lie along the hot wet coastal lowlands. The interior highlands are covered with dense tropical forests where transportation is difficult.
3. Farming is the chief industry. Sugar cane, rice, cacao, bananas, manioc, vegetables, and fruits are grown, for home use principally.
4. Some minerals are mined in the Guiana Highlands: gold in French Guiana, diamonds in Guyana, and bauxite (for aluminum) in both Guyana and Surinam.

5. People of many races make up the population of the Guianas, but altogether they are fewer in number than in the city of Boston. Most of the people live in the capital cities, namely: Georgetown, Guyana; Paramaribo, Surinam; and Cayenne, French Guiana.

What *have I learned?*

On a numbered piece of paper name:
1. the country lying south of the Guianas
2. the capital of Surinam
3. the country with the largest population
4. the mineral ore from which aluminum is obtained
5. the chief food of the plantation workers
6. the largest of the Guianas
7. the fiber used for making sleeping hammocks
8. a valuable mineral of French Guiana
9. the capital of French Guiana
10. the chief industry of the people of the Guianas

Facts *to understand*

Give a reason in a complete sentence for each of the following statements.
1. People of the Guianas live in the lowlands rather than in the highlands.
2. River transportation is poor in the Guianas.
3. Balata sap is used to make insulation for electric wires.
4. The population of the Guianas is small.
5. Some of the people of the Guianas are Orientals.

Unit Three Review

Questions for Discussion and Review

1. Why is Portuguese spoken in Brazil, while in the remaining South American republics Spanish is the official language? 2. Why do most Brazilians live in the southern part of their country? 3. What conditions may bring about an increase of population in the interior of Brazil? 4. Why is São Paulo a more pleasant place to live than Santos? 5. In what way does São Paulo need Santos? 6. Why is the iron ore mine near Belo Horizonte so valuable to Brazil? 7. Describe the

harvesting of coffee in Brazil. **8.** Compare the Amazon River with the Mississippi in length, size of drainage basins, and amount of water carried to the sea. **9.** Describe how the Indian families of the Amazon region live and work. **10.** Why is transportation difficult in the Guianas? **11.** Why were native peoples brought from the Far East to live in the Guianas? **12.** Why is there little manufacturing done in the Guianas?

Using the Maps and Globe

1. What is the northernmost latitude of Brazil?
2. What is the name of the largest island in the mouth of the Amazon River?
3. What city of Brazil lies as far south of the equator as New Orleans lies north of it?
4. What large cities in Brazil lie close to the Tropic of Capricorn?
5. What is the longitude of Recife?
6. On a world map follow this degree of longitude north until you come to a land body. What is it?
7. On what river is Manaus? How many degrees south of the equator is it?
8. Name two countries of South America that do not border on Brazil.
9. What part of Brazil is lowland?
10. In what part of Brazil are the Iguássu Falls?

Using Geography Words

Here is a list of special words that have been used in this unit. Write a sentence using each to show that you know its geographic meaning.

punts	latex	Tropic of Capricorn
fazenda	babassu	balata
carnauba	manioc	bauxite
reef		

Getting Information from Books

Use reference books such as *Compton's Pictured Encyclopedia* for information on these topics. Prepare to give a report on one of them.
Animals of the Tropical Rain Forest
The Steel Mills at Volta Redonda
Making Chocolate
Airlines from Natal
Names of Brazil's Twenty States
Iguássu Falls
Brasilia
The Amazon River

Final Test

Name it! Write your answers on a numbered paper.
1. largest city in Brazil. **2.** longest river of South America. **3.** fraction of South America's population in Brazil. **4.** chief money crop of Brazil. **5.** milky juice from rubber tree. **6.** uncultivated food product from the forests of Brazil. **7.** largest manufacturing city in Brazil. **8.** shortest distance from South America to Africa. **9.** gateway city to the Amazon region. **10.** tree from which wax is obtained. **11.** part of manioc used for food. **12.** mineral imported by the United States from Surinam. **13.** largest colonial country in South America. **14.** mountains in which the Amazon River has its source. **15.** former rubber city in the interior of the Amazon region. **16.** coffee capital of the world. **17.** crop from which chocolate is made. **18.** name given to a coffee plantation. **19.** chief tributary of the Amazon. **20.** hardest mineral known to man.

Applying Christian Principles

Choose the best ending for each incomplete sentence. Then write the sentence on your answer paper.
1. Spain and Portugal solved their boundary problems best when they **a.** sent explorers to examine them **b.** submitted them to a ruling by the Holy Father **c.** threatened to go to war over them.
2. Brazil is one of the outstanding countries in the world because it **a.** raises coffee for the United States markets **b.** has much unoccupied land **c.** has a mixed population of different races that respect each other.
3. The people of Brazil will be helped most when **a.** all have an opportunity to learn to read and write **b.** more iron and steel mills are built **c.** they can export more coffee.
4. The best reason for improving transportation routes to the interior of Brazil is that **a.** more land and natural resources will be available for a growing population **b.** tourists can see the country more easily **c.** more automobiles can be sold.
5. When the white colonial people found it difficult to work on the sugar cane plantations of the hot wet coastal lands, the worst thing they did was to **a.** urge the Indians to do the work **b.** bring Hindus from India to work the plantations **c.** enslave the Negroes from Africa.

Neighbors in Africa

**In this Unit
you will learn that:**

1 Africa is the second largest continent and has over 300 million people. Only 5 million are members of the white race who live chiefly on the northern and southern fringes of the continent.

2 Despite the large population, Africa is not densely populated. Large cities are few and are located only near the coast.

3 African nations have gradually become independent. There are now thirty-eight African-ruled nations.

4 Africa is chiefly a large plateau with scattered groups of mountains. Several large rivers flow from the interior to the sea.

5 Africa's location on and near the equator gives it a hot, moist climate except in the northern and southern areas. There high elevations tend to temper the heat.

6 Africa is rich in mineral resources. Until they were discovered, farming and grazing were the only occupations.

It is only in modern times that our neighbors in Africa have achieved their great importance among the peoples of the earth. The people of Africa are just catching up with civilization, as we know it. Because of this, Africa is a land of contrasts.

Although it is the world's second largest continent, Africa remained unknown to outsiders for many centuries. Because they had not thoroughly explored it, many generations of Europeans called Africa the "Dark Continent."

It is not hard to understand why Europeans were slow to reach the heart of Africa. Explorers entering the continent from almost any direction had to cross wide, hot deserts or steaming, unhealthy jungles. Very few natural harbors mark the long coast line, and steep cliffs block the way inland from the coast on the west and south. Frequent waterfalls prevent long trips on the rivers.

Today we realize that Africa is a great storehouse of raw materials, especially valued by countries which have nearly used up their own resources. When a way is found to live in its deserts and jungles, Africa may also provide a home for many people from the now over-crowded parts of Europe and Asia. Native Africans are now learning how to educate and govern themselves. Some day soon Africa may be renamed the "Bright Continent."

129

AFRICA

Africa, the "Dark Continent," can be seen in clear detail on this global map. It is surrounded by the Indian Ocean and the Red Sea to the east, and the Atlantic Ocean to the south and west.

North of Africa, across the Mediterranean Sea, is Europe. Notice how close Africa is to Europe, especially at the Strait of Gibraltar on the west, and how close it is to Asia at the Isthmus of Suez. The peoples of southern Europe and southwestern Asia have influenced the history of North Africa for centuries, since these areas are but a short distance away.

Africa's great rivers and lakes can also be seen clearly. The Nile River, in northeastern Africa, flows north and empties into the Mediterranean Sea. In western Africa the Niger River forms a large curve and empties into the Gulf of Guinea. The Congo River flows through central Africa and has its mouth on the western coast. In southeastern Africa are three great lakes: Victoria, Tanganyika, and Nyasa.

In the north are the Atlas Mountains, and in the southeast, the Drakensberg Range. The high plateau of Ethiopia can be seen in the east, and in east central Africa, the Ruwenzori Range.

Notice the contrast between these high lands, the barren desert land that stretches across all of northern Africa, and the green belt of vegetation across central Africa. As you will learn, Africa is indeed a land of many contrasts.

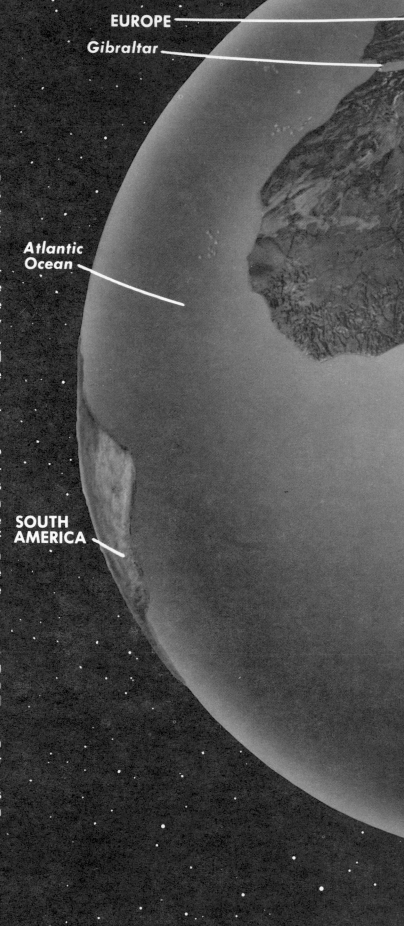

EUROPE

Gibraltar

Atlantic Ocean

SOUTH AMERICA

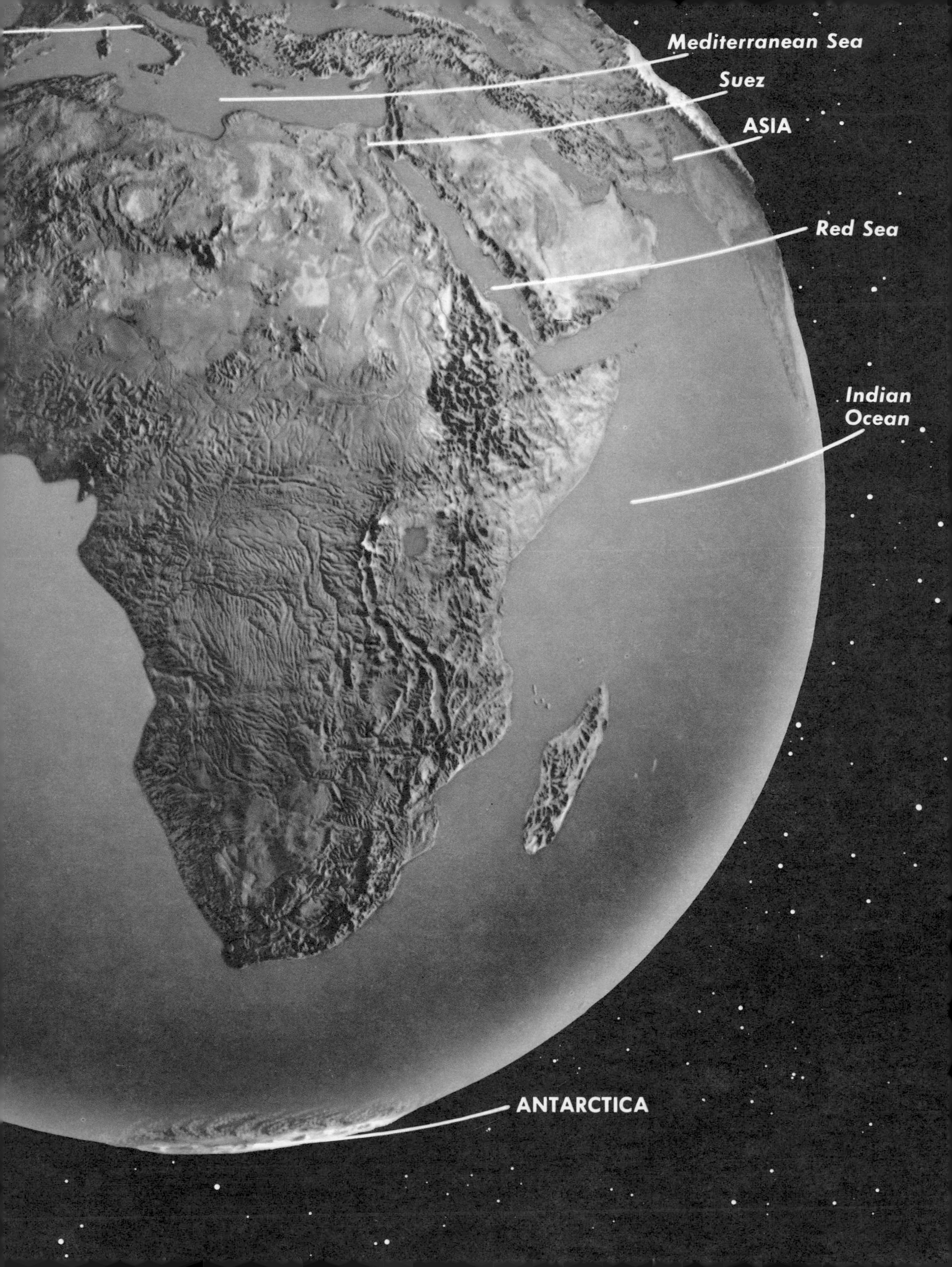

Mediterranean Sea

Suez

ASIA

Red Sea

Indian
Ocean

ANTARCTICA

1

Let's Learn About Africa

David Livingstone was a Scottish missionary and explorer. In 1841 he made his way far into the interior of Africa and spent the next thirty years traveling over unexplored parts of the continent. One of his many discoveries was Victoria Falls on the Zambezi River.

At one time Livingstone was believed lost. A New York newspaper then sent another explorer, Henry Stanley, to look for him. The story of Stanley's search for Livingstone is an exciting adventure story.

Stanley found Livingstone ill with fever. These two men became friends, and Stanley learned about the Congo River from the missionary. This made Stanley want to explore the great river. Returning to Africa a few years later, Stanley found the source of the Congo and paddled a boat to its mouth.

Other explorers traveled through Africa. Soon much of the continent was explored. The people of Europe wanted more land, raw materials, and markets for their own products, and felt that Africa could provide them.

Some European countries built settlements along Africa's coasts. When they realized the richness of Africa's resources, there was intense competition among them for colonial possessions. Great Britain, France, Belgium, Germany, Spain, Portugal, and Italy soon established colonies throughout this promising continent.

Location and Surface. Northern Africa is separated from Europe by the Mediterranean Sea. At the Strait of Gibraltar, the narrow western opening of the Mediterranean, Africa is less than ten miles south of Europe. On its northeast edge Africa is joined to the continent of Asia by the Isthmus of Suez. The Suez Canal was dug across this isthmus to join the Mediterranean Sea with the Red Sea, permitting ships from the Mediterranean to sail to the Far East without making the long trip around the southern tip of Africa. The Red Sea, the Gulf of Aden, and the Indian Ocean border the eastern coast of Africa.

Africa is the second largest continent in area. Only Asia is larger. Africa extends about 5000 miles from north to south. In the northern part, where it is widest, the continent stretches from east to west about 4000 miles. A huge part of northern Africa juts far out into the Atlantic Ocean on the west. Like South America, Africa becomes narrower toward the south.

Most of Africa is a high plateau with narrow lowlands along the coast. Large parts of the interior are desert wastelands. In the north is the world's largest desert, the Sahara, and in the south is the Kalahari Desert.

The Ruwenzori Range in tropical Africa is higher than our Rocky Mountains. Mt. Kilimanjaro, the highest peak in Africa, is 19,000 feet high. This is only 1000 feet less than Mt. McKinley, the highest peak in North America. The Atlas Mountains lie in northwestern Africa between the Mediterranean Sea and the Sahara. The Drakensberg Mountains, near the southwestern coast, form the highest part of southern Africa.

Natural Wealth. Africa is rich in natural resources. Diamonds, gold, copper, pitchblende (uranium ore), and many other minerals are found in the earth in abundance. Rubber and cacao grow well on tropical plantations. Valuable hardwoods are found in the tropical forests. The continent's riches cannot be obtained without great danger and much hard work, however. The hot equatorial sun, the scarcity of fertile farmland, dread diseases such as the sleeping sickness, yellow fever, and malaria, poisonous snakes, and wild animals all combine to make life very difficult in many parts of this continent.

Africa, with its many falls and rapids, abounds in sources of hydroelectric power but few of them have yet been put to work. The desert camel, the horse, the donkey, the buffalo, and cattle, sheep, and goats help supply man's needs for domestic animals in different areas. Wild animals live in the grasslands and jungles of central Africa. These are favorite regions for big game hunters.

The Wealth of Africa. At Kimberley, in the south of Africa, a polished diamond (being held) is compared with some rough diamonds from a mine.

Studying the Map

A. 1. Where is Africa located with respect to Europe? With respect to Asia? **2.** What large body of water separates Africa and Europe? Africa from the Arabian peninsula in southwestern Asia? **3.** What canal joins these two bodies of water? Of what importance is this canal to the people of eastern Africa? **4.** What ocean touches the western coast of Africa? the eastern coast? **5.** Notice that both the Tropic of Cancer and the Tropic of Capricorn cross the continent of Africa. In what climatic zones are northern, central, and southern Africa located? In what climatic zone is the largest part of the continent? **6.** About how far would a pilot fly in making a non-stop trip from the city of Cape Town to the city of Cairo?

B. 1. What does the map tell you about the surface of a large part of Africa? **2.** In what part of Africa are the highest elevations? **3.** Find Mt. Kilimanjaro, the highest peak in Africa. What is its height? How does it compare with the highest mountain peak in Asia? Are there any mountain peaks in the United States as high as Mt. Kilimanjaro? **4.** What is the name of the mountain range in northwestern Africa? What is its approximate height? **5.** The world's largest desert is located in northern Africa. What is its name? What small desert is in southern Africa? **6.** There are only a few lowland regions in Africa. Use the map key to discover the locations of these regions. **7.** How can you account for the lack of good seaports on the coast of Africa?

C. 1. The few large rivers of Africa flow over the steep edges of the highlands as waterfalls and rapids on the way to the lowlands. How does this help to explain why the interior of Africa remained unexplored for many centuries? **2.** Name the large river that flows through the equatorial region of Africa into the Atlantic Ocean. Through what country does this great river flow? **3.** What large river flows northward from central Africa into the Mediterranean Sea? What countries does it flow through? What land feature has this river built at its mouth? **4.** On what river is Victoria Falls located? How can the people of Zambia, Rhodesia, and Bechuanaland benefit from the use of this wonderful waterfall? **5.** Three of the world's large lakes are located in central Africa. Name them. Which of the lakes is crossed by the equator?

134

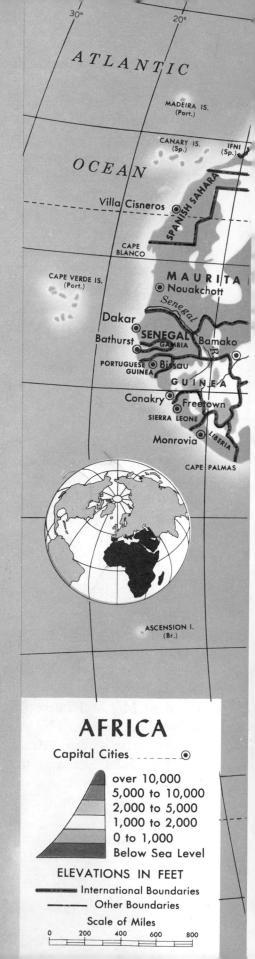

AFRICA

Capital Cities ⊙

over 10,000
5,000 to 10,000
2,000 to 5,000
1,000 to 2,000
0 to 1,000
Below Sea Level

ELEVATIONS IN FEET

International Boundaries
Other Boundaries

Scale of Miles

0   200   400   600   800

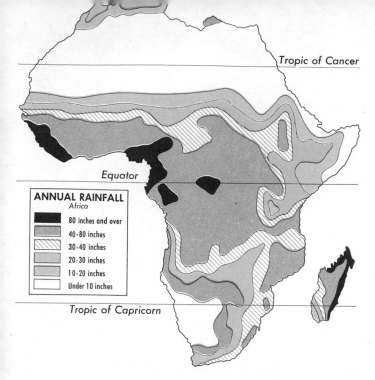

ANNUAL RAINFALL
Africa

- 80 inches and over
- 40-80 inches
- 30-40 inches
- 20-30 inches
- 10-20 inches
- Under 10 inches

Tropic of Cancer

Equator

Tropic of Capricorn

Variety of Climate. Africa lies on both sides of the equator. The northernmost part of Africa lies about as far north as the Virginia-North Carolina boundary. Its most southern point is as far south as Buenos Aires, Argentina. Much of the continent lies in the Tropical Zone. Part of northern Africa lies in the North Intermediate Zone, and part of southern Africa is in the South Intermediate Zone.

Snow in Africa. This is Mount Kilimanjaro, whose altitude is 19,710 feet. Although it is almost on the equator, snow usually covers this peak.

Much of this continent is hot, but many parts of central Africa have high plateaus and mountains where the climate is cooler. No part of Africa is far enough north or south of the equator to be very cold at any time of the year, except in the very high mountains. The peaks of the lofty Ruwenzori Range, for example, are often snow-covered throughout the year.

The Rain Forests. The equator crosses central Africa. This part of the continent is the region where the heaviest rains fall. During certain times of the year the rains come almost daily in the afternoon, usually accompanied by thunder and lightning. Here are broad, swampy areas, numerous streams, and dense forests.

The trees and vines of the forests grow very close together in this region, making travel difficult except along the wider rivers. Even the sunlight is kept out in many places by the thick masses of vines and branches. Only on the cooler plateaus of this region is the land covered with grass and a thinner growth of trees and bushes.

The rain forests of central Africa are the home of dangerous wild animals and large snakes. Huge crocodiles live in the waters and swamps. Monkeys, gorillas, and chimpanzees roam the dark jungles.

The Grasslands. Just north and south of the equatorial forests are the tropical grasslands. They are called *savannas*. On the savannas the rainfall is lighter, and there are few trees. There is a short rainy season during which the grass grows rapidly, but during the long dry season it stops growing and dries out, forming hay.

Many animals wander over the savannas and feed upon the grass. Among them are herds of antelopes, giraffes, and zebras. The rhinoceros roams over the grasslands while the huge hippopotamus stays near

African Rain Forest. In this picture you can see how dense and thick the vegetation grows where tropical heat and frequent rain are the rule.

the swamps and rivers. Herds of elephants roam the edge of the grasslands and the more open forest areas. The lion, the leopard, and other flesh-eating animals make their home on the savannas and prey upon the herds of grass-eating animals for food. The grasslands are good hunting grounds.

Wildlife of Africa. This continent is famous for its numbers of wild animals. On the grasslands these tall giraffes wander in search of food.

Desert Scene. The complete dryness of the desert becomes even more noticeable when you contrast it with an occasional spring or oasis.

The Deserts. Still farther north and south in Africa the rainfall is even lighter, and the land is desert. These deserts, among them the Sahara in the north and the Kalahari in the south, cover a large part of the continent. Few plants and animals live in the deserts because food and water are so scarce. When it rains in the desert, plants grow very rapidly, but they die or stop growing in a few days. Bunch grass, thorny plants, and a few small bushes are the only kinds of plants that can live in the desert. They have long roots that reach deep down into the ground for water, and thick leaves which do not allow much water to be lost through evaporation.

African River. The calm waters of the Tana River in Kenya make their way slowly past the deep forests. The men are filling their water cans.

Rivers and Lakes. The desert regions of Africa have few rivers, but there are many in the rainy equatorial regions. The largest rivers of the continent rise in the high mountains and plateaus of central Africa, and flow a great distance before reaching the sea. These rivers are the Nile, the Congo, the Niger, and the Zambezi. With their tributaries, they drain a large part of the continent and are navigable on the plateaus and in the coastal lowlands. Many rapids and falls prevent travel, however, especially where the rivers flow from the plateaus to the coastal lowlands.

The Nile, which is the longest river in the world, flows north across Sudan and Egypt to the Mediterranean Sea. The Congo flows north and circles west through the Republic of the Congo to the Atlantic. The Niger flows northeastward through Guinea and Mali, making a large curve before it flows southeast through Nigeria to the Gulf of Guinea. The Zambezi River flows east through Zambia, Rhodesia, and Mozambique to the Indian Ocean. Trace the course of these rivers on the map on page 135.

Africa, like North America, has a system of great lakes. They, too, lie near the central rainy section of the continent and have long been navigated by the native people. Lake Victoria is the second largest fresh water lake in the world. Only Lake Superior is larger. Other important African lakes are Nyasa, Tanganyika, and Chad. Locate each of these lakes on the physical-political map on page 135.

The People of Africa. The population of Africa is over 300,000,000. Most of the people are Negroes who live in the central and southern parts of the continent. About three fifths of all the Negroes in the world live in Africa. They are members of many tribes who differ greatly in size, looks, language, and ways of living. Farming, herding

Africans in Native Costume. These men are dressed for a traditional tribal ceremony. Notice the jewelry, horns, and feathers they are wearing.

and hunting are the chief occupations. Many are also employed in mining and other industries.

Only five million white people live in Africa. Most of them are in the northern and southern parts of the continent. Many of them came from Europe as missionaries, traders, or government workers of the countries that have had or now hold possessions in Africa. Others came to Africa to work on farms or in the mines. Still others came as workers in transportation and in communication, as overseers on plantations, or as managers in industries.

White Students at the University of Johannesburg. These young people, resembling American college students, are typical white Africans.

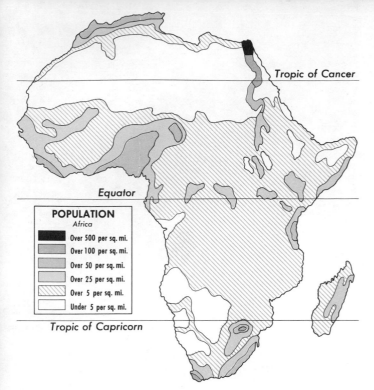

Tropic of Cancer

Equator

POPULATION
Africa

■	Over 500 per sq. mi.
	Over 100 per sq. mi.
	Over 50 per sq. mi.
	Over 25 per sq. mi.
	Over 5 per sq. mi.
	Under 5 per sq. mi.

Tropic of Capricorn

There are only three African cities with more than a million people. The inland cities are few and small. Trade is mostly with countries outside of Africa because transportation among the different lands in the interior is difficult.

Africa is such a large continent that to study it we must divide it into three parts. These will be Northern Africa, Central Africa, and Southern Africa.

Facts *to remember*

1. Much of Africa remained unknown for many years because of its hot deserts, poor harbors, unnavigable rivers, unfriendly natives, and tropical diseases.

2. European countries established colonies in Africa as soon as they realized it had valuable resources. France, Great Britain, Belgium, Portugal, and Spain have claimed much of the continent but today Africans are working toward independence. The Europeans have helped to develop the resources and make them available for use.

3. Africa is chiefly a large plateau with only narrow lowlands along the coast.

4. A large part of Africa is hot and rainy. It lies near the equator, and dense forests grow in these

hot, wet lands. The tropical grasslands called savannas lie north and south of the rain forests. Still farther to the north and farther to the south are the desert lands.

5. Several large rivers rise in the high mountains of central Africa. They are the Nile, the Congo, the Niger, and the Zambezi. Rapids and falls in these rivers make transportation difficult in many places. Lake Victoria is one of several large lakes in central Africa.

6. The population of Africa is over 300,000,000. Of this number, 5,000,000 are members of the white race. The few large cities are near the coast. Trade and transportation are difficult in the interior.

7. The Negro people of Africa are members of many tribes that differ greatly in appearance and ways of living. They are, however, all members of the same human race to which we belong.

8. Farming, herding, and hunting are still the chief occupations of the native peoples.

What *have I learned?*

Answer each of the following questions in a complete sentence.

1. What strait separates Europe from Africa?

2. What canal connects the Mediterranean with the Red Sea?

3. How does Africa rank in size among the continents?

4. What is the world's largest desert called?

5. What is the highest mountain peak in Africa?

6. What are Africa's tropical grasslands called?

7. What African river is the longest in the world?

8. What is the name of the largest fresh water lake in Africa?

9. What word describes the coast line of Africa?

10. What region has the heaviest rainfall?

Facts *to understand*

Give a reason for each of the following facts.

1. The countries of Europe wanted to establish colonies in Africa.

2. Africa has great differences in climate.

3. Most of the white people live in the northern and southern parts of the continent.

4. Transportation for long distances on Africa's rivers is difficult.

5. The climate is cool in certain parts of central Africa.

2

Northern Africa

The Nile River Near Aswan. This sailing boat, with the odd-shaped sail, is an Arabian *dhow*. There is much passenger and cargo traffic on the Nile.

If you were to travel westward from southwestern Asia, you would cross the Isthmus of Suez into Africa. Continuing along the Mediterranean coast of North Africa, you would pass through Egypt, then Libya, and finally Tunisia, Algeria, and Morocco. This area is closely connected to the Mediterranean countries of Europe and Asia. Its climate is similar, and for many

Europeans, North Africa was like home. For years the French, the Italians, and the Spanish colonized and developed different sections of North Africa. Even among those lands of northern Africa that have become independent, the influence of European manners, customs, and methods of government is still quite strong. In addition, the people of northern Africa have their own customs and ways of life. Some of them are eager to take over government, business, education, and other tasks which European nations once did for them.

EGYPT

The Work of the Nile. Beyond the great pyramids of Egypt lies a vast expanse of desert, but water from the Nile irrigates a green, fertile oasis.

Egypt is the oldest and most important of all the countries in northern Africa. It is a member of a new union called the United Arab Republic. Seven thousand years ago Egypt was already a civilized land. As far back as 5000 B.C., the people of Egypt knew how to irrigate their farms, weave flax and other fibers into cloth, and make fine pottery from clay. They were among the first to study mathematics and geography. The ancient Egyptians knew how to measure off their land and to draw good maps. They learned how to keep time by measuring the positions of the sun, moon, and stars. Egyptian civilization was one of the most advanced of ancient times.

The Nile Is Egypt. Most Egyptians today live along or near the Nile River, just as they did in ancient days. The Nile is the longest river in the world. It measures 4037 miles from its source near the equator to its rich delta where it flows into the Mediterranean Sea.

Near its source the Nile flows through a swampy region of heavy rainfall. Plants grow thickly in the swamps, and here a layer of vegetation grows even on the surface of the water.

As the Nile continues its course northward, rainfall decreases until the river reaches the drier region of grasslands. Then it flows through a desert area with little or no rain. Between Khartoum and Aswan there are rapids and falls, but the Nile becomes a gentle stream as it flows from Aswan, through the delta, into the Mediterranean. Here its flat valley and delta are the most densely populated part of Egypt because of the rich soil.

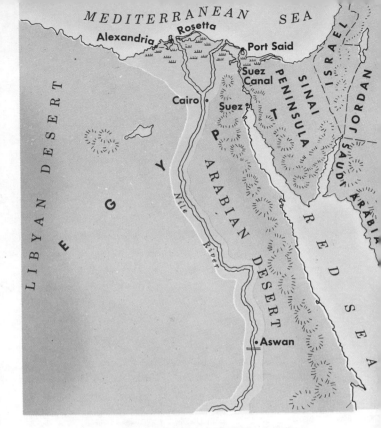

The Nile Oasis. A fertile spot in a desert is called an *oasis*. The northern valley of the Nile is an oasis. The land along this part of the river is crowded with flat fields of cotton, clover, grains, and vegetables which grow and thrive under the hot sun.

Day after day the Egyptian farmers can be seen bending over the rich soil, planting and plowing, hoeing and reaping. Travelers along the northern or *lower* Nile see palm trees waving their branches. Little boats move silently on the broad, blue waters. Beyond the green fields along the river, hundreds of miles of yellow desert sand lie in the sunlight. Overhead is the almost cloudless blue desert sky.

On the map, Egypt looks like a very large country, but the area where the people can earn a living by farming is smaller than the Netherlands. The Nile Valley is so fertile, however, that it can feed twice as many people as there are in the Netherlands. This narrow strip of land along the Nile, less than ten miles wide, forms the largest oasis in the world. There are more than 1400 people to the square mile in this area. This oasis, irrigated by river water which has been stored behind large dams, makes up about one thirtieth of Egypt's total area.

Floods and Fertile Soil. Recently dams have been built at Aswan and Sennar to control the waters of the Nile. Until then the river would rise at the same time each year and flood the farmlands along its northern banks. These floods were a mystery in ancient times because they always occurred at the hottest time of the year, after the river had flowed through a desert and no large tributaries had joined it for hundreds of miles. When the flood waters receded, they left a thin layer of silt which made the soil fertile. This rich silt made Egypt the "Gift of the Nile."

Most of the Egyptians have always lived in the area made fertile by the Nile floods. Today the modern system of flood control makes it possible to grow crops the year round, but now the land must be fertilized.

Desert Monuments. These ruins are all that remains of an ancient Egyptian temple. They still show, however, the art of Egypt's early civilization.

Harnessing a Mighty River. Just above Aswan, this dam backs up the Nile's water, which is piped out over the thirsty soil in the nearby fields.

Egypt's Blessing. Irrigation is necessary in this region. Egyptian farmers have several ways of lifting water from the Nile. One is the simple device of using a bucket attached to the end of a long pole. This is called a *shadoof* and is operated by one man.

Basin irrigation, another ancient method, is still used in some places. The land along the river is divided into basins with dirt walls around them. The basins are connected by canals. When the river overflows, it fills the basins. After the flooding, the water is drained off the basins and a layer of fertile soil remains.

The Nile overflow is gentle because the flood waters are controlled by the dams. This has been a blessing to Egypt. In this the Nile differs from China's Hwang River with its sudden raging floods. The Hwang is China's Sorrow; the Nile is Egypt's Blessing.

Crops sown in autumn grow during late fall and winter and are harvested in February and March. As we learn in the Bible, famines were common in ancient times. The waters of the Nile usually provided plenty of food in Egypt, however, even when neighboring lands suffered from lack of rain.

New Methods of Farming. In recent years Egyptians have been trying new methods of irrigation. A dam has been built on the Nile at Aswan. A huge new dam is also being built there to form an artificial lake three hundred miles long. During the winter, when the ground is dry, canals are used to carry the water to the farmlands.

Since the dams make water available at any time of the year, Egyptian farmers can now raise two or three crops on the same land each year. After one crop is harvested, another is planted, since Egypt has warm weather throughout the year.

Although more crops are now grown because of new methods of irrigation, the practice may ruin Egypt's soil. Irrigation all year long often spoils the land by crusting it with chemical salt in which no plant will grow. The Egyptians have been farmers for more than six thousand years. Their land was always kept fertile by the silted flood waters. Now, for the first time, Egyptians are having trouble with their soil, and many farms need fertilizer.

Egyptian Crops. Cotton is the chief money crop and export of Egypt. It is grown mainly on the delta lands near the mouth of the Nile. An Egyptian farmer usually rotates cotton with other crops. This means that if a field is used for cotton one year, wheat and clover are grown on it during the next two years. In this way the farmer keeps his land from wearing out, since clover helps to renew the fertility of the soil. Egyptian cotton is famous for its long fiber, and is exported to Great Britain, the USSR, the United States, and other textile-manufacturing countries.

Other crops grown on the delta and in the Nile Valley are rice, wheat, corn, sugar cane, tobacco, tropical fruits and vegetables. Some farming is also carried on in scattered oases where dates and figs are raised.

Egyptian farmers have little livestock because all the land is needed for crops. They may keep one or two cows for milk or for use as draft animals. Nomadic desert herders, however, raise cattle, sheep, camels, and donkeys.

Other Egyptian Industries. Egypt is poor in minerals. There is no coal or iron. Some gold and copper are mined, and building stones are quarried. Manufacturing in Egypt is limited by the small amount of raw materials available. Egypt must import such needed products as machinery, tools, medicine, and automobiles. In Cairo, and in the other smaller cities, we find some cotton mills and factories that produce cottonseed oil. Other manufactured products include cigarettes, perfumes, and pottery. Fine quality products like silk shawls and ornaments trimmed with gold, silver, and ivory are made by hand in homes and in small shops.

Heavy Industry in Egypt. This is a view of one of the many refineries in Suez. This city, at the southern end of the canal, is an oil center.

THE SUEZ CANAL

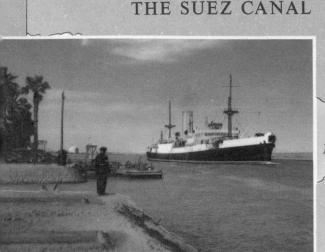

Freighters in the Canal. A constant procession of large ships steams slowly through the busy Suez Canal. The trees at the landing are date palms.

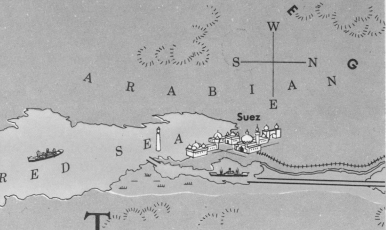

The Suez Canal cuts across Egyptian territory and links the Mediterranean Sea on the north to the Red Sea on the south. It shortens the water route to Asia by several thousand miles. The Suez Canal is a little more than one hundred miles in length, and is deep enough and wide enough for ocean-going ships.

Chief Cities. Cairo, the capital and largest city, is near the delta of the Nile, not far from the Mediterranean Sea. This ancient city of two million people is more densely populated than any other African city. The city has good land and water transportation. Its nearness to the Suez Canal and to southwestern Asia makes it an important center for trade. Cairo has many modern government buildings, large hotels, and lovely European-style homes. Tourists visit the capital during the comfortable winter season. Not far from Cairo are the pyramids and other ancient ruins of historical interest.

Alexandria is the chief port on the Mediterranean coast. It is only a few miles west of the mouth of the Nile, and about 130 miles from Cairo. Through Alexandria passes most of Egypt's import and export trade. It was a great port in ancient times, but lost much of its trade when the new route to India was discovered around the Cape of Good Hope. When the Suez Canal was opened, about a hundred years ago, however, Alexandria's trade began to grow again. Port Said, a city at the Mediterranean end of the Suez Canal, provides a harbor for many of the huge vessels waiting to use the canal.

Old Section of Cairo. Ancient Moslem mosques are most evident in this view of Egypt's capital. Note the modern electric power lines, however.

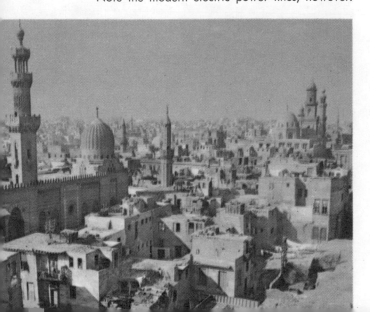

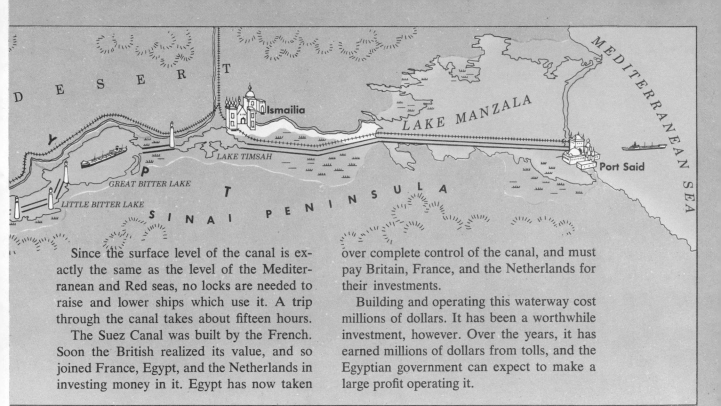

Since the surface level of the canal is exactly the same as the level of the Mediterranean and Red seas, no locks are needed to raise and lower ships which use it. A trip through the canal takes about fifteen hours.

The Suez Canal was built by the French. Soon the British realized its value, and so joined France, Egypt, and the Netherlands in investing money in it. Egypt has now taken over complete control of the canal, and must pay Britain, France, and the Netherlands for their investments.

Building and operating this waterway cost millions of dollars. It has been a worthwhile investment, however. Over the years, it has earned millions of dollars from tolls, and the Egyptian government can expect to make a large profit operating it.

The People and the Government. The population of Egypt is about 22 million. The Egyptian people speak the Arabic language, and many of them are descendants of the Arab conquerors of long ago. The beautiful Moslem churches with their slender towers called *minarets* can be seen all over Cairo.

Today there are only a few thousand Catholics in this strongly Moslem country. They belong to the ancient Egyptian branch of the Catholic Church called the Coptic Church. They are descended from the Egyptians who received the Faith from the Apostles themselves.

Egypt was governed by a king until 1953. It was not always an independent country, and several nations have fought for control of Egypt at one time or other. Great Britain was most interested in Egypt and once held a protectorate over the country. In 1953 the Army of Egypt drove out the King and proclaimed it a republic. It is a dictatorship, however, and not really a republic. Early in 1958 the leaders of Syria, Yemen, and Egypt formed a single government called the United Arab Republic, with the Egyptian ruler as its head.

The Oldest Church in Egypt. This ancient building marks the spot where the Holy Family rested on the flight to Egypt. A synagogue is next door.

Omdurman, Sudan. A street scene in the largest city in Sudan reveals the typical African open market. Notice the buildings made of dried mud.

SUDAN

Sudan became an independent country on January 1, 1956. Formerly it had been ruled by Great Britain and Egypt.

Sudan has an area about three times as great as Egypt, but its population is only a little more than that of New York City. On the map we see that Sudan lies south of Egypt. Eritrea, Ethiopia, and the Red Sea form its eastern boundary. To the south are Uganda, Kenya, and the Belgian Congo, and French Equatorial Africa and Libya are on the west.

The name of the country comes from Arabic words meaning "Country of Negroes." In the northern, desert part of Sudan the people are Arabs and Negroes, while in the south the population is largely Negro. Years ago the native chieftains of Sudan used to grow rich by raiding other tribes and selling their captives into slavery.

The British, the Germans, and the French who settled in Sudan and surrounding areas put an end to this evil custom.

From Desert to Forests. Sudan is a region of deserts, grasslands, and some tropical rain forests. It is crossed by the White Nile and the Blue Nile. The climate is hot all year.

The northern part near Egypt is a desert. In the south, near the equator, there is abundant rain and dense forests. Between the northern and southern part is a great grassland where the rainfall is light.

Much of Sudan is fertile wherever there is irrigation or sufficient rainfall. In these areas, farming is carried on. The Negroes raise a corn-like grain called *durra,* for they are not rice-eaters like the people of Asia. They prefer foods made of durra meal, which they call *mealies.* Wheat and barley are also grown, and cattle, sheep, and goats are raised on the grasslands. The chief crop of Sudan is cotton, which is grown on irrigated land near the rivers. While the British were in Sudan they built a large dam on the Blue Nile near Sennar to supply water for irrigation.

The native people obtain a product called *gum arabic* from small trees that grow in certain areas of Sudan. Most of the world's supply of gum arabic comes from this country. The hardened gum is exported to our own country and to countries of Europe where it is used to make a special type of glue.

Other products of Sudan are medicinal herbs, skins and hides, nuts, and some gold. Recently iron ore has been found in the old worn-down mountains of the western part of the country.

A Useful Tree. In Sudan as well as other parts of Africa grows the *baobab*, one of the world's oddest but most useful trees. The wood of the baobab holds water like a sponge. A thirsty traveler can drill holes in a baobab and get good drinking water. This tree has fruit which tastes like gingerbread. Fever medicine is made from its outer bark, and rope is sometimes made from fibers of the soft inner bark. Even the baobab leaves are good to eat.

Baobab trees do not grow very tall, but the trunk is enormous, often as much as thirty feet thick. Natives sometimes hollow out the trunk of a living tree and use it for a house. Many African houses are built beside a baobab tree. The dense foliage provides pleasant shade and coolness for the family. The baobab can be truly called the all-purpose tree.

Cities in the Sudan. Khartoum, the capital of Sudan, is in a hot region with little rainfall. It is located where the White Nile and the Blue Nile join. It is a center for trade. Caravan and water routes meet at this city which is about 1300 miles south of Cairo, Egypt. Railroads extend north

Africa's Famous Baobab Tree. You can get an idea of the huge size of this tree by noticing the size of the woman standing by its thick trunk.

and south from the city. Most of the people who work in Khartoum live across the river in Sudan's largest city, Omdurman. It has a population of about 125,000.

Port Sudan, a city on the Red Sea, is the country's only important port. Most of Sudan's foreign trade passes through this city which is connected by railroad with Khartoum.

The Church in Sudan. In the western regions of Sudan the White Fathers carry on mission work among the native tribes. The work of spreading the Faith is also done by Italian missionaries called the Sons of the Sacred Heart. Both groups have had a good measure of success in the southern parts of Sudan where Islam is not yet rooted among the Negro people. In the northern sections, however, where all are Moslems, there are few conversions.

OTHER NORTHERN LANDS

The City of Marrakech. This wide market place, or *bazaar*, is covered with stalls and tents where Moroccans buy, sell, and trade important goods.

In ancient history we learn about the Phoenicians and the Greeks who had settlements along the coast of northern Africa more than a thousand years before the birth of Christ. Later the Romans took control of this region and built roads, reservoirs, and aqueducts. Parts of northern Africa once helped to feed the Roman Empire with wheat and other food crops. Today these once productive lands are little more than dry deserts, made this way by warring armies who ruined the irrigation systems. Slave labor and bad management also helped to ruin the land. Summer winds and winter rains carried away the fertile soil.

After the fall of the Roman Empire, Arab peoples moved into northern Africa and gained control of the coastal area.

In more recent years, the French conquered and settled the region. Although Arabs form the largest part of the population, there are many French, and some Spanish and Italian people living here.

Moslem Lands. At one time the lands of northwestern Africa that bordered the Mediterranean were known as the Barbary States. The Arabs called this region "The Western Isle." This area is in fact a kind of island, surrounded by seas of water and of sand. The people of Tunisia, Algeria, and Morocco were once Catholic, with many Bishops directing thriving dioceses. Today the Barbary Coast is the western outpost of Islam, the Moslem religion.

For centuries, the Barbary Coast was a center for two criminal activities—piracy and slave-trading. Slave dealers sold thousands of captured people into bondage.

Religious Orders were founded in Europe to ransom the poor slaves. Saint Vincent de Paul, the great French saint of the poor, was one of the many Europeans who spent years in Moslem captivity. The rulers of the Barbary States also demanded tribute of every passing ship, and their pirate vessels made the seas unsafe. During the early years of our country, the United States fought a war against these pirates. By defeating them, Americans helped to keep the high seas safe and free for the ships of all nations.

The People and Their Homes. The Arabs and the Berbers are the native people of the Atlas lands. The Berbers were once Christians, but today most of them are Moslems like their Arab neighbors.

The Berbers are peasant farmers and live inland in villages on the mountain slopes and plateau lands. Their homes are one-room huts made of dried mud with thatched roofs. They are placed close together, and often the villages are walled to protect them against robbers.

Some of the Arabs are nomads, who wander over the lowlands with their herds of cattle, camels, sheep, and goats in search of grass. Others live in small villages which are sometimes not much more than a circle of tents. Still other Arabs live in the larger cities.

The Europeans live in the newer sections of the large cities, usually some distance from the homes of the natives. The streets where the Europeans live are well planned, and are much more attractive, with their white-walled houses, than those of the older sections.

The market place is an important part of any town. It is usually located on a long, narrow street with booths and stores on each side. In the large cities there are a number of such market streets.

The Atlas District. The Atlas Mountains are in northwestern Africa. The region extending a few hundred miles in from the coast is known as the Atlas District. It lies along the Atlantic and western Mediterranean coasts. To the south of this district is the great desert called the Sahara.

The countries in this region are Morocco, Tunisia, and Algeria. Morocco and Tunisia are independent countries. While the French and the Spanish controlled separate parts of Morocco, the city of Tangier on the Atlantic coast of northwest Africa was an international city. Today it is considered part of independent Morocco. Algeria, once a part of France Overseas, achieved its independence in 1962 and now has its own government.

From the Tell Inland. The narrow strip of plains and hilly land that borders the Mediterranean coastal region of northern Africa is called the Tell. This is a good name because *tell* means hill in Arabic. South of the Tell are higher lands consisting of plateaus and the Atlas Mountains.

Typical Berber Town. Ait-ben-Haddou is a fortified town in the foothills of the Atlas Mountains. In the distance, notice the Berbers' farmlands.

The coastal lands of the Tell have some rainfall during the mild winters. Summers are hot and dry. This is the same Mediterranean climate as in some of the countries of southern Europe. There are some well populated areas in the Tell covered with green trees, farms, and gardens.

As you travel inland from the coast to the plateau and mountain areas, the climate changes. On the slopes of the Atlas Mountains facing the coast there is plenty of rain because the winds from over the water rise, become cool, and drop their moisture. Some of these windward slopes are covered with trees, and farming is carried on in the mountain valleys. The southern slopes of the Atlas Mountains and the areas on the plateau between the mountain ridges, however, have little rain. This is because they are sheltered from the moisture-bearing Mediterranean winds. These areas are used chiefly to graze animals, except where irrigation has made farming possible.

A Farming Region. Farming is an important occupation of the people in the Atlas lands. French farmers brought in

Fine Morocco Leather. Craftsmen are working here at their ancient art of leather tooling. These fancy bindings for books are famous everywhere.

modern machinery, but crude plows pulled by oxen are still used by many of the natives. The farmers frequently make use of irrigation to grow their crops.

Many different kinds of crops are grown. Grapes are raised and made into wine, or are sun-dried for raisins. The main cereal crops are wheat and barley. Vegetables are grown and shipped to France and England. Such Mediterranean crops as oranges, lemons, olives, figs, nuts and tobacco are grown in the coastal region. Dates are raised on the desert oases south of the Atlas Mountains. The cork oak tree grows on slopes of mountains where there is enough rain. Cork is obtained from these

152 Africa

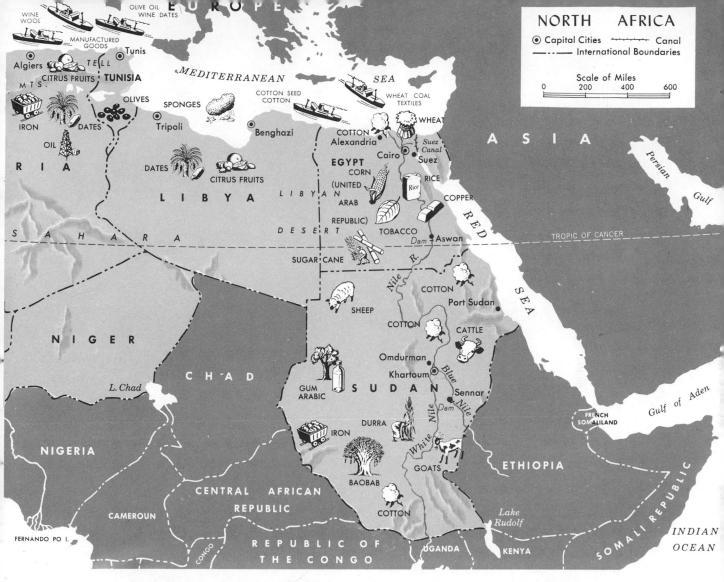

trees, and also an extract used in the process of tanning leather.

Other Occupations. Much of the hilly Atlas region receives very little rain. It is suitable for grazing. Herders take their animals over the hills and plains in search of grass. Hides and leathers are exported. Camels are not so important as they once were because of the introduction of automobiles, trucks, and airplanes.

On the high plateaus, where little rain falls, *esparto* grass grows. When it is about two feet high, it is cut and used to make paper, shoes, and cord. Some is shipped to France and England.

Northwestern Africa is poor in coal and oil, but large deposits of phosphate rock and iron ore are found there.

Principal Cities. Casablanca, on the Atlantic Ocean, has an excellent harbor and is the chief port of Morocco. It is the largest city in this part of Africa. In addition to its old Arab section, Casablanca has a modern section where many Europeans live.

The city of Rabat is the capital of Morocco. The principal cities of Algeria are Algiers, the capital, and Oran. Both cities are important seaports on the Mediterranean. Tunis, the capital and chief city of Tunisia, is another important port on the Mediterranean.

LIBYA

Bedouins at a Libyan Well. These tribesmen of the Libyan desert have stopped at a well to fill up with water, a scarce item among these people.

Libya lies between the Atlas lands and Egypt. It once belonged to Italy, and during that time peasant farmers came from the over-crowded mother country and settled here. They worked and toiled on irrigated lands, and made the desert sands bloom and produce. Since it was on the losing side in World War II, Italy had to give up Libya and its other colonies in Africa, but the farm families remained.

Most of Libya is a desert. For this reason it is thinly settled. The Moslem population makes a living by raising cattle, sheep, goats, and camels, and by selling wool, hides, and skins. Some farming is done on the scattered oases and near the coast. Deep wells are dug from which water for irrigation is obtained. Dates, olives, citrus fruits, wheat, barley, and tobacco are the chief crops.

There are few cities and towns along the coast. The chief city is Tripoli, sometimes called the "White City" because of its white-walled buildings and mosques.

THE CHURCH IN NORTHWESTERN AFRICA

While the French were in control of this part of Africa, some cities had large French populations. Catholic churches and schools grew up, and there is a shrine of Our Lady of Africa looking out over the blue Mediterranean Sea towards France.

In Algiers there is a monastery of the White Fathers, one of the great mission societies at work in Africa. Those who work among the Moslems may spend thirty or more years of toil tending the sick and wounded, feeding the poor, teaching, and praying, and win no more than two or three converts during the whole time.

THE SAHARA

Making Camp in the Sahara. These desert nomads are busy feeding the camels and setting up tents. Colorful rugs hang on the tents' inner walls.

The Sahara occupies much of northern Africa. It is the world's largest desert. The word *sahara* is Arabic, and means "the great desert." It is larger in area than the United States, and stretches from the Mediterranean Sea and the Atlas Mountains on the north to the grasslands of Sudan on the south. It reaches from the Atlantic Ocean on the west to the Red Sea on the east. The physical-political map on page 135 shows that the Sahara extends into many countries of Africa. Among them are Morocco, Algeria, Tunisia, Libya, Egypt, Sudan, Niger, Mali, and Mauritania.

Surface and Climate. The Sahara is one of the driest regions of the world. It has less than ten inches of rain per year and this comes in short heavy showers at certain seasons. The summers are very hot, and the winters are warm. The sun heats the rocks and sand, and the air sometimes reaches a temperature of 130 degrees. After sunset, the sand and rocks lose some of their heat, and the air cools.

Some parts of the Sahara are covered with drifting sand dunes, while other parts are stony. Large areas are nearly level but there are sections that are hilly and even mountainous. Except where water can be obtained from springs or wells, few people live on the Sahara.

BEDOUIN FAMILIES

Wandering herders called Bedouins live on the edge of the Sahara or on the higher lands where grass grows. The families live in tents of cloth spun and woven by hand from the dark hair of their goats. Herders move often, so they carry few bulky possessions. Their food is chiefly meat and milk, the products of their flocks. They trade rugs, leather products, animals, and meat for dates, grain, and clothing.

Here, as in Arabia, the Bedouins make their way from oasis to oasis, herding their flocks along the edge of the desert, where a little grass grows. Bedouin families live together and move together; families group together in tribes, under the direction of a chief or *sheik*. Children are born in tents and grow up on the backs of camels.

When a grassy place with a well or spring is found, the nomads stop. Camp is set up in minutes. Fires are made, and meals cooked. Children, with legs cramped from long riding, run about wildly, help carry water from the wells, gather dry plants for fuel, and drive or lead animals here and there.

Typical Bedouin Family. This nomad is not so shy of cameras as his family who peer out from the ragged tent. Notice the lambs they are raising.

Desert Oases. An *oasis* as we have learned, is a fertile place in the desert, with water. Some oases depend upon rivers for

One Important Job at an Oasis. These women make use of the waters of an oasis near Tunis to do something impossible in the desert—the wash.

water; some are at the foot of mountains where springs furnish water, and others depend upon deep wells. The French have dug many wells in the Sahara. Most oases are green with plants, especially the date palm trees whose fruit provides useful food. Some are surrounded by walls as protection against robbers.

The people on an oasis live in stone or adobe (sun-dried mud) dwellings. The walls and roofs are made thick to keep out the heat of the sun. Inside the house it is cool and dark because there are few windows. Roofs are flat because there is no need to shed rain or snow. The dwellings are often located on the edge of the oasis to leave all the land near the springs or wells for farming.

After a few days in one place the grass may all be eaten. Early the next morning tents are packed, everything is stowed away, and again everyone mounts his camel, the "ship of the desert." Camel bells tinkle, the beasts' feet plod softly on the sand, and the riders jerk and sway in a slow motion. As the sun rises in the sky, the day grows hot. The Bedouins wear head veils and loose clothing to keep out some of the heat and let the air circulate around the body, but they feel the heat from the hot sand.

There are places on the desert where there is enough rain for a few crops. Here some of the Bedouin families stay for a while. They sow wheat or barley, and harvest it to make their bread.

Desert women and girls as well as the men carry on handicrafts. They spin and weave cloth from the wool of the sheep and the hair of the goats and camels. They make rugs, tents, and clothing from this material.

A visit to the market in an oasis town is a great event for a Bedouin tribe. Some of the handicrafted articles, as well as some animals from the herds, are sold in the market. There the Bedouins buy sugar, coffee, fine rifles, and ammunition. The women buy trinkets for themselves and toys for the children, and sometimes a silk scarf from France or China. All members of the family can get the small phonographs and records that they like. While in town, the Bedouins all may enjoy cooling soft drinks which are sold everywhere. Soda water is especially popular among Moslems who cannot drink wine.

The desert nomads know little about our civilized comforts but, like the Gypsies, they prefer their own way of life. They are in no hurry. They do not rush to catch trains. They take time to visit and to give banquets for their friends, serving whole boiled sheep on huge mounds of rice, and plenty of black coffee. At these feasts, laughter and good talk go on for hours. Sometimes guests at parties make up poetry and songs. Each one sings his own composition to see which is best.

Nomad children have their schools and teachers. Their schools are mostly out of doors. They study the Moslems' holy book, the *Koran,* and often learn to write by tracing letters in the smooth sand.

Desert Travel. Until recent years camels were the chief means of transportation in the Sahara. Large caravans crossed from north to south carrying products to market. There are no railroads connecting the edge of the desert with the sea. The first automobile crossed the Sahara a few years ago, travelling from Algeria to Timbuktu in the Mali Republic, a distance of about 1200 miles in 20 days. Today, automobiles struggle along, stopping often because of boiling radiators, or tires which burst from the heat of the sand. No one crosses the Great Desert without risk; anyone may be caught in a sand storm, or may run out of water. Airplanes skim above the sandy wastes, but their crews dread a forced landing in this thirsty wilderness.

Auto busses make the trip from Timbuktu, on the Niger River, across the desert to Marrakech in Morocco, or from

Desert Caravan. Masked and hooded against the sun and sand, these drivers lead their camels over the shifting dunes of the Sahara near Algeria.

Camels at Timbuktu. These "ships of the desert" are resting between caravan trips. Timbuktu is an important center of trade routes in the Sahara.

Kano in Nigeria to Tunisia. The old camel caravans took eight weeks. The bus makes it in a week, and the airplane in less than a day. Passengers on busses have to be hardy, for there is no good road on which to travel. On the rim of the desert some wild life may be seen. Slender, graceful gazelles race beside the bus and leap across in front of it.

Bus drivers start out across desert territory about three o'clock in the morning. Much of each day's journey is done before the dreaded sunshine begins to make sand and rocks glow like a white-hot furnace. Stations are set up in the desert at places where bus passengers can pass the night. Some of these stations are little hotels in oases, while others are merely buildings

Dakar, Republic of Senegal. This city is a major Atlantic seacoast port in west Africa. In the center of the city, there is an open-air market.

surrounded by desert sand, where no grass or tree lives, and no bird or beast or even leaf stirs to break the stillness.

A few camel caravans, carrying freight, still cross the desert or travel from one oasis to another. Caravans travel mostly at night when it is cool. Since there is no guide post, the men find their way by the sun and stars.

Timbuktu. Timbuktu is a city on the southern edge of the Sahara. It is near the northern bend of the Niger River in the Republic of Mali on a hot plain where little rain falls. Many caravan routes meet there. The dwellings are of sun-dried mud, and the streets are narrow and winding. Salt, gold, cloth, and many other products are brought to the market in this city.

The arrival of a caravan bringing salt is a great event, for salt is scarce and therefore precious in Africa. For many years caravans have been bringing salt from mines in the Sahara. Some mines are 425 miles north of the city, a journey of ten days. There used to be more than 4000 camels in some caravans, and each camel carried at least two great blocks of salt.

Dakar. Dakar on the Atlantic coast is the most western port on the continent. It has a large man-made harbor and serves as a port and naval base for the lands along the west coast. It is the leading city of this part of Africa, and capital of Senegal.

The location of Dakar is important to us because it is only about 1000 miles from the South American continent. It is as near to Brazil as it is to Europe. Airplanes that fly between Africa and South America take off from Dakar. Goods bound for the interior of western Africa go through this port, and a railroad runs from Dakar to the Niger River. Boats then carry the products on the Niger to Timbuktu and other interior towns.

ISLANDS NEAR NORTH AFRICA

Outer Harbor, Funchal. Funchal, the capital of the Madeira Islands, is the third largest city of Portugal. It attracts many tourists like these.

The Madeira Islands, the Cape Verde Islands, and the Canary Islands are west of North Africa. The Canaries are owned by Spain, while the others are Portuguese colonies. The Madeira Islands and the Canary Islands have a large Catholic population. The people are Europeans, mostly of Spanish or Portuguese background. The islands have fine old churches, monasteries, and schools. Although the Cape Verde Islands have a European colony, most of the natives are of the Negro race.

The islands were formed by volcanoes. They have fertile soil and mild climates. All of them ship fresh fruits and vegetables to Europe. The word *Canary* came from the Latin "canis" meaning dog, on account of the large wild dogs living there. The

Tomb of Father de Foucauld in the Sahara.

CHARLES de FOUCAULD

In the Sahara, along the camel route from Tunis to Kano, is a high, sandy plateau. Across it, fierce Moslem nomads ride from oasis to oasis with their faces veiled against the blowing sands. Here, in modern times, a French priest, Father Charles de Foucauld, lived a life of prayer and penance as a hermit in the desert.

In his youth, he had been a brilliant army officer who gave up his Faith for a life of sin. After he repented, he studied and became a priest. Then he became interested in the souls of the nomads he had known in his army days.

Father de Foucauld found that there was no hope of converting the Moslems through preaching. He decided to live the life of a saint in the desert, to offer Mass, and be one Christian soul in this land. He fasted on dates and water, did penance, kept silence, and thought of God daily.

When the Bedouins visited him, Father was kind, gay, and helpful. The Moslems respected him for his holiness. During the first World War, some war-like Arabs martyred him. French officers found his body in the sand. The Moslems who knew and loved Father de Foucauld still honor his tomb.

dogs were on the islands at the time they were settled, and it is believed they were left there by ancient sea rovers. The yellow song birds called *canaries* received their name from these islands where they were first found.

Facts *to remember*

1. The chief countries of northern Africa are: Egypt, Sudan, Morocco, Algeria, Tunisia, Libya, Senegal, Mauritania, Mali, and Niger.

2. The Nile River, the longest river in the world, flows northward to the Mediterranean Sea. It irrigates the valley of Egypt.

3. Egypt's 22 million people live close to the Nile. Cotton is the chief crop of Egypt. Others are rice, wheat, corn, sugar cane, tobacco, tropical fruits, and vegetables. Minerals are scarce and manufacturing is limited. Cairo is the largest city in Egypt and in Africa. Alexandria, on the Mediterranean, is Egypt's chief port.

4. The Suez Canal extends 100 miles from the Mediterranean Sea to the Red Sea and shortens the water route between Europe and Asia.

5. Egyptians speak Arabic and are strongly Moslem. Most of the people are poor and cannot read or write. At present they are ruled by a dictator.

6. Sudan lies south of Egypt. Here various tribes of Negroes live by farming. The principal food crop is durra, a corn-like grain. Khartoum is the capital city and largest trading center of Sudan. Port Sudan on the Red Sea is the only seaport.

7. The Atlas lands are Morocco, Algeria, and Tunisia. They border on the Mediterranean Sea. Along the coast, where there is a Mediterranean climate, fruits, olives, and vegetables are raised. Inland are plateaus and mountain areas. Animals graze on the mountain slopes and some farming is carried on in the interior valleys.

8. Casablanca, on the Atlantic coast, is Morocco's chief port. Algiers is the capital and chief port of Algeria.

9. Libya lies between the Atlas lands and Egypt. It is a desert land with few settlers. The Moslem population raises animals for their hides, wool, and skins. Some farming is carried on near the coast and at the oases. Tripoli, on the Mediterranean, is the chief city of Libya.

10. The Sahara desert extends across northern Africa. Travel over this dry expanse of sand and rocks is difficult, and only a few people live in this region. Timbuktu is a city on the southern edge of the Sahara. Dakar, the capital and chief city of Senegal, is the most western port on the continent.

11. The Madeira, Canary, and Cape Verde island groups are off the northwest coast of Africa. Many Spanish and Portuguese settlers live on these islands.

What *have I learned?*

Write the answers in one word on your paper. Do you know the . . .

1. longest river in Africa?
2. largest city in Africa?
3. chief money crop of Egypt?
4. salt city at the southern edge of the Sahara?
5. chief port of Egypt?
6. most useful tree in Sudan?
7. capital of Sudan?
8. mountains in northwest Africa?
9. religion of most Arabs?
10. chief port of Morocco?
11. desert country just west of Egypt?
12. name given to a fertile spot in a desert?
13. capital of Senegal?
14. most useful desert animal?
15. name given to the wandering herders of northern Africa?

Facts *to understand*

Answer each of the following questions in a sentence or two.

1. Why are people able to live in a desert oasis?
2. Why do most of Egypt's people live near the Nile?
3. Why have dams been built at several places along the Nile?
4. Why was the Suez Canal built?
5. Why do Egyptian farmers rotate cotton with other crops?
6. Why are the herders of northern Africa nomads?
7. Why is the location of Dakar on the west coast of Africa important to the Americas?
8. Why does the climate along the coast of North Africa resemble that of southern Europe?

3

Central Africa

Native Village of Central Africa. Here members of a tribe in Kenya sit in the sun outside their huts. The metal shed is used for storing food.

Central Africa means the middle area of the continent. This area, which has been called "darkest Africa" or the "Heart of Africa," has only recently been explored and settled. It is crossed by the equator, and the climate, the vegetation, and the danger of disease make it very difficult for white men to live here. Gradually, however, Europeans and natives have begun to make central Africa a useful, productive region.

The native peoples of central Africa are Negroes. They have suffered many injustices. Often they were captured and sold into slavery by unscrupulous European and American slave traders. Sometimes the members of one tribe would be enslaved by those of another stronger tribe. Happily, there is no trace of this vicious trade in human lives left in central Africa today.

The background of all these peoples remains very primitive, however. Since their language is a spoken language only, very few can read or write. They are not well educated. They have very few of the conveniences and advantages of modern civilization which we take for granted. Some areas of central Africa are rich in minerals and other resources. Many areas, however, have few resources and poor farm land; making a living in these places is very difficult.

France, Britain, and Belgium are three countries of Europe that have had control over most of central Africa. In recent years, however, many African nations have achieved independence. Many Africans have had problems in running their own governments. It takes some time for people to learn the difficult job of self-government. In some cases the European mother country has trained the native people to handle their own business and political affairs. These trained people helped provide good government for everyone.

In this chapter we shall study the peoples and lands of central Africa, beginning with the Republic of the Congo.

The mighty lion is known as "the king of beasts."

The elephant has often been hunted for his ivory.

Giraffes are found in no other place but Africa.

THE REPUBLIC OF THE CONGO

The Congo, as this land was once known, is the leading country of central Africa. In the past, the Belgian government developed much of the resources of the Congo Republic. They found that they made no mistake in sending men to this territory and investing money in it.

Forests and Wild Life. The Albert National Park is a reserve region of 1500 square miles set apart by the Belgian government and named after a Belgian king. Here the animals of Africa's rich wild life live in peace, undisturbed by the rifles of game hunters.

The great mahogany trees of this region shelter herds of baboons. Here the great-eared elephants make the earth tremble when they stamp down the trails to water-holes. The mighty buffalo—the most dangerous of all wild animals—the lion, the leopard, and the huge gorilla all live in these forests.

Along the borders of the Republic of the Congo and nearby areas are the Great Lakes of Africa, and a mighty range of

The lazy hippopotamus enjoys a warm sunbath.

One of Africa's strongest animals is the gorilla.

mountains. The Ruwenzori Range, nearly 17,000 feet high, always has its peaks wrapped in snow, even though it stands almost astride the equator. Nearby, a chain of volcanoes rises thousands of feet high.

The Pygmies. The jungles of the Congo are the home of tribes of dwarfs called Pygmies. These little people are only about three feet tall when fully grown. Ages ago they fled from stronger and fiercer war-like tribes and made their homes deep in the forests. Since then their customs and ways of living have changed little.

The Pygmies make small nest-like shelters for protection during bad weather. The rest of the time they live outdoors.

These people support themselves by hunting and gathering fruits and nuts.

The Pygmies have not adopted civilized ways partly because they have been cut off from the progressive ways of other people. The missioners who are working among them report that the Pygmies are intelligent and eager to learn. Whole tribes of them have become Catholics.

The Bantus. The Bantus are another people who are scattered throughout the central part of South Africa. Although taller than the Pygmies, those from the Republic of the Congo are not very tall. These people may belong to the same branch of the human family as the natives of certain South Sea Islands and Australia.

In the past, the Bantu tribes have driven into the forests smaller and less civilized peoples, including the Pygmies, the Bushmen, and the Hottentots. The Bantus are farmers and makers of dugout canoes, pottery, and cloth. They do not herd cattle.

Africa's Little People. The pygmies are very shy, and this tiny hunter had to be coaxed to have his picture taken standing with a tall stranger.

Riverboat on the Congo. The steamer has docked at a landing to pick up passengers and cargo. The wood, conveniently piled, will be used as fuel.

The Congo River. Through the hot rainy section of central Africa flows the mighty Congo River. The river rises in the Great Lakes of eastern Africa and flows northwest, west, then southwest in a great semi-circle; finally it empties into the Atlantic Ocean. Although the Nile River is longer than the Congo, it does not carry as much water to the sea as the Congo. In fact, of all the rivers in the world, only the Amazon in South America empties more water into the sea than the Congo. The waters of the Congo are colored by the brownish red silt it carries.

The native people use the Congo to go from place to place in long boats made from hollowed-out logs. There are also many steamboats plying the river.

A steamship traveling from the Atlantic up the Congo River might start at Banana, a small port at the river's mouth. Here the river is four or five miles wide, and there are many small islands. Often a hippopotamus may be seen swimming in the water.

Our steamship stops at several ports. One is Boma, about 60 miles up the river.

There many people on their way to Leopoldville will transfer to airplanes for a quicker journey. Another stop is made at Matadi, 95 miles from the ocean. This city is the farthest point reached by ocean ships. Beyond Matadi there are rapids and waterfalls on the river. The ship may unload machinery, cotton goods, gasoline, and canned goods, and then sail back from Matadi with a load of sugar, rubber, ivory, cotton, gold, copper, and other exports.

Matadi has many European residents, beautiful concrete homes, shops, fine hotels, and theaters. At Matadi, travelers bound for the interior board a train for a 250 mile ride around the river falls. Twelve hours later they reach Kinshasa on the Congo River. It is an important modern river port. Across the river from Kinshasa is Brazzaville, the major city and river port for the previous French territory now called Congo Republic.

From Kinshasa smaller ships can travel up the Congo for about a thousand miles before coming to the Stanley Falls and Rapids. At Stanleyville, near the equator, passengers again must change to a train, since another series of rapids and waterfalls begins there.

River boats on the Congo burn wood for fuel and travel only by daylight. The nights are very dark, and it is not safe to travel then because of floating logs, sand banks, and little islands along the way. The river is very wide in some places, and it is hard for the pilot to keep the boat in the main channel. The shore is lined with thick, green forests, where many beautiful birds and wild animals live.

Here and there along the Congo, crews of native boatmen, holding paddles, stand gracefully in canoes which they have made of hollowed-out logs. They shoot the rapids and avoid the rocks with great skill and ease. A drummer always sits in the bow and beats his drum with stirring rhythm. The crew swing their paddles in rhythm with the drum, and the craft glides along like a swift-flying bird.

Farming. The Republic of the Congo, situated on the equator, has a hot, rainy climate. Most of the Congo natives are farmers, who also herd cattle and do some hunting. Native farms are usually small, since the work is done by hand. A heavy hoe is used to dig and cultivate. A long heavy knife, called a *machete,* is used to cut weedy growths and harvest the crops.

It was once the custom for a farmer in the Republic of the Congo to clear a space of forest or grassland and grow crops in it for a few seasons without rotation until the soil lost its fertility. Then the farmer would move on. This was not a good practice, because it left much plowed land unused, causing loss of valuable topsoil.

Some modern practices are just as bad. Today's machines, irrigation, and year-round use of the land grow more food per acre, but they also wear out the soil too rapidly. In the tropics, wherever the land has been plowed it must be covered or shaded by some vegetation. Otherwise the hot sunshine burns up the humus in the soil, and the torrential rains wash away the plant food.

European settlers are finding that they must help the native farmers by teaching them to raise better crops without spoiling the land. Rotating crops, using compost, and some other practices produce better results. The native farmers of the Congo Republic region raise corn, manioc, sweet potatoes, sugar cane, peanuts, tobacco, cotton, coffee, and vegetables.

Forest Products. Many products come from the forests of the Republic of the Congo. These forests have trees which would make good lumber. Few trees are cut however, because of the difficulty in carrying the logs to market.

The palm oil tree, one of the most useful trees of the Congo region, thrives in the poor soil. It grows wild and is also raised on plantations. This tree bears fruit about the size of a large plum with a kernel surrounded by pulp. Oil is taken from the pulp and exported to Europe to be made into soap and other toilet articles. Oil is also obtained from the kernel, and this is used in making salad oil and substitutes for butter in cooking.

Jungle Car Near Kinshasa. A strange sight in the dense African forest is this trolley car, which must be prepared to meet wild animals.

Metal Industry. At a mine in the Katanga Region, Africans and Europeans are engaged in smelting tin. Notice the modern factory and equipment.

Mineral Resources. The Republic of the Congo is rich in minerals. One of the richest mining regions of Africa is the Katanga Region in the southeastern part of the

Tin Mining in the Congo. This open-pit mine and ore-crushing plant produce 10,000 tons a year. The trucks and machinery were made in America.

country. The city of Elizabethville is the center of this region. Large quantities of copper, gold, silver, tin, cobalt, and pitchblende are mined.

This country not only ranks first among the countries of the world in the production of cobalt, fourth in tin, and fifth in copper; but a single pitchblende mine of the Katanga Region produces more than half the world's supply of uranium ore. Most of this mineral is sold to the United States, where it is used to produce atomic energy.

In the southwestern part of the Republic of the Congo are mines that yield the world's largest supply of industrial diamonds. Industrial diamonds are used in machines and tools to cut steel, saw stone, shape bowling balls, polish dental fillings, and make needles for record players. They are the hardest natural material known to man.

Natives in Industry. Although most of the Congo natives are still farmers, many work in the mines of the Katanga area. Thousands of Africans have left their forest homes to work in the mining industry.

The natives are good workers, learning quickly to operate machines, to care for the great furnaces, and to direct parts of the work. Formerly they were not well treated by some employers. However, Belgian government agents and some good Christian employees cooperated with the Church to improve conditions for the African mine laborers. Workers are helped to settle on company farms with their wives and children. Neat brick cottages are furnished for the families. The women are given garden plots to cultivate.

The mining company supplies all the food needed by the families as part of their wages. This food consists of the things the Africans like, including white ants which they fry and eat as a great treat. It is interesting to learn that the natives in various

parts of Africa eat ants, caterpillars, beetles, locusts, water bugs, and other kinds of insects. Not only do they like such food, but they also find it very nourishing.

The workers' children are taught in Catholic schools. They receive three free meals daily and free medical care. Each camp has a church and a priest to care for the natives.

The mines and smelters have safety devices which protect the lives and health of the workers. Formerly many workers, coming from the outdoor jungle life to work in industry, became ill and died. The company heads were then made to pay a large fine for each worker who died. As a result of this policy, the executives soon took steps to protect native life and health. Even at its best, however, work in industry is not very good for the African. He seems better off in his jungle village, cultivating his farm.

Government and Church. The Congo government working with Catholic missioners, had set up many research stations as well as hospitals and clinics to cure people and animals afflicted with the sleeping sickness. The Sisters who do nursing in the mission hospitals give injections which can cure cases of sleeping sickness in the early stages. Native helpers are trained to find these early cases. They take a sample

Sisters in the Congo. These are Sisters of Saint Joseph of Cluny, in Brazzaville. They must wear helmets and white habits because of the hot sun.

of blood and examine it under a microscope. The government pays them a bonus in money for each such case they detect.

The Congo government has built roads throughout the Congo, encouraged merchants to sell to the natives, and provided hospitals, doctors, and medical care. The Church has provided priests and teaching Sisters, and built mission schools throughout the area. The education of the young people will promote progress and stability in the African nations.

Throughout the Republic, many natives have been trained for skilled labor and desk jobs. They work as railway engineers and conductors, as policemen, overseers, factory clerks and foremen, as typists and teachers. Slowly but surely, the Belgians, a Catholic nation, have brought the African natives out of savagery into civilization. They treated the natives as younger brothers who needed education and training. Now, the Africans of the Congo are managing their own political and business affairs. There are many problems and obstacles to overcome, but with time and patience, the Africans should do well.

Nigerian Jungle. Here you can see one of the most important features of the Guinea Coast lands: dark, wet jungles. Natives wash in the river.

LANDS ALONG THE GUINEA COAST

The hot, rainy lands along the west coast of central Africa border on the Atlantic Ocean and the Gulf of Guinea. Among them are the former British colonies of Gambia, Sierra Leone, and Nigeria. All three are now independent nations in the British Commonwealth of Nations. Other new lands were once part of French Equatorial Africa and French West Africa. Togo and Cameroun were once French colonies, and still have close ties to France. The independent countries are Liberia, Ghana and Guinea. The last two have become leaders in a drive toward the formation of a union of free African nations.

The lands along the Guinea coast are heavily forested and infested with mosquitoes and other germ-carrying insects. Diseases like malaria and yellow fever are still common in this part of Africa, although they are not so widespread today as they once were. The people have learned to fight the disease-bearing mosquito by wearing special boots and nets. Since they know that water often carries germs, they boil it before drinking. They wear helmets to prevent sunstroke, and they keep in mind the "three F's"—fingers, flies, and food,—any one of which can carry and spread disease germs.

Jungles and Plantations. In many of the lands along the west coast of central Africa, the thick growth of trees and vines makes travel very difficult for Europeans. Only the African forest-dweller can make his way easily through the jungle.

Although some trees are cut for timber, the lumbering industry is not important. Palm oil trees grow wild, but they are also raised on plantations where the jungle has been cleared by exporting companies.

Another chief plantation crop is cacao, from which cocoa and chocolate are made.

Cacao trees are grown in many villages. They are planted in rows, and begin to bear fruit after five or six years. The cacao beans grow in pods. When the pods are cut, the beans are removed and dried. The dried cacao beans are then carried to the coastal ports, where they are packed and shipped to the countries of Europe, the United States, Canada, and other lands. More cacao is produced in this part of Africa than anywhere else in the world.

Here, as well as in other rainy parts of Africa, rubber trees can be grown on plantations. Another tropical plant, the banana, furnishes a livelihood for thousands of families of planters.

Native Farmers. Most of the natives in the western part of central Africa work on farms. Soil here is more fertile than in the Congo. Land is cleared and used for several years until it begins to lose its fertility. Then the natives move on to a new farm. They have little trouble in moving from place to place, since their homes are made of light wood thatched with palm leaves and grass. Since they spend little time indoors, these people require very little furniture, making it easy to move.

Trees on a piece of land to be farmed for the first time are burned during the dry season, and the land is prepared for planting. The crops are planted on the cleared land at the start of the rainy season. Among the crops are rice, sweet potatoes, beans, peanuts, and vegetables. Women do most of this work and the children help by chasing away the birds and animals who would eat the seeds and the crops. The men herd cattle and hunt wild game.

Nigeria. Among the new countries that border the Gulf of Guinea, Nigeria is the largest in area and population. It stretches inland for a distance of 600 miles. Over 30,000,000 people live there.

Unusual Wedding Ceremony. In Nigeria, a bridegroom is going to join his bride at her parents' home. Members of his family bring the gifts.

The lead mines of Nigeria are very rich in ore. Coal is also mined in the colony. Transportation is better in Nigeria than in other lands along the Guinea coast. Some very good highways and railroads lead to the busy mines.

Nigerian planters produce palm oil, cacao, peanuts, hides, skins, and rubber. These products, along with tin, coal, and lead, are exported through Lagos, the chief port and capital city.

Nigerians in Industry. This young Nigerian woman is being taught how to work a textile machine. More and more Africans are working in industry.

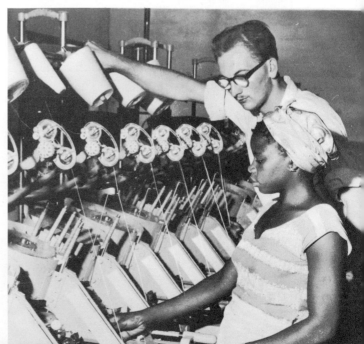

Fishermen of Ghana. Accra, on the Gulf of Guinea, is the center of a lively fishing trade. These men are arranging their nets before a voyage.

Ghana. This country, once known as the Gold Coast, was one of the richest of the British colonies. Ghana gained its independence in 1957. Ghana is still a member of the British Commonwealth of Nations, however, and many of its departments of government are modeled on Britain's. If the government and people use their great natural resources wisely, this new country may show that educated Africans are ready for freedom.

Water Line. In this small town in Ghana, children line up to draw purified water from government tanks. In the tropics, water must be purified.

Ghana is the world's largest producer of cacao. More than one third of the world's supply is now produced there. It is the main money crop of the country. Other crops are rubber, palm nuts, and coffee.

Ghana also possesses great mineral wealth, including bauxite, manganese, gold, and diamonds. The country could become one of the world's largest producers of aluminum if the waters of the Volta River were harnessed to produce hydroelectric power. As you know, a great deal of electric power is necessary in order to produce aluminum from bauxite ore.

On the flat coastal plain stands the city of Accra, the capital and chief port of Ghana. It is a colorful, untidy city with some modern buildings and streets. It is known as the Cacao Capital of the world.

Guinea. The country of Guinea was once a part of French West Africa. Now it has achieved its own independence, and manages its own government and business affairs. The people of Guinea have close ties with the people of Ghana which is nearby. These two nations may soon join in a union with other free African lands.

Liberia. This small republic is located on the west coast of central Africa. The United States has always been interested in Liberia because it was started as a home for freed slaves from our country.

Liberia has been called the "Garden Spot of West Africa" because of its fertile soil and abundant rain. Dense forests provide fine hardwood timber. Coconut trees grow near the coast, and palm oil trees and rubber trees grow in the interior.

Many of the Liberian people are farmers. Some of them work in mining and other industries. American tire companies own large rubber plantations in this country. Recently a mountain of high grade iron ore was discovered near Monrovia, the capital. American businessmen are now building a railroad to develop Liberia's iron and steel industry.

At the time this colony was set up, the Bishop of Philadelphia sent three missioners to care for the Catholic people of Liberia. His action marked the beginning of the great contribution of American Catholics to the foreign missions. At the same time, one of the Church's missionary orders, the Society of the Holy Ghost, was directed by a very great and holy priest, Father Francis Liebermann. A convert son of a Jewish rabbi, he was full of zeal like Saint Paul. His Society did much for the African people in this area.

Health Protection in East Africa. A white Sister and the chief surgeon of a health station talk over the problems of caring for sick natives.

African "Witch Doctor." In spite of the fact that modern methods of medicine are now quite usual, tribal doctors are still consulted by Africans.

ETHIOPIA

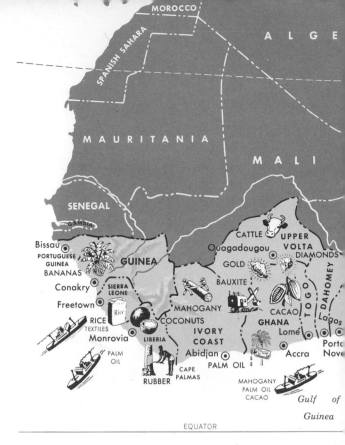

Ethiopia, or Abyssinia as it is sometimes called, is located on high plateaus and mountains. Its location helped keep out invaders until shortly before World War II, when Italy invaded and conquered this country. It was freed during the war by the Allied armies. Today Ethiopia is independent and is governed by an emperor.

The People. This country on the east coast of Central Africa has a very ancient civilization. Deserts and mountains cut Ethiopia off from the rest of the continent, so the people have always had more dealings with Arabs to the northeast than with other African nations. Many of the eighteen million Ethiopians have a mixture of Arabic blood. Many are copper-colored, have long hair, and long thin noses. They are tall and handsome, and wear gracefully draped garments.

Ethiopia has been a Christian land since the Fourth Century, when missioners brought the Faith from Egypt. Today the Church there is separated from Rome, like that of Greece and some other eastern lands. A number of Moslems live in Ethiopia, but the King and other officials are Christians. There are only a few Catholics.

Some of the Bantu people of central Africa live on the edge of the wilderness in Ethiopia. They are mostly pagans. These people belong to the same family of nations as other tribes in the wide strip of central Africa reaching from coast to coast, including those of the Congo and of Uganda. All these people use the Bantu language, with some differences.

CENTRAL AFRICA
⊙ Capital Cities
International Boundaries
Other Boundaries
Scale of Miles
0   200   400   600

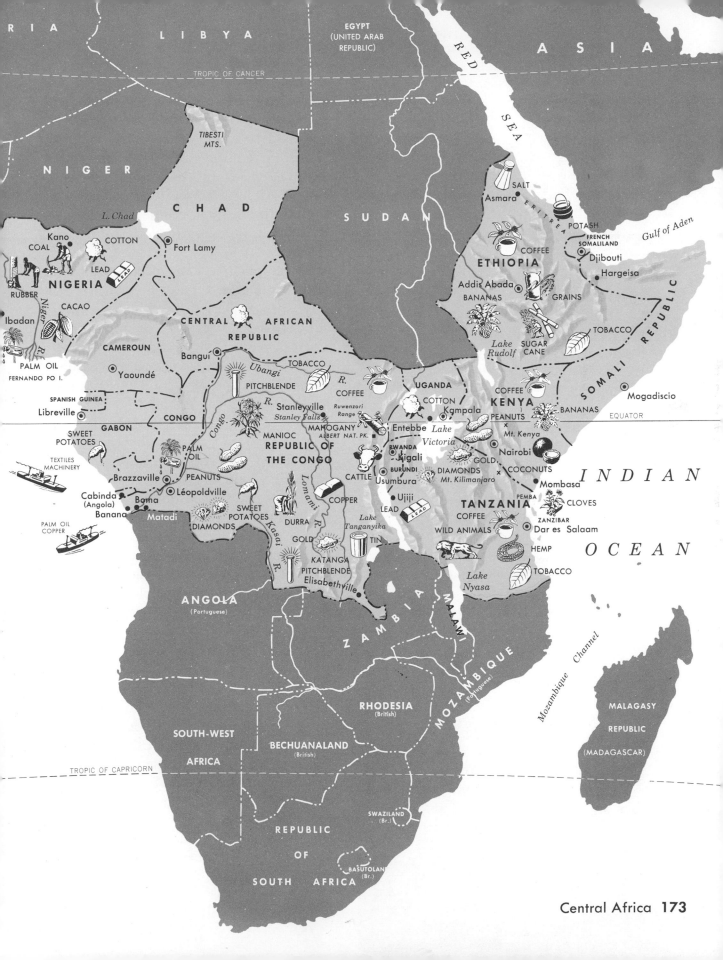

Central Africa **173**

Trade in Ethiopia. A large number of people have gathered together for the exchange and sale of necessary goods—food, cloth, and farm animals.

Hot Land and Cool Land. There are three levels of climate in Ethiopia. Where the land is less than 5000 feet high, the weather is hot. On the plateau land between 5000 and 8000 feet where most Ethiopians live, the climate is mild. Land

Ethiopian Village. Notice the unusual clothes the people wear. Women use parasols for protection against the harmful rays of the noonday sun.

above 8000 feet is rugged and has a cool climate.

The lower ground near the southern border is hot and rainy. Here bananas, sugar cane, and tobacco grow. In this country the first coffee was grown on the slopes of the plateaus. Arabs used it in early times. However, it was only after Brazilians began to raise the famous little red berry that coffee-drinking became a world-wide habit, and the coffee trade became a big business.

On the plateau, cattle feed on the fine grass. At this level the soil is fertile, and crops such as barley, corn, millet, wheat, and tobacco grow well because of the cooler climate.

The high mountainous land is seldom used. The few people who live in this cool area raise sheep and goats.

The Chief City. Addis Ababa is Ethiopia's capital and chief trading center, located in the central part of the country. It is connected with the Red Sea by a railroad. There is air transportation from Addis Ababa to the more settled parts of Ethiopia, as well as to Egypt and Kenya. The other cities of Ethiopia are little more than towns. There are few good highways. Most of the roads are trails suitable only for the mules and ox-carts that carry products from town to town.

Eritrea. This land borders on Ethiopia and extends along the Red Sea for more than 600 miles. Eritrea was an Italian colony for some years before World War II. After the war, its million people decided to join in a federation with Ethiopia.

The low areas along the coast are hot and almost without rain. Malaria and other tropical diseases keep these areas from being well settled. The cooler uplands, however, are settled by farmers and herders. In the coastal regions, mining companies produce and export salt and potash.

EASTERN CENTRAL AFRICA

Uganda, Kenya, and Tanzania lie on or near the coast of the Indian Ocean. All three were once British colonies but are now free and independent countries. Tanzania, which includes the islands of Pemba and Zanzibar, was formerly called Tanganyika.

Together, these three countries include some of the highest mountain peaks and largest lakes in Africa. Lake Victoria, the largest lake, touches all three countries. Mount Kilimanjaro, Africa's highest peak, is in Tanzania.

Along the coast of Kenya and Tanzania, and partly in the interior of Uganda, the climate is hot and rainy, and the lowlands are thickly forested. Most Europeans who still live in these countries make their homes on the plateaus where the climate is milder. African animals such as the giraffe, lion, rhinoceros, and deer are found on the milder uplands.

Kenya. For the last ten years or more, this unfortunate land has been the scene of violence and disorder. Several tribes of natives once banded together into a terror society known as *Mau Mau* and caused many deaths among the British settlers and the less violent natives. However, after the police restored order, peaceful means were applied in the drive for independence, and the people govern themselves today.

New Homes in Kenya. This is Kamiritho Village, a model of neatness and comfort. Not all villages in this part of Africa, however, look like this.

Central Africa **175**

Lake District of Uganda. Central Africa isn't all jungle, as you can see from this photo. Gentle, grassy hills surround lovely lakes and streams.

The native farmers of Kenya raise the same kind of crops as the native farmers of Uganda. From Nairobi, the capital city of Kenya, big game hunters begin their hunting safaris into the jungles and grasslands of central Africa. Mombasa, the chief port, has a good harbor on the Indian Ocean.

Drying Cloves in Zanzibar. It is said that seamen can smell the spicy odor of cloves while they are still miles away from this African Island.

Uganda. Many British settlers still remain in Uganda. They help the elected native government to rule the people, and give advice on farming and industrial methods. Kampala, near Lake Victoria, is the capital. Entebbe is another leading city.

The native Africans of Uganda are fine, intelligent people. Most of them live well on the products of their farms and herds. They grow bananas, coconuts, and tobacco in the lowlands. On the plateaus they grow coffee, cotton, and peanuts, which they call *ground nuts,* and raise cattle and sheep.

Tanzania. This country was taken over as a territory by Great Britain after World War I. Parts of Africa's three Great Lakes, Victoria, Tanganyika, and Nyasa, lie within its borders.

The farm products of Tanzania are similar to those of Uganda and Kenya. In addition, there are valuable mineral resources including gold, lead, tin, tungsten, salt, and even diamonds.

The capital and chief port of Tanzania is Dar es Salaam on the Indian Ocean.

Off the coast of Tanzania lie two small islands that were formerly British colonies. Zanzibar and Pemba achieved their independence at about the same time as the territory of Tanganyika achieved independence. They all united to form the country of Tanzania. The two islands have fertile soil and hot, rainy climates. Much of the world's supply of the spice called cloves comes from Zanzibar and Pemba.

The clove tree is an evergreen which grows thirty to forty feet high. The buds are picked before blossoming. When dried and packed, these buds become the cloves which we buy in grocery stores for flavoring. Entire areas of these islands are sweet with the spicy aroma of the clove trees. Sailors even say they can smell it far out at sea.

Facts to remember

1. The largest country of central Africa is the Republic of the Congo. The Congo River crosses it. It is a land of rain forest and wild animals. The chief means of transportation is by river boats on the Congo, but rapids and falls make travel difficult and dangerous.

2. The Republic has many rich resources. Farm products are corn, manioc, sugar cane, tobacco, cotton, and coffee. Oil from the palm oil tree is exported. The mineral resources of the Katanga region are copper, gold, silver, tin, cobalt, and pitchblende (uranium ore). The city of Elizabethville is the center of the mining region. Industrial diamonds are mined in the southwestern part of this country.

3. A number of smaller countries of Central Africa lie along the Atlantic Ocean and Gulf of Guinea in the west. They are Gambia, Portuguese Guinea, Guinea, Sierra Leone, Liberia, Ivory Coast, Ghana, Togo, Dahomey, Nigeria, Cameroun, Gabon, Spanish Guinea, and Congo. Upper Volta lies inland. Palm oil, cacao, and rubber come from these hot, rainy lands.

4. Nigeria was once a large British colony with over thirty million people. It recently took over its own government. Valuable products of Nigeria are lead, tin, coal, oil from palm trees, peanuts, hides and skins, and rubber. Lagos is the chief port and capital.

5. Liberia is the oldest independent country of Africa. Hardwoods, rubber, palm oil, and iron ore are important products. Monrovia is the capital and chief city.

6. Ghana, an independent member of the British Commonwealth of Nations, produces and exports cacao, rubber, palm nuts, and coffee. Its mineral wealth includes bauxite, manganese, diamonds, and gold. Accra is its capital.

7. Guinea, an independent member of the French family of nations, produces palm-oil, cacao, bananas and rubber.

8. Ethiopia is in east central Africa. Most of its 18 million people live on the cool plateau. Here fine grass grows for the cattle, and fertile soil produces grains and tobacco. Sheep and goats are raised in the colder mountain areas. On the hot moist lowlands crops of bananas, sugar cane, and tobacco grow. Coffee grows on the plateau slopes.

Addis Ababa is the capital and chief city. Eritrea has joined Ethiopia for protection.

9. Uganda, Kenya, and Tanzania are the major lands of east central Africa. Lake Victoria and Mt. Kilimanjaro are found in this region. These countries produce bananas, coconuts, tobacco, and cotton, and raise cattle and sheep. The former Belgian colony of Ruanda-Urundi split into Rwanda and Burundi. Rwanda is now a republic, and Burundi is a monarchy under a native king.

10. Zanzibar and Pemba are islands off the coast of east Africa, part of the country Tanzania. They produce most of the world's cloves.

What have I learned?

Following is a list of brief descriptions of countries studied in this chapter. Copy this list and write after each the name of the country that matches the description.

1. largest producer of cacao
2. richest deposits of minerals
3. island noted for cloves
4. former British colony with large population bordering on the Gulf of Guinea
5. country established for our free slaves
6. former colony of French West Africa, now closely allied with Ghana
7. Lagos, its chief port and capital
8. Nairobi, its capital city
9. a former Italian colony now joined to Ethiopia
10. Mt. Kilimanjaro on its northern border
11. Brazzaville, its capital
12. former British colony bordering Liberia
13. Country made up of former colonies of Tanganyika, Pemba, and Zanzibar
14. Accra, its capital city

Facts to understand

Give reasons for these statements.

1. Although Addis Ababa, the capital of Ethiopia, is near the equator, it does not have a hot climate.
2. The Republic of the Congo is important to the production of atomic energy in the U. S.
3. White men find it difficult to live in many parts of Central Africa.
4. The United States is interested in Liberia.
5. Little lumber is cut in the tropical rain forests of Central Africa.

4

Southern Africa

The story of southern Africa is closely bound up in the lifework of one man. He is Cecil Rhodes, an Englishman who is often called "The Empire Builder."

Rhodes had a grand and daring plan to unite Africa. One feature of his plan was a transcontinental railroad linking Cape Town with Cairo. These two cities are five thousand miles apart, which is twice the distance between New York and San Francisco. The difficulties Rhodes met in central Africa made the railroad impossible at that time, but his work in developing the southern part of Africa produced remarkable results.

Rhodes was largely responsible for the growth and development of southern Africa. This region was hardly known a century ago, but today it is already beginning to make good use of its natural resources and, in some places, even to take part in its own government. Although the people still have many problems to overcome, they are making Rhodes' dreams come true.

Surface and Climate. Much of the southern part of Africa is a high plateau. The southeastern edge has very rugged land. The highest sections form the Drakensberg

Mountain Range. The only lowlands in southern Africa lie along the coast, and they are merely narrow strips of land.

No part of southern Africa is more than thirty-five degrees from the equator. It is about as far to the south of the equator as our state of North Carolina is to the north of it. Therefore, southern Africa does not have very cold winters. The interior plateaus have hot summers and mild winters.

In the region around Cape Town, along the southwestern coast, we find a Mediterranean-type climate. It has hot, dry summers and mild, rainy winters. The interior parts of South Africa have light rainfall. Southeastern Africa has a heavier rainfall.

The coastal areas and the windward sides of the mountains get most of this rainfall.

The Kalahari Desert in the interior of southern Africa is for the most part stony. Most of the region is covered with desert brush or scrub growth. The little rain that does fall comes in short, heavy showers. Many low places fill with water and become lakes after such rains, but this water rapidly disappears after the shower.

The rivers of southern Africa are not of much use, for they become swift torrents in winter when the rain falls, and dry up in summer. Most of them have to tumble over rocky cliffs before reaching the sea, so there is no way to use them for travel.

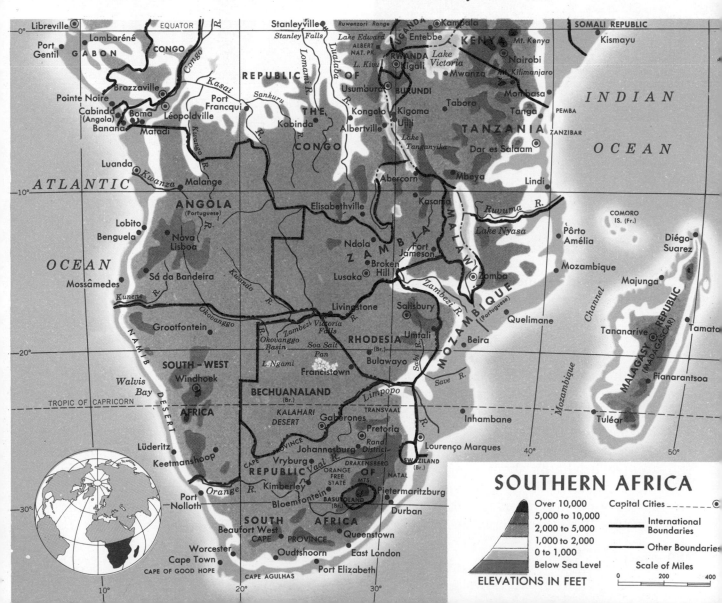

SOUTHERN AFRICA

ELEVATIONS IN FEET

Over 10,000
5,000 to 10,000
2,000 to 5,000
1,000 to 2,000
0 to 1,000
Below Sea Level

Capital Cities
International Boundaries
Other Boundaries

Scale of Miles
0   200   400

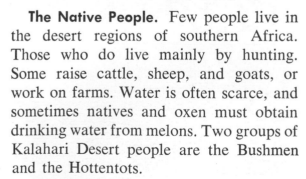

The People of South Africa. (upper l.) Native women proudly display their national dress, with fancy circlets and jewelry. (lower l.) Buying fruit and vegetables at an open-air market in Lourenco Marques. (above) A young girl of the Bushman tribe is drinking water from a strange container made from the shell of an ostrich egg instead of a plain drinking glass.

The Native People. Few people live in the desert regions of southern Africa. Those who do live mainly by hunting. Some raise cattle, sheep, and goats, or work on farms. Water is often scarce, and sometimes natives and oxen must obtain drinking water from melons. Two groups of Kalahari Desert people are the Bushmen and the Hottentots.

The Bushmen are small, achieving an average height of about five feet. They once wandered all over southern Africa, but have now been forced into the desert. Bushmen live in crude huts made of bushes or tree branches. They form groups of about fifty to hunt game food. The Bushmen are rapidly decreasing in number. The Hottentots, who are a little taller, raise livestock for a living.

In many parts of southern Africa, white men from Europe have driven back the natives and have taken possession of much of the land. However, there are still six times as many natives as whites. Perhaps for this reason the white inhabitants of southern Africa feel strongly about the natives. Because they worry about what may happen to them if the native peoples gain control, they allow the natives very little opportunity in government or business.

English and Dutch. Southern Africa was settled first by the Dutch, who bought the land around Cape Town from the Hottentots. The Dutch farmers, who were known as Boers, drove out the Hottentots and the Bushmen. Later the Dutch were themselves driven north by the English. Now there is growing a new race of white men in the region, neither Dutch nor English, but South African, just as we of the United States are American. Today, as a general rule, the South Africans of Dutch descent are farmers, and those of British descent are merchants. The Dutch live in the country, and the British live in villages or cities. The Dutch are now known as the Afrikanders.

Southern Africa is a white man's land. Although the population is made up mostly of Negroes, they are forced to live in small restricted sections called *reserves*. There they may carry on farming, but overpopulation and poor land keep them from making a good living. Those who work in mines and other industries live in city slums segregated from the white people. Their poverty and misery are great. They are not allowed to learn skilled trades nor to prepare for desk jobs. They do only the hard labor on white men's plantations, dangerous work in mines and industry, or servant's work in homes, and all for low wages.

One of the great problems of southern Africa is to bring about just living and working conditions so native and white peoples may live together in peace.

The People of South Africa. (below) Afrikander dress is worn on a holiday which celebrates the Dutch struggles to settle in southern Africa. (upper r.) Historic home built in the original Afrikaans style. (lower r.) Here an Afrikander farmer directs the watering of his grapevines. Many Afrikanders manage large farms.

THE REPUBLIC OF SOUTH AFRICA

Downtown Johannesburg. This is Townhall Square in the business district. The buildings, streets, and cars are similar to those in our country.

The most important country of southern Africa is the Republic of South Africa. It is a self-governing nation, once a member of the British Commonwealth of Nations. It has an area of about one sixth that of the United States and a population of over twelve million people, only two million of whom are white.

The Republic of South Africa is made up of four states or provinces—Cape Province, Orange Free State, Transvaal, and Natal. Each was once a separate British colony. The Republic of South Africa also governs the dry, poorly settled region called South-West Africa.

Farming. Only a small part of the Republic of South Africa is farmland. Over a large part of South Africa crops cannot be grown without irrigation. In many places the soil is poor and the surface is too hilly. The great distance to European markets and the expenses involved in shipping make it difficult for farmers to dispose of large crops at a profit.

Grape growing is a big industry along the southwestern coast because of its Mediterranean climate. Some years ago an insect destroyed most of the vines, which were replaced by grape plants from the eastern part of the United States. Fresh grapes are shipped to the United Kingdom. Some are dried to make raisins. Wines are produced in large quantities. The area also has some irrigated orchards which produce peaches, pears, apricots, and oranges. Tobacco and winter wheat are also raised in some parts of South Africa.

The eastern coastal region with its hot, rainy climate produces tropical crops. Here the farms are like those in southern Asia. The farmers raise sugar cane, cotton, tobacco, bananas, pineapples, and grapefruit. A small amount of tea is grown on the hillsides.

The chief crop of the Republic of South Africa is durra. Over half the cultivated land is used for this crop, which resembles corn, as you have already learned. Durra is raised mostly for home use, but some of the crop grown on farms run by European people is shipped to Great Britain.

Much of the durra crop is grown on the eastern part of the plateau region called the veld. *Veld* is the Dutch word for prairie land. This area resembles our own Corn Belt and has plenty of the showery summer rain which soaks into the level ground and helps the plants to grow well.

A Grazing Land. Large areas of South Africa are too dry or hilly to allow farming. In such areas the people raise sheep, goats, and cattle. Merino sheep were imported from Europe, since the native sheep were of poor quality. Today the sheep produce fine wool and high grade meat. Much wool is exported to Great Britain to supply the textile mills that make fine woolens.

Angora goats from Asia Minor are also raised. Mohair, the fine hair of these goats, is an important export. The goat skins are also exported.

At one time ostriches were brought from northern Africa, and ostrich farms were started. This business depended on the changing styles worn by women and girls in Europe and North America. When hats with feathers were in style, the ostrich business prospered. Today the demand for feathers has decreased, and ostrich-raising is no longer important.

South African Home. This is a native hut, called a *kraal*, in Zululand, State of Natal. Note the brightly colored blossoms on the cactus plant.

Rich Mines. The Republic of South Africa is the richest gold and diamond area of the world. It is also very rich in pitchblende, which is found in some of the gold mines. Other minerals mined are coal, iron, platinum, copper, and manganese.

About one third of the world's gold comes from this country, mainly from the Rand District near Johannesburg in Transvaal. Gold is found mixed with hard rock. Waste rock is removed, and the gold ore is pounded by large machines which crush it into powder. The powder is passed over mercury, which clings to the gold particles. Pure gold is then separated from the mercury. Natives come from various parts of the country to work in the mines.

Many of the world's gem diamonds come from Kimberley and Pretoria, although there are also mines in other areas. Diamonds are found mixed with blue clay in old volcano craters. The clay is loosened by dynamite blasts, then taken to the surface and spread on the ground to dry. Then the clay is broken up, and the diamonds are removed by passing the crushed material over greased boards. Diamonds stick to the boards. In some places diamonds are found mixed with gravel and sand near the surface. The diamonds of the gem variety are shipped to Amsterdam in the Netherlands to be cut and polished.

The country has much coal. Several million tons are mined each year. Some coal is exported through Durban and other ports.

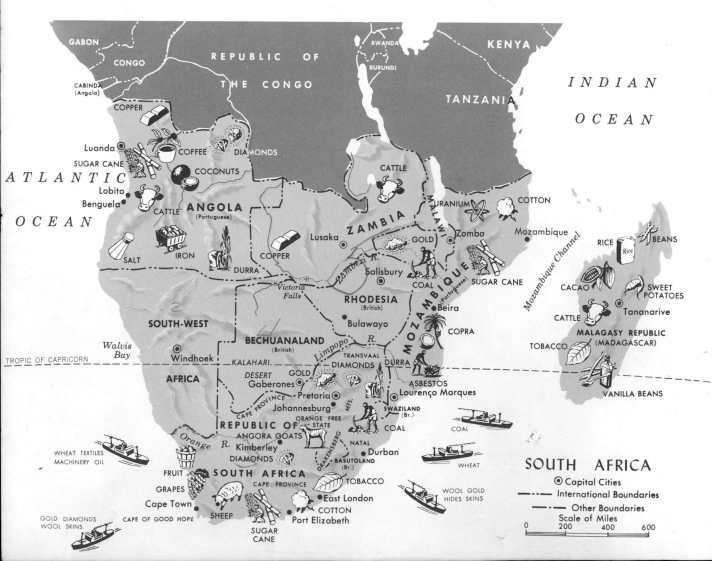

SOUTH AFRICA

⊙ Capital Cities
--·--·-- International Boundaries
—·—·— Other Boundaries
Scale of Miles
0   200   400   600

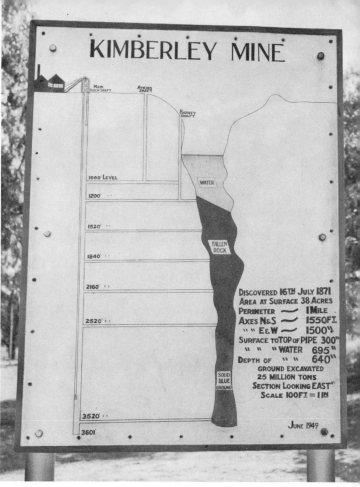

Diamond Mining. The huge open hole (left) contains blue ground, in which diamonds are embedded. Diagram (right) shows a side shaft to the pit.

Transportation. Lack of good inland transportation has been a great handicap to parts of South Africa. Most of the rivers do not have enough water during the dry season, and during the rainy season the many rapids make travel dangerous.

In some places roads follow animal trails and wagon tracks. Travel on the plateau is mainly by carts or wagons drawn by oxen. In the more developed parts of South Africa, highways have been built, and automobiles and trucks are used.

Certain parts of the country have railroads, but there are also large areas without them. The ports of Cape Town, Port Elizabeth, East London, and Durban are connected by railroads to interior cities. The railroads follow valleys in passing from the coastal lowlands to the plateau. Johannesburg is the chief railroad center.

Many steamship lines and airlines connect the Republic of South Africa with other parts of the world.

Street Scene, South Africa. In downtown Durban, in the State of Natal, men work to draw taxis. Durban is fast becoming a popular resort town.

"City of Gold." Johannesburg is the center of the South African gold mining industry. After gold is taken from the ore, piles of residue remain.

Cities. Johannesburg, a gold mining center, is the largest city of southern Africa. In a little over sixty years it has grown from a mining town of small wooden buildings to a modern city with a population of over 1,000,000. Johannesburg is near the coal fields, iron mines, and corn-producing lands. The steel industry and many other manufacturing industries are centered here.

Like Denver, Colorado, Johannesburg

One Capital of South Africa. Laws for the Republic are made here at the city of Cape Town. It is an old city, but still growing rapidly in size.

is a "mile high city." It lies only 26 degrees south of the equator but in July and August light frosts may occur because of the high elevation.

Cape Town, the oldest city, ranks second in population. It is known as the "City of Sunshine," because its summers are dry, and its winter rains are only moderate. A sea wall protects the deep harbor, and many ships refuel at Cape Town.

Gold, diamonds, and other products are shipped from the port of Cape Town which handles most of South Africa's trade with Europe and the Americas. The Republic of South Africa has two capitals. Laws are made in Cape Town, but the governor and government officials live in the inland city of Pretoria, not far from Johannesburg.

Durban is the leading east coast port. It has good rail connections with farming and grazing sections and exports much wool and corn. The port has a deep harbor and many ships take on coal and other cargo there for export. Durban is a resort city, since it has a mild and sunny winter. It has fine hotels, homes, and boulevards.

Two other ports on the eastern coast are Port Elizabeth and East London.

OTHER SOUTHERN LANDS

Victoria Falls, on the Zambezi River. Here, on the Zambezi River between Zambia and Rhodesia, a mighty cascade of water drops over 350 feet.

To the north of the Republic of South Africa are three former British territories, now free countries with different forms of government. Zambia, with its capital at Lusaka, and Malawi, with its capital at Zomba, are completely self-governing. Rhodesia has the largest number of British inhabitants and maintains closer ties between its government and the British Commonwealth. Rhodesia's capital is Salisbury.

The Zambezi River separates Zambia and Rhodesia. On this river is the famous Victoria Falls, which is a 350-foot cascade of water. Some day these falls may be used to produce electric power, and the river may be used for irrigation. Development of the Zambezi River would help bring out the great resources of this part of southern Africa.

Zambia and Malawi are nearer the equator than Rhodesia, and share a hot, dry climate. In each, the population is made up mostly of natives, and farming and cattle raising are the main occupations. Zambia is rich in copper ore.

Rhodesia has a milder climate, because it is farther from the equator and is mostly higher ground. It has a better climate for the Europeans there who engage in farming and mining.

Botswana and Lesotho are two new independent nations. Swaziland is a British protectorate, with some self-government.

MALAGASY REPUBLIC (MADAGASCAR)

Tananarive, Malagasay Republic. Tananarive is the capital and chief city of this republic on the island of Madagascar. French is spoken here.

Southeast of Africa in the Indian Ocean about 240 miles from Mozambique lies the island of Madagascar. Now called the Malagasy Republic, the island is a member of the French community and is the world's fourth largest island. Only Greenland, New Guinea, and Borneo are larger.

The east coast lowland has a hot, rainy climate and tropical forests. The west

MARIANNHILL

Near the city of Durban, in Natal, a state in the Union of South Africa, a group of buildings stands on a tract of fertile farm land. This is the monastery called Mariannhill. Monks from Germany and other European countries live here, and they pray, sing, and labor in the fields nearby. Like the ancient monks, they teach and minister to the people who live near the monastery.

Father Bernard Huss, with other monks of Mariannhill, started an agricultural school to teach the natives better ways of farming. Before long, there were twelve hundred acres of fertile land, a large herd of pure-bred dairy and beef cattle, equipment, farm buildings, and a boarding school. The monks of Mariannhill tried to persuade the natives to leave the city slums, go to country villages, and work as free men farming their own land.

coast lowland has wet and dry seasons. The interior rises to a height of 4000 feet above sea level and has cooler weather and a moderate amount of rainfall.

Many of the people are farmers and herders. The chief crops are rice, corn, beans, sweet potatoes, vanilla beans, cloves, coffee, tobacco, cacao, and sugar cane. The forests yield cabinet woods, tanning fluids, and naval stores. Graphite, mica, and precious stones come from Madagascar's rivers.

The people are dark-skinned, and probably belong to the same race as some of the Indonesians. Most of them are pagans. Portuguese and French missioners have worked here for hundreds of years, and there are now a number of fine native Catholic families. The Christian Brothers and other orders run schools where the children learn Christian living.

White employers, however, did not like to see their workers move away.

Next, the monks started Catholic Action groups among the natives so that they would be able to help each other more easily. Father Huss traveled through the countryside, teaching Christ's message to the natives. Agricultural schools were started in other parts of Africa, and soon the monks opened a monastery for native African priests and Brothers. The monastery building they erected completely by hand. It is a thriving monastery today, with native monks supporting themselves completely.

A great modern movement is under way to bring Christianity and Western culture to Africa. The wisdom and zeal of such efforts are examples of the contribution of the Church to the progress of Africa.

PORTUGUESE LANDS

Angola is sometimes called Portuguese West Africa. Its four million people, many of whom are Bantus, live in an area almost twice the size of our State of Texas. There is a narrow coastal lowland in the south where the climate is hot and dry, and irrigation is necessary for farming. The northern coastal lowland receives heavy rainfall. The interior is a high plateau, where the climate is cooler with more moisture.

The main crops of Angola are sugar cane, coffee, corn, bananas, and other fruits. The trees yield palm oil and coconuts. There are deposits of copper, iron, and salt, and diamonds are mined. Fishing is carried on off the coast, and dried fish are exported. Luanda, the capital, and Lobito are the chief ports. They have railroad connections with the interior.

Mozambique is also known as Portuguese East Africa. It has a population of six million, largely Bantus. Because the climate is not suited for Europeans, the white population is small.

Lourenco Marques, Mozambique. The chief port and capital of this Portuguese land on the Indian Ocean is also a business and industrial center.

The northern and southern parts of Mozambique are separated by the Zambezi River, which flows through the center of this country. The country is not well developed. In fact, large areas have not yet been carefully explored.

Much of Mozambique is a lowland with a hot climate. It has heavy rainfall. Thick forests are found near the streams, and tall grasses grow in most other parts.

In the hot, moist coastal lands, there are plantations where sugar, cotton, and coconuts are raised. Mozambique has some deposits of coal, uranium, tin, gold, silver, and asbestos that have been only partly developed. Mozambique has two important ports, the capital, Lourenco Marques, and Beira, a seaport.

Facts *to remember*

1. The most important country in southern Africa is the Republic of South Africa, a self-governing nation. It was once a member of the British Commonwealth of Nations. Of its twelve million people, two million are white.

2. Along the southwestern coast farming is important. The climate here is Mediterranean. Citrus fruits, tobacco, grapes, and wheat are among the chief crops. Irrigated orchards produce peaches, pears, apricots, and oranges.

3. Durra, a corn-like grain, is grown on the plateau region of South Africa called the *veld,* or prairie land. It is the principal food of the natives.

4. Sheep, goats, and cattle are raised on the hilly lands of South Africa. Much wool is exported. Mohair and goat skins are other important exports.

5. About one third of the world's gold comes from South Africa in the district near Johannesburg. Many of the world's gem diamonds come from the mines near Kimberley. Coal is exported through the port of Durban. Iron, platinum, copper, and manganese are also mined in South Africa.

6. Southern Africa's inland transportation is poor. There are only a few good roads. Railroads connect only the large cities.

7. Cape Town is the oldest city of South Africa. It handles most of the region's export trade with Europe and the Americas. South Africa has two capitals. One of them is Cape Town, where the laws are made, but most of the government officials live in the other capital, Pretoria.

8. Rhodesia, Zambia, and Malawi make up a large area of southern Africa. In these former British territories, farming and mining are the chief occupations. Victoria Falls is located on the Zambezi River, between Rhodesia and Zambia.

9. Madagascar, a large island off the southeast coast of Africa, is a French territory. Many of the people are farmers and herders. Chief crops are rice, corn, beans, cloves, tobacco, and cacao. Forest products are cabinet woods and naval stores.

10. Angola and Mozambique are Portuguese territories. Most of the people are Bantus. Most of Angola is plateau land. The main crops are sugar cane, coffee, corn, bananas, and tree crops. Mozambique is a hot, moist land where sugar cane, cotton, and coconuts are raised. Both countries have deposits of coal, tin, gold, and pitchblende, but will need help in developing these resources.

What *have I learned?*

I

Answer each of the following in a complete sentence.

1. Name the most important country of Southern Africa.

2. What name is given to the Dutch who live in South Africa?

3. What part of South Africa has a Mediterranean-type climate?

4. Who planned a Cape Town-to-Cairo railroad?

5. What is the Dutch word for prairie land?

6. What do the natives of South Africa call corn?

7. Name a Portuguese colony in southwest Africa with mostly a Bantu population.

8. What Portuguese colony borders on the Indian Ocean?

9. What is the chief export at Durban in South Africa?

10. Near what city are the gold mines of South Africa?

11. Name the two capitals of the Republic of South Africa.

12. What river separates Zambia to the north from Rhodesia to the south?

13. Name the capital city of Rhodesia.

14. What is the chief industry on the island of Madagascar?

15. For what may Victoria Falls be used?

II

Choose the correct word or name in parentheses to complete each statement.

1. South Africa was first settled by the (English, Dutch, French).

2. The largest city of the Republic of South Africa is (Cape Town, Johannesburg, Pretoria).

3. The Republic of South Africa leads the world in the mining of (gold, iron, coal).

4. The chief crop of South Africa is (fruit, wheat, durra).

5. Victoria Falls is located on the (Congo, Zambezi, Nile), River.

Facts *to understand*

Give a reason in a complete sentence for each of the following statements.

1. No part of South Africa has a cold climate.

2. The Cape Town-to-Cairo railroad was never completed.

3. Many people raise sheep, goats, and cattle instead of farming.

4. The rivers of southern Africa cannot be used for travel.

5. There is discontent among the native peoples of the Republic of South Africa.

Unit Four Review

Questions for Discussion and Review

1. How does Africa compare in size and population with the other continents? 2. Why was most of this continent left unexplored for so many centuries? 3. Why is the climate of much of Africa hot? 4. Why is the Nile River called Egypt's Blessing? 5. Compare the coast line of Africa with that of Europe. 6. Why is Egypt more important than other African countries bordering the Mediterranean? 7. Why is Egyptian cotton highly prized in world markets? 8. Why are the rivers of southern Africa of less value than those of the rest of Africa? 9. What mineral resources bring wealth to the Republic of South Africa? 10. Name an African country famous for each of the following products: coffee, cotton, cocoa, cloves. 11. Why is the vegetation so dense near the equa-

tor? 12. What makes the Congo more valuable than Angola? 13. Which countries in Europe still have African territories to govern? 14. Why should other peoples help the native peoples of Africa?

Getting Information from Globes and Maps

1. List the countries a Cape Town-to-Cairo railroad would cross.

2. Give the latitude and longitude of the city of Accra.

3. Through what countries does the Niger River flow?

4. Name the African countries crossed by the equator.

5. What African countries border on the Red Sea?

6. Use the scale of miles to determine how far Africa extends along the equator.

7. Name and locate two mountain ranges in Africa.

8. Name the water bodies that surround Africa.

9. How many cities in Africa have over a million population? over one half million? (Use the Appendix, if necessary.)

10. Arrange a list of the five largest countries in Africa according to area; according to population.

Using Geography Words

Write a sentence using each of the following to show that you understand its geographic meaning:

isthmus	Koran	oasis
veld	Pygmy	Tropic of Capricorn
Bedouins	baobab	cacao
savanna	pitchblende	Bantu
pyramid	machete	shadoof
tsetse	manioc	trusteeship

Using Your Encyclopedia

Refer to Compton's or another encyclopedia to make special reports on one of the following topics.

1. Stanley and Livingston

2. Building the Pyramids

3. Ancient Life in Egypt

4. Work of Missionary Orders in Africa

5. Victoria Falls

6. Kruger National Park

7. Diamond Mining and Cutting

8. Sahara Desert

9. Mining Pitchblende

Name That River

Number your paper from 1 to 15. After each number, tell which river is described.
1. It flows into the Indian Ocean.
2. It is the second largest river in Africa.
3. It crosses the equator twice.
4. Its course was explored by Stanley.
5. It is used to irrigate much land.
6. It empties into the Gulf of Guinea.
7. It flows chiefly through the rain forests.
8. It flows north to the sea.
9. Victoria Falls belongs to it.
10. It has a densely populated delta.
11. It rises near Sierra Leone.
12. It flows through Mozambique.
13. It rises in the lake region and flows north.
14. Leopoldville is on its bank.
15. Livingstone is on its bank.

Final Test

Choose from the parentheses the correct word or words to complete each sentence. Write the complete sentence correctly on your answer paper.

1. Most of Africa's desert land is in the (northern, central, southern) part. 2. An African country with an old civilization is (Liberia, Egypt, Belgian Congo). 3. The chief export of Ethiopia is (coffee, cotton, coal). 4. The (northern, central, southern) part of Africa receives the most rain. 5. The largest island of Africa is (Zanzibar, Madagascar, Angola). 6. The African country that mines a large amount of pitchblende is (Congo Republic, Rhodesia, Egypt). 7. The climate of (northern, central, southern) Africa is most difficult for white inhabitants to endure. 8. The Congo Republic is noted chiefly for (agricultural, mineral, manufactured) products. 9. (Ghana, Libya, Liberia) was never a European colony. 10. Addis Ababa is the capital of (Ethiopia, Angola, Togoland). 11. Mozambique is a (French, Spanish, Portuguese) territory. 12. Ghana's capital city is (Monrovia, Lagos, Accra). 13. The (northern, central, southern) part of Africa is the home of the Bedouins. 14. From north to south, Africa measures about (5000, 3500, 7000) miles. 15. The chief crop of the Nile delta is (sugar cane, cotton, rice). 16. The narrow belt of plains and hills along the northern coast of Africa is called the (Said, Atlas, Tell). 17. A mineral obtained in the Atlas Mountains is (coal, bauxite, phosphate). 18. The Republic of South Africa leads the world-production of (coffee, rubber, diamonds). 19. The coastal region of northern Africa has (an oceanic, a continental, a Mediterranean) type of climate. 20. Explorers from (France, England, Portugal) first sailed around Africa to India. 21. Large rubber plantations are found in (Egypt, Liberia, Ethiopia). 22. The former French possession off South Africa is (Zanzibar, Eritrea, Madagascar). 23. The surface of Africa is largely in (plains, plateaus, mountains). 24. A plant that grows well on a desert oasis is (sugar cane, date palm, cacao). 25. The world's largest producer of cacao is (Ghana, Liberia, Nigeria).

Applying Christian Principles

Choose the correct ending for each of the incomplete sentences below. Then copy the sentences on your answer paper.

1. The best way for the white race to help the African natives is by a. employing them as laborers, b. sharing knowledge with them, c. buying their products.
2. Europeans mistreat the Africans most when they a. do not recognize them as brothers, b. enrich themselves at the expense of the Africans, c. force the natives to work for them.
3. Christian living in Africa is practiced best when a. surplus goods are exported to other countries, b. natives, Europeans, and missionaries pray, sing, and work together, c. all business is done through co-operatives.
4. Christian living in Africa is ignored most when a. the natives are forced to live separated from the whites, b. native workers are underpaid, c. poverty exists in slum areas.
5. The Congo Government helps the natives most by a. providing hospitals and clinics, b. building roads, c. assisting missionaries to educate the people.
6. Conditions in Africa will improve most when a. Europeans free their colonial territories, b. transportation to the interior improves, c. all unite to raise the standard of living for the Africans.
7. We can help the Africans most by a. learning more about their lives, b. praying for the missionaries there, c. seeing African movies.

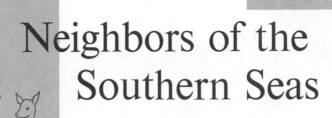

Neighbors of the Southern Seas

AUSTRALIA   NEW ZEALAND
SOUTH PACIFIC ISLANDS
ANTARCTICA

In this Unit
you will learn that:

1 Australia is an island continent in the Southern Hemisphere about the size of the United States.

2 Australia's best land is on the eastern side of the continent far from the trade routes of the world. Deserts cover much of the interior. There are only two rivers of importance, and they dry up at certain seasons of the year.

3 More than half of Australia's nine and one half million people live in a few large cities along the eastern coast.

4 Australia's seasons are the reverse of ours with summer starting in December and winter in June.

5 Animals and plant life in Australia are different from those found anywhere else in the world.

6 There are sixteen times as many sheep as there are people in Australia. One fourth of the world's wool comes from this continent.

7 New Zealand is made up of two main islands lying southeast of Australia. The islands are mountainous. They have snowy peaks, great glaciers, dense forests, and blue mountain lakes.

8 New Zealand has a cool, moist climate, well-suited to farming. Most of New Zealand's two million people earn their living by raising sheep and cattle.

9 Many of the people of the South Pacific Islands make a comfortable living from the great ocean that surrounds them. They are fishermen and sailors.

Australia is the only continent in the world that is also a single country. It is a lonely continent, separated from all the others by miles of ocean waters. The journey to Australia by ship, or even by plane, is always quite long; it is almost two days by plane from our country or Europe. Nevertheless, Australia is a very up-to-date, modern land. Its people are very much like Americans in their customs and way of life.

Southeast of Australia, over 1200 miles away, lies a group of islands called New Zealand. This island country is closely related to Australia. The people, the government, and the geography of these two countries are very similar. East of New Zealand, stretching for thousands of miles into the vast areas of the South Pacific Ocean, are many more islands. These islands are both large and small, populated and deserted, modern and primitive. They form a kind of island world of their own.

At the most southern part of the world we will find the strange and almost unknown continent called Antarctica. Beneath Antarctica's icy, rocky surface, it is believed that great mineral riches are stored, waiting for men to overcome the freezing climate in order to obtain them.

NEW GUINEA

Great Dividing Range

Indian Ocean

ANTARCTICA

AUSTRALIA

Notice the wide expanse of ocean water which separates Australia and New Zealand from each other and from most of the world.

Far to the south lies the ice-bound land of Antarctica. To the east are some of the tiny islands which dot the far reaches of the South Pacific Ocean. Asia lies just to the north, but several days' travel separates Australia from Europe or America.

Pacific Ocean

NEW ZEALAND

Farther south, the Pacific Ocean and the Tasman Sea separate Australia from New Zealand's two main islands by 1200 miles. The Indian Ocean lies to the west.

The wide brownish area in the interior of Australia shows the extent of desert land. The mountains of the Great Dividing Range in the east and the smaller ranges in the north cut off the moisture-bearing winds before they can reach Australia's dry interior.

The Murray-Darling river system irrigates the southern part of Australia, and empties into the Indian Ocean. In the summer, however, it often dries up to a mere trickle. The northern part of Australia has a hot climate, very similar to that of New Guinea. Here the rainfall is quite heavy, and the vegetation is almost tropical.

New Zealand and Tasmania enjoy more rainfall and better farming conditions than most of Australia. Although there are many mountains in New Zealand, no part of it lies far from the sea. It enjoys a mild climate.

This lonely continent is called "the land down under" because it lies completely in the Southern Hemisphere. The equator passes just north of the large island of New Guinea, which is separated from Australia by the Timor Sea and the Arafura Sea.

Along the northeastern shore can be seen the Great Barrier Reef. Beyond this is the Coral Sea, scene of a famous naval battle in World War II.

Australia

Melbourne, One of Australia's Chief Cities. This view of Melbourne demonstrates the beauty and design which its founders planned to achieve.

It took a long, long time to discover Australia. Spanish, Portuguese, and Dutch sailors were the first Europeans to see it, but they did not like its sandy deserts and tropical swamps. No European country claimed Australia until Captain James Cook, an English explorer, visited it in 1770. That was just a few years before our Revolutionary War began.

Cook gave Australia its name and told the people in England about it. At first they were not interested because it was so far away. Then someone thought it might be a good place to banish the prisoners who were crowding British jails.

Australia grew very slowly from this beginning. Many of the prisoners sent to Australia were not real criminals at all. They had committed only small offenses, or were too poor to pay their debts. As soon as they gained freedom in Australia, they settled down to build the land. Other people came from the British Isles as colonists, looking for new land and the opportunity to work. Some brought sheep with them and started ranches. Others built cities. Among them were British, Irish, and Scots, but English was their common language. They called themselves Australians, just as the colonists in the early days of our history called themselves Americans.

South of the Equator. At first the British called the continent *Terra Australis* meaning "Southland." Later they shortened the name to Australia. On your globe you will find that it is in the Southern Hemisphere between the Indian and Pacific oceans. In size it is almost the same as the United States without Alaska, but in population it numbers 9½ million people, which is only about a million more than the City of New York.

Nearly half of Australia lies in the Tropical Zone. The Tropic of Capricorn passes north of the widest part of the continent.

A Small Continent. Australia is the smallest of the seven continents. It is thinly populated with fewer people than any continent except Antarctica. Large parts of Australia have no people at all. Most Australians live in the eastern part and along the southeastern and southwestern coasts where the weather is mild and the rainfall moderate.

Australia is the only continent covered entirely by one country. This self-governing, democratic nation is a member of the British Commonwealth of Nations. The country is divided into six states and two territories. The states are New South Wales, Victoria, Queensland, South Australia, Western Australia, and the island state of Tasmania, which is separated from the mainland by the Bass Strait. The two territories are the Northern Territory and the small Australian Capital Territory set aside for the capital city, Canberra.

Surface and Climate. Most of Australia is a dry, hilly plateau country. The Eastern Highlands are low mountains somewhat like the Appalachians of the United States. The main range of the Eastern Highlands is known as the Great Dividing Range. This is a good name because it divides the small rivers that flow east into the Pacific from those that flow west. The eastern slopes are steep, but the western slopes descend gradually to the lowlands and plains of the dry interior. These lowlands extend from the Gulf of Carpentaria on the north southward to the Indian Ocean.

Since the continent is in the Southern Hemisphere, Australians must travel north to find their hottest weather and south to find their coolest.

The far northern part of the continent lies in the tropics and therefore has a hot, moist climate along the coast and a short distance inland. Much of the rest of the

continent is on the leeward side of the Eastern Highlands. The winds from the Pacific lose most of their moisture on the windward side of these mountains leaving the interior extremely dry. More than one third of the continent receives so little rain that it is a desert. A still larger area has only enough rain for grass or small bushes. Farmers and ranchers are continually hoping and praying for rain; the weather is a constant topic of conversation.

The coastal regions of southern and southwestern Australia receive the most rain in winter. This gives them a Mediterranean type of climate. The coast of southeastern Australia has a climate like that of the windward side of the state of Florida. The island of Tasmania always has plenty of rain, except in the interior valleys.

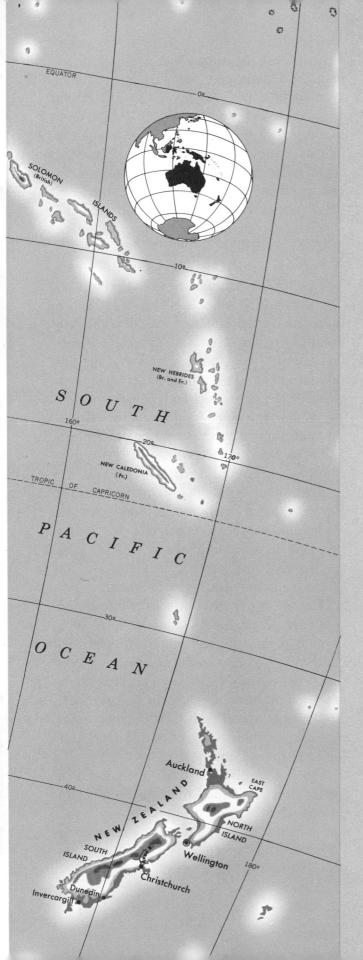

Studying the Map

A. 1. Australia is the only continent that is a single country. Use the scale of miles to find the distances across the continent from east to west. How does this compare with the distance across the United States? **2.** Find where the Tropic of Capricorn crosses Australia. What part of Australia is in the Tropical Zone? What part of the continent is in the South Intermediate Zone? **3.** Which ocean lies to the east of Australia? Which ocean lies to the south and west of the continent? **4.** What important island group lies north of Australia? **5.** Name the large island that lies north of Australia. To whom does it belong? **6.** Use the map key to find whether Australia is largely highlands or lowlands. What mountain range is located in the eastern part of the continent? How does the height of this mountain range compare with the Alps? the Himalayas? the Rockies? the Andes? **7.** The continent of Australia has only a few rivers. The longest river system drains the southeastern part of the continent. Name this river system. Into what ocean does it flow? **8.** Where is the Great Barrier Reef located? How was it formed? Explain why there are no important ports in this part of Australia.

B. 1. Most of Australia's people live in the cities. What part of Australia has the greatest number of cities? Why do so few people live in the interior of the continent? **2.** Name six important Australian cities. For each give the Australian state in which it is located. **3.** Which city serves as the Australian capital? **4.** What island part of Australia lies just off the southeastern coast? What strait separates the island from the continent? Name an important city located on the island's southern coast.

C. 1. New Zealand is not part of Australia but a separate island country that lies southeast of the continent. Use the scale of miles to find approximately how far New Zealand is from the Australian coast. **2.** In which zone does New Zealand lie? **3.** What are the two largest islands of New Zealand called? **4.** How does the surface of New Zealand compare with that of Australia? Where are New Zealand's lowland areas located? **5.** Name three important cities of New Zealand. Which one serves as its capital?

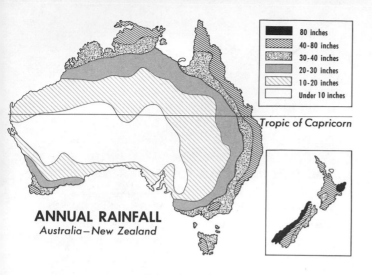

ANNUAL RAINFALL
Australia – New Zealand

Legend:
- 80 inches
- 40-80 inches
- 30-40 inches
- 20-30 inches
- 10-20 inches
- Under 10 inches

Tropic of Capricorn

Water Is Scarce. During some years very little rain falls in Australia, and the sheep and cattle have a hard time getting enough grass to eat or water to drink. Thousands of cattle and sheep have died in the past for lack of water. Today, when dry weather comes, the rancher tries to sell most of his animals before they die of starvation or thirst.

Water for the animals is collected and stored in ponds which are dug for this purpose. Rain water is caught in tanks placed a few feet above the ground. Streams are dammed to hold back the water, and deep artesian wells are dug.

This lack of rainfall causes a serious problem for humans, too. This is one reason why large areas are underpopulated.

Rivers and Irrigation. It is believed that twenty million people could make a living in Australia, if there were a system of irrigation and conservation such as our Tennessee Valley Authority. A look at the map will show you why such a project is unlikely, even in the future. Australia has only one important river system—the Murray River with its main tributary, the Darling. This provides water for irrigation only to the farm lands nearby. Artesian wells provide some water for irrigation in other parts of Australia.

Australian Farmers. The lack of water explains why only a small part of the land is used for farming. Wheat is the Australian farmer's most important crop. More than two thirds of the cultivated land is planted in this grain. It is grown on the plains, some miles inland from the southeastern and southwestern coasts. There the soil, temperature, and rainfall are favorable, for wheat does not require much moisture in order to flourish.

Farmers use modern machinery in harvesting and threshing the wheat. They do not store much wheat in elevators, as we do in the United States. Sacks of wheat are usually loaded into high-wheeled ox-wagons or trucks, and carried to a market or railroad train. Railroads carry wheat to some of the coastal cities. More wheat is raised than is needed by the Australian people, and the surplus is exported to Britain and other countries of Western Europe that cannot raise enough for themselves.

Australians grow many kinds of fruit. Farmers raise such large quantities of apples and pears in Tasmania that it has been called the "Orchard State." Apples are barreled and shipped to Great Britain where fresh fruit is in great demand.

The coastal regions of southwestern and southern Australia have about the same climate as the coastal lowlands of southern California. There the farmers raise Mediterranean-type crops. Many excellent fruits are dried in the sun during the hot weather. Fresh fruits, dried fruit, jams, jellies, marmalades, and wines are exported from this region to many countries.

The hot, moist coast of Queensland in northeastern Australia has some large plantations where such tropical crops as bananas, pineapples, rubber, and sugar cane are produced and exported. The climate here is not favorable to farming other crops.

The Rabbit Pest. There were no rabbits in Australia until English settlers brought them. For years rabbits were protected, and a man was even fined in court for shooting one. Today the people spend huge sums to get rid of them.

It is said that ten rabbits will eat as much grass as one sheep. To conserve the grass, ranchers drive rabbits from their land, and destroy them with traps and guns. They have built thousands of miles of rabbit-proof wire fences. Some people make their living by catching these animals. Millions of frozen rabbits are shipped to the United Kingdom every year, and many skins are exported. The fur is used to make cloth or felt hats.

Foxes and dingoes that kill the sheep are also hunted and shot. The dingoes attack without yelping, which gives the sheep no warning. When the sheep are plentiful, the dingoes prefer to eat only the tongues of their victims.

Raising Cattle. Although there are seven or eight times more sheep than cattle in Australia, cattle raising is also a great industry. There are many large cattle ranches in the drier regions, where herds of cattle roam over the land in search of grass. One cattle station, the world's largest, is nearly as large as the state of New Jersey.

The big event of the year is the roundup, or *muster,* as it is called in this part of the world. It is then that the cattle are gathered, branded, and counted. Driving cattle to market is not an easy job, if the ranch is far from the railroad.

The cattle are watered from wells which are dug along the travel routes and from tanks which hold rain water. The animals graze as they move slowly along. It takes ranchers from several days to several weeks to drive cattle to market. In recent years some of the long drives have been eliminated by building slaughter houses and chilling plants in the cattle country. The chilled beef is then shipped out by airplane.

Cattle Ranch, Australian Style. There is not much difference between this picture of cattle at a watering trough and one of an American ranch.

The Animals of Australia. (above) The koala bear. (right, above) The kookaburra bird. (right, below) The emu, a bird which runs swiftly along the ground. (far right, above) The kangaroo. (far right, below) A very rare mammal, the platypus.

Strange Animals, Fish, and Birds. Scientists think that Australia has been separated from the rest of the land on our planet for a very long time. They believe that many animals and plants found today in Australia once existed in other parts of the world. On this "lonely continent," set far apart in the southern part of the Pacific Ocean, these plants and animals did not die out. They are much the same today as they were ages ago.

The platypus has a duck-like bill, webbed feet, fur, and a beaver-like tail. It growls like a puppy, and lays eggs. The spiny anteater digs for ants with its long beak and longer tongue. The kangaroo jumps twenty feet, runs forty miles an hour, and carries its young in pouches. The Australians call them "roos " The koala looks like a toy teddy bear and lives in trees.

Australia has many strange lizards, tortoises, snakes, and fish. The lungfish can live out of water for a long time because it breathes air. There are also many strange kinds of birds, large and small, brightly colored and very beautiful. One of them is the emu, which cannot fly but runs swiftly over the plains. The kookaburra has a big bill and makes sounds like a person laughing wildly. The beautiful lyre-bird can mimic almost any sound it hears, even an automobile horn.

Strange Plants. Australia has strange trees as well as strange animals. The study of these strange plants interested the early explorers, and for this reason the bay

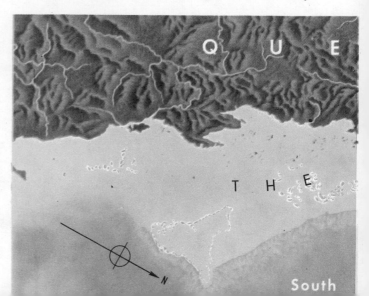

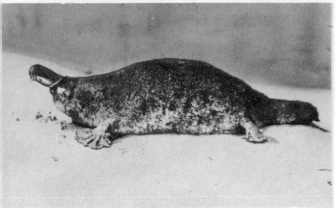

chemical used in tanning leather, is obtained from the eucalyptus bark. Oil and gum used in medicines are taken from the leaves, so some types of eucalyptus are known as gum trees. Eucalyptus leaves turn to the sun, so they cast little shade.

The bottle tree is another unusual Australian tree. It has a bottle-shaped trunk and its pulp is full of water, which thirsty travelers sometimes draw out and drink.

Ferns are also common in Australia. Some grow as tall as trees.

The Great Barrier Reef. The Great Barrier Reef, another of Australia's natural wonders, stretches for more than 1200 miles along the northeastern coast. This reef has been built up during the ages from the skeletons of tiny sea animals. The masses of coral rock, formed by millions of these skeletons, are in different shapes. Some look like sponges and some resemble many small pipes packed close together. Other coral rocks look like deer horns or small plants. One kind of coral is called "brain coral" because it looks so like a human brain.

Navigators of ships along the northeastern coast of Australia must be very careful or they would run aground on the coral reefs hidden below the water surface. These sharp reefs can punch holes even through thick steel hulls.

south of Sydney was called Botany Bay. The word *botany* means the study of plant life.

A common Australian tree is the eucalyptus, of which there are hundreds of varieties. Some are very small, but others grow 300 feet high. The eucalyptus is an evergreen which sheds its bark but not its leaves.

Some eucalyptus trees make fine, hard lumber, which is used for railroad ties and posts. The lumber is also used to build docks and piles in the harbors. Tannin, a

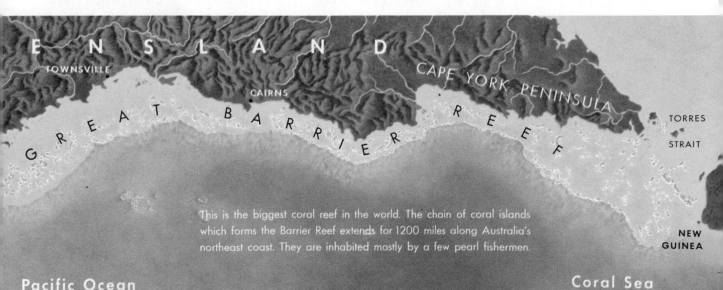

This is the biggest coral reef in the world. The chain of coral islands which forms the Barrier Reef extends for 1200 miles along Australia's northeast coast. They are inhabited mostly by a few pearl fishermen.

Pacific Ocean

Coral Sea

Australia's Great Sheep Industry. (above) Sheep are herded by ranchers on horseback. (right) A ram's fleece is displayed. Note its depth and thickness, qualities which go to make excellent material when woven. (far r., above) A team of sheep shearers at work. These skilled workers travel from station to station on their job. A sheep is almost hidden by the huge pile of wool which is sheared from it. (far r., below) Sheep ranchers proudly display their prize sheep at a fair. The first two have been awarded blue ribbons.

Sheep Ranches. Australia is one of the great sheep-raising countries of the world. There are 16 times more sheep than people. Much Australian land is better suited for grazing sheep than for raising farm crops. Large areas have enough rain for scattered patches of grass and dry scrub, but not enough for crops.

The winters are mild, and sheep can find forage to graze on all year. Sheep ranches or *sheep stations,* as they are called by Australians, are often very large. When rainfall is light, it takes many acres to grow enough feed for one sheep. The greatest number of sheep are raised in the states of Victoria, New South Wales, and Queensland, all in the eastern part of the country.

Merino sheep are raised in Australia. These sheep produce a very good grade of wool. The fiber is long, fine, and strong and is used in the manufacture of high grade cloth. The quality of mutton from these sheep is poor, however. Other breeds of sheep which yield good mutton are also raised, but their wool is not so high in quality as merino wool. Some mutton is exported, but wool is the leading export. Australia produces over one fourth of the world's supply of wool.

Sheep require much attention. Some of the workers, called *boundary riders,* help keep the fences in good condition. Secure fences are very necessary to keep out rabbits, foxes, and wild dogs called *dingoes.*

goorlie and other desert mining towns. Today, western Australia is the country's greatest producer of gold. Some gold is still mined in eastern and southeastern Australia, but the best deposits have been used up.

The gold rush caused the country to grow rapidly. Many who came found no gold, but settled in Australia to work on farms and ranches, or take jobs in cities. Gold mining caused better roads and railroads to be built.

Other Minerals. Another important mineral found in Australia is coal. There are large coal fields near the cities of Sydney and Newcastle in New South Wales. Newcastle is said to be the gateway to the most valuable coal field in the Southern Hemisphere. The coal is used in the iron and steel industry centered in Newcastle, to supply power for factories, to run railroads, to produce electricity, and as fuel for steamships that sail to and from Australia.

Iron Knob is the center of a deposit of almost pure iron in South Australia. The country also has large deposits of tin, lead, copper, zinc, and silver. Today Australian minerals are almost as profitable as wool.

Gold Brings Settlers. Gold was discovered in eastern Australia in 1851, just a short time after it was discovered in California. Forty years later, in western Australia, two campers found some nuggets and soon discovered that that region was also rich in gold. A statue of one of them, Paddy Hannon, has been erected at Coolgardie. One large gold nugget, called "Welcome Stranger," was worth $50,000 to the miner who found it.

People rushed to Australia after gold was discovered. Since the gold region was in a desert, early miners had a difficult time obtaining water. Years later a large reservoir was built at Perth. A pipeline 350 miles long carries water from Perth to Kal-

Golden Mile, Kalgoorlie. This area is thought to be the world's richest square mile. More than 300 million dollars in gold has come from it.

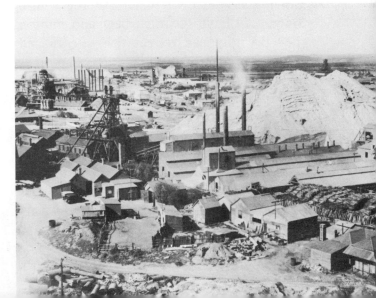

Fishing. Only a few Australians fish for a living in the cool waters of the south. Since they have so much beef and mutton they do not need to eat fish. Pearl-shell fisheries are found in the warm ocean areas for about 1000 miles along the northwestern coast and the Great Barrier Reef. Here, men dive for oysters in which the precious pearls are sometimes found. Buttons and other products are made from oyster shells.

Manufacturing and Trade. World War I and World War II brought many changes to Australia. During these two world wars the Australians could not get manufactured goods from Britain and other countries. They had to begin manufacturing needed articles and war materials at home. After World War II, manufacturing grew in Australia to the point where today there are now more people working in the factories than on the farms and ranches. Despite this increase some kinds of manufactured goods are still imported.

Australia's principal manufactures include textiles, steel, electrical and radio equipment, farm and other machinery, and

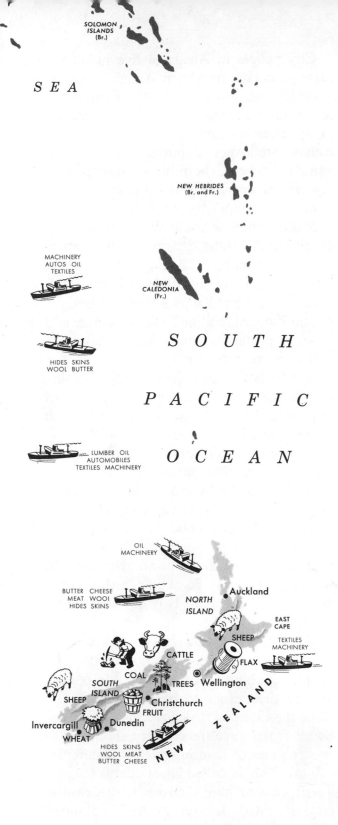

SEA

SOLOMON
ISLANDS
(Br.)

NEW HEBRIDES
(Br. and Fr.)

MACHINERY
AUTOS OIL
TEXTILES

NEW
CALEDONIA
(Fr.)

HIDES SKINS
WOOL BUTTER

SOUTH

PACIFIC

LUMBER OIL
AUTOMOBILES
TEXTILES MACHINERY

OCEAN

OIL
MACHINERY

BUTTER CHEESE
MEAT WOOL
HIDES SKINS

NORTH
ISLAND

Auckland

EAST
CAPE

SHEEP

TEXTILES
MACHINERY

CATTLE

FLAX

SOUTH
ISLAND

COAL

TREES

Wellington

SHEEP

Christchurch

FRUIT

Invercargill

Dunedin

WHEAT

HIDES SKINS
WOOL MEAT
BUTTER CHEESE

NEW ZEALAND

Capital Cities
State Boundaries
Scale of Miles
0   200   400   600

motor cars. Foods are processed, and wine is made from grapes.

The chief exports are raw materials and processed foods. Wool, wheat, flour, hides and skins, butter, meat, fruit, gold, and lead are shipped to Britain and other countries. Although Australians export their products all over the world, most are sent to this country's near neighbors in India, Indonesia, and other parts of southeastern Asia. Among the imports are gasoline, iron ore, cotton goods, paper, chemicals, airplanes, automobiles, and other products. Many of these are imported from Britain. Since World War II, the United States has been an important source of Australia's imports.

Transportation. The most important cities of Australia are on the coast, and travel between them is easily accomplished by boat. Inland water transportation is poor, however, since there are few rivers and many of these dry up during part of the year.

Most railroad lines are in the eastern, southeastern, and southwestern parts of the country where most of the people live. Transportation in Australia suffers from the use of different railroad gauges. The gauge of a railroad is the distance between the two rails in the track. Some tracks have narrow gauges, some use wide gauges. This prevents a car on one line from using the tracks of another railroad. In recent years, however, the Australians have been replacing tracks so that all will be of the same gauge. A transcontinental railroad runs east and west across the southern part of the country joining the eastern cities to Perth on the west coast.

In some areas, people still use trails and dirt roads. In the desert regions, camels pull wagons. Good highways have been built in the larger populated districts. Travel by

Oldest City in Australia. This is an air view of Sydney, the capital of New South Wales. Notice the long bridge spanning Sydney's busy harbor.

airplane has made the greatest advances. The chief cities of Australia now have excellent air transportation. Australians have become the most air-minded people in the world. A greater part of the population travel by plane in Australia than in any other country.

Chief Cities. Almost half of the people live in the six state capital cities of Sydney, Melbourne, Brisbane, Adelaide, Perth, and Hobart. Sydney and Melbourne have large populations of over a million people each.

Adelaide, South Australia. This city is a center of industry, railroads, and commerce for central and southern Australia. Here is its shopping area.

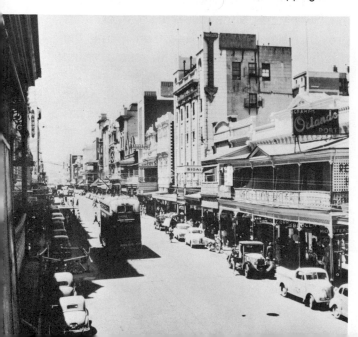

City people in Australia live much the same as do the people in American cities. The cities are modern, and the standard of living among the people is high. There are many churches and good schools. Australians are lovers of sports. Their national game is cricket. School boys grow up playing cricket on vacant lots just as the boys in our country play baseball.

Sydney, in New South Wales, is the largest city of Australia. It is only a little more than 150 years old. The city was started in a forested area along the banks of a small stream that flowed into a wide harbor. It has all modern facilities and buildings, and is an important manufacturing center as well as a great wool market.

Sydney is also the chief port of Australia, and it has a fine harbor. Many foreign ships stop there. One of the largest bridges in the world has been built across the harbor at Sydney. Visitors to the city admire the many beautiful parks and gardens.

Melbourne, in Victoria, is the second largest city. It was formerly the capital of Australia. It has a good harbor, and is the second most important port. It is a beautiful city with many parks and beaches. In winter people may go skiing in the mountains, which are only two or three hours away from the city.

When the different regions of Australia united to form the Commonwealth, the people of both Sydney and Melbourne wanted their cities to be the capital. To settle the question, the government of New South Wales gave the country about 1,000 square miles of land in which to locate the capital. This is called the Federal Capital Territory and here Canberra, the capital city, is located. It is one of the few planned cities of the modern world, and was laid out by an American architect. Canberra is like our capital city, Washington, D.C.

Brisbane is a meat-packing center and the chief city of Queensland, while Adelaide is a large industrial city of South Australia. In Western Australia the leading city is Perth, and nearby is the port of Freemantle. Hobart is the chief port and capital of Tasmania. Fruit is shipped from this city.

The Australian People. Today, at least two thirds of the people live in towns and cities. Those who live outside, however, lead lonesome lives. The nearest neighbor may be many miles away.

Most of the people in Australia work hard but always manage to find time for play and relaxation. Many games played by Americans are also enjoyed by Australians, especially tennis. Like us, they also enjoy the "movies." They spend time out of doors going to the rivers, lakes, wooded places, and seashore for bathing and picnics. Horse racing is very popular in Australia. People travel by the thousands to the larger cities where races and other sporting events take place.

The Natives of Australia. When the English first came to Australia, they found dark-skinned people already living there. These people still live in small groups in wild and desert places of the continent. The white Australians call them the *Blackfellows.*

The Blackfellows never learned to produce or use metals. They use wooden spears, clubs, and stone hatchets for hunting. Their most interesting weapon is the *boomerang,* a throwing stick carved and shaped so that it returns to the hunter if it misses its target. These Australian natives are skillful hunters with the boomerang. Usually the natives are not farmers, but follow instead the simple hunting culture of the more uncivilized peoples. They have no domestic animals, except man's earliest

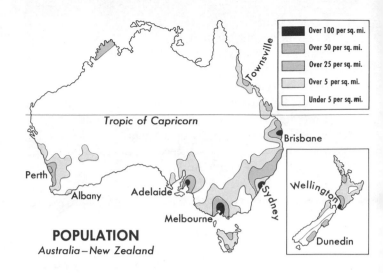

POPULATION
Australia—New Zealand

friendly beast, the dog. They catch fish, hunt the kangaroo and many smaller desert animals, and gather seeds and roots of wild plants for food.

These native Australians have remembered rather well some of the things about God that Adam learned and handed down to his children. They know God as their Father and Creator. They have many pagan practices, however, and, like certain Indians of California, they see signs of God especially in rainbows and in lightning.

Australian Natives. Although they are educated by the government in the ways of modern living and farming, the natives still do primitive dancing.

THE CHURCH IN AUSTRALIA

Irish prisoners brought the Faith to Australia. A very great number of Irishmen who spoke out and fought for their country's freedom were banished to Australian prison camps. Here they were not allowed to practice their Faith, but were made to attend the services of the Church of England. Those who refused were starved, beaten, and made to work on the roads in chain gangs.

Today, in Australia, people of all Faiths may worship freely. Catholics have built fine churches and schools. Colleges, homes for the old and poor, and other charitable institutions form part of the Church's work here.

Possessions. Eastern New Guinea, called Papua, as well as some neighboring small islands are under the control of Australia. Much of New Guinea has never been explored. These island possessions have a hot, moist climate. A few white settlers have plantations where they raise tropical crops. The natives are forest and mountain dwellers who make small clearings, farm the land for a few years, and then move on, in the manner of primitive peasant-hunters. Missioners are at work in New Guinea today, making Christians of these people.

Facts *to remember*

1. Australia is an island-continent in the South Pacific Ocean. It is about the same size as the United States, but has a population of only 9½ million. Australia is composed of six states and two territories: New South Wales, Victoria, Queensland, South Australia, Western Australia, the island of Tasmania, Capital Territory, and Northern Territory. It is a member of the British Commonwealth of Nations.
2. Since Australia lies south of the equator, its seasons are the reverse of ours. Most of the country is a dry plateau. The Great Dividing Range runs north and south near the eastern coast and prevents the moist ocean winds from carrying rain beyond the mountains. The heaviest rainfall is along the northern and eastern coasts. One third of Australia is desert land and three fourths of it is too dry for growing crops.
3. On the dry grasslands millions of sheep and cattle graze. Australia supplies one fourth of the world's wool. Much of it is the fine quality wool from merino sheep.
4. The Murray-Darling river system is the only important one. It is used more for irrigation than navigation. Australia has underground water, but it is difficult to obtain.
5. Most Australians live in large cities along the eastern and southeastern coasts. Sydney is the largest city with more than a million people. Canberra is the capital. Melbourne is the second largest city. Brisbane is a meat-packing center. Adelaide is an industrial city on the south coast. Hobart is a fruit center on the coast of Tasmania. The western gateway city is sunny Perth with its port of Freemantle.
6. The natives of Australia are called Blackfellows and live in a primitive way, hunting and fishing, and gathering roots and seeds for food.
7. Only a small part of the land is farmland. Wheat is the chief crop and some is exported. Meat, dairy products, sugar, and fruits add to the export list.
8. Abundant supplies of coal, iron, copper, tin, lead, and zinc have helped the growth of manufacturing in recent years. Factories supply clothing, hardware, and other needs of the people.

What *have I learned?*

Answer each question about Australia in a complete sentence. Do you know . . .
1. the ocean to the west?
2. the capital?
3. the gold center?
4. the largest city?
5. the principal export?
6. the most important cereal crop?
7. the animal pest?
8. the name of the natives?
9. a fine breed of sheep?
10. the origin of most of the settlers?
11. the important river system?
12. the capital of New South Wales?
13. the island state?
14. a duck-like animal?
15. the country receiving most of its surplus food products?

2

New Zealand

Mountain Lake in New Zealand. The islands of New Zealand are very mountainous. This country has many such lakes, which make good vacation spots.

In 1642 a great Dutch navigator, Abel Tasman, discovered a group of islands in the South Pacific Ocean. He called them New Zealand. In 1769 the famous Captain James Cook visited the islands. Some years later sealers and whalers ventured into the seas around New Zealand. Some of them settled in the islands. Missioners came to convert the native peoples.

In 1840 England claimed the islands as a colony. Since 1840 a fairly steady stream of settlers from the British Isles has sailed to this far-away land. Today New Zealand has become a self-governing nation within the British Commonwealth of Nations. Let us visit this land of high mountains, green valleys, and narrow coastal plains.

Southern Hemisphere Land. If you look at the map of the world, you will find New Zealand in the southern Pacific Ocean, halfway between the equator and the South Pole. It is over 1200 miles southeast of Australia and halfway around the world from Great Britain. When it is midnight in Britain it is noon in New Zealand.

Two main islands, North Island and South Island, together with a number of smaller islands, form this nation. Its population is slightly over two million people, or about one fourth that of Australia. Two thirds of its people live on North Island. The total area of New Zealand is twice that of the State of New York and is larger than that of Great Britain.

New Zealand is a mountainous country. South Island is more mountainous than the others. Several peaks rise above 10,000 feet. From mountain ice fields and glaciers, numerous rivers run swiftly to the sea. Hundreds of lakes provide pleasant fishing and swimming areas.

North Island has numbers of geysers, hot springs, and three active volcanoes. Occasional earthquakes shake the islands.

Natural Boiling Water. A young woman of the *Maori* people, the native people of New Zealand, shows how the islands' hot springs can cook an egg.

A Mild Climate. New Zealand lies in about the same latitude south of the equator as the United States lies north of it. Therefore its seasons are just the reverse of ours. It is in the westerly wind belt with winds always blowing from the ocean. This helps keep the summers from getting very hot and the winters from becoming very cold. In some places on the west coast, there is no great difference between summer and winter temperatures.

There is plenty of rainfall on the western or windward slopes of the mountains. The eastern or leeward slopes have less rainfall. Unlike Australia, New Zealand has no scarcity of water.

Forests and Farms. Mountain forests supply timber for buildings and wood pulp for paper. The government buildings at Wellington, the capital, are large wooden structures.

Some workers still collect gum from the tall kauri tree and use it to make resin for varnishes. Gum is also dug from the ground where many years ago pine trees and lumps of gum were buried. The trees decayed, but the gum remained. The gum is no longer as important as it once was, because resins are now being produced chemically.

New Zealand is a farming country. About one third of the surface is well suited to crops and pastures. Most of the farms in New Zealand are small, except for a few large dairy farms. The chief crops are wheat, barley, oats, corn, peas, and potatoes. Various kinds of fruits such as peaches, pears, plums, and apples are raised. A small amount of flax is grown.

Sheep and Cattle. New Zealand, like Australia, is a grazing country. Sheep and cattle graze out of doors all the year round, because the climate is so mild that they do not need shelter during the winter. There is plenty of rain, and the soil is good for grass. The use of refrigerated ships spurred the raising of animals in faraway New Zealand. These ships made it possible to export frozen meat and dairy products to other countries.

Sheep are raised for both wool and mutton. Shearing is done in the late winter or early spring. The wool is hauled to ports where it is exported. Some sheep are slaughtered at the ports, and mutton is exported.

Cattle are raised for meat and milk. The dairy animals are given more attention than ordinary beef animals and are carefully fed. On some of the larger dairy farms, the cows are milked by machinery. Some milk is sold fresh in the cities. Much of the milk, however, is used for making butter, cheese, and condensed milk. There are co-operative creameries where the farmers send their cream. Much New Zealand butter and cheese is exported to Britain and other countries of Western Europe. During recent years the dairying industry has grown to the point where it rivals the sheep industry in the value of its products for home use and export.

Few Minerals. New Zealand is poor in minerals. Some coal and gold are mined. To make up for a lack of coal, water power is used. About 95% of all the electricity used is produced by hydroelectric power. Metals and heavy machinery for manufacturing must be imported, usually from Australia.

Cities. Auckland is the chief port and largest city of New Zealand. It is on a narrow neck of land on North Island. Ships sailing between San Francisco and Sydney, Australia, often stop at Auckland. This city has railroad connections with Wellington and other cities on North Island.

Butter, cheese, meats, wool, and lumber are exported through Auckland. Automobiles, textiles, clothing, and iron and steel products needed by New Zealanders are imported here. Its factories turn out rope, brick, varnish, soap, boots and shoes, and some machinery. Shipbuilding is also an important industry in Auckland.

Wellington, the second city in size, is New Zealand's capital. Situated at the south end of North Island, it has a good central location. The city has a good harbor and imports and exports the same kind of products as Auckland. Some manufacturing is carried on in Wellington.

Christchurch is the most important city

Strange Bird of New Zealand. The Kiwi bird does not appear in any other part of the world. The kiwis have no wings, but run swiftly like ostriches.

on South Island. It is on the Avon River, about seven miles from the ocean. It is smaller than Auckland or Wellington.

People of New Zealand. Nine tenths of the people of New Zealand are of English origin. The native people are a tall, strong, and brave people called Maoris. They belong to the same part of the human family as the brown people of the Hawaiian Islands. The Maoris may be related to some of our American Indians. They fought many fierce wars against the white

Capital of New Zealand. Wellington is located on North Island. Outside its harbor, you can look across the narrow passage toward South Island.

Shearing the Sheep. In the spring in New Zealand the winter coats of the sheep are ready to be cut. Here a rancher's son helps with the job.

invaders. Now, however, they take part in the country's government. They are intelligent and make good leaders. Several thousand live on the islands.

New Zealand gave women the right to vote many years before this right was gained by American women. This little southern country also has some of the world's most progressive social laws, regulating wages for workers and providing insurance to pay expenses in times of sickness or accident. Widows, orphans, old people, and unemployed persons are cared for by law. Parents receive extra money for each child in the family, and all medical treatment is free. New Zealanders have a very high standard of living, and are said to be the best fed people in the world.

Irish Catholic settlers brought the Faith to New Zealand, and French priests did

The Natives of New Zealand. These girls, who are Maoris, display their colorful native costume. Notice the intricately carved wood on the house.

missionary work among them. French Marist Fathers and English priests work among the Maoris. The Church has grown very fast in New Zealand, and there are fine churches and schools. Most New Zealanders are Protestants, and everyone is free to worship as he pleases.

Facts *to remember*

1. New Zealand, a member of the British Commonwealth of Nations, lies in the South Pacific Ocean 1200 miles southeast of Australia. Its area is larger than Great Britain's, but its population numbers only two million.
2. Most of the islands are mountainous. One third of the land is used for crops and pastures. A mild, moist climate provides green pastures. Sheep and dairy products are important exports.
3. New Zealand forests provide building timber, pulp for paper goods, and gums for varnishes.
4. Auckland is the chief port and largest city of New Zealand. Wellington is in the center of the country, and is the capital and also a shipping port. Christchurch is the most important city on South Island.
5. Although nine tenths of the people are of British ancestry, there are several thousand descendants of the native people, the Maoris. They take part in the government and make fine intelligent leaders. Irish, French, and English Catholics have brought the Faith to New Zealand where the Church is growing fast.

What *have I learned?*

Answer each question in a complete sentence.
1. What are the two main islands of New Zealand?
2. New Zealand has what season in July?
3. On what island is the capital city?
4. What is the population of New Zealand in comparison with your state?
5. Is New Zealand chiefly plains or mountains?
6. Did New Zealand become a Dutch or English colony?
7. Who are the Maoris?
8. What product is obtained from the kauri tree?
9. Name two important domestic animals raised in New Zealand.
10. Is New Zealand rich or poor in minerals?

3 Islands of the South Pacific

Shoreline of Tahiti. An islander's outrigger boat is beached, awaiting its next fishing trip. In the distance, the surf crashes over the reef.

A glance at the globe shows us that most of our earth's surface is water. A little more than one fourth is land. Moreover, most of this land lies north of the equator. The Southern Hemisphere is a vast watery expanse where small areas of land lie widely separated by the sea. Early explorers who sailed after Columbus had discovered America made daring voyages into the unknown waters of the South Pacific. These men suffered starvation, thirst, sickness, and even mutiny among their crews.

It was the Portuguese, Ferdinand Magellan, who named the Pacific Ocean. Magellan's men on their heroic voyage, the first around the entire globe, passed among these islands without seeing any of them until they came to the Marianas. Before that, however, they suffered many hardships and came to such extremes of hunger that they boiled and ate the leather straps that held the sails in place. Magellan himself never completed the voyage around the world, because he was killed by natives in the Philippine Islands.

These hardy adventurers were followed later by the Englishman, Captain Cook, who might be called a collector of islands because he discovered or visited so many of these charming places. We have seen how he surveyed the coast of Australia, and brought it and New Zealand to the attention of his countrymen. Cook was finally murdered by natives on one of the lovely islands. Little by little the South Pacific was explored; and each group of islands added a little more to the map of the world.

High Islands and Low Islands. There are two kinds of islands in the South Pacific, high mountainous islands and low coral islands. The mountainous islands are larger, and some have active volcanoes. They have rich soils at the base of the mountains, abundant rainfall, and are more densely peopled because the forests and patches of cleared land yield many kinds of food.

The coral islands are small and low and seem to come up right out of the ocean. Coral polyps are tiny creatures living in warm, shallow waters. When they die, their skeletons add to others and build up a reef from the bottom of the sea. The gradual accumulation of these skeletons brings the coral reef above the level of the water, forming a string of islands, like the Great Barrier Reef. Elsewhere, in deeper waters, the peaks of huge, underwater volcanic mountains reach close enough to the surface for the coral to form a broken circle of islands around them.

A ring of coral islands is known as an *atoll*. The water it encloses is called a *lagoon*. Lagoons often make good harbors. Drifting coconuts and plant seeds brought by wind, water, and birds take root in the coral sands and grow.

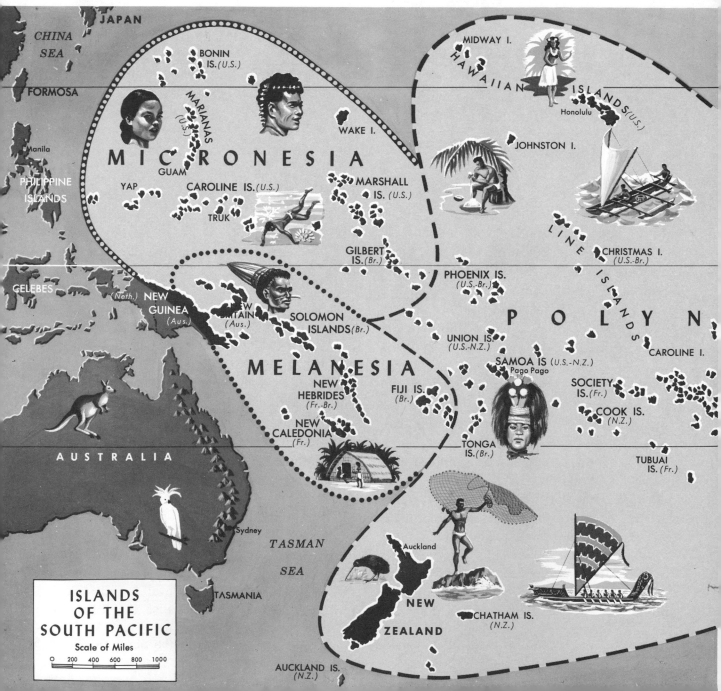

ISLANDS
OF THE
SOUTH PACIFIC

Scale of Miles

0   200   400   600   800   1000

The Island People. It is said that the first inhabitants of many South Pacific islands were small people of the black race called Negritos. Larger, fiercer, brownish men came later to some islands, killed the black men, and took the women for wives. Today the islands of this far-flung region can be classified, roughly, according to the different peoples who inhabit them.

Melanesia is the name that is given to the area where the black race has been least affected by civilization. The areas where the tall, pale brown people have taken over are called Polynesia. Other groups of islands, where the population is a mixture of Melanesians, Polynesians, and Malays, are called Micronesia.

Melanesians, or Negritos, are the least civilized of the island people but they are the most hard-working. They are good farmers who raise pigs, taro, sweet potatoes, bananas, squashes, and pumpkins.

The Micronesians have few resources and lead primitive lives. The Polynesians, called Kanakas, are tall and sturdy with lighter skins. They are very intelligent and are among the world's best swimmers, sailors, and fishermen.

We often call the South Sea islands by the name Oceania, meaning land of the ocean. The islands of the South Pacific are all closely connected with the great ocean that surrounds them. The sea—its products, its means of transportation, its storms and its climate—is part of the lives of the island people.

South Sea Islanders have long been expert seamen and great travelers. In their frail outrigger or double canoes they sail from island to island, catching fish and collecting rain water on the way. It is thought that some may even have reached the shores of Central America and South America long before Columbus, and that they settled there and were the ancestors of some tribes of Indians.

The Lure of the Islands. People love to visit the Pacific Islands to enjoy their restful beauty and their charm. White coral beaches, waving palm trees, rich vegetation, and sunny skies have always been the attractions which lure travellers to these lands. The islands have been called a "tropical paradise" even though there are several bad points about life there.

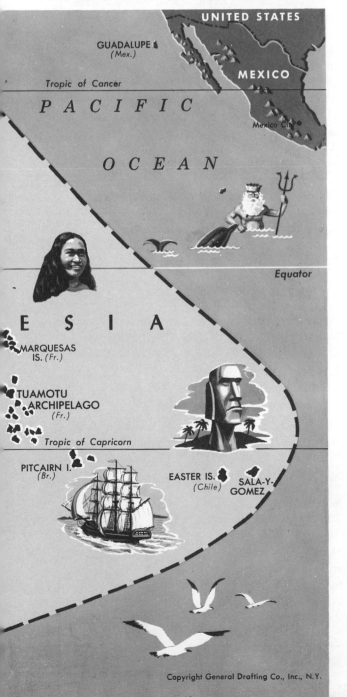

UNITED STATES

GUADALUPE I.
(Mex.)

Tropic of Cancer

MEXICO

P A C I F I C

Mexico City

O C E A N

Equator

E S I A

MARQUESAS
IS. (Fr.)

TUAMOTU
ARCHIPELAGO
(Fr.)

Tropic of Capricorn

PITCAIRN I.
(Br.)

EASTER IS.
(Chile)

SALA-Y-
GOMEZ

Natives of the Fiji Islands. The people of these islands are mostly of the Melanesian type. The thatched hut is built to withstand heavy rain.

On some of the islands, food and drinking water are scarce, and some islands are overcrowded. In addition, some of the islands of the South Pacific suffered greatly during the fierce battles of World War II, and the population of other islands has had to be moved because of radiation dangers from atomic tests in the Pacific areas.

Like man's first paradise on earth, these islands also suffered from the sin of Adam. Witchcraft, devil worship, and headhunting have long held the people in terror. For centuries, many natives ate human flesh. It was the fate of many early missioners to end up as a feast for a party of island savages.

Christianity in the Islands. After the first discovery of these islands, a vicious group of white men cheated, robbed, and molested the simple islanders. At first, the early Protestant and Catholic missioners were suspected of being the same type as those who abused the natives. Soon, however, the islanders came to respect the missioners and many natives are now Christians. Catholic missioners have been especially helpful to the victims of leprosy, a disease which is common here.

Facts *to remember*

1. There are thousands of high and low islands in the South Pacific Ocean. Low coral islands are built of a rock-like material that was once the skeleton of a tiny creature called a polyp. The high islands are mostly mountainous, and some have volcanoes. Rich soils at their base produce food for many people.

2. A ring of coral islands is known as an atoll, and the water in the center is called a lagoon. Coconut palm trees grow on these islands.

3. We divide the people who live on these islands into three classes. The Melanesians who look like Negroes are called Negritos. They work hard as farmers. The Micronesians are a mixture of the races in this area. They have few resources and lead primitive lives. The Polynesians are more intelligent, with lighter skin and stronger bodies. They are the world's best swimmers and fishermen.

4. Food, clothing, and shelter are easy to obtain on many of these islands. Tropical fruits, fish from the sea, and the coconut furnish abundant food. Copra, the dried nut meat of the coconut, is exported.

5. Hundreds of Europeans and Americans have spent their lives on these islands teaching the Faith.

What *have I learned?*

Write the numbers 1 to 10. After each number write the name that matches the description.

A
1. "tiny islands" of mixed races
2. dried meat of the coconut
3. water in the center of an atoll
4. many islands inhabited by Kanakas
5. polyp that builds reefs in warm water
6. largest ocean in the world
7. islands closest to Australia
8. a tropical fruit
9. people teaching Christianity
10. naval and air base for the United States

B
Micronesia	Pacific
copra	Melanesia
lagoon	pineapple
Polynesia	missioners
coral	Samoan Islands

ANTARCTICA

Antarctic Ice Sheet. This photo, which was taken from an airplane, shows a common feature of the Antarctic scene—huge, moving, masses of ice.

Antarctica, the great land mass that lies around the South Pole, is the world's southernmost continent. Few people realize that the area of Antarctica is about 6,000,000 square miles, or almost twice the size of the United States. It is much larger than Europe or Australia, and almost as large as South America. The map shows that practically the entire continent is within the Antarctic Circle in the South Polar Zone.

Antarctic Explorations. Antarctica was the last continent to be discovered. At about the time of the Revolutionary War in the United States, Captain Cook, the British explorer, sailed around the continent through icy waters without seeing the land. This was the same Captain Cook who sailed along the coast of Australia and claimed New Zealand for the British. Other explorers from Britain, the United States, Russia, France, and Germany sailed along the irregular coast of Antarctica. They discovered various islands, peninsulas, and two large seas, Weddell Sea and the Ross Sea. None were able to reach the interior.

Learning More About Antarctica. Rear Admiral Richard E. Byrd, America's great explorer of the Polar Regions, was the first to fly over both the North Pole and the South Pole. His first flight over the South Pole was made with three companions in 1929. Since then, Byrd and others have made many flights over the South Pole.

During his exploration trips to Antarctica, Byrd maintains a camp which he calls Little America. It is located near the edge of the continent on the Ross Ice Shelf. Here sleeping quarters, a dining hall, weather

Travel in Antarctica. In the distance an icestrip has been smoothed off for airplanes to land on. Most Antarctic travelling is done on tractors.

observation stations, repair shops, and hospital facilities have been set up. There are even such modern conveniences as electric lights and telephones.

The latest of the expeditions under the leadership of Admiral Byrd began in 1955. It was known as Operation Deep Freeze. Its purpose was to build a series of new bases in Antarctica from which scientists could work to gather weather information as part of a program for the International Geophysical Year (1957-58). One of their biggest tasks was the building of a mile-and-half-long runway for large airplanes.

Much new information about the geography of Antarctica has been learned from aerial photographs and new maps that were prepared as the result of these international explorations. Today, every part of Antarctica has been mapped, even if all parts have not yet been explored.

A Land of Ice and Snow. Antarctica was first thought to be a number of islands covered with ice. Today we know it is a great continental land mass. Much of the area is a plateau with an average altitude of 6000 feet. Along the border of the plateau are high mountain ranges. Some of the mountain peaks rise to heights of 15,000 feet or more. There is even an active volcano which gives off steam and gases.

Most of Antarctica is covered with layers of snow and ice which in places are believed to be several thousand feet thick. At the edges of the continent large masses of ice break off and form icebergs which float away in the surrounding waters. Some of the glaciers are hundreds of miles long and many miles wide. In a few places large sheets of ice extend over thousands of square miles. It is on one of these, Ross Shelf, that Little America, our most important base in Antarctica, is located. The top of the ice is smooth in some places, rough in others. Large cracks in the ice, sometimes hundreds of feet deep, make travel dangerous.

The weather is cloudy and very windy. Much snow falls. Blizzards occur when the falling snow is blown about by strong winds. Along the coast there are a few places where the land is bare and rocky, but for the most part no land can be seen because the ice reaches far out to sea.

Antarctica is one of the coldest lands in the world. On many winter days the temperature falls to 50° or 60° below and has been known to sink as low as 126° below zero. Even in the summer, temperatures are usually below zero and it is very rare for temperatures to rise above freezing, even along the coast.

Of course, Antarctica's seasons, like those of the other continents south of the equator, are the opposite of ours in the Northern Hemisphere. The coldest month in Antarctica is August, and the mildest is January. South Polar expeditions usually take place during our winter because then it is summer in Antarctica.

At the South Pole, the sun remains above the horizon for six months in the summer, and there is continuous daylight. For the remaining six months the sun is below the horizon, and the continent has continuous night.

Life on the Continent. Although Antarctica has an area of 6,000,000 square miles, no human beings have ever lived on the continent the year round, until the recent "Operation Deep Freeze." Early explorers and scientists who visited Antarctica were there only for the summer months of December, January, and February. During these months, temperatures rise above zero, and the ever-present sun made exploration and work possible.

The only plant life to be found on Antarctica are little patches of mosses and lichens. These are similar to those that grow on the tundra of the Arctic regions of North America and Eurasia. No land animals live on the Antarctic continent, and the few land birds remain only during the summer and leave before winter begins. Many penguins live along the shores of Antarctica. These sea birds walk like men and can swim very rapidly. Their white breasts and black backs make them look as though they were wearing full-dress suits. The emperor penguin, largest of sea birds, often grows four feet tall and weighs 80 or 90 pounds.

Most of the whales caught today come from the cold southern waters that surround the Antarctic continent. During the past sixty years many whaling ships have sailed to Antarctic waters. Today, some of the ships use airplanes to help locate the whales.

Harpoons, fired from guns, are used to capture the great animals. The carcasses are towed to the ship, where they are cut up. Oil is obtained from the *blubber* or fat

Antarctica's Rare Living Creatures. The penguins seem to be talking about the ship they see. It is the U.S.S. *Bear* on a voyage of exploration.

by heating it in large kettles. It is then stored in tanks. Animal foods are made from the flesh, and fertilizer from the bones. Livers are saved for making medicines. A large ship has been known to catch more than 1,000 whales. Seals and fish are also abundant in Antarctica.

Antarctica's Future. We have learned much from the explorers and scientists who have been to Antarctica in recent years. Coal has been found in the rocks at the surface, and it is believed that there is plenty below the surface. Rock samples indicate that the continent may have other mineral deposits. Some day when the scientists find ways of living on the continent throughout the year it may be possible to obtain the minerals. At present it would not be profitable to send men and machinery to this cold, barren, far-off land.

What *have I learned?*

Answer each of the following questions in a complete sentence.

1. Why do Antarctic explorers make their expeditions to the continent during our winter season?
2. What fishing industry is carried on in Antarctic waters?
3. How does Antarctica compare in size with the other continents?
4. What mineral resource has been discovered on the Antarctic continent?
5. How do winter and summer temperatures compare in Antarctica?

Unit Five Review

Questions for Discussion and Review

1. Compare Australia with the United States as to size, population, and location.
2. Explain why Australia's seasons are the reverse of ours.
3. Why are Australia's large cities located on the coast?

ANTARCTICA

The dazzling whiteness of this view of Antarctica demonstrates its chief physical features—ice and snow. Antarctica is a continental land mass, larger than Europe or Australia. This land mass is completely covered with a layer of ice and snow.

The South Pole is located almost exactly in the center of the continent. Antarctica, therefore, suffers an extremely cold climate. Extending out from the mainland of Antarctica is a dangerous area of crumbling drift ice. Here the many pieces of ice broken off from Antarctica's frozen crust slowly melt as they reach warmer waters.

In the lower part of the picture is the famous Ross Ice Shelf, bordering on the Ross Sea. The United States base called Little America is located here, and it is across this area that the first overland trips to the South Pole were made.

Many brave men have risked their lives exploring "the world's last frontier." Their efforts may someday show that Antarctica is really a valuable and important part of the world in which we live.

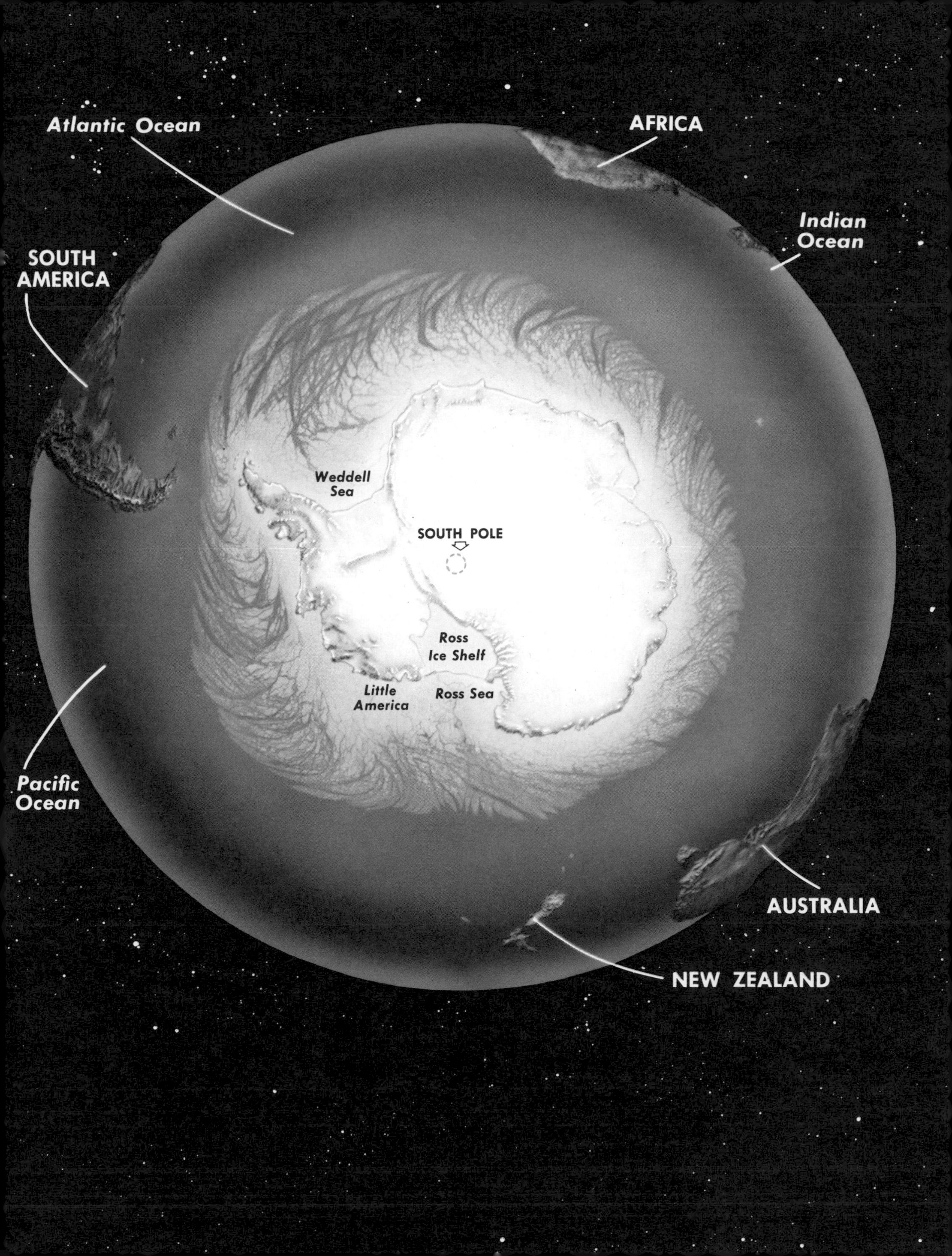

Atlantic Ocean

AFRICA

Indian
Ocean

SOUTH
AMERICA

Weddell
Sea

SOUTH POLE

Ross
Ice Shelf

Little
America

Ross Sea

Pacific
Ocean

AUSTRALIA

NEW ZEALAND

4. Explain how Sydney has become a large city.
5. Describe the capital city of Australia.
6. Why is Australia such a dry country?
7. Why did the raising of sheep become the chief industry of Australia?
8. Why is southern New Zealand often compared with Switzerland?
9. How was the Great Barrier Reef formed?
10. Compare New Zealand with Australia as to size, population, and industries.
11. Explain the value of the coconut tree to the South Sea Islanders.
12. Why should we be interested in the people of the South Sea Islands?
13. Explain why foreign countries are interested in the South Pacific Islands.
14. Explain how the sea plays an important part in the life of the people of these islands.
15. Discuss the importance of recent discoveries in Antarctica.

Using the Maps and Globe

1. Name each of the Australian states and their capitals.
2. Name the water bodies that surround Australia.
3. In what direction is Australia from New Zealand?
4. Into what ocean does the Murray River flow?
5. What is the latitude of the city of Adelaide?
6. What island state lies south of Australia?
7. Using your Scale of Miles, find the distance across Australia along the Tropic of Capricorn.
8. Where are the lowland areas in New Zealand?
9. Name three groups of islands to the north of New Zealand.
10. Draw a map of Antarctica and label Ross Shelf, Little America, and the Weddell Sea.

Using Geography Words

Here is a list of special words that have been used in this Unit. Use each one in a sentence to prove you know its meaning in geography.

platypus	Maoris	Melanesia
eucalyptus	mutton	Polynesia
coral	cisterns	Micronesia
merino	lagoon	dingoes
artesian	Blackfellows	sheep stations
atoll	koala	blubber
kauri gum	copra	penguins

Final Test

A

Write each sentence on your paper, choosing the correct word or words in parentheses.

1. New Zealand's chief exports are products of its (farms, animals, mines).
2. The Great Barrier Reef is formed of (coral, lava, rock).
3. Most of Australia is a very (wet, cold, dry) land.
4. Australians travel (south, west, north) for warmer weather.
5. The Tropic of Capricorn passes through (New Zealand, Australia, New Guinea).
6. New Zealand is a (continent, an island group, an isthmus).
7. A polyp is a (sea animal, plant, bird).
8. (The greatest number of sheep are raised in the eastern, southern, northern) part of Australia.
9. Australia's most valuable export is (gold, wool, wheat).
10. The only forms of plant life found in Antarctica are (vegetables, trees, mosses and lichens).

B

Copy the following list on your paper. After each item write whether it applies to Australia, New Zealand, or both.

1. Canberra is its capital.
2. It exports sheep and dairy products.
3. It has many high mountain peaks.
4. It has its summer in January.
5. Native Maoris live there.
6. There is a serious water problem.
7. There are many swift-flowing rivers.
8. It is a member of the British Commonwealth of Nations.
9. It has valuable mineral resources.
10. Wellington is its capital.

Applying Christian Principles

Select the best ending for each sentence. Then write the complete sentences on your paper.

1. One of the best features of the New Zealand government is that it **a.** provides extra money for each child in a family **b.** allows each person to worship God as he pleases **c.** grants women the right to vote.
2. Countries owning island groups help them most by **a.** buying their products **b.** sharing their knowledge **c.** building roads and railroads.

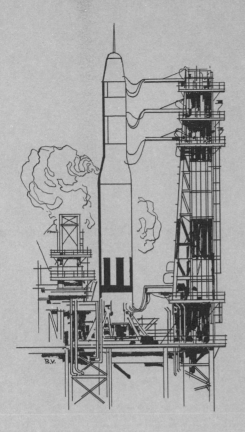

Geography for the Space Age

**In this Unit
you will learn that:**

1 The universe includes all things which exist in space—everything which God created, from the greatest stars to the tiniest atoms.

2 Our earth is part of the Solar System. It is one of an orderly group of bodies moving with the sun through space.

3 The earth travels around the sun as it spins on an axis. The seasons change as the earth changes its position with respect to the sun's rays.

4 It is important that we learn how to use the globe and maps for location, for measuring distance and direction, for finding out about surface features, and for figuring out differences in time.

5 Water covers much more of the earth's surface than land. The land surface changes as the result of erosion. Worn-away materials are carried from the land to the ocean.

6 Changes which take place in the earth's atmosphere affect weather and climate all over the earth.

Five, four, three, two, one . . . By now, the calm voice calling the countdown has become familiar to everybody. It heralds the departure of another rocket-powered vehicle—perhaps on its way to circle the earth, look at the moon, or reach to Venus.

Your study of geography has been concerned with the world we live in—the earth and its people. This is right, of course, because *geography* means "the study or science of the earth." But you are now living in the Age of Space.

Almost everything that scientists learn about space has some meaning for each of us on the earth as well. For example, by means of radio, a satellite sends back information on electric impulses in outer space. We discover that these impulses have an effect on the earth's weather, causing our storms.

You must now learn to study and measure the earth as part of the entire universe. In the following chapters, you will see the earth in its true appearance, as a tiny speck in the huge system of heavenly bodies which surround it. From your study of the earth and the universe, you should become more and more aware of the great glory of God, and of the wonders of His Creation.

SPACE AGE CHALLENGE

Not very long ago, the event which you see in this picture would have been considered fantastic and impossible. Nowadays, everybody knows that travel in space is nearly a reality.

News that another rocket has been fired into the heavens, or that another satellite has been guided into orbit by man, is hardly even exciting any more. Plans for exploring space, the moon, or other planets seem quite ordinary and commonplace. This is truly the Space Age we are living in.

The rocket in this picture has been fired from the earth. You can follow its trail back to a spot on the east coast of Florida. Perhaps it is Cape Kennedy , starting point for so many bold ventures into the unknown.

To the right, the craters and seas of the moon seem bleak and unwelcoming. We are quite sure there is no life on this cold, arid body. Other planets, however, challenge man to find their secrets. Perhaps passengers in a vehicle such as this one will come back to tell us their fascinating stories.

Perhaps you, the young people of the Space Age, will take part in this great adventure of the Twentieth Century.

1 Let's Learn About The Universe

Universe means *everything*. All of the Creation of God, all space, all heavenly bodies, including our earth and everything on it, taken together are called the universe.

Men of all countries and all times have been curious about the universe. Through the years, many facts have been learned which add to our knowledge of the universe. However, we still know very little.

Scientists today are discovering many facts about our universe through the use of satellites, giant telescopes, and television cameras. Unfortunately, the more we learn, the more difficult it is to explain the whole universe. One thing is sure—science by itself can never tell who made the hot stars, the gas clouds, or the whirling dust. Science can study the chemicals of space, and measure its light, heat, air, and moisture. Science can guess at the master plan which controls the vast workings of the universe. Only God knows the beginnings, the first moment of Creation.

The Beginnings of God's Universe. "In the beginning God created the heavens and the earth" (Gen. 1:1). These words begin the first part of the Bible, the Book of Genesis. The writer of the Book of Genesis, inspired by God, gives us an account of the origin of the universe, of our earth, and of all living things. However, the Book of Genesis was not meant as a science textbook. It was meant to inspire us with awe and wonder at the power and glory of God. In Genesis, the story of Creation is told in simple, poetic language.

You will remember reading of the six days in which the Creation took place. This may be confusing until you learn that each "day" may have taken millions of years. Some "days" occurred before the sun and the earth were fixed in place; that is, before there were days as we count them.

God in His great wisdom thus made known to us the fact of creation in a way that our limited minds could grasp. He left much for us to discover with the wisdom He gave us. But nothing that man has discovered, or will discover, can ever change what we know—God is the creator of all things. Our discoveries help us gradually to learn more and more about God's marvelous plan. It is this plan which directs the workings of the universe, from the tiniest atom to the largest star.

As you begin to study the universe and the laws which govern it, remember that man's knowledge is puny and small when compared to the vastness of God's space and the secrets still unlearned. Remember also the purpose of the universe, as the psalmist sang: "The heavens declare the glory of God, and the firmament proclaims his handiwork" (Ps. 18:2–3).

Measuring the Universe. At great distances, appearances of objects can deceive us. The sun, for example, seems very small when we see it in the sky. Actually, it is more than a million times larger than our earth. It appears small only because of its great distance from us. Many of the stars which we see as mere pin points of light are really many times larger again than the sun. Our ideas of size and distance are limited by the things we see close to us.

Light travels faster than anything we know, but with modern instruments its speed can be measured. Light travels at the amazing speed of 186,000 miles per second. Count "one, two," and in that second of time, light could travel a distance of more than seven times around the earth. The speed of light is sometimes used to express distances in space. A *light year is* the distance which would be covered in a year by a beam of light, traveling at 186,000 miles per second.

We begin to get some idea of the extent of the universe, then, when we realize that the *nearest* star (not counting the sun) is so far away that its light takes over four years to reach us. Yet this light is traveling through space at 186,000 miles per second! Other stars are so far away that they can be seen only by the most powerful telescopes. Light from them may still take a million years or more to reach the earth. Our "little" earth, moving around our "little" sun, is only a speck in the vast universe.

The Milky Way. This photo, taken through a telescope, shows a tiny part of our galaxy. This cloud-like mass of matter is called a *nebula*.

Galaxies and Stars. The sun, like all the stars, is rushing through space at a speed of more than 46,000 miles per hour. Of course, the earth and the other bodies which revolve about the sun are also rushing through space. The "family of the sun" travels together. The sun's family is only a tiny part of a huge, wheel-shaped group of stars called a *galaxy*.

At times the earth faces in such a direction that we can see much of our galaxy arranged like a belt of light across the sky. This is the famous "Milky Way." The white path we seem to see is really the light of about ten billion individual stars. These stars are separated from each other by vast distances. They are so far away from us, however, that we do not see them separately, but as a single white mass. Each of these millions of stars may in turn have its own "family" of bodies rotating around it.

Even though our galaxy is 100,000 light years in diameter, it is not the only one in the universe. Great numbers of other galaxies have already been discovered and photographed by the use of powerful telescopes like the one at Mount Palomar, California. Each galaxy contains millions of stars. The galaxies move through space at speeds that are difficult to imagine.

The Old Earth. *Geologists* are men who study the many materials which make up the rocky crust of the earth. They have made careful examinations of all the different layers of rock and soil. From these studies, they estimate that the earth is several billion years old. Our period of recorded history is just a tiny part of this.

For the first billion years, geologists think there was no life of any kind on this planet. The earth may have been a hot ball of liquid gas which took a very long time to cool off. Most likely, conditions on earth were not yet ready to support life. At any rate, God took His time preparing the earth for His precious gift of life.

The Beginning of Life. Nobody knows exactly when life first came to earth. Remains of once-living creatures have been found embedded in layers of rock. These remains are called *fossils*. They help us to judge at what time in the earth's history different forms of life were abundant. Judging from many fossil signs, life seems to have burst out all at once in many simple forms: sea weeds and worms in the water, fern-like plants and simple creatures.

Soon (that is, within a few million years!) the earth was swarming with reptiles, birds, plants, and animals; great elephants, fierce tigers, and big monkeys walked the earth. A billion years at least had passed, and still man did not appear.

God lives in eternity, not in time. To Him, a day is like a thousand years. Our ordinary methods of measuring time fail when we consider the time period of the Creation, just as ordinary means of measuring distance fail when we consider the extent of God's universe.

The First Human Beings. Scientists estimate that man has now been on the earth from 100,000 to 600,000 years. They think that during the ages, more perfect plants and animals kept developing from simpler forms. It is possible that God made the

Ancient Animals. Long before written history, western Canada was covered by an inland sea. Here lived huge creatures which we call *dinosaurs*.

body of Adam through millions of years of slow changes, bringing out more and more perfect forms all the time, until He brought forth the first man's shape. Adam and Eve were the *first human beings* because God gave them a *soul*. They had bodies like other living creatures, but their soul made them completely different. God gave them and their descendants reason and intelligence, free will, and power to know Him.

Early Man. From various bones which have been dug up, scientists have put together a model in clay of early man as he might have appeared.

WHAT IS AN ATOM?

There are 92 natural elements and 8 man-made elements. Elements are composed of atoms of different kinds and sizes.

An atom has at its center a nucleus made up of one or more *protons,* (+),

and

the same number, or a larger number, of *neutrons,* (neutral),

and

one or more *electrons,* (−), circling around the nucleus in tiny orbits.

Depending on the kind of atom—gold, oxygen, or some other—there is a set number of protons and neutrons. There is one electron for every proton.

Hydrogen is the simplest atom. It has one proton, one electron, no neutrons.

This is a carbon atom:

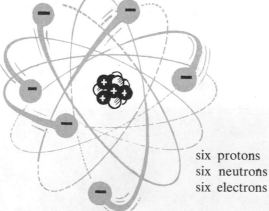

six protons
six neutrons
six electrons

The uranium atom has 92 protons, 92 electrons, and 146 neutrons. In atomic *fission,* this atom's nucleus is given an extra neutron. The upset arrangement causes changes which lead to the release of tremendous energy. This is called *nuclear energy.*

The Material of Creation. All matter is composed of certain substances. It may be living matter, like human bodies, plants, and animals, or it may be non-living matter, like rocks, water and air. These substances are made up of *elements.* Examples of elements are oxygen, iron, and uranium.

Some elements we see and use in their pure state. Most matter, however, is made of combinations of different elements. For example, water is a combination of the elements hydrogen and oxygen; table salt is a combination of sodium and chlorine. The cells of our bodies are made of very complicated combinations of different elements, such as calcium, iodine, and sodium.

For a while, scientists thought they had discovered the smallest piece into which any element could be divided. This thing they called the *atom.* They thought the atom could not be divided any further. Nobody ever saw an atom, even with a microscope. Scientists knew, however, that the atom of any one element was different from the atom of any other element. Later, a number of astonishing things were discovered about atoms.

Atomic Structure. We know now that every atom is composed of tiny particles, some charged with electricity. These particles are in constant motion. An atom resembles a tiny solar system. There is one central part, called the *nucleus.* Particles located at the nucleus are called *protons* and *neutrons.* Particles which are whirling around the nucleus are called *electrons.*

It is difficult to understand that all matter is composed of these tiny, whirling systems of atoms. Yet we are all familiar today with the effect produced when scientists "split the atom." Upsetting the arrangement of the particles in the nucleus of a certain atom can release a fantastic amount of energy. This is an atomic explosion. We are even learning to harness and use the amount of energy given off by atoms in this way. Scientists think, too, that it is a constant changing of the structure of atoms which produces the sun's heat and light.

All matter is made up of elements and mixtures of elements; elements are composed of atoms. The atom of any particular element has a certain size, a certain weight, and a certain arrangement of parts. Elements combine into compounds to form cells in living things; the human body is made up of large numbers of cells, each doing a certain job in the process of life.

Center of Creation. Man appears in Creation between the very large and the very small. The very large is the vast universe of space and distant stars; the very small is the tiny world of atoms. One world is so vast we can see only a little of it, and guess at the rest. The other world is so small we cannot see it at all, but can only find out about it through scientific experiments.

Man, then, stands about half-way between the atom and the star. Yet man is greater and more wonderful than either of these, for he has a soul. Man alone can reason and make decisions. He alone in creation is free to choose between good and evil. He alone can know and love God, the Creator of all things.

Galaxies go slipping silently and smoothly through space; millions of worlds whirl about the distant suns; atoms split and release frightful amounts of energy. Yet God knows each one of us, calls us by name, and keeps watch over us.

Facts *to remember*

1. The earth is only a small part of the universe. The sun and other stars are much greater in size than the earth. They appear small because of their great distance from us.

2. Distances in the universe are so great they are measured in light years. Light travels 186,000 miles per second. A light year is the distance light travels in a year.

3. A huge wheel-shaped group of millions of stars is called a galaxy. There are many galaxies in the universe. The sun, earth, and moon are located in the Milky Way Galaxy.

4. Scientists estimate the age of the earth as several billion years. This estimate is based on studies of the rock layers of the earth's crust.

5. The remains of once-living plants and animals (fossils) have also been studied by scientists to trace the history of life on the earth.

6. The material from which the universe was created is called matter. Matter is made up of simple substances called elements. Elements, in turn, are made up of atoms.

What *have I learned?*

Answer each of the following questions in a complete sentence.

1. What are some of the new methods scientists use to discover more about the universe?

2. How fast does light travel across space?

3. How does the sun compare in size with other stars?

4. What name is given to our galaxy of stars?

5. What are fossils and where are they found?

6. How long do scientists estimate that the earth was inhabited by man?

7. In what way do human beings differ from other living things?

8. Name the tiny parts of atoms.

9. When do atoms give off great energy?

10. In what book of the Bible does the story of Creation appear?

Facts *to understand*

Give one reason in a complete sentence for each of the following statements.

1. Science can never explain completely the workings of Creation.

2. The "six days" of Creation, as told in Genesis, was probably a much longer time.

3. Light from some stars may still take a million years or more to reach the earth.

4. The first human beings had bodies like other living creatures, yet they were completely different.

5. The individual stars of the Milky Way appear to us as a single white mass.

MILKY WAY GALAXY

SOLAR SYSTEM'S LOCATION

JUPITER

MERCURY

MARS

SATURN

EARTH

VENUS

PLUTO

URANUS

SOLAR SYSTEM

The Sun and Its Family. The nine planets are the most important members of the Solar System. They revolve about the sun, each in its own orbit. Some of the planets have one or more moons revolving about them. The Solar System is located in one of the great families composed of millions of stars, called the Milky Way galaxy.

NEPTUNE

2 The Family of the Sun

Because it is difficult to learn much about the vast areas of outer space, we concentrate first on learning all we can about our nearer neighbors in space. The earth, the sun, and earth's nearer neighbors can be grouped together and called the *solar system*. *Sol* is the Latin word for sun, and we call this group of bodies in space the solar system because they are all centered in some way upon the sun.

The Sun's Family. The solar system is made up of the sun and all the bodies which revolve about it. These bodies range in size from tiny grains to giant balls of rock or gas thousands of miles in diameter.

All the members of the sun's family have one thing in common—they travel in orbits, or circular paths, around the sun at tremendous speeds. As the different bodies whirl rapidly through space, they build up *centrifugal force*. This is a force which makes them tend to fly off into space, straight out from their orbit. However, God in His infinite wisdom created another force called *gravity*. It balances against centrifugal force and keeps all the members of the solar system in their orbits. As they revolve about the sun, the "push-pull" effect of these two forces works on all of them.

Gravity is the same force that keeps people on the rapidly spinning earth from flying off into space—the same force that brings down a ball we throw up into the air —the same force that keeps the moon revolving in its orbit around the earth.

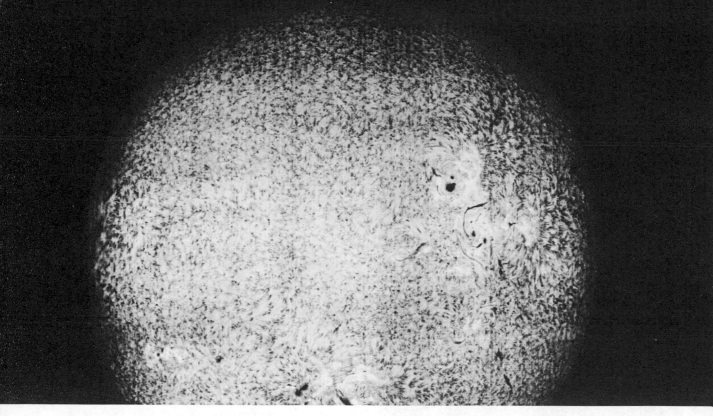

Close-up Picture of the Sun. This photograph of the dense glowing star at the center of the solar system was taken with a special camera.

The Star of the Family. Although the sun is only a medium-sized star, it is by far the largest member of the solar system. It is a huge round ball of dense, hot, glowing gases. Scientists tell us the temperatures on the surface of the sun approach 10,000 degrees.

Here and there on the surface of the sun are dark patches called *sun spots*. These change in size and appearance from year to year. It was a study of photographs of sun spots which brought about the discovery that the sun rotates on its axis from west to east.

The sun is about 93,000,000 miles from the earth, but this is not a great distance when we consider the vastness of space. For example, the next nearest star to us, after the sun, is almost 300,000 times as far from the earth as the sun. It is easier

now to understand why the huge stars appear at night as mere pinpoints of light.

The Source of All Energy. The most important thing to remember about the sun is that it is the source of all the energy and heat which are necessary for life on earth. The sun is made up of some of the same chemical substances we find on the earth. The sun is so hot that these substances exist only in the form of glowing gases. Over the centuries there have been many different explanations given for the heat of the sun.

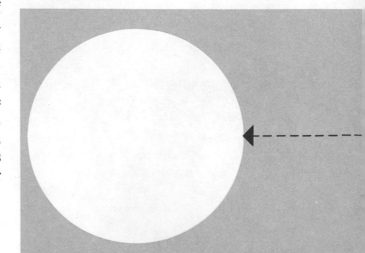

Because of its great distance, however, it has been impossible to learn much about the sun. Only by the use and improvement of telescopes and other instruments have we gradually built up our store of solar information.

Scientists who study the skies are called *astronomers*. Today most astronomers believe the heat of the sun is produced by the energy given off during changes in the structure of atoms within the sun. Just as the atom bomb gives off tremendous amounts of heat and light, so does the sun. Even though the sun is so far away from the earth, its energy reaches us in the forms of heat and light. If God had not created the sun, the earth would be cold and dark. Just the right amounts of heat and light from the sun make life on earth possible.

The Planets. A *planet* is one of the major bodies of the solar system. There are nine planets. Each planet travels in its own orbit around the sun. The four planets closest to the sun are Mercury (nearest to the sun), then Venus, Earth, and Mars. These four planets are bodies composed of solid materials. Beyond Mars are Jupiter, Saturn, Uranus, Neptune, and Pluto (farthest from the sun). These five planets are made up mostly of gas, with perhaps a solid core.

Millions of miles of space separate the Earth from Mercury, Venus, Mars, Jupiter and Saturn. Even so, these planets can be seen with the naked eye. The other planets are too far away from the Earth to be seen without a powerful telescope.

Planets give off light, of course, or we couldn't see them at all. However, they do not shine with their own light, since they are not burning masses like the stars. Planets can be seen in the night sky only because their surfaces reflect the sun's light. If we were standing on another distant body in space, we could look out into the heavens and see our own earth shining brightly. It would not be shining with its own light, but with light from the sun which it reflects.

Ancient people recognized that planets were different from stars. They noticed that the planets changed their positions among the constellations of stars. The ancient Greeks gave them the name "planet," which means *wanderer*. The planets revolve in orbits about the sun. They change their position among the stars from season to season.

The farther a planet's orbit is from the sun, the more slowly it appears to move across the sky. Thus, the planets which are farther away from the sun take much longer to complete their journey around the sun than those which are nearer. There is plenty of space—millions of miles—between the different planets, so there are no collisions. There are really very few large masses like the planets, and they are widely separated.

If the sun were this size, the earth would be a mere dot 13.4 feet away.

DISTANCE=13.4 FT.

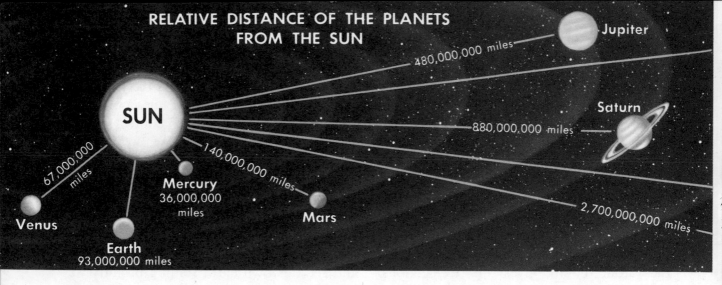

RELATIVE DISTANCE OF THE PLANETS
FROM THE SUN

Jupiter
480,000,000 miles

SUN

Saturn
880,000,000 miles

67,000,000 miles

140,000,000 miles

2,700,000,000 miles

Mercury
36,000,000
miles

Mars

Venus

Earth
93,000,000 miles

Innermost Planets. Mercury is a small planet, so near to the sun that it takes only three of our months to travel around the sun. The air we breathe on earth is called the *atmosphere*. Mercury has no atmosphere, so it is unlikely that any forms of life known to us exist there. Our life depends on the air we breathe.

Venus, a beautiful, bright planet, comes closer to the earth than any other. It is nearly as large as the earth, and it seems to be covered with a cloudy atmosphere. About every nineteen months Venus is in a position to shine in our evening sky. It is usually visible for a period of three or four months. It gleams brilliantly white, almost

as bright as the moon. Then we call it the "evening star."

At other times Venus shines in the morning sky—the beautiful "morning star" that comes before the dawn. The word "star" is used here only in its popular sense, of course, since Venus is actually a planet.

Our earth is the third planet in distance outward from the sun. Mars, the fourth, is a rather bright planet which shines with a reddish glow. It can often be seen in the evening sky. It seems to have a thin atmosphere and a little water on its surface.

There are ice caps at the poles of Mars which grow larger in the Martian winter, smaller in summer. Mars and Venus are

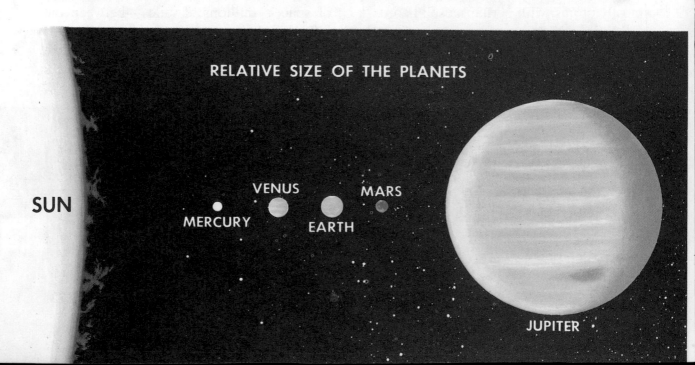

RELATIVE SIZE OF THE PLANETS

SUN

VENUS

MARS

MERCURY

EARTH

JUPITER

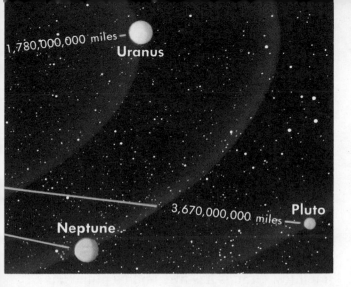

1,780,000,000 miles — Uranus

3,670,000,000 miles — Pluto

Neptune

Outermost Planets. Jupiter, although it is far away from us, can easily be seen in the sky because of its size. The ancient peoples of the world knew this great planet and named it after the king of their pagan gods because of its great size.

Jupiter is the largest planet, many times the size of the Earth. This planet, viewed in the telescope, appears purplish white. Much of its bulk is thought to be made up of dense gases, with perhaps a rocky core at the center.

Saturn, when viewed without a telescope, looks like a reddish pin-point of light. In a telescope it appears as a reddish globe circled by beautiful rings. Its surface is probably composed of a cloud of dense vapor. The rings are believed to be formed by millions of tiny pieces of rock and metal, held in place by the planet's force of gravity. Some astronomers say these rings are satellites, or moons, "in the making."

The beauty and perfection of this magnificent ringed globe in the heavens gives praise to God's glory. As the Bible says, "The heavens declare the glory of God."

Uranus, Neptune, and Pluto are so far away from earth that they can be seen only with a telescope. We know little about them.

the only two planets, besides the Earth, which seem to have atmosphere and temperatures suitable for some forms of life. There is, however, no proof that life exists on either of these planets.

God may of course create life on other planets if He chooses. However, among the millions of heavenly bodies very few seem to be suitable for life. Every detail on our planet is delicately and perfectly arranged to keep us safe and to feed and shelter us. This state of affairs is no accident. The more we learn of God's world through scientific discoveries, the more we appreciate the majesty, power and wisdom of God, bringing order to all Creation.

SATURN

URANUS

NEPTUNE

PLUTO

Pieces of a Broken Planet. These planetoids, too numerous to count in this picture, may be fragments of a planet once between Mars and Jupiter.

The Planetoids. Besides the nine planets, astronomers have discovered over 1500 small planet-like bodies which they call *planetoids*. Planetoids, like the planets, revolve about the sun in fixed orbits, or paths. They are too small and too far from the earth to be seen with the naked eye, but many of them have been photographed and charted by means of high-powered telescopes.

The planetoids are not scattered throughout the solar system. Most of them revolve in orbits located between the orbits of Mars and Jupiter. Some astronomers believe that another planet may once have existed between Mars and Jupiter. They believe it may have broken up, and that the broken fragments became planetoids which continued revolving around the sun. More and more planetoids are being discovered each year with the aid of new and more powerful telescopes.

Satellites. Just as the planets move in orbits around the sun, satellites revolve in orbits around most of the planets. They travel with them around the sun. There are about thirty-one satellites in the solar system. The two innermost planets, Mercury and Venus, have no satellites, and none have yet been discovered around Pluto.

The moon is the Earth's satellite. It has a diameter of over 2,000 miles, and revolves in an orbit around the earth, about a quarter of a million miles away.

Mars has two tiny satellites revolving about it, each less than 15 miles in diameter. Jupiter, the largest planet, has twelve satellites. Four of them are as large or larger than our moon. Saturn has nine satellites, Uranus has five, and Neptune has two. Some of these satellites have only been discovered in very recent years with the aid of powerful telescopes. More may yet be found by the astronomers as they continue to search the heavens.

Man-made Satellites. On October 4, 1957, Russian scientists fired *Sputnik I* out into space by means of a powerful rocket. The rocket carried this man-made satellite far out into space, where it went into an orbit around the earth. It was held for some time by the same forces—centrifugal and gravity — that keep the moon revolving about the earth and the planets about the sun. *Sputnik I* remained in orbit for three months before it was burned up by the friction of the atmosphere as it fell toward the earth's surface.

Since then, the "race for space", especially between the Soviet Union and the United States of America, has absorbed the attention of people all over the world. Many different kinds of space shots have been fired, and many satellites have been placed into orbit around the earth and around the sun.

Most spectacular, however, have been the "manned" orbital shots, in which American and Russian astronauts have ridden in capsules placed in orbit around the earth by high-powered rockets. As man learns more and more about space, the time when he can land on the moon comes closer and closer.

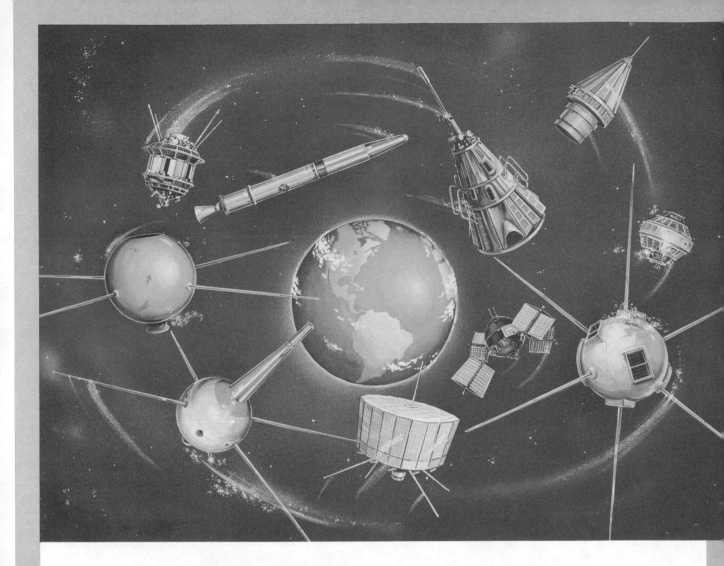

WORLDWIDE COMMUNICATIONS

In 1962, scientists in the Bell Telephone Laboratories designed and built an amazing satellite, *Telstar*. This was the world's first communication satellite, launched from Cape Kennedy on July 10, 1962. *Telstar* can relay many kinds of information from the United States to countries in Europe. For example, a newspaper in New York City can transmit text for its foreign edition in Paris, via *Telstar*, at about the rate of 60,000 words in one hour. Previously, it could transmit only 36 words in one hour!

Early Bird, a United States TV satellite, and *Molniya*, Russia's satellite, were both launched in 1965. These two satellites opened up a new era of worldwide communication. The European television network became connected with the American system for the first time. Millions of people in North America and Europe were united in a cultural, news, and educational exchange.

These satellites also serve other useful purposes. *Early Bird* has made it possible for the Royal Canadian Mounted Police, Scotland Yard in London, and the FBI in the United States to exchange important information concerning criminal activity throughout the world.

The United States, the Soviet Union, and other nations of the world plan a cooperative program for further research and development of these wonderful satellites.

In 1966, America launched *Lunar Orbiter I*. It relayed lunar shots back to earth. The Russian *Lunar II* was launched on August 24, 1966.

Meteor "Showers." Sometimes in August, September, and December there are enough "shooting stars" to make astronomers call them *meteor showers*.

Other Solar System Bodies. Many small bodies composed of iron, nickel, and other minerals drift about in space. Some of these are no larger than a grain of sand; others are very sizable chunks of matter. They are called *meteors*. Those which get close enough to the earth are pulled towards it at great speed by the force of gravity. As these swiftly-moving bodies come into our

A Good Look at a Meteorite. This young girl is inspecting a meteorite. Very seldom does a meteor escape burning up before it strikes the earth.

atmosphere, they begin to heat up by friction and soon turn white hot. They reach such high temperatures that most of them burn up before reaching the earth's surface. You have probably seen them shooting across the sky and mistakingly called them "falling stars." Sometimes large numbers of meteors appear in the sky. This occurs most often in the months of August, October, and December. Astronomers call them meteoric showers.

Occasionally, larger meteors reach the earth's surface without completely burning up in the atmosphere. These explode on striking the surface of the earth and the large chunks bury themselves deep in the ground. They are called *meteorites*. Meteorites are rock-like in structure with varying amounts of iron and nickel in them.

The most mysterious of all the bodies of the solar system are the comets. In some parts of the world they are treated with superstition and fear. Comets are bodies, smaller in size than the planets, which travel in long, oval orbits around the sun. Only occasionally do their orbits bring them anywhere near the earth. When a comet gets close enough to the earth to be

Halley's Comet. Looking somewhat like a star with a long fiery tail, this famous body was last seen in 1910, and will appear again in 1986.

seen, it looks like a star with a long, bright tail.

Some comets come back regularly, while others are seen only once and never return. Halley's Comet approaches the earth every 76 years. Its last appearance was in 1910 and its next one will be in 1986.

Other Solar Systems. Many astronomers believe other solar systems may exist. Some of the billions of stars in the universe may be surrounded by a family of planets as our sun is. But this they cannot prove, at any rate not with the instruments now in use.

The earth is so distant from the other stars it is impossible to see planets that may revolve around them. Remember that planets are not seen by their own light but only by light they reflect. This reflected light is dim by comparison with the light of the stars themselves.

A Visitor's Orbit. In this diagram, you can trace the path of Halley's Comet as it crossed the orbit of the earth in its last appearance.

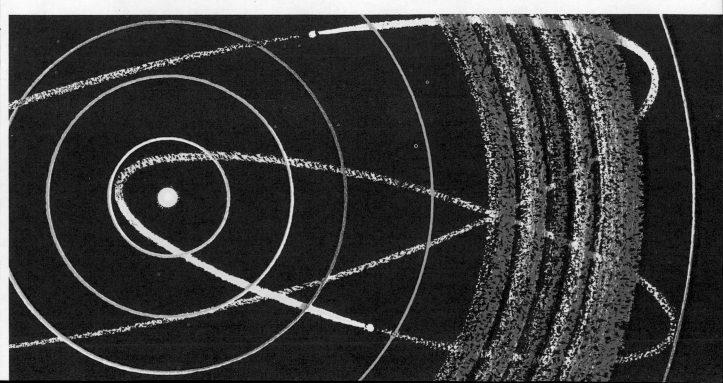

Facts *to remember*

1. The sun is the center of the Solar System. It controls the movement of the planets, planetoids, satellites, comets, and meteors which revolve about it.

2. The surface of the sun is very hot. It gives off energy, in the forms of heat and light, which travels through space for millions of miles. Some of this energy falls on the earth's surface. It is necessary for life on earth.

3. The planets, in order of their distance from the sun, are: Mercury, Venus, Earth, Mars, Jupiter, Saturn, Uranus, Neptune, Pluto. Scientists still have much to learn about the more distant planets.

4. Planetoids are small, planet-like bodies which revolve about the sun. Their orbit is between the orbits of Mars and Jupiter. Over 1500 planetoids have been discovered.

5. The moon is the earth's satellite. All the planets except Mercury, Venus, and Pluto have satellites. Jupiter has the most satellites—twelve.

6. Man has recently made small satellites, some of which have been sent into space by rockets. Some of these man-made American satellites are: *Explorer I, VI,* and *VII; Vanguard I, II,* and *III;* and *Tiros I.* A Russian satellite, called *Sputnik III,* is in orbit around the earth, also.

7. Meteors are small masses of rock and metal drifting about in space. When they come close enough to the earth they are pulled toward it by gravity. Most of them burn up when they enter the earth's atmosphere. Some, however, have struck the surface of the earth. They are called *meteorites.*

8. Comets have long glowing tails. They travel around the sun and are seen only when they come close to the earth. The best known is Halley's Comet which is seen every 76 years.

9. There may be many other solar systems besides ours. However, we do not know that any other stars have planets in orbit around them. They are all too far away for us to see details such as orbiting planets with our present telescopes.

What *have I learned?*

I

Complete each of the following sentences, choosing the correct word or words in the parenthesis.

1. Scientists who study the skies are called (geologists, astrologers, astronomers).

2. (Jupiter, Venus, Mars) is nearest in size to the earth.

3. (Planetoids, meteorites, galaxies) revolve about the sun in fixed orbits.

4. The planet with the greatest number of satellites revolving around it is (Jupiter, Mars, Saturn).

5. (Meteorites, stars, comets) travel in long oval orbits around the sun, occasionally coming close enough to the earth to be seen.

II

Number your paper from 1 to 15. Copy the items in column A. After each one, write the matching item from Column B.

A	B
1. Mercury	largest planet
2. Venus	planet with conditions most like the earth
3. Earth	man-made
4. Mars	farthest planet
5. Jupiter	planet that comes nearest to the earth
6. Saturn	third in distance from sun
7. Pluto	earth's satellite
8. Sun	smallest planet
9. Planetoids	long glowing tail
10. Meteor	beautiful rings
11. Comet	sometimes called a "falling star"
12. *Sputnik I*	planet-like body
13. Moon	explodes when it strikes earth's surface
14. Orbit	Center of solar system
15. Meteorite	path of a planet

Facts *to understand*

Give one reason in a complete sentence for each of the following statements.

1. Planets remain in their orbits around the sun.

2. Planets can be distinguished from stars in the night sky.

3. Man could not live without the sun.

4. Man-made satellites are important to us.

5. Meteors burn in the earth's atmosphere.

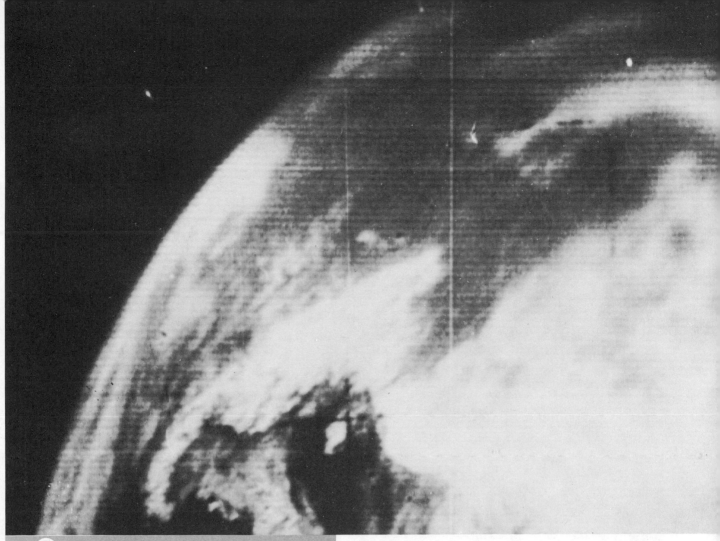

3 The Earth in Space

Picture of the Earth. This is the Mediterranean area, photographed by an American satellite called *Tiros I*, from a height of 450 miles.

For many reasons, our planet seems to have an ideal position in the family of the sun. Of the nine planets, the earth is third in order of distance from the sun. It gets, therefore, neither too much nor too little of the sun's energy. The earth does not have the searing heat nor the intense cold which astronomers have estimated on some of the other planets.

Of all the planets, the earth seems to be the only one that has an atmosphere containing oxygen. *Oxygen* is a chemical element vital to life as we know it on earth. Also, our planet seems to be the only one which has oceans. Moisture from the oceans forms the clouds which bring rain over the land, and this also is vital to life as we know it.

Without the correct amounts of heat and light, oxygen and moisture, no forms of life can exist, as far as we can now tell. The earth, then, seems to be the only planet which has the proper conditions suitable for man to live and work.

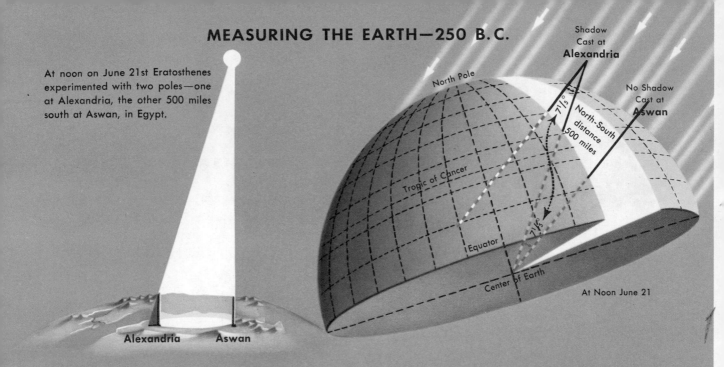

MEASURING THE EARTH—250 B.C.

At noon on June 21st Eratosthenes experimented with two poles—one at Alexandria, the other 500 miles south at Aswan, in Egypt.

Shadow Cast at **Alexandria**

No Shadow Cast at **Aswan**

North Pole

North-South distance 500 miles

Tropic of Cancer

Equator

Center of Earth

At Noon June 21

Alexandria   Aswan

At ALEXANDRIA the pole cast a shadow. Eratosthenes measured the angle of the shadow. It was 7 1/5°.

At ASWAN the pole cast no shadow. This was because the sun was straight overhead.

So Eratosthenes concluded that since the angle of the shadow was 7 1/5° and a whole circle has 360°, it was 1/50 of a circle. If 1/50 of a circle is 500 miles, the whole circle or globe would be 500 miles x 50 or 25,000.

Mathematicians know that these angles are always the same on June 21st.

Today, scientists with their exact and delicate instruments measure the circumference of the earth and say it is 24,899 miles.

24,899 miles

The Planet Earth. Like the rest of the planets, the earth is shaped like a ball. First-hand proof of the shape of the earth is now being supplied by photographs taken in space. These are made by radio cameras sent to great heights above the earth in rockets.

The diameter of the earth (distance through the center) is about 8,000 miles. The circumference of the earth (distance around) is about 25,000 miles. To understand how the size of the earth was first measured read the picture story above.

The earth's core, or center portion, is believed to be composed of nickel and iron kept very hot by high pressure. On the outside of the earth, there is a solid crust, or shell, about 35 miles thick. This crust extends even under the deep oceans. Hot gases and melted rocks exist in pockets within the earth's crust. Sometimes they explode from open volcanoes or ooze forth from cracks in the shell. These cracks are often opened by earthquakes.

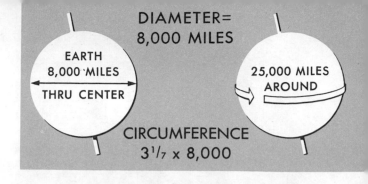

DIAMETER= 8,000 MILES

EARTH
8,000 MILES
THRU CENTER

25,000 MILES
AROUND

CIRCUMFERENCE
3¹/₇ x 8,000

The Axis and Rotation. Many years ago most people who looked up at the sun thought that it moved while the earth stood still. In fact, we usually say, out of habit, that the sun "rises" and "sets." Actually, the sun is still, and the earth is turning. This is what makes the sun appear to rise in the east and set in the west.

The *axis* is an imaginary line through the center of the earth, and about which the earth spins. It extends from the North Pole through to the South Pole. The axis is tilted about 23½ degrees from an upright position. This tilt is called the *inclination* of the earth's axis, and its effect upon life on the earth will be taken up later.

Remember that the north end of the axis is called the North Pole and the south end the South Pole. The North Pole of the axis always points in the direction of the North Star.

The imaginary circle drawn like a belt around the earth midway between the poles is called the *equator*. The equator divides the earth into the Northern and Southern Hemispheres. A *hemisphere* means half of a sphere, or of a ball.

The spinning motion of the earth on its axis is called *rotation*. The earth rotates from west to east. It makes one complete rotation on its axis in every twenty-four hour period. This determines the length of a day. Rotation of the earth makes the sun seem to rise over the horizon every morning and set below it every evening. Remember, however, that the earth travels around the sun—not the sun around the earth.

THE EARTH'S ROTATION

The spin of the earth on its axis causes day and night.

Night on this side of the earth.

Dusk or twilight.

Day on this side of the earth.

Equator

SUN

Star Trails. When a camera is aimed at the sky at night and a time exposure taken, this picture results; it proves the earth's rotation.

Proofs of Rotation. How can we prove the earth rotates on its axis? Perhaps you have played "Crack the Whip" on skates. If so, you noticed that the child at the end of the "whip" traveled faster than one closer to the center. The reason is that the one at the outer end was farther from the center than the one cracking the whip. The

same thing applies to the rotating earth. A point on the outside surface of the earth moves faster than a point near the center. It travels a greater distance in the same amount of time.

For example, a person who drops something from the roof of a very high building discovers that it does not fall to a point exactly below. It tends to fall a little toward the east. The reason is that the roof of the building, which is farther from the center of the earth, is traveling slightly faster from west to east than the ground is. If the earth were not rotating, objects would fall to a point directly below the point from which they were dropped.

At night, if we focus a camera on the North Star and take a time exposure of the sky, a very surprising picture results. Instead of the stars appearing as points of light, they appear as curved circles of light. In order to have made such a picture, either one of two things would have to be true: either the stars were moving across the sky, or the earth was turning under the stars. We have already learned that the stars maintain a fixed position. Therefore the circles of light in our picture (called *star trails*) are another proof that the earth rotates on its axis.

Day and Night. Since the half of the earth turned toward the sun is always lighted by the rays of the sun, the other half turned away from the sun is in darkness. Thus if the earth did not rotate, the sun would always shine on the same part of the earth, where there would always be daylight. The other part would always have darkness or night.

The rotation of the earth also determines the length of our day. If the earth rotated either more rapidly or more slowly it would make our day shorter or longer than it is now.

Revolution Around the Sun. The movement of the earth around its axis is called *rotation*. The forward motion of the earth in its orbit around the sun is called *revolution*. One complete revolution of the earth around the sun is called a *year*. One revolution of the earth takes 365¼ days. We make a year consist of 365 even days. Every fourth year, called a *leap year,* has 366 days.

The revolution of the earth takes it through all the different positions in its orbit. This partly accounts for the unequal length of day and night and the change of the seasons. However, revolution alone would not give us unequal day and night, nor a regular change of seasons.

If the earth's axis were not inclined, or tilted, the sun's rays would always reach from North Pole to South Pole. Days and nights would then be equal in length all over the world. There would always be twelve hours of darkness and twelve hours of daylight everywhere. It is the inclination of the axis, together with revolution, that causes days and nights to vary in length and brings about a change of seasons on the earth. In addition, the North Pole always points to the North Star. See the diagram of revolution below.

THE EARTH'S REVOLUTION
THE SWING OF THE EARTH AROUND THE SUN CAUSES THE CHANGING SEASONS

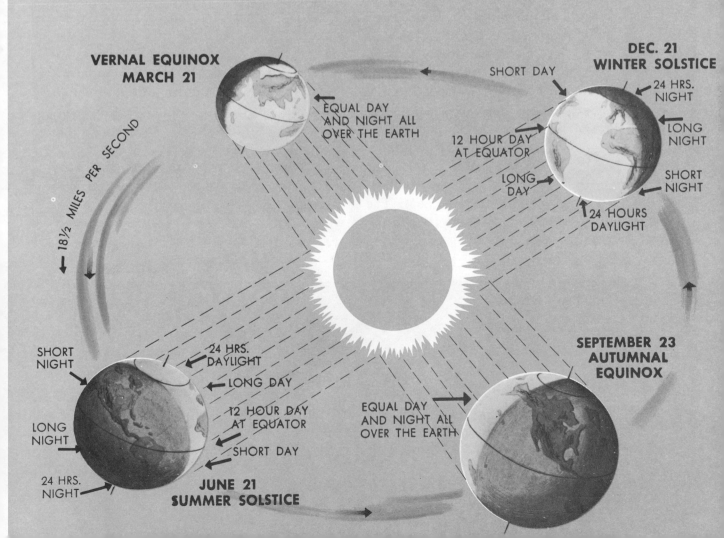

VERNAL EQUINOX MARCH 21
EQUAL DAY AND NIGHT ALL OVER THE EARTH

18½ MILES PER SECOND

DEC. 21 WINTER SOLSTICE
SHORT DAY
24 HRS. NIGHT
LONG NIGHT
12 HOUR DAY AT EQUATOR
LONG DAY
SHORT NIGHT
24 HOURS DAYLIGHT

SHORT NIGHT
24 HRS. DAYLIGHT
LONG DAY
12 HOUR DAY AT EQUATOR
LONG NIGHT
SHORT DAY
24 HRS. NIGHT
JUNE 21 SUMMER SOLSTICE

SEPTEMBER 23 AUTUMNAL EQUINOX
EQUAL DAY AND NIGHT ALL OVER THE EARTH

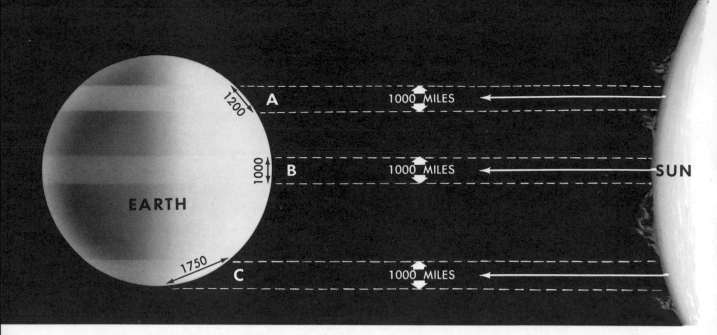

The Sun's Rays Striking the Earth. The rays of the sun which are striking the earth straight on cover a smaller area and deliver more heat.

The Angle of the Sun's Rays. The sun's rays are almost parallel to each other as they strike the earth's surface. However, the earth's surface is curved, and the rays hit different parts of the surface at different angles. Look at the diagram on this page. The rays of the sun that strike the earth's surface almost straight on deliver more heat because they cover a smaller area. The slanting rays are spread out over a larger area and therefore deliver less heat. The diagram on this page also shows why areas of the earth receiving vertical rays are warmer than areas receiving slanting rays.

As the earth revolves around the sun, the area on which the more vertical rays fall shifts from north to south, between the Tropic of Cancer and the Tropic of Capricorn. At the same time, the angle of the slanting rays is also changing. The diagram of the earth's revolution seen below shows how the rays of the sun shift north and south on the earth's surface as the earth moves forward in its orbit. This helps bring about the regular change of seasons.

Unequal Days and Nights. All places on the earth, except those located on the equator, have unequal days and nights. As we go north and south from the equator we find a greater and greater difference

June 21

between the length of day and the length of night. At the North Pole and the South Pole there are six months with the sun above the horizon and six months with the sun below the horizon. You may have heard it said that the poles have six months of day and six of night.

In the Northern Hemisphere the days are longer than the nights from March 21 to September 23. In the Southern Hemisphere the days are shorter during that same period. Throughout the Northern Hemisphere the greatest number of hours of daylight occurs on June 21.

In the Southern Hemisphere the days are longer than the nights from September 23 to March 21. In the Northern Hemisphere they are correspondingly shorter during this period. The greatest number of hours of daylight throughout the Southern Hemisphere occurs on December 21.

However, no matter where man lives on earth, he will have an hour of darkness in winter for every hour of daylight he has in summer. If his longest period of summer daylight is 18 hours in one day, his longest period of winter night will be 18 hours.

The Change of Seasons. Let us consider why our summer days are warmer than our winter days in the Northern Hemisphere. There are two reasons for this. During the summer in the Northern Hemisphere the sun's rays are more nearly vertical (at right angles to the earth). Therefore, the rays have a greater heating effect. In addition, the number of hours of sunlight is greater (day is longer than night). This helps to explain why we have our warmest weather from June to September.

During the winter in the Northern Hemisphere, the sun's rays are more slanting. Then they have less heating effect. In winter also, the number of hours of sunlight is less (night is longer than day). This explains why we have our coldest weather from December to March.

In the Southern Hemisphere the seasons are the reverse of those in the Northern Hemisphere. More slanting rays and shorter days occur from June to September (winter in the Southern Hemisphere). More nearly vertical rays and longer days occur from December to March (summer in the Southern Hemisphere).

Spring and Autumn occur when the vertical rays of the sun are nearer the equator, and days and nights are almost equal in length. The sun's energy is more or less evenly divided between Northern and Southern Hemispheres at this time. Almost all places in both hemispheres have in-between temperatures in Spring and Autumn.

Summer and Winter. The illustration below shows the position of the earth at two different times of the year. Notice where the seasons occur.

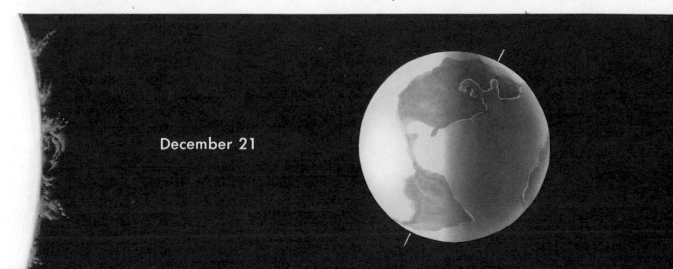

December 21

The Summer Solstice. The diagram on page 249 shows the position of the earth with respect to the sun on June 21. Notice that in this position the North Pole and the Northern Hemisphere are nearer the sun. The South Pole and the Southern Hemisphere are farther away from the sun.

The most direct rays of the sun (vertical rays) are shining directly on the Tropic of Cancer which is 23½ degrees north of the equator. June 21 is called the *summer solstice,* which means the "sun stand-still." The vertical rays go no farther toward the North Pole. They appear to stop at the Tropic of Cancer, and then move back toward the equator.

The more slanting rays of the sun pass 23½ degrees beyond the North Pole so that the entire region north of the Arctic Circle is lighted by the sun at the same time. Although the sunlight is continual, there is very little heat. The sun's rays strike this area at a wide slant.

In the Southern Hemisphere, on June 21, the rays of the sun extend only as far south as the Antarctic Circle. This means that the entire South Polar region south of the Antarctic circle is in darkness.

Land of the Midnight Sun. On June 21, when this picture was taken, the sun could still be seen shining at midnight over Advent Bay, Norway.

The Winter Solstice. The diagram on page 249 shows the position of the earth with respect to the sun on December 21. December 21 is called the *winter solstice.* Notice that in this position the South Pole and the Southern Hemisphere are nearer the sun. This time the North Pole and the Northern Hemisphere are farther away from the sun. The North Pole, however, continues to point toward the North Star, which is to the upper right of this diagram.

The vertical rays of the sun are now shining directly on the Tropic of Capricorn, which is 23½ degrees south of the equator. On December 21 the vertical rays go no farther toward the South Pole. They appear to stop and then begin to move back toward the equator.

The slanting rays of the sun pass 23½ degrees beyond the South Pole so that the entire region south of the Antarctic Circle is lighted by the sun at the same time. In the Northern Hemisphere on December 21 the rays of the sun extend only as far north as the Arctic Circle, so that the entire North Polar region is in darkness. This begins summer in the Southern Hemisphere and winter in the Northern Hemisphere.

The Equinoxes. The sun is directly over the Tropic of Cancer on June 21 and directly over the Tropic of Capricorn on December 23. On all the other days of the year the sun is directly overhead somewhere between the Tropic of Cancer and the Tropic of Capricorn.

On March 21 and September 23 the sun's vertical rays strike the equator and the slanting rays reach each pole. On these dates every place on the earth has exactly twelve hours of daylight and twelve hours of darkness. That is why March 21 and September 23 are called *equinoxes,* which means equal nights. Of course, if the nights are equal, then the days are equal, too.

The Earth's Satellite. The earth has one satellite, the moon. The moon is not very large, and does not have an atmosphere. On any body in space, gravity is a strong or weak force depending on the size of the body. Only a very large body, like the earth, has enough gravity to hold the light gases which make up an atmosphere.

No water, no air, no wind, no erosion, and no life exist on the moon. Mountains and craters stand high and bare in the light of the sun on one side, and in the cold darkness on the other.

The Cold and Lifeless Moon. Earth's satellite has always fascinated and puzzled mankind. We know now that there is no life on this airless body.

The moon makes only one complete rotation on its axis while it revolves once around the earth. Therefore, the moon always presents the same side toward us as it revolves about our earth. We have never seen its other side. Recently, however, an earth satellite launched by the Russians, *Lunik III,* photographed the far side of the moon and radioed the photo back.

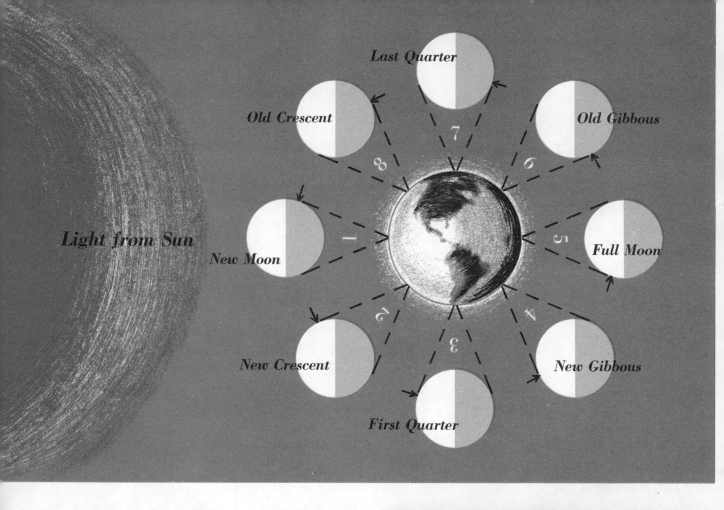

Last Quarter

Old Crescent

Old Gibbous

Light from Sun

New Moon

Full Moon

New Crescent

New Gibbous

First Quarter

The Phases of the Moon.

The moon revolves in its orbit around the earth, completing its journey in approximately twenty eight days. In fact, the word "month" comes from the word "moon." The measure of time which we call a month really means the approximate time from one "moon" to another. Savage tribes and civilized nations alike use this measure in some form or other.

When the moon is on the same side of the earth as the sun, none of the moon can be seen from the earth. This is because the dark side of the moon is turned toward the earth. This phase is called *new moon*. As the moon moves forward in its orbit, a small part of the lighted portion becomes visible. The visible portion grows larger until we can see half of the lighted part, which is really one fourth of the entire

Last Quarter

Phases of the Moon as Seen from the Earth

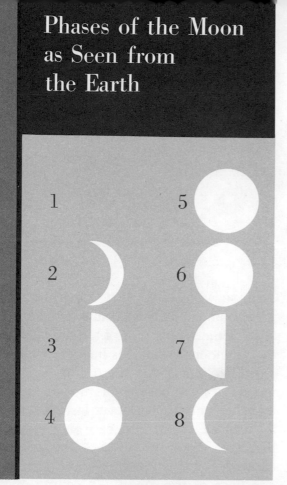

moon. This is called the *first quarter phase* and occurs about a week after the new moon. The lighted portion continues to grow larger until we can see the entire lighted part of the moon from the earth. This is called the *full moon phase*, and it takes place about two weeks after the new moon phase.

After the full moon we begin to see less and less of the lighted portion until once again only one half of the lighted part is visible to us on the earth. This is called the *last quarter phase*. About three weeks have passed since the new moon. Now the lighted portion seen from the earth continues to grow smaller and finally only a thin crescent is visible. The crescent soon disappears and once again we are at a new moon phase in about four weeks.

The Phases of the Moon. These photographs show how the moon appears during its various phases. Notice the rugged surface, craters, and valleys.

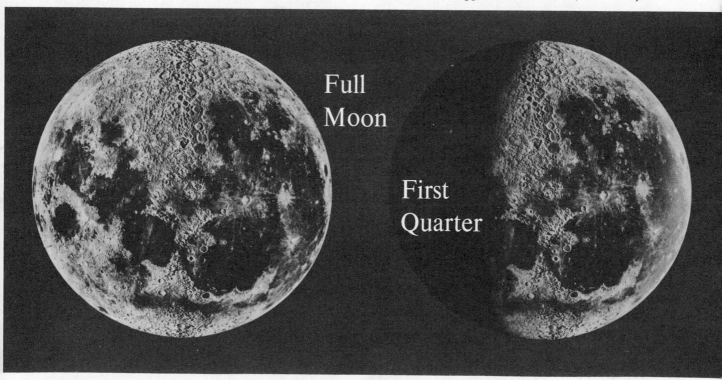

Full Moon

First Quarter

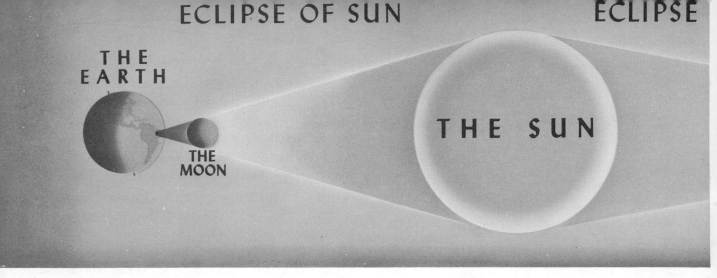

THE EARTH

THE MOON

THE SUN

Eclipse of the Sun and of the Moon. The diagram shows what happens in a total eclipse of the sun (left), and an eclipse of the moon (right).

Eclipse of the Sun. As the moon revolves around the earth, it sometimes gets directly between the earth and the sun. When this happens the moon blocks off sunlight and the shadow of the moon is cast on a small part of the earth's surface. The people on the earth who are in this shadow cannot see the sun because the moon is in the way. This is called an *eclipse* of the sun.

When the light of the sun is entirely blocked out we say that the eclipse is total. During a total eclipse of the sun it becomes almost as dark as night for the people in the eclipse area. Even the stars become visible. However, the total eclipse area on the earth is very small. It is only on very rare occasions that we are located in this area, so we get very few opportunities to witness an eclipse of the sun.

Sometimes only part of the sun is hidden by the moon. When this happens we say a *partial eclipse* of the sun occurs. Since the moon is a small body and is moving rapidly, an eclipse of the sun never lasts very long. An eclipse of the sun can only occur at the new moon phase. See the diagram above to find why this is so.

Eclipse of the Moon. An eclipse of the moon may also occur. At the full moon phase the moon is on the opposite side of the earth from the sun. When the shadow cast by the earth falls upon the lighted part of the moon an eclipse of the moon takes place. Sometimes only a part of the lighted portion of the moon falls into the shadow cast by the earth. When this happens, the people on the earth see a partial eclipse of the moon.

A total eclipse of the moon takes place when the entire lighted part of the moon falls into the shadow cast by the earth. Then none of the moon can be seen from the earth. People on the earth are much more likely to see an eclipse of the moon than an eclipse of the sun.

Astronomers can figure out exactly when eclipses will occur. We can find out for ourselves when to expect an eclipse by consulting an almanac.

Eclipse of the Sun. During the eclipse, all we can see of the sun is this brightness at its edge. It is the sun's *corona*, a Latin word for crown.

THE EARTH

THE MOON

Facts *to remember*

1. The earth seems to be the only planet with conditions needed to support life. It is not too hot or cold, and has an atmosphere containing oxygen and water.

2. The earth is shaped like a ball. Its diameter is 8,000 miles. Its circumference is 25,000 miles.

3. The earth has two principal motions. It rotates on its axis once every 24 hours and revolves around the sun in an orbit once every year. Rotation causes day and night. Revolution causes unequal day and night and the change of seasons.

4. Vertical rays of the sun heat the earth more than slanting rays. This causes places near the equator to be warm and places near the poles to be cold.

5. The summer season occurs in any part of the earth when the sun's rays are almost vertical. It is winter when the sun's rays are most slanted.

6. As the moon revolves around the earth we see different portions of its lighted side. The portions we see are called the phases of the moon. When we see none of the lighted portion it is called new moon; when we see all of the lighted portion it is called full moon.

7. An eclipse of the moon occurs when it falls into the dark shadow that the earth casts into space. An eclipse of the sun occurs when the moon casts its shadow on a part of the earth.

What *have I learned?*

I

The word in italics in each sentence is right or wrong. If it is wrong, rewrite the sentence using the correct word.

1. The spinning motion of the earth on its axis is called *revolution*.

2. On June 21 the vertical rays of the sun are on the Tropic of *Capricorn*.

3. Days and nights are equal in length all over the earth on *March 21*.

4. During our *summer* season the Southern Hemisphere has long days and short nights.

5. A *lunar* eclipse occurs when the moon casts its shadow on the earth's surface.

6. The phases of the moon are caused by the *revolution* of the moon.

7. The most heat is delivered to the earth's surface by *vertical* rays.

8. The greatest differences between the length of day and night occurs at the *equator*.

9. When the moon is on the same side of the earth as the sun, it is *full* moon.

10. More people can see a *lunar* eclipse when it occurs than an eclipse of the sun.

II

Answer each of the following in a complete sentence.

1. Which star never changes its position in the night sky?

2. How much toward or away from the sun does the earth's axis tilt?

3. If the earth's axis were not tilted, what would you notice about the length of night and day?

4. Which part of the Northern Hemisphere never receives vertical rays of the sun?

5. How many days does it take for the earth to make one complete revolution of the sun?

Facts *to understand*

Give reasons for these statements.

1. Vertical rays heat the earth's surface more than slanting rays.

2. While the Northern Hemisphere is having its summer season, the Southern Hemisphere has its winter.

3. The sun appears to rise in the morning and set in the evening.

4. No life can exist on the moon.

5. The same side of the moon is always seen from the earth.

A Mapmaker looks at the Earth. Throughout history, men have been trying every means to represent the earth we live on by a flat picture, or *map*.

4 Mapping the Earth

It was the explorers who first took careful note of the shape of sea and land, rivers and mountains. They made measurements, wrote down what they saw, and drew maps for the use of those who followed them. Each generation of adventurers added a little more to the hard-won knowledge of those who went before. Adventure and map making went hand in hand.

The Global Earth. It was impossible to make correct maps of the earth until men knew its shape. Contrary to what most people think, Columbus was not the first man to believe that the earth is round.

In fact, five hundred years before Christ (which was two thousand years before Columbus), a learned Greek named Pythagoras discovered that the earth is a sphere. Possibly he had noted the round shadow on the moon at the time of an eclipse and decided that it must be the shadow of a global earth.

Aristotle, another famous Greek teacher, taught the same idea two hundred years after Pythagoras. He pointed out that certain stars which are above the horizon in Egypt were blocked from view in places farther north. Therefore, he reasoned, the earth's surface must be curved.

In the centuries that followed, other brilliant men including Pope Pius II, Copernicus, and Galileo taught that the earth is a sphere. Map makers began to work out arrangements by which the entire surface of the earth could be shown.

Maps Are a Problem. A map is a kind of picture made on a flat sheet showing all or some part of the earth's surface. Because the earth is a sphere, it is not easy to make such a map. Imagine the earth's surface as being like the skin of an orange, but vastly larger. To make a flat map of even half the earth would be like trying to take the skin of a half an orange and make it lie flat on a level surface such as a table top. It cannot be done unless the skin is torn in several places or stretched out of shape. The problem would even be greater in making a map of the whole earth. The illustration on this page shows one way it might be done.

Making good maps of smaller areas of the earth is somewhat easier, just as a smaller piece of the orange skin can be flattened more easily than a larger piece. That is why maps of smaller areas are always more accurate than maps of large parts of the earth's surface.

Whatever size the area to be mapped, however, the earth's surface is spherical everywhere and can never be drawn exactly true on a flat surface. A globe is the only truly accurate way to show the world. No flat map, even of a small area of the earth, can be perfect. Maps are necessary, however, for the following reasons: they are easier to work with and carry around than globes; they can give more detailed information about a certain part of the earth's surface than globes, which must be limited in size; they are cheaper to make and buy.

From Globe to Flat Map. This illustration shows one way to represent the round globe as a flat surface. Why is it not a very practical method?

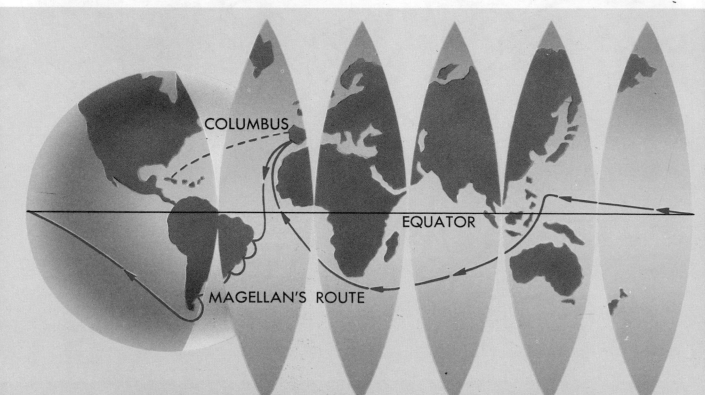

COLUMBUS

EQUATOR

MAGELLAN'S ROUTE

The Early Map Makers. We are often told that learning did not advance until modern times. Nothing could be further from the truth. For example, geographers of ancient times made maps of the world, as they knew it, that are almost as good as our modern maps.

The Greek Strabo wrote about the geography of those lands known to the Mediterranean peoples who lived about the time of Our Lord. In his writings can be found directions for making a globe. On the surface of a globe he drew a map of all the regions of the world then known and inhabited. He even gave directions for making a flat map with straight lines as parallels and meridians. Thus almost 2000 years ago, we had directions for maps almost the same as we use today! On Strabo's map of course, many areas were inaccurately

MAP MAKING AND EXPLORATION

Which came first, the map maker or the explorer? It is almost impossible to find the answer to this question. Map makers always depended upon explorers returning from long journeys to bring information about the lands and seas they had crossed. After hearing the travelers' accounts, the map makers would draw their maps according to the new

drawn or missing altogether. These areas, however, represented the parts of the world which had not yet been explored.

Almost 1500 years after Strabo's time, just after Columbus' discovery of America, Spanish ships began to sail to the New World for trade and business. The King of Spain hired a group of navigators to draw maps of the newly discovered lands and seas, coasts and harbors. The chief map maker was Amerigo Vespucci, who made several voyages to the New World Columbus discovered.

The two continents of the Western Hemisphere were named after Amerigo Vespucci rather than Columbus. This is because he was better known to the people of the time. His name appeared on the corner of every map he drew of the New World.

information they received.

Explorers, however, also depended upon the makers of maps and charts. They could not have journeyed far without trustworthy maps and charts to guide them. Columbus, sailing across an unknown ocean, depended on the charts of Spanish waters to get started in the right direction.

As more and more of the world became known, adventurers were encouraged to sail forth and find the unexplored places. In our time, brave men have gone to the frozen wastes of Antarctica to find out what they could about this unknown continent.

Explorers who go to Antarctica today are indebted to the men who went before them, recording the locations of bays, mountains, and other important features. They are indebted also to the map makers who patiently added details, little by little, to the maps of Antarctica. Quite often, these maps mean the difference between life and death to a man driving a snow tractor through a blizzard, or a pilot looking for his base.

Gerhard Kraemer, a Flemish map maker who called himself Mercator (Latin for merchant), drew a map in 1569, which is still used. He curled a piece of paper around the globe and marked off the equator and all the meridians as they cross the equator at right angles. He then marked off all the lines of latitude at right angles with the meridians. He then projected the land area from each section on the globe onto the equivalent rectangle on his map. As indicated on the globe and map opposite, the land masses were correct near the equator, but to the north and south, the land was increasingly distorted.

Look at Greenland on the map. Then find South America. Actually South America is about 10 times as large as Greenland, but on Mercator's map, Greenland appears to be much larger.

Mercator made Greenland look like this.

But Greenland is actually this size.

General Drafting Co., Inc.

Map Projections. Since the discovery of America and Magellan's voyage around the world, map makers have developed many different ways to show all or part of the earth on a flat surface. The different methods of showing the curved surface of the earth on a flat sheet are called *map projections*.

A good map projection should show shapes of lands and waters, distances between places, and directions, all as correctly as possible. As we have already learned, however, no flat map can do all of these things at the same time. Projections can be drawn to show true direction but not true shapes and distances. Others may show true shapes of continents but distances and directions will not be correct. Still others may give accurate shapes and distances. Such maps, however, are not continuous and use a scheme similar to the one shown on page 259.

As was stated before, flat maps of small areas can be made with greater accuracy than maps of larger areas. Map projections of various kinds are used throughout your geography book. Compare them with each other and with a large globe. Notice that there is more detail in a map of a small area.

Maps of the World. Gerhard Kraemer, a map maker of Germany, called himself Mercator, the Latin word for merchant. He drew and published a flat map of the world in 1569. The projection he developed is still widely used today, called the *Mercator projection*. A study of the diagram on this page will help you to understand the method used by Mercator to map the lands and water areas of the curved surface of the earth on a flat paper. Although the far

northern and far southern sections of a Mercator projection are drawn very much out of shape, it is still a very useful map. A Mercator projection shows the whole world (except the extreme polar regions) in one single flat map. It is very useful to navigators, because any straight line drawn on the map always shows true direction.

Since Mercator's time, many other kinds of map projections of the world have been worked out. Not one of them shows everything correctly. That is why we should always compare the map we are using with a globe or with other maps.

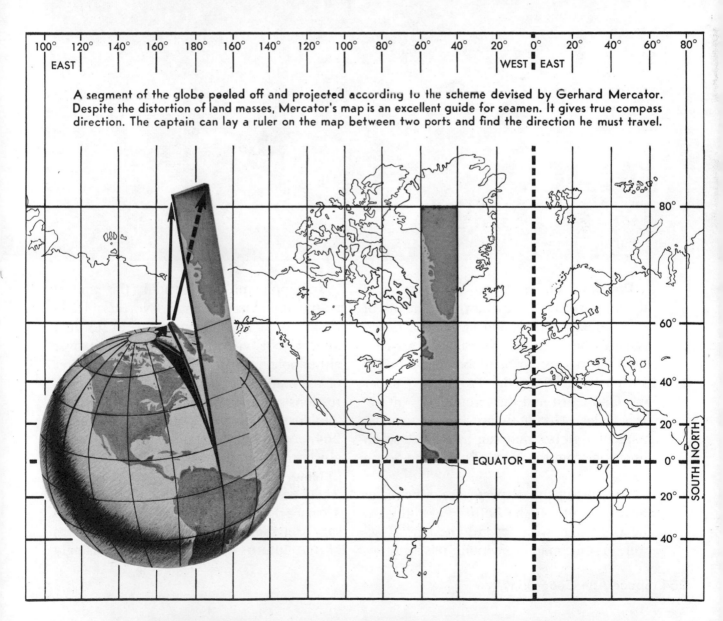

A segment of the globe peeled off and projected according to the scheme devised by Gerhard Mercator. Despite the distortion of land masses, Mercator's map is an excellent guide for seamen. It gives true compass direction. The captain can lay a ruler on the map between two ports and find the direction he must travel.

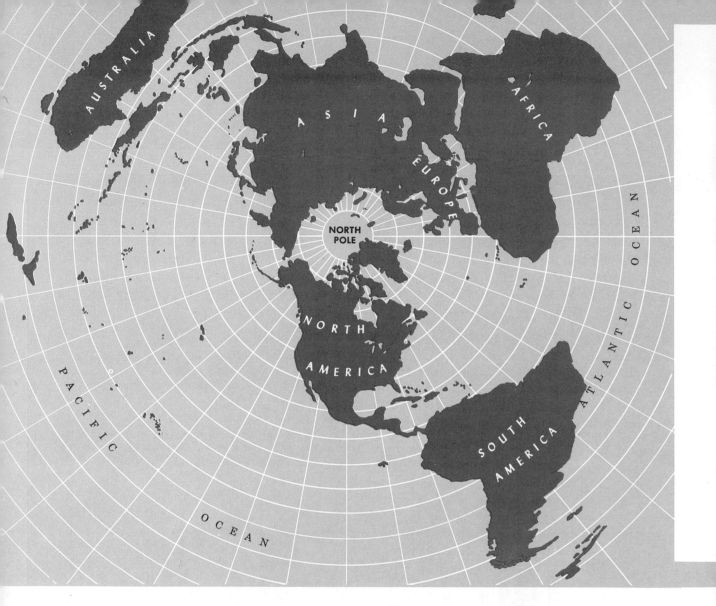

Direction on a Map. On maps and globes, directions are shown by means of lines called parallels and meridians. *Parallels* are the lines that run in an east-west direction on a map or globe. The equator is a parallel. So are the Tropics of Cancer and Capricorn and the Arctic and Antarctic Circles. *Meridians* are lines drawn on maps and globes that run in a north-south direction from the North Pole to the South Pole.

On most of the maps we use, north is at the top; south at the bottom; east toward the right and west toward the left. However, in some map projections, this is not so.

In a polar projection map (the kind of map that pictures either the Northern Hemisphere or Southern Hemisphere as it would appear to a viewer far off in space over either pole), north or south is at the center of the map. East and west are opposite directions along the meridians. By studying the North polar projection shown on page 264, you will understand why north is not always at the top of a map.

New Maps for a New World. Today, when we are passing from an "air age" to a "space age," new kinds of maps are necessary. Jet planes, rockets, and space ships of the future will travel at increasingly

POLAR PROJECTION

The unusual map on the opposite page is often called a *polar projection*. This means that the North Pole is at the center of the map, the meridians extend out from it like spokes from the hub of a wheel, and the parallels appear as circles. Map makers refer to it by its exact name—*polar equidistant map*. It is called this because all distances measured from the North Pole are shown correctly.

On a polar equidistant map, a person could draw a straight line from the North Pole, at the center of the map, to any other point on the map. The line would represent a "great circle"—the shortest distance always between any two points on the globe. By referring to the scale of miles, the true distance between the pole and the other point could then be measured.

Today, many airline flights in the Northern Hemisphere cross the Arctic Circle. Lay your ruler on the map in a straight line between the west coast of North America and the North Pole. Measure the distance in inches. Now turn the ruler and measure a straight line from the North Pole to the Mediterranean area of Europe. The sum of the two straight lines represents, approximately, the great circle route between San Francisco and Rome. Now trace with your finger the route a plane would take if it flew across the United States east from San Francisco, then across the Atlantic Ocean, and through the Mediterranean to Rome. This is the route we might ordinarily expect a plane to take, but you can see how much longer it is than the great circle route across the Arctic region.

Equidistant maps can also be made which show true distances from other points as well as the North Pole. For example, this kind of projection might be drawn with Washington, D.C., at its center. Then, a straight line drawn from Washington to any other point on the map would represent the great circle route between Washington and that point. The exact, shortest distance between them could easily be measured. Can you see why the airlines especially are making use of this kind of map?

Mercator Projections are still in use today, mostly by seafaring people, because they show true compass direction. However, many other new and interesting maps, like the polar projection, are now being used. It is necessary for astronomers, geographers, engineers and other map users keep developing better and better maps.

greater speeds from one part of the world to another. They may even travel from the earth to another part of the universe.

We have found during the present air age that the shapes of land and water areas and the positions of harbors are not so important as they once were. For example, it is unnecessary for an airplane to travel around the edges of a continent to arrive at its destination. Instead it flies directly from place to place using the shortest possible way. Such a route is called "a great circle route" because it follows the curved surface of the earth. It is the shortest distance between any two points on the earth's surface. A *great circle* is any line on a sphere drawn around its widest part. Longitude lines, for example, are great circles.

Map projections which show true distances between places on the earth's surface are being used more and more. In addition to the mercator projection and the other kinds of maps in our geography books, we need maps like the Air Age map opposite. Straight lines always show "the great circle routes" airplanes now use in traveling to distant parts of the earth. Distances which once were measured in thousands of miles and weeks of travel are now measured in mere hours of flying time.

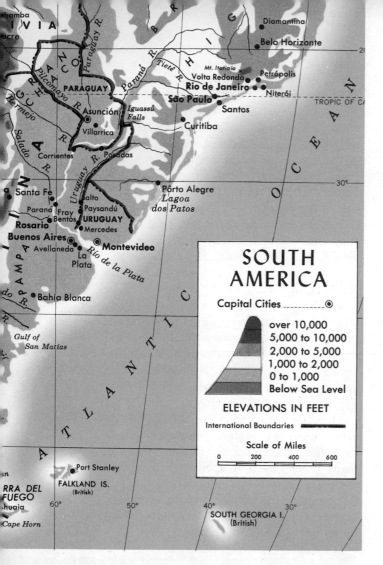

SOUTH AMERICA

Capital Cities .... ◎

over 10,000
5,000 to 10,000
2,000 to 5,000
1,000 to 2,000
0 to 1,000
Below Sea Level

ELEVATIONS IN FEET

International Boundaries ━━━━

Scale of Miles

0   200   400   600

Map Skills. It is more important than ever for us to learn how to use maps. We have been learning how to get information from maps since we began studying geography several years ago. Let us review some of these map skills and, in addition, develop some new ones.

Maps are much, much smaller than the parts of the earth's surface they represent. To give an accurate picture of size and distance, a map must be drawn *to scale*. The map scale compares the distance on a map with the actual distance on the earth. The larger the scale used, the larger each feature appears on the map. Maps of the world or of large sections of the earth's surface

must therefore be drawn to a smaller scale than maps of a country, a region, or a state. If not, the world map would be so huge it would be clumsy to use.

The scale to which a map is drawn can usually be found in the map key or legend. This is a special box somewhere along the margin of the map. Check several of the maps in this geography and find the scale of miles in the legend for each. It should always be studied before a new map is used.

On physical maps the legend also shows how different colors, ranging from greens to brownish-reds, show elevation. Dark green to lighter green to yellow indicate surface elevations from below sea level to about 2000 feet. Light brown to darker browns show elevations between 2000 and 10,000 feet. Reddish-brown indicates the highest elevations on a physical map, those over 10,000 feet.

Check the legend of the maps in this geography book for the color tints used to show elevation. They will help you to get a better picture of the surface features of the area shown on the map.

The maps in the atlas at the back of this geography book also make use of different colors, but not for the purpose of showing elevation. Blue on these maps represents oceans, seas, bays, and large lakes just as it does on the other maps. Black lines usually show rivers, boundaries, parallels and meridians. Other colors represent the different countries, and make it easier to distinguish one from the other. Such maps are called *political* maps.

One of the most important map skills is to be able to find exact location. By using the parallels and meridians on maps and globes, places can be accurately located by their latitude and longitude. Let us learn some more, therefore, about latitude and longitude.

Latitude. You have learned that parallels of latitude extend as circles around the earth in an east and west direction. These lines are called parallels because they are equally far apart for their entire length and never meet. The equator is the parallel that extends around the earth midway between the North Pole and the South Pole. Distance measured north and south of the equator is called *latitude*. If we wish to find the latitude of any place on the earth we must study a map or globe in order to find which parallel the place lies on or near.

Degrees of Latitude. Geographers and map-makers find it helpful to divide all circles into 360 equal parts. They call each part a *degree*. One degree, therefore, equals one 360th part of the circumference (distance around) of a circle. Each degree is further divided into 60 minutes; each minute into 60 seconds.

Since the earth is a sphere, the parallels and meridians we draw on it are circles. Latitude and longitude are measured along these circles, which appear as straight lines on a flat map. The unit we use to measure latitude and longitude, then, is the degree.

When we measure distance from the equator to the North Pole we are going one fourth the way around the earth. This is the same as going one fourth the way around a circle which contains 360 equal parts called degrees. Therefore, we can refer to this distance along the curved surface of the earth as one fourth of 360, or ninety equal parts. Each of these equal parts is called a degree, so we can say that the North Pole is ninety degrees from the equator, which is zero degrees.

Places near the equator are said to be in the low latitudes (zero to thirty degrees). Places near the poles are said to be in the high latitudes (sixty to ninety degrees). Places between the low latitudes and the

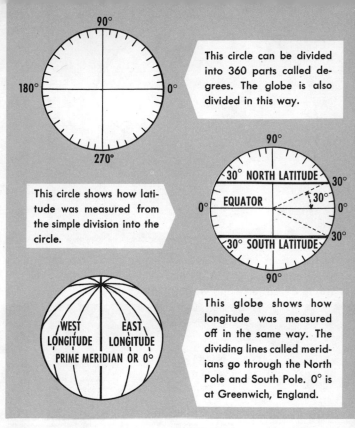

This circle can be divided into 360 parts called degrees. The globe is also divided in this way.

This circle shows how latitude was measured from the simple division into the circle.

This globe shows how longitude was measured off in the same way. The dividing lines called meridians go through the North Pole and South Pole. 0° is at Greenwich, England.

Degrees of Latitude and Longitude. When we measure a part of a circle in degrees, we are measuring an angle formed at the center of the circle.

high latitudes are said to be in the middle latitudes (thirty to sixty degrees). The United States is in the middle latitudes.

In order to tell the difference in location between places north and south of the equator we say that those north of the equator are in north latitude and those south of the equator are in south latitude. The symbol for degrees is °. The equator is 0°, the North Pole 90° north, and the South Pole 90° south.

Thus, the latitude of Chicago is about 41° north. You will not find the parallel for 41° north on most maps, however. Usually only the parallels of some of the degrees of latitude are shown on maps and globes.

Since the earth is about 25,000 miles in circumference (measured all the way around), one degree of latitude equals 1/360 of 25,000. A degree of latitude is therefore a little less than 70 miles.

Parallels are lines of latitude that extend around the earth in an easterly and westerly direction.

Meridians are lines of longitude that extend north and south to meet at the poles.

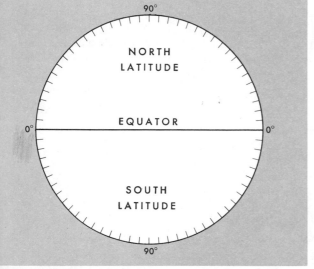

Latitude is distance north and south of the equator measured in degrees, minutes and seconds.

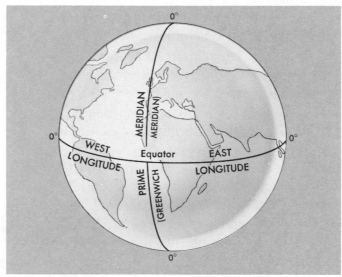

Longitude is distance east or west of the prime meridian measured in degrees, minutes and seconds.

Longitude. Meridians are imaginary lines extending north and south, and crossing at the poles. Remember that parallels and meridians exist only on maps and globes. We cannot find these imaginary lines on the earth itself. Just as latitude is measured north and south from the equator, or 0°, longitude is measured from the prime meridian. Like the equator it is marked 0°. The prime meridian passes north and south through Greenwich, a suburb of the city of London. It is sometimes called the Greenwich meridian instead of the prime meridian.

Distance measured east or west of the prime meridian is called longitude. If we wish to find the longitude of any place on the earth we must study a map or globe in order to see what meridian it is on or near.

Suppose two people start from the same place on the prime meridian and travel along the same parallel—one to the east and the other to the west. If they travel at the same rate of speed they would meet at a meridian halfway around the world from the prime meridian. Each person would have traveled halfway around the circle, or 180°. That is why the greatest longitude a place can have is 180°. The longitude of New York City is 74° west.

Length of a Degree of Longitude. Now look again at the lines on a globe. You will see that the parallels that go around the earth in an east-west direction become smaller circles as you go from the equator toward the poles. You will also see that the meridians which go around the earth in a north-south direction are farthest apart at the equator and meet at the poles.

A person traveling around the earth along the equator would travel a distance of 25,000 miles. However, a person traveling around the earth along a parallel between the equator and the pole would travel a shorter distance. In both cases he would go 360 degrees because he would be going around in a circle. This means that the distance for a degree of *longitude* is not the same everywhere on the earth as it is for a degree of latitude. It is 1/360 of 25,000, or a little less than 70 miles, at the equator; it is 0 miles at the poles where the meridians meet. Only along the equator is the distance for a degree of longitude equal to the distance for a degree of latitude.

How We Use Latitude and Longitude. If we know the latitude and longitude of any object we can find it easily on a map. This is true of a place, of an airplane, or of a ship at sea. Also, if a person knows the latitude and longitude of his own position on the earth, he knows exactly where he is.

Latitude can be determined by observing the position of certain stars by night, or the height of the sun above the horizon at noon. The instrument used to observe the position of the sun or stars is called a *sextant*.

Longitude can be found by comparing the ship's time (which is obtained from the position of the sun by day and the position of certain stars by night) with the time at the prime meridian. A ship generally carries a clock set with the time of the prime meridian (which is called Greenwich time). Such a clock is called a *chronometer*.

To show that you understand how to locate a place by using parallels and meridians, use a map to find the latitude and longitude of the place where you live.

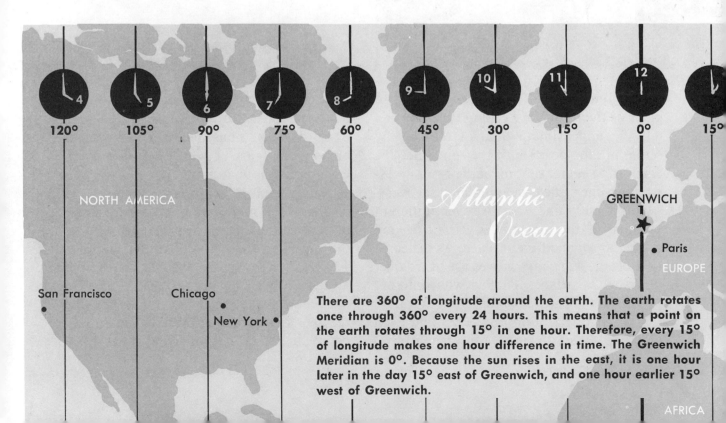

There are 360° of longitude around the earth. The earth rotates once through 360° every 24 hours. This means that a point on the earth rotates through 15° in one hour. Therefore, every 15° of longitude makes one hour difference in time. The Greenwich Meridian is 0°. Because the sun rises in the east, it is one hour later in the day 15° east of Greenwich, and one hour earlier 15° west of Greenwich.

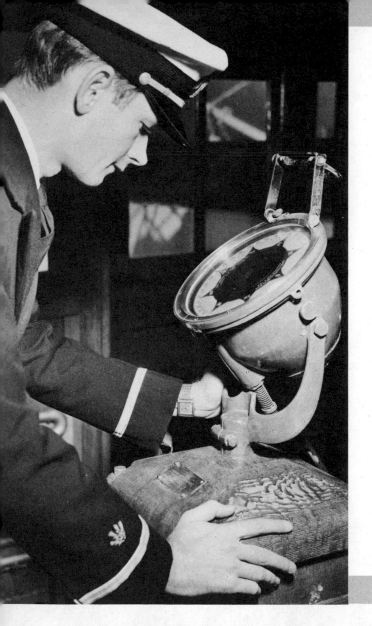

NAVIGATION

Navigation is the science of travel. Because of this science, ships and planes can safely travel through fog and blinding weather, confident of reaching their destination exactly as planned. To many seamen and pilots, navigation is important even in good weather. A ship or an airplane is often out of sight of any landmarks which would help to show the way. At these times, the science of navigation is their guide.

The ship's officer to the left is using a navigation instrument familiar to all—a *compass*. The officer in the picture to the right, above, is laying out his ship's course on a chart. He uses *parallel rulers* and *dividers*. At the bottom, an officer measures the angle of the sun over the horizon with a *sextant*. In this way, he can find the ship's longitude.

Longitude and Time. Longitude also gives us the means of keeping time. We can tell the approximate time of the day by observing the position of the sun. Since the earth is a sphere, the sun cannot rise everywhere at the same time, nor can it set everywhere at the same time. At every different moment of the day, the sun is rising and setting at some different place. As the earth rotates, the sun's rays moves westward over the earth's surface. That is why different places on the earth have different times.

There are 24 hours in a day, and each place on the earth turns a distance of 360 degrees in a day. This means that in one hour each place turns 1/24 of 360 degrees, or 15 degrees. Thus, for every 15 degrees of longitude east or west there is a difference of one hour in time.

For example, when it is 12 o'clock noon on the prime meridian (0°) it is 11 A.M. at the meridian 15° West, and 10 A.M. at the meridian 30° West. At the meridian 15° East it is already 1 P.M. The time is always earlier in places to the west of us and later in places to the east of us. Remember that when we watch the sun rise, people to the west of us cannot yet see it.

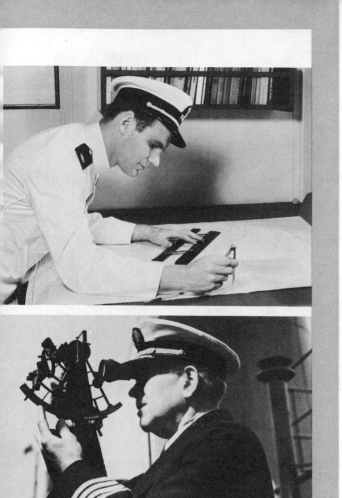

When the sun is directly overhead at a certain place, it is noon at that place. All places located on the same meridian have noon at the same instant. To the east of this meridian it is already afternoon and to the west it is still morning. However, if all people set their clocks and watches according to exact sun time, we would have a great deal of confusion. One place would have noon at a different time from another place just to the east or west of it. Travelers from place to place would have to change their watches constantly in going to the east or to the west.

Standard Time. Some years ago, in order to avoid confusion about time, the United States adopted *standard time*. Many other countries are now using standard time. According to this plan, the world is divided into *standard time belts*. Each belt has an average width of 15 degrees. Since there are 360 degrees around the world, this makes 24 standard time belts.

The meridians on maps and globes are generally drawn 15 degrees apart. Each 15° meridian is just about in the middle of a standard time belt. All places in a standard time belt have the same time. When a person travels westward he sets his

Therefore, it is earlier in the day for them. Thus, if we know the longitude of a place we can always determine its time as compared to our own. East of us, it is later in the day; to the west it is earlier.

Sun Time and Sundials. In ancient times people used the sundial, an instrument for telling time. They observed the shadow cast by the sun moving around a fixed dial. Sundials are still used in some places, but they seldom agree with our clocks and watches. They give the *sun time* for their locality. Sun time is the exact time at any given place on the earth.

Standard Time Belts of the United States. The small clocks show the differences in time. For daylight saving time, add one hour to the time shown.

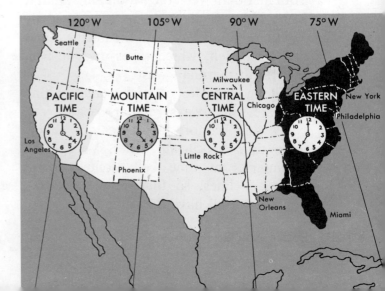

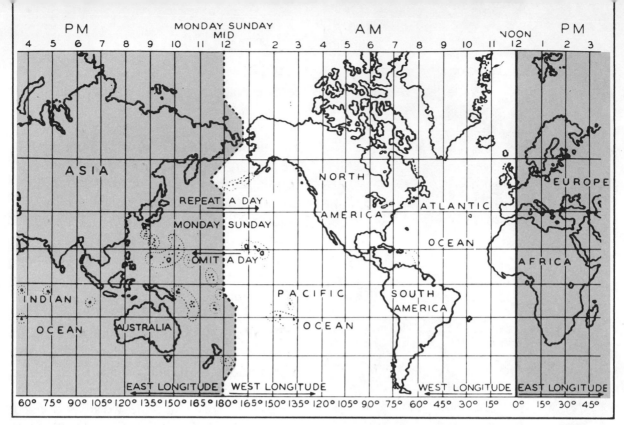

Time Zones of the World. On this map, every 15 degrees of longitude means an hour's difference in time. Note the International Date Line.

watch back one hour when he comes to another time belt. When a person travels eastward he sets his watch ahead one hour when he comes to the next time belt.

In our country there are four standard time belts. They are: the Eastern Standard Time Belt, which takes its time from the 75th meridian west; the Central Standard Time Belt, which takes its time from the 90th meridian west; the Mountain Standard Time Belt, which takes its time from the 105th meridian west; and the Pacific Standard Time Belt, which takes its time from the 120th meridian west.

The boundaries of each standard time belt are not always regular because railroads find it more convenient to change their time at certain cities. Very often, boundaries of time belts follow county boundary lines, so that people within a county will all have the same time.

The Calendar Day. A new calendar day must begin somewhere. The line where the new calendar day begins is called the International Date Line. The nations of the world have agreed that the International Date Line should be located on or near the 180th meridian, which runs through the middle of the Pacific Ocean. It was located there for convenience, so as not to run through the important countries.

Look at a map of the world. You will notice that the Date Line is not a straight line. It generally follows the 180th meridian but bends to the east or west of it so that certain islands can have the calendar day that is most convenient for them.

Let us see how this works out. A ship sailing westward from California to Japan crosses the International Date Line at 1 P.M. on Monday. The time which is determined by the sun remains the same but it immediately becomes Tuesday, the next calendar day, as the ship crosses the line.

Facts *to remember*

1. The earth is a sphere. A map of the whole earth or any part of it cannot be drawn perfectly on a flat surface.

2. Maps which attempt to show the curved surface of the earth on a flat surface are called map projections. Some projections show directions correctly. Others may show correctly the shapes of continents or distances.

3. A Mercator projection shows true directions. However, the shapes of continents and oceans are distorted on a Mercator especially in the far north and far south.

4. A Polar projection shows either the northern or the southern hemisphere. North or south appears at the center of such a map rather than at the top.

5. The shortest distance between two points on the curved surface of the earth is called a "great circle route." Special map projections are used to show great circle routes.

6. Maps are drawn to scale. The scale compares distance on the map with actual distance on the earth.

7. Color tints, ranging from green for low elevations to reddish browns for the highest elevations, are used on physical maps.

8. Latitude is distance measured north or south of the equator in degrees. Numbered east-west lines called parallels are drawn on maps and globes to help us find the latitude of a place, a ship at sea, or an airplane.

9. Longitude is distance measured in degrees east or west of the prime meridian. Numbers of north-south lines called meridians are drawn on maps and globes to help us find the longitude of a place. By means of latitude and longitude the exact location of any place on earth can be determined.

10. Longitude also helps us keep time on the earth. For every 15 degrees of longitude there is a time difference of one hour.

11. The world is divided into twenty-four standard time belts. Each belt takes its time from the meridian that crosses it. We can find the time anywhere in the world at a given instant by counting the meridians, then considering the time at Prime meridian or some other meridian.

12. A new calendar day begins and ends at the International Date Line which roughly follows the 180th meridian.

What *have I learned?*

Answer each question in a complete sentence. Do you know the . . .

1. name of the map projection most useful to navigators?

2. shortest route between any two places on the earth's surface?

3. name of the part of a map legend that helps you measure distance on a map?

4. color used on a physical map to show lowlands?

5. ocean through which the International Date Line runs?

6. name of a line drawn on maps and globes running from pole to pole?

7. map projection with north at the center of the map?

8. unit used in measuring latitude and longitude?

9. name of the line from which latitude is measured?

10. word used to describe the shape of the earth?

11. city through which the prime meridian passes?

12. name of a clock set with the time of the prime meridian?

13. name of the standard time belt in which you live?

14. place where a new calendar day begins?

15. name of the lines drawn on maps and globes that run in an east-west direction?

Facts *to understand*

Give a reason in a complete sentence for each of the following statements.

1. A globe is the only truly accurate map of the world.

2. Maps are needed as well as globes.

3. A degree of latitude equals about 70 miles.

4. Mercator maps may confuse Geography students.

5. Standard time belts were established.

6. Airplanes follow great circle routes.

7. Sundials seldom indicate the same time as a clock.

8. Boundaries of time belts are not always regular.

9. The length of a degree of longitude varies.

10. The International Date Line was located in the Pacific Ocean.

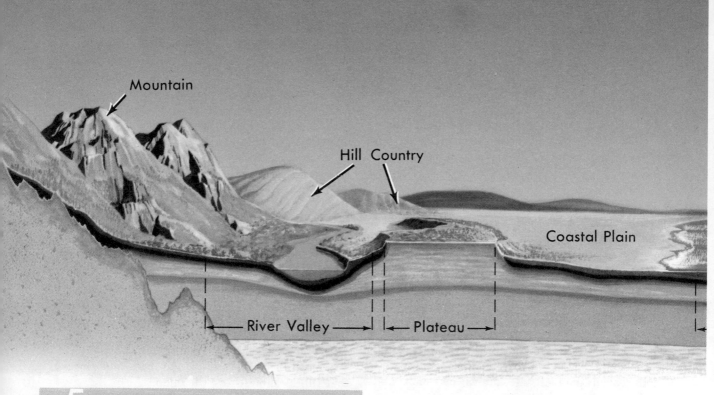

Mountain

Hill Country

Coastal Plain

River Valley | Plateau

5 Land and Water

The earth's surface is made up of land and water. The land masses cover a little more than one fourth of the earth's surface; the oceans and seas occupy the other three fourths. Of the land area of the earth, nine tenths lies north of the equator. The Southern Hemisphere is largely covered with water.

Asia, the largest of the continental land masses, is small in area when compared to the largest ocean, the Pacific. The Pacific Ocean would cover all the continents. Even the smaller Atlantic Ocean is larger in area than the continents of Asia and Africa together.

Continents. We have already learned that the huge bodies of land on the earth are called continents. Many geographers believe that all the continents were at one time joined into one great land mass. With the cooling and shrinking of the earth's surface, they drifted apart. Eurasia and North

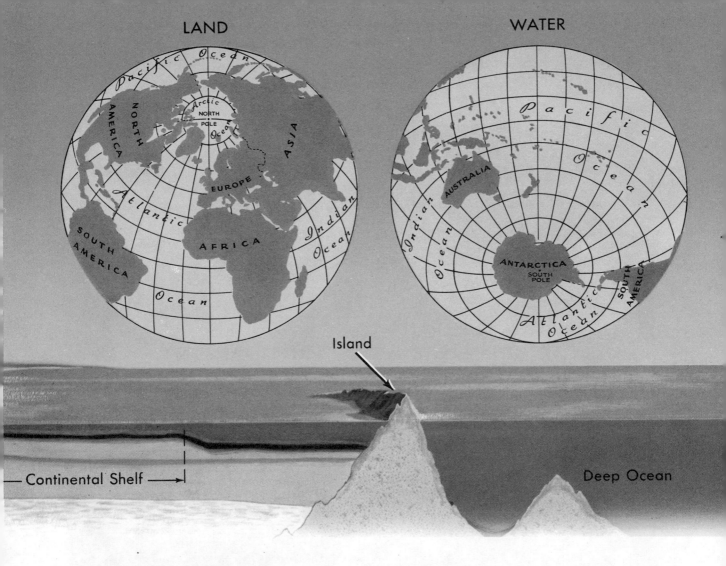

LAND

WATER

Island

Continental Shelf

Deep Ocean

America, separated now only by the narrow Bering Strait, formed at one time a single great land mass. All the other continents, except Australia and Antarctica, are joined either to Eurasia or to North America by narrow necks of land. A narrow strip of land connecting two larger bodies of land is called an *isthmus*. Africa is thus connected to Asia by the isthmus of Suez. South America is connected to North America by the isthmus of Panama.

All the continents, except Antarctica, are widest in the north and become gradually narrower toward the south. Pieces of land called *peninsulas* jut outward into the sea from all the continents. Most of the peninsulas extend southward. Some examples of

peninsulas are Iberia, Italy, Scandinavia, India, and Florida.

The edges of all the continents extend out under the oceans. Instead of dropping steeply into deep water, the coastlines gradually extend underwater for a certain distance. This extension of the land underneath the sea is called the *continental shelf*. The water over the shelf is shallow. The continental shelf may extend outward for several hundred miles, as it does in many places along the eastern American and western European shores facing the Atlantic Ocean. In other places the shelf is very narrow or does not exist at all. This can be seen along the western coasts of North and South America.

Land and Water 275

The Grand Canyon of the Colorado River. This canyon is one of the most dramatic examples of erosion caused by the cutting power of water.

The Earth's Changing Surface. The earth's surface is constantly changing. We do not notice most of the changes because they take place slowly over long periods of time. The forces of nature which cause these changes are always at work. Some of them build up the surface of the earth; others cut and wear it down.

The forces that build up mountains and other surface features come from the interior of the earth. One of these forces is the action of volcanoes. Sometimes the hot lava (melted rock) erupts from openings in the earth's crust. It cools and hardens, building up to great heights on the surface. At other times the lava moves toward the surface but does not escape. Instead it causes the upper layers of the earth's crust to bulge upward. Still other forces make the rock layers at the surface wrinkle or fold. Sometimes, large blocks of the earth's solid crust are cracked, lifted up, dropped down, tilted, or pushed over other rock layers.

The force that breaks up, cuts, and wears away the surface of continents is called *erosion*. The force which moves the eroded

Volcano Erupting in Hawaii. The forces under the surface of the earth can cause great changes on the surface when they erupt like this volcano.

Hard-hit Shoreline. The shores of the continents, as a result of the constant pounding of the waves, are continually being worn away, little by little.

material and places it elsewhere is called *deposition*. The effect of erosion is to wear down the high areas of the earth's surface. Deposition fills in the low areas.

Erosion is accomplished in the following way: the first step is weathering — the breaking up of rocks by temperature changes, frost, and chemical change. After weathering breaks up and loosens rock materials, other agents continue the work by cutting and wearing them away. Among these agents are running water (rivers and streams), moving ice (glaciers), air in motion (winds), ocean waves and currents, and gravity. They often carry the loosened materials great distances. When they lose their cutting or pushing force, deposition takes over. The materials are dropped, and the surface is filled in.

Thus we see how the forces which build up are opposed by the forces of erosion which grind down. The result is constant change in the surface of the earth.

Major Surface Features. Mountains, plateaus, and plains are considered the major surface features of the continents because of their great extent and area. These major features were created by great uplifting forces that occurred within the earth's crust.

Plains. The areas of low-lying land that occupy large portions of the earth's surface are called *plains*. Two of the great plain regions of the world are the Central Plain of North America extending from the Gulf of Mexico to Hudson Bay, and the European Plain extending from the Atlantic Coast far into Asia. These great expanses of nearly level land were formed by slight uplifts of areas once beneath the sea.

Most of the world's people live on plains wherever the climate is favorable. The low level lands are usually quite fertile. Where there is enough rainfall, they provide ideal conditions for food production through farming and the animal industries. Plains are also easier to travel over than rough, hilly, or mountainous lands; crops and other goods can be easily transported across them from place to place.

Panorama Showing Surface Features. In this illustration of an imaginary region of the earth, each of the major surface features is clearly shown.

Plateaus. A *plateau* is a kind of plain. Because plateaus sometimes have a higher elevation above sea level, they are often called "raised plains." It is wrong, however, to think of plateaus only as high level land. In fact, some plains actually have higher elevations than plateaus.

The chief difference between plains and plateaus is the way the streams and other agents of erosion work on each. On a plain, streams are usually shallow, and do not cut deep paths as they cross the surface of the land. On a plateau, the streams cut much deeper into the surface, and they often cause deep gullies, called *canyons,* to appear. Because of the steep sides of these canyons, a plateau that is crossed by many streams may resemble a mountainous area, although its top surface is really a plain. It will not have the high peaks and ridges found in neighboring mountains, however, nor will it be so high above sea level. The plateau of Tibet, in Asia, is the highest in

the world. Its elevation is 16,000 feet above sea level. Other high plateaus are the Altiplano of South America, 14,000 feet, and the Colorado plateau of North America, 6000 feet.

Mountains. Mountains are layers of rock on the earth's surface which have been disturbed and pushed upward by forces in the earth's interior. They don't appear singly but in groups, or systems. The great mountain systems of the earth lie near the edges of the continents. One of these great mountain systems appears to surround the Pacific Ocean. It includes the Andes of South America and the Rockies and other ranges of Western North America. In Asia, it includes ranges in eastern Siberia, Japan, and the Philippines. Sections of this huge system appear thousands of miles apart.

Another system encircles the Atlantic Ocean. The Appalachians of the eastern United States are part of it. A great east-west mountain system extends from Central America and the West Indies and disappears from sight under the Atlantic Ocean. It reappears in Europe and North Africa, more or less following the shores of the Mediterranean Sea. The famous Alps are part of it. Crossing into Asia by way of Turkey and Iran, this east-west system extends into northern India and Tibet where we find the Himalayas, the highest range in the world. It ends finally in the volcanic peaks of Indonesia.

Hill Country. Sometimes an old, eroded, worn-down mountain area is called *hill country*. Sometimes, hill country is the remains of an eroded, stream-cut plateau. Like mountainous areas, hill country has narrow valleys and very little area at the summits, or peaks. The peaks are very much lower in elevation, however, than in mountain areas. Examples of hill country in the United States are the Cumberland hills of eastern Kentucky and Tennessee, and the Ozarks of Missouri and Arkansas.

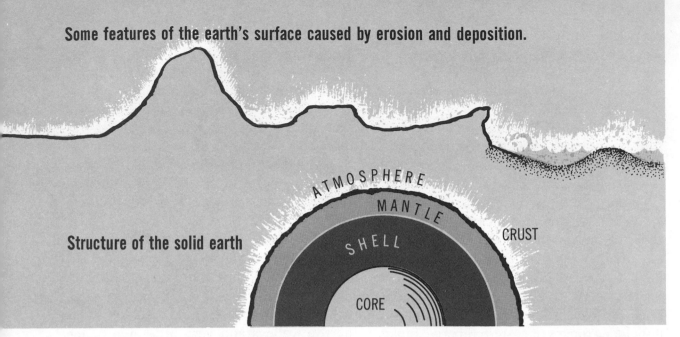

Some features of the earth's surface caused by erosion and deposition.

Structure of the solid earth

ATMOSPHERE

MANTLE

SHELL

CRUST

CORE

Some of the Earth's Surface Features. This cutaway view of the earth shows how the outstanding parts of its surface would look in profile.

Minor Surface Features. A closer examination of mountains, plateaus, and plains shows smaller features which are part of the major surface divisions. Among these minor surface features are hills and valleys, cliffs and slopes, flood plains and deltas, beaches and sand bars and many others. They have been formed gradually by the agents of erosion and deposition. The earth's surface, then, is constantly undergoing change.

One of the "Steppingstones." This tiny coral island, or *atoll*, is one of the Marshall Island group in the South Pacific. Note the circling reef.

Steppingstones Between the Continents. Small bodies of land which are completely surrounded by water are, as you know, called *islands*. There are many thousands of islands on the earth. Most of them are very small — no more than small rocks sticking out of the ocean waters. However, a few islands are very large. One of them is Greenland, the largest island in the world. Two other very large islands are New Guinea and Borneo.

Some islands have large populations, while others have few people living on them; many are entirely uninhabited. Certain islands have become very important as bases for airplanes and ships. The Virgin Islands in the West Indies are important to our country for the protection of the Panama Canal.

The location of our fiftieth state, the Hawaiian Islands, gives them the title "Crossroads of the Pacific." The large planes which fly between North America and Asia use the Hawaiian Islands and the smaller islands of Midway, Wake, and Guam as "steppingstones" in the Pacific Ocean.

"The Lonely Sea and the Sky." A seaman realizes the vastness of the ocean when he sees it stretch to the horizon on all sides, with no land in sight.

The Oceans. The water which covers much of our planet is divided into oceans, seas, and other bodies with different names. These divisions are not separated, however, as are the continents. They are all connected with one another and flow into one another, making one vast world ocean. We often call this continuous body of water simply, "the sea."

The oceans are of great importance to man. They were once known as the "highways" between the continents, a title they must now share with the atmosphere since the invention of the airplane. However, water transportation is still the cheapest and most convenient way to ship large amounts of inexpensive, bulky materials like coal, ore, and wheat. Shipping lanes are still busy thoroughfares, and seaports still handle a large part of the world's trade.

The oceans have a very important effect on climate. The rain waters that fall on our land come from the ocean. From the ocean come the winds which cool and moisten the dusty atmosphere, cleanse away the smoke, and freshen up the world. Cool or warm currents affect the climate of lands they pass.

From the ocean comes the fish which furnishes man with food and many of the vitamins that are so necessary for healthful living. The ocean is also the source of certain salts and other minerals. In fact, it is believed that scientists will develop more and more ways for man to make use of the wealth of minerals and foods which the sea contains, and which have just barely been discovered. "Farming the sea" will probably be one way to provide enough food for the earth's increasing population.

The seas are a gift of God's careful providence without which we could not live.

Man and the Ocean. The oceans of the world are fertile and very rich in animal and vegetable life. To date, these riches have merely been mined, not farmed. That is, men have taken from the sea as from a mine, but they have not tried to use the sea to grow food as farmers use the soil. One exception is oyster farming, a growing industry in certain seashore areas. Men put oysters in beds of shallow water, feed them, protect them from natural enemies like the starfish, and harvest a crop of oysters.

It is possible that much more could be done to use our vast oceans to support human life. Many millions of people in the world today are hungry all the time through no fault of their own. Perhaps men may develop better ways to cultivate the millions of acres of sea water, in order to feed the world's starving people.

Minerals and salts from the land are being continually washed into the sea. When sea water evaporates and passes away into clouds, the minerals and salts are left behind. They stay in the ocean. The sea is,

therefore, gradually becoming more and more salty. The minerals in sea water happen to be those most needed for strong plant and animal growth, so that food taken from the sea is very healthful.

Sea weed, for example, is one of the finest fertilizers for crops; vegetables grown upon it are both nutritious and tasty. In fact, it is believed that all life on earth originated from the sea or from swampy lands along its edges. The very blood in our veins is a chemical composition much like sea water.

The sea is a great storehouse, full of riches untapped as yet by man.

Charting the Oceans. One of the great dangers to a ship in unknown waters is running aground. At one time, all ships made use of a simple system to find the depth of uncharted waters. A seaman would throw a weighted line overboard, and wait until the lead would strike the bottom. As the line ran through his fingers, he counted the knots on it which had been tied at regular intervals. This method of telling depth was called "sounding." In this way, the depths of the sea were measured and charted over the centuries.

Today these soundings are taken more

Diving for Ocean Treasures. These brave men descend to great depths, searching for the precious gems called pearls. They learn to work quickly.

easily and swiftly by means of sonar. A sound wave is sent down through the water, and the seaman can tell the depth of the water by the length of time it takes for the "echo" of the wave to bounce back from the ocean floor.

A *chart* is a map of any water area. Depths of water and safe sea lanes are indicated on charts. Dangerous rocks, reefs, and sand bars are also marked. Floating buoys with bells or lights are chained to underwater rocks to warn sailors away from danger. Lighthouses have also been built at certain points all along the shores of continents and islands, to warn sailors of danger in coming too near, and to help them find direction. Navigators can tell where they are by timing the flashes of light. They can identify the lighthouse they see because most lighthouses blink their light a certain number of times per minute.

Lighthouse keepers, sometimes with their families, live lonely lives surrounded by the waves and storms. Many have sacrificed themselves through great dangers, sickness, and hardships, for the sake of their duty—to keep the light burning. In some places the coast guard takes care of the lighthouses.

Teeming Life in the Ocean. Throughout almost every part of the world's oceans, many different kinds of plant and animal life find means of existence.

How Deep Is the Ocean? Three quarters of the earth's surface is covered by the sea. This vast area of restless water is not only wider than all the land, it is so deep that if earth's highest mountains were dropped into it in some places, they would make only a mighty splash and then disappear from sight.

The average altitude of the land on earth is only about one half mile; the average depth of the sea is two and a half miles—five times as great. The greatest known ocean depth in the Pacific Ocean, just off the Philippine Islands, is about seven miles. Mt. Everest in the Himalayas, earth's most towering peak, rises less than six miles into the sky. Of course, the oceans do not seem deep when we consider that it is 4000 miles down to the center of the earth!

Land and Water 283

The Bottom of the Ocean. The floor of the ocean is not level. It is made up of mountains, plains, valleys, and canyons. Some of the underwater mountains reach right up out of the water, where their peaks form islands. We have learned how the edges of the great continents extend out under shallow water for miles. At the edge of this continental shelf the ocean floor slopes down sharply into deep water.

The shallow waters of some of the continental shelves are the great fishing banks of the world. Here there is always plenty of plant life upon which the fish can feed.

In warm, clear, shallow ocean waters formations called coral reefs are often found. They are built up from the skeletons of millions of tiny sea animals known as *coral polyps*. Great formations of coral are found along the northeastern coast of Australia, among the islands of the South Pacific Ocean, and in the West Indies.

Marine life is not nearly so plentiful in deeper parts of the ocean, however. The heavy pressure of the tons of water overhead, and the almost total absence of light, makes plant life very difficult. Even in these great depths, however, there are strange and wonderful living creatures. How do we know of them?

Some men have dared to explore the ocean depths, going down in globes of

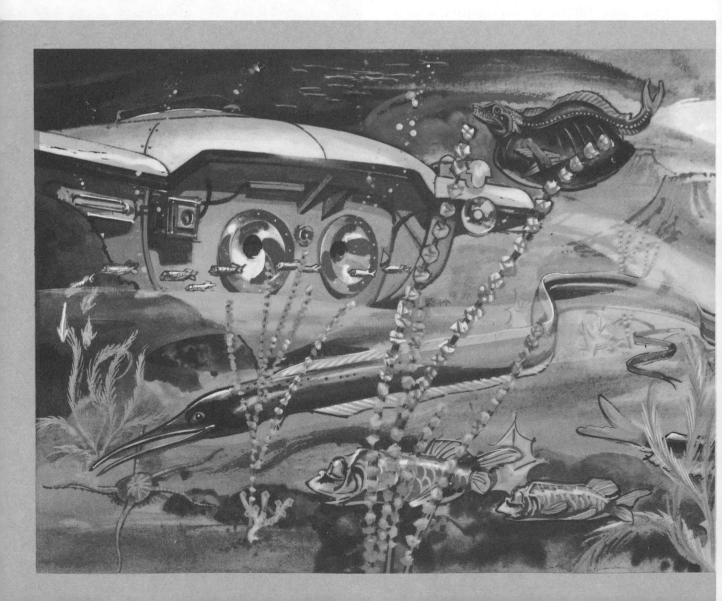

metal and thick glass to observe and take photographs. Others have used dredges to bring up samples of matter and small creatures from the sea bottom. Much of the ocean floor is deeply covered with ooze formed by millions of skeletons of tiny sea creatures. When living, these creatures float about near the surface of the open sea or cling to underwater rocks and seaweed. When some of them die, their bony shells or skeletons sink to the bottom. Wherever part of the ocean floor was pushed up to form part of a continent or an island, this kind of ooze formed soil which is exceedingly fertile. A great part of the world's food is grown in soil formed this way.

Movements of the Sea. The waters of great oceans or seas are in constant motion. Cold water is always sinking to the bottom because it is heavier than the warmer water which remains near the surface. Ocean currents, resembling rivers in the ocean, flow all around the world.

Winds whip up tremendous sea waves during storms. The level of the sea is constantly changing as the rotation of the earth and the pull of gravity from the moon and the sun cause the high and low tides to move westward around the earth. These movements of the sea have a great effect upon shipping, upon harbors, and upon the climate of places located along the coast.

CREATURES OF THE OCEAN FLOOR

Men have always been curious about the bottom of the ocean. One of the most fascinating questions has always been: What kind of life exists fathoms down in the deepest water?

In recent years, scientists called *oceanographers* have invented different ways to go down to the bottom of the ocean and study its life. Previously, they had to rely on specimens of strange fish which were accidentally caught, or plain guesswork.

One of the vessels which was invented for this purpose is shown in this illustration. Behind its thick hull of steel and glass, men breathe oxygen from a tank, and look out comfortably at the life around them on the bottom. Their reports tell of a strange world, with creatures whose bodies are weird-looking, but capable of supporting life in the cold dark waters.

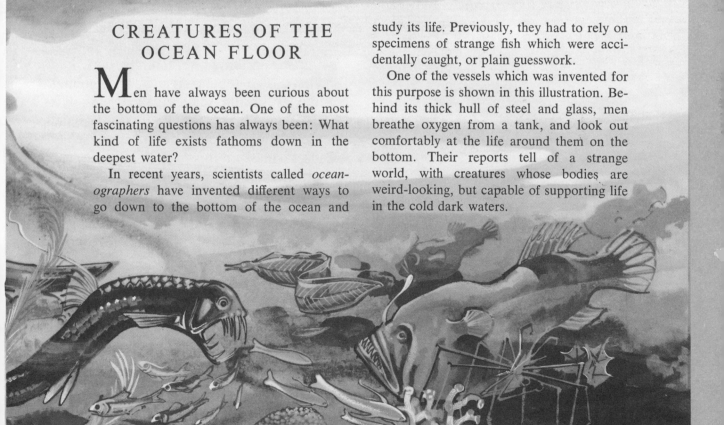

When you attach a weight to a string and whirl it, it tends to fly away. This tendency to fly away is called centrifugal force. The string prevents the weight from flying off and also holds it in its circular path. It is this same force that keeps the earth and moon in their orbits and keeps them from falling apart or crashing together. The balance between centrifugal force and gravity keeps the earth and moon from flying apart, just as your string controls the weight. On the side of the earth nearest the moon, the moon's pulling force is strongest. This causes the water to be pulled up into a bulge producing high tide there.

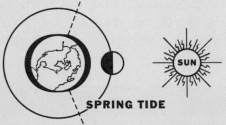

SPRING TIDE

The pulling force of the sun also affects the tides. When the sun and the moon are in a straight line and exert their pulling force together as a team, spring tides occur. At this time the highest high tides and the lowest low tides occur. Spring tides come at new moon and full moon.

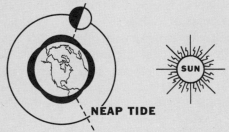

NEAP TIDE

When the sun and the moon are exerting their pulling force at right angles to each other, there is no team work and they are working against each other. At this time neap tides occur and high tides are not so high nor are the low tides so low. This occurs at first and last quarter phases of the moon.

Waves. As we stand on the shore and look toward the sea we can see that the surface of the water is seldom still. Regular up-and-down movements of the surface of the sea are called waves. These are caused by the wind blowing over the surface of the water. When the wind does not blow with great force, the ocean may become quite calm. When it is stormy at sea the waves grow to great heights. Even the big ocean liners are tossed about by these giant waves.

A cubic foot of ocean water weighs about sixty-four pounds. When the waves dash against the shore with great force, the weight of the water pounds the rocks and gradually wears them away. The beautiful white sand on many ocean beaches was formed there by the breaking up and crushing of the rock along the coast by ocean waves. In other places the waves wash out beaches and the sand is carried back into the sea, only to be deposited again on another shore.

When waves roll up on a gently sloping shore, their motion is interfered with and the waves roll over to form breakers. The breakers that form along a sand beach are called the surf. Perhaps you have enjoyed swimming in the white, foaming surf.

Tides. The regular risings and fallings of the level of the sea are called tides. The pull of gravity by the moon is the chief cause of tides. Study the diagram "What Causes Tides" on this page. It will help you to understand why tides occur.

The level of the sea gradually rises for about six hours and then gradually falls for another six hours. This movement of the water goes on all the time and is most noticeable along the shore.

Out in the middle of the ocean, tides are not noticed because the water rises and falls only two or three feet. Near the shore the tides often rise much higher than this. At high tide the water comes into the shores and at low tide it flows out. The lowland along the shore is likely to be covered with water during high tide. The average level of the oceans between high tide and low tide is called *sea level*.

Spring and Neap Tides. The water on the side of the earth facing the moon tends to bulge out because the attraction of the moon—its force of gravity—is greatest at that point. The water on the side of the earth turned away from the moon also tends to bulge out because the solid part of the earth might be said to pull away from it. That is why there are always two high tides on the earth at the same time. The high tides gradually move westward around the earth because of the earth's rotation.

The sun is farther away than the moon, and so it does not affect the tides so strongly. However, it too plays an important part in producing tides. Sometimes the sun helps the moon to cause even higher tides or lower tides than usual. For example, when the sun and moon are in the same straight line, their attraction on the earth is greatest. Then the high tides are highest and the low tides are lowest. The difference between low tide and high tide is greatest when this occurs. Such tides are called *spring tides*. The name has no relation to the spring season.

When the force of the sun and the force of the moon are working at right angles, they are not pulling together but against each other. The pulling effects of the moon and the sun are in different directions. At this time, the high tides are not so high, nor are the low tides so low. Such tides are called *neap tides* and the difference between low tide and high tide is not so great as at spring tides. (See diagram of spring and neap tides on opposite page.)

How Tides Affect Shipping. At sea, tides have little effect on shipping because the average rise and fall of water is only about two or three feet. It is the bays and inlets along the coast which feel the greatest effect of tides. There the difference between high and low tides may be many feet. All ships entering or leaving a harbor must take the tide into consideration. Large vessels generally enter and leave shallow harbors only at high tide to make movement easier and avoid running aground.

The docks where ships load and unload may have movable platforms. Then, when the ships rise and fall with the tide, the cargo can still be transferred. In some bays and inlets the difference between high and low tide may be so great that a ship could not dock properly without such platforms.

High Tide and Low Tide. These two photographs were taken several hours apart at Friendship, Maine. Between tides the difference is about ten feet.

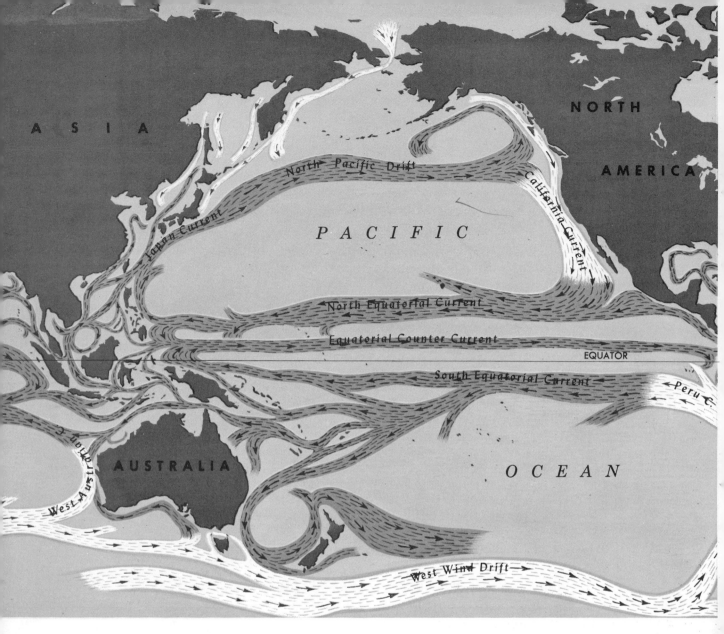

Ocean Currents. Besides waves and tides, great rivers, called currents, flow and swirl through the oceans. Warm currents flow through cold waters, and cold currents flow through warm waters. These currents raise or lower the temperature along the shores of the lands they touch. They also cool or warm the air that blows over them.

Ocean currents are caused chiefly by steady prevailing winds, and their direction is influenced by the rotation of the earth. Warm currents in general move out from the equatorial regions toward the poles.

Cold currents move from the poles toward the equator.

Ocean currents move slowly and steadily along the surface like very wide rivers in the ocean itself. Great, almost circular currents flow in each of the three large oceans—the Atlantic, the Pacific, and the Indian. The ocean currents of the Northern Hemisphere flow generally in the direction taken by the hands of a clock. Those in the Southern Hemisphere move in the opposite direction. The map you see above shows the most important ocean currents.

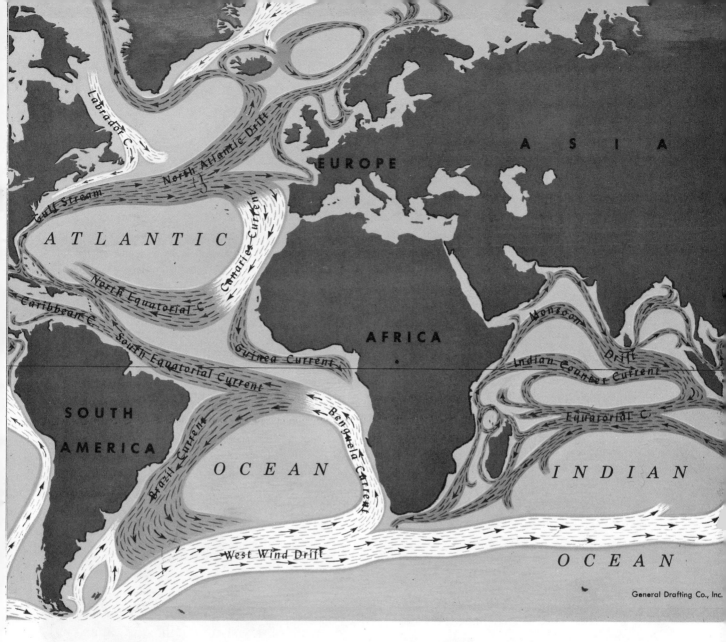

The Gulf Stream. The best known ocean current of the North Atlantic Ocean is the Gulf Stream. This warm current flows from the Gulf of Mexico through the Florida Strait at a rate of about five miles per hour. The Gulf Stream then moves northeastward, passing near the eastern coast of the United States. Just south of the island of Newfoundland, it turns more to the east, becomes the North Atlantic Drift, and starts its journey across the Atlantic toward the northwestern part of Europe, finding its way into the cold northern waters.

The North Atlantic Drift helps to keep the waters along the coast of the British Isles and other western European countries warmer than they would normally be. The harbor at Hammerfest in Norway, north of the Arctic Circle, is ice-free throughout the year because the warm waters of the North Atlantic Drift wash the coast. The winds blowing over this current are warmed; as a result, coastal areas in western Europe enjoy milder climate than is normal for their latitude. The climate of the British Isles is strongly influenced by this current.

Land and Water 289

A Treacherous Foe. Torn from the glacier and carried south by the Labrador Current, this iceberg, a menace to ships, will be sunk by the Coast Guard.

The Labrador Current. Another important ocean current of the North Atlantic is the Labrador Current. This cold current flows southward from Baffin Bay and Greenland along the coast of Labrador. This current sometimes carries the icebergs which have broken off the Greenland glaciers into waters farther south.

One Effect of the California Current. This family enjoys mild breezes which strike the Pacific Coast, lowering the temperature in the summer.

Another interesting effect of this current is the production of dense sea fogs in the vicinity of Newfoundland. They are caused by the mixing of cold air over the Labrador Current with the warmer air over the Gulf Stream. The Newfoundland fogs, as they are called, have long been a hazard to North Atlantic shipping, especially to the fishing vessels that come to the Grand Banks for their catch. However, the use of radio and radar have reduced the number of shipping accidents in recent years.

The Japan Current. The most famous current of the North Pacific, the Japan Current, starts in the vicinity of the Philippines, and passes near Japan. This warm current then becomes the North Pacific Drift, and flows eastward. Part of it turns north and warms the waters along the western coasts of Canada and Alaska. Part of the ocean current turns southward to become the California Current. The winds that blow over this current help to make the winter climate milder along the western coast of North America. However, in the summer, the California current is generally cooler than the shores it flows past.

Facts *to remember*

1. The surface of the earth is three fourths water and one fourth land. Most of the land lies in the Northern Hemisphere. The Southern Hemisphere is largely water.

2. Asia is the largest continent. The Pacific is the largest ocean.

3. The edges of continents that extend under the oceans are called continental shelves. The water covering the shelves is shallow. Many fish live on the continental shelf.

4. The surface of the earth is always changing as the result of erosion. The agents of erosion are rivers, glaciers, winds, waves, currents, and gravity.

5. Plains are low nearly level lands; plateaus are higher lands with nearly level tops; mountains are high areas with uneven peaks and ridges.

6. Islands are land areas completely surrounded by water; peninsulas are pieces of land that extend outward from continents into the sea; isthmuses are narrow strips of land that connect two larger bodies of land.

7. Oceans are important to man as highways and as sources of food and minerals. They affect the climate of the lands near them.

8. The average depth of the ocean is greater than the average height of the land.

9. Movements of the sea include waves, tides, and currents. Waves are caused by wind; tides by the attraction of the moon and the sun; and currents by steady winds.

10. Ocean currents which flow toward the poles are warm. Ocean currents which flow toward the equator are cold. An example of a warm current is the Gulf Stream. An example of a cold one is the Labrador Current.

What *have I learned?*

I

Answer each of the following in a complete sentence.

1. In which hemisphere are most of the continents located?

2. What name is given to a narrow strip of land that connects two continents?

3. Name the world's largest island.

4. Does a neap tide or a spring tide occur at full moon?

5. About how long a time passes between one high tide and the next?

6. What effect does erosion have on the surface of the earth?

7. How could you tell the difference between a plateau and a mountain?

8. Give one reason why oceans are important to man.

9. How does the height of the land compare with the depth of the sea?

10. How do neap tides compare with spring tides?

11. What effect does the North Atlantic Drift have on the coastal waters of Western Europe?

12. How is sea level along any coast determined?

13. In what kind of waters are coral reefs formed?

14. What causes ocean currents?

15. Does the moon or the sun have the greater effect on tides?

II

Complete each of the following sentences, choosing the correct word or words in the parenthesis.

1. The ocean current closest to the east coast of the United States is the (North Atlantic Drift, Japan Current, Gulf Stream).

2. An example of hill country in the United States is (the Ozarks, the Rockies, the Catskills).

3. The force which moves material on the surface of the earth and places it elsewhere is (erosion, deposition, gravity).

4. The (Indian, Atlantic, Pacific) is the largest ocean in the world.

5. The greatest known ocean depth is about (seven, five, ten) miles.

Facts *to understand*

Give reasons in a complete sentence for each of these statements.

1. More people live on plains than in plateau or mountain regions.

2. Higher tides occur at the full moon and new moon phases.

3. Waves cause a great deal of erosion along a coast.

4. More fish are found along the continental shelf than in deeper waters.

5. High tides move westward around the earth.

6 Weather and Climate

Violent Change in Weather. A familiar sight in the summer is the sudden thunderstorm, with lightning flashes, strong winds, and heavy rains.

Nothing is more important to us than the earth's atmosphere — the air, as we more commonly call it. Without air to breathe, even for a short time, man and all living things would soon die. The atmosphere is a mixture of gasses surrounding the land and water surface of the earth. It is a sort of layer or skin around the earth.

The weather we have from day to day is the result of changes which take place in the atmosphere. The changes influence our choice of clothing, our methods of carrying out our daily tasks, the materials we use to build our homes,—in fact, almost anything we try to do. The kind of weather a region has year after year is called its *climate*. We have already learned how climate affects the way people live and the kind of work they engage in.

In this chapter we will study what causes changes in the earth's atmosphere and how the changes affect weather and climate.

The Atmosphere and Life. About one fifth of our atmosphere is composed of a gas called oxygen. The oxygen in the air is necessary for life. We breathe air with its oxygen into our lungs. There, it enters the blood and is carried to every part of the body where it is used in the processes of living. Oxygen is also important to us in other ways. For example, fires cannot burn without the oxygen in the air. Oxygen also causes the decay by which dead plants and other waste materials are returned to the soil to be again used by growing plants.

The most abundant gas in the atmosphere is *nitrogen*. It makes up almost four fifths of the air. Nitrogen is necessary for plant life. In the soil, nitrogen combines chemically with oxygen and other substances to form *nitrates*. These dissolve in ground moisture and are taken up into plants through their roots. Plants use nitrogen in this form as food.

A gas which forms only a very small fraction of the atmosphere, far less than one hundredth, is *carbon dioxide*. Even though the amount of this gas is not great, it is nevertheless very important. Green plants take carbon dioxide from the air through openings in their leaves. At the same time, as we just learned, water enters the plant through its roots. Helped by the energy of the sun, the carbon dioxide and water combine chemically to form sugar. The sugar in turn changes to starch, and is stored by green plants in leaves, stems, and roots. Man needs the starches in plants and could not live without them.

Water in the form of a gas (called water *vapor*) is also present in the atmosphere. The amount of water vapor in the air varies from time to time and from place to place. Water vapor is the source of rain, snow, clouds, fog, and other forms of moisture which come out of the atmosphere.

The Gases in the Atmosphere. Our air is really a mixture of several different gases. Two important ones—oxygen and nitrogen—are shown here.

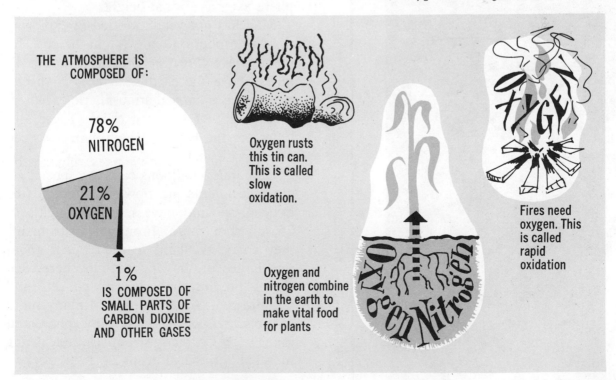

THE ATMOSPHERE IS COMPOSED OF:

78% NITROGEN

21% OXYGEN

1% IS COMPOSED OF SMALL PARTS OF CARBON DIOXIDE AND OTHER GASES

Oxygen rusts this tin can. This is called slow oxidation.

Oxygen and nitrogen combine in the earth to make vital food for plants

Fires need oxygen. This is called rapid oxidation

PHOTOSYNTHESIS

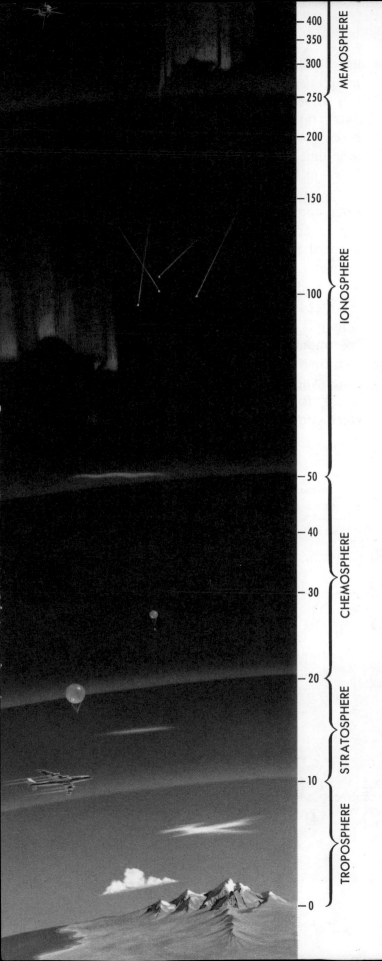

The diagram's altitude scale (in miles) and atmospheric layers:

- 400
- 350
- 300
- 250 — MEMOSPHERE
- 200
- 150
- 100 — IONOSPHERE
- 50
- 40 — CHEMOSPHERE
- 30
- 20
- 10 — STRATOSPHERE
- 0 — TROPOSPHERE

Height of the Atmosphere. It is still impossible to find out exactly how far up the atmosphere extends from the surface of the earth. It is estimated, however, that the layer of air surrounding the earth is *at least* two hundred miles in height, and probably extends to over six hundred miles. See the diagram on this page.

The estimate of two hundred miles is based upon the observation of meteors. Meteors can be seen only when they enter the earth's atmosphere from outside space, because then the friction of the air causes them to burn. Then we see the bright, burning trail. Since meteors are seen at heights of at least two hundred miles, we must conclude that the atmosphere extends at least that far.

The *Aurora Borealis,* or "Northern Lights," is seen at heights of over six hundred miles. Scientists tell us that these lights are caused by discharges of electricity through thin gases. This would seem to indicate that at least some very thin atmosphere extends to that height.

Man has not yet succeeded in exploring the atmosphere to any great height. Jet planes have flown at heights of about 15 miles above the earth's surface. A special balloon once carried atmospheric explorers to a height of fourteen miles. These altitudes are the highest which man has been able to rise so far.

Unmanned balloons carrying special radio instruments are now sent up into the atmosphere and have reached heights of 25 miles or more. From the instruments they carry, we have learned much about the nature of the upper atmosphere. Scientists predict that manned rockets and satellites will some day reveal many more of the secrets of the upper atmosphere and outer space. Already scientists are learning more about the atmosphere from rockets.

294 Space Age Geography

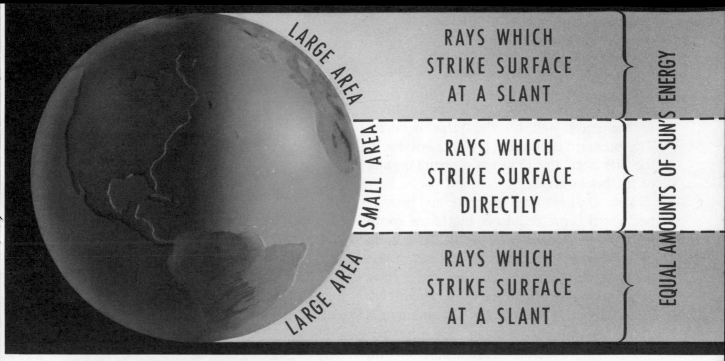

LARGE AREA

SMALL AREA

LARGE AREA

RAYS WHICH
STRIKE SURFACE
AT A SLANT

RAYS WHICH
STRIKE SURFACE
DIRECTLY

RAYS WHICH
STRIKE SURFACE
AT A SLANT

EQUAL AMOUNTS OF SUN'S ENERGY

How the Air Is Heated and Cooled. The sun's energy, called *insolation,* travels across space at a speed as great as the speed of light. This light-energy strikes the atmosphere, the land surface, and the water surface of the earth. Some of it is absorbed and changes to heat.

The regions near the equator receive nearly vertical rays of insolation while the polar regions always receive slanting rays. Vertical rays do not spread their energy over so great an area as slanting rays. Therefore, more of the sun's energy is brought to the regions near the equator and less to the polar regions. The more slanting the rays, the greater the thickness of the atmosphere they have to pass through, and the more energy they lose before striking the surface of the earth. Hence there are cold polar regions, and much warmer tropical regions.

Air does not absorb much of the sun's energy, although a small amount of heat does get into the atmosphere as the sun's rays pass through it. Generally, the land and water surfaces of the earth absorb most of the sun's heat, and then they in turn transfer it back into the atmosphere.

The Heating Effect of the Sun's Rays. The rays of the sun which strike the earth directly cover a smaller area; more heat results in that area.

Land surfaces are better absorbers of the sun's energy than water surfaces. They heat up more quickly and become hotter than water surfaces. For that reason the Northern Hemisphere, where most of the land surface is located, has a warmer summer than the Southern Hemisphere, which is mostly water. However, a good absorber of heat also loses heat quickly. That is why winters in the Northern Hemisphere are colder than winters in the watery Southern Hemisphere. During a long winter night, the land surfaces lose more heat than they have gained during the day.

Water, which takes more time to heat than land does, also takes longer to cool. Temperature differences from season to season are, therefore, much greater over the land than they are over water.

Because no heat is coming from the sun at night, the atmosphere loses some of the heat which it gained by day. The heat loss continues throughout the night, and the hour just before sunrise is the coolest.

Pressure of the Atmosphere. The atmosphere presses down on the earth, just as a stack of books presses down on each book in the stack and on the table beneath. The pressure on the book at the bottom of the pile is greater than the pressure on any of the books above it.

The air at sea level is denser and heavier because it is pressed down by the air above it. That is why the pressure at the bottom of the atmosphere at or below sea level, is greatest. Air becomes thinner and lighter as we go higher above sea level. The higher we go above sea level, the less air there is above us, and therefore the less pressure.

Air exerts pressure because of its weight. It weighs only 1¼ ounces per cubic foot at sea level, but the atmosphere extends to a height of several hundred miles. The pressure of the atmosphere at sea level, therefore, is approximately fifteen pounds per square inch. This amounts to almost a ton of pressure on each square yard of the earth's surface. We are not usually conscious of this great pressure because air is everywhere around us. Since the air pressure is equal inside and outside our bodies, it does not cause us any great physical discomfort.

The human body is accustomed to normal air pressures. That is why people who live near sea level have difficulty breathing at high altitudes. Airplanes that fly at great heights above sea level have specially built cabins where normal sea level pressures can be maintained mechanically.

Why Air Pressure Changes. Air pressure is not always or everywhere the same, however. It changes from day to day and from place to place on the earth's surface. When air is heated, it expands and becomes lighter. Lighter air, of course, exerts less pressure than heavier air. In the same way, when air is cooled it contracts and becomes

PREVAILING WINDS

At the equator, the air becomes heated and rises. It cools as it rises, and releases moisture in the form of daily rainfall. The area of rising air, or *low,* is called the Doldrums. Some of the rising air from the Doldrums is pushed all the way to the poles.

heavier than the warm air. You can see, therefore, how temperature changes in the atmosphere are bound to cause changes in the air pressure. An air pressure less than normal (less than 15 pounds per sq. inch) is called "low pressure." An air pressure more than normal is called "high pressure." Scientists and weather observers use a *barometer* to measure air pressures.

How Winds Get Their Start. The air over a highly heated portion of the earth receives more heat from the surface than air over a cooler surface. The heated air expands and becomes lighter. This creates an area of the atmosphere where the air pressure is lower, called a *low.* Where air is cooler and heavier, the pressure is higher. An area of cool, heavy air is called a *high.* Air always moves from where the pressure is high to where the pressure is low. When this air moves across the earth's surface it is called *wind.* The greater the difference

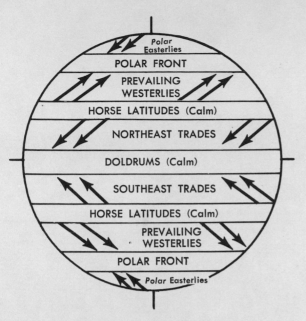

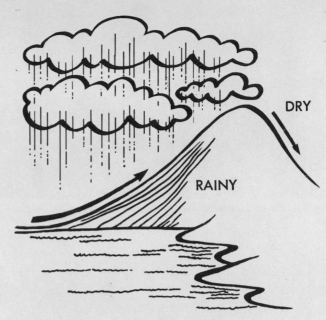

Here, the cooled air descends. This area of descending air is a *high*.

Some air from the Doldrums does not reach the polar highs. It descends in the Horse Latitudes, another belt of calm highs. The polar easterlies, the steady trades, and

the prevailing westerlies move air away from the highs.

In addition to these regular wind patterns, high mountains, large bodies of water, and other local conditions also have a strong effect on wind force and direction.

in pressure between the high and the low, the greater the strength of the wind. Wind should not be confused with the up and down movement of air called a *current*.

Winds are named by the direction from which they blow. A wind that blows from north to south is called a north wind, a wind that blows from east to west is called an east wind, and so on.

Wind and Calm Belts. In order to understand how the air is circulated over the earth's surface, we must locate the great areas of low and high pressure. In the equatorial region, there are always vertical or nearly vertical rays of the sun striking the surface and heating the atmosphere. Temperatures here are always high. The air in this region is highly heated, expands, and becomes lighter. This causes a belt of low pressure called the *doldrums* to develop in the vicinity of the equator. The doldrums are a belt of calms around the earth where

only light, variable winds develop. The most important air movements in the doldrums are the upward currents. The air is forced to rise by the cooler and heavier air from the north and the south that flows into this belt of low pressure.

The rising air in the doldrum belt overflows at higher levels. It cools and becomes heavier as it moves northward and southward. It begins once again to settle back in currents to the earth's surface. This causes belts of high pressure known as *horse latitudes*. They form where the air is settling north and south of the equator. Like the doldrums, the horse latitudes are calm belts where only light, variable winds may develop.

Part of the air which settles to the earth's surface in the high pressure horse latitudes moves along the surface, as a wind, toward the low pressure doldrums. The rest moves along the surface toward the poles. The

DAY: Hot air rises over land. Cool Breeze flows in to replace it.

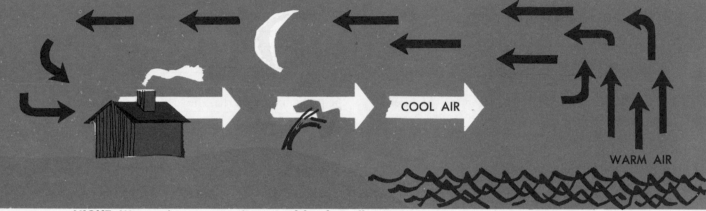

NIGHT: Warm air over sea rises. Cool land air flows out to sea.

Land Breezes and Sea Breezes. Small boat owners are familiar with this effect. At night, a steady land breeze blows; in the daytime, it reverses.

winds that blow from the horse latitudes toward the doldrums are called *trade winds.*

In the Northern Hemisphere the trades blow from the northeast and in the southern hemisphere they blow from the southeast. Those that move toward the poles from the horse latitudes are called westerlies. The cold polar regions are high pressure areas from which the air flows outward. The place where the warmer westerlies meet the cold air flowing out from the poles is called the *polar front.* Stormy and unsettled conditions always prevail at the polar fronts of both hemispheres

The trades and the westerlies are known as *prevailing winds* because they always blow fairly steadily from one direction.

Shifting of Winds. The winds do not always blow as shown in the diagram of the prevailing winds on page 297. As the sun's vertical rays move north and south over the earth's surface, the centers of the low pressure doldrums and the high pressure horse latitudes shift northward and southward. This causes the trade and westerly wind belts to shift accordingly. Because of the shifting of the wind belts and the calm belts, it is possible for certain places to be in one belt for part of the year and in another belt for another part of the year.

In addition to shifting of the wind belts, local conditions also affect wind circulation. An example of this is the sea and land breezes experienced by people who live along the coast. The diagram on this page will help you to understand why these winds blow from opposite directions during the day and the night.

How Moisture Gets Into the Air. The atmosphere always contains some water vapor. We are not conscious of it because we usually cannot see, feel, taste, or smell it. Water vapor is a colorless and odorless gas. The process by which a liquid or solid, such as water or ice, is changed into a gas, or vapor, is called *evaporation*. The water vapor in the atmosphere evaporates from the oceans, lakes, and rivers and from the surface of the earth itself. Of course, most of the water vapor comes from the oceans since they cover three fourths of the earth's surface.

The word *humidity* is used to describe the condition of the air with respect to the amount of water vapor in it. When we say the air is humid we mean that it has a lot of water vapor in it.

Evaporation is influenced by different conditions of the air. The warmer the air, the greater the rate of evaporation because warm air is "thirstier" than cool air—it can hold more water vapor. Perhaps you have noticed how, on a windy day, wet clothes dry very quickly. Air in motion increases the rate of evaporation. Dry air can take up more water vapor than air which already contains a large amount of water vapor.

HOW MOISTURE GETS INTO THE AIR

Evaporation is the term we use to mean the process by which moisture, in liquid form, is changed into a gas in the atmosphere. This process is going on all the time. Water from the oceans, lakes, rivers, and streams is absorbed into the air in varying amounts and at varying speeds, according to the temperature of the air, the speed of the winds, and other conditions.

In this illustration, energy from the sun heats the surface of the water, the land, and the air above them. As the air is heated, it becomes able to absorb more moisture. Evaporation takes place—water passes into the air as vapor.

Higher up, the air cools. It can no longer contain as much moisture. The excess moisture condenses in liquid form onto tiny dust particles, forming clouds.

Relative Humidity. When we compare the amount of water vapor the air is holding at a given temperature with the amount the air can hold at that temperature, we call the comparison *relative humidity.* Remember that relative humidity is always expressed as a *ratio,* or comparison, of two things. For example, if the air is holding one half as much water vapor as it could hold at a certain temperature, we say the relative humidity is fifty percent. If the air is holding all the water vapor it can, it is said to be *saturated;* its relative humidity is one hundred percent. Relative humidity is always written as a percent rather than as a fraction.

When the relative humidity is very high, the air is holding nearly all the moisture it can. The air then feels sticky and muggy, and we say it is humid. On such days, people feel uncomfortable and lazy. High relative humidity slows up the evaporation of perspiration from our skin, so that we feel damp and warm. People feel more uncomfortable as the result of high relative humidity than as the result of high temperature. In the same way, high humidity can make the winter's low temperatures more uncomfortable. A relative humidity of about fifty percent seems best for human comfort.

How Moisture Leaves the Air. We have all noticed how water droplets sometimes form on cold window panes, glasses of soda, or other cold surfaces. This happens where water vapor comes out of the air and forms as moisture on a cold surface.

The process by which water vapor leaves the air and changes to some form of water or ice is called *condensation.* Condensation is just the reverse of evaporation. Above the earth's surface vapor condenses onto tiny dust particles floating in the atmosphere. These serve as a cold surface upon which the water vapor can form.

Clouds and Fog. When the droplets of moisture are so small in size that any slight motion of the air keeps them floating, they form clouds or fog. Clouds and fogs are alike except that clouds form at higher levels, while fogs form near the surface.

Many types of clouds form at varying heights above the surface of the earth.

KINDS OF CLOUDS

One of the most accurate ways to forecast weather is ready to be used at all times—the clouds in the sky. (Left, top)—*Cirrus* clouds. These form at altitudes of 5 to 6 miles and are thin and fleecy. They usually mean a gradual change in the weather. (Left, middle)—*Cumulus* clouds. These are fleecy on top, flat on the bottom, and usually form about one mile high. They indicate fair weather. (Left, bottom)—*Stratus* clouds. These occur at low altitudes, and usually bring steady rain.

(Below)—*Cumulo-nimbus* clouds. *Nimbus* means a cloud from which rain is falling. These are darker than cumulus, and usually extend vertically to a great height. They are often called *thunderheads,* and their appearance means a violent change in the weather.

These clouds are signs that changes are taking place in the atmosphere and are of great importance in predicting weather.

Fogs are really low clouds. They are more likely to occur at night. That is when the lower air cools off, losing some of the heat it gained during the day. The moisture in the air then condenses because the cooler air can no longer contain all the moisture it could when it was warm. Other fogs are the result of cold air coming into contact with warm air and mixing with it. Fogs lift when the air is heated by the rays of the sun. The warmer air is then able to hold more water vapor. Fog droplets evaporate and again become part of the atmosphere.

Hail and Sleet. Hail generally occurs during the summer. It is believed that hail forms when raindrops are lifted up into high, cold atmosphere by the strong up-currents which develop during a thunderstorm. When the raindrops reach freezing levels, they turn into hail. They may be blown into upper and lower levels several times, so that additional layers of ice form on them. When the hailstones become heavy enough, they fall to the earth. Hailstones have been known to grow to the size of golf balls and larger. They sometimes cause severe damage to buildings, animals and crops.

Sleet is different from hail. It is really frozen rain and occurs during the winter.

Rain and Snow. Rain consists of large particles of water that form within clouds when droplets combine. When these particles of water grow too heavy to stay in the air they fall as raindrops. Very often rain falling from clouds evaporates back into the air as it falls toward the earth. Sometimes, drops of rain are so small that they seem to be floating toward the earth rather than falling. This kind of light rain is called drizzle.

Snow forms in the same manner as rain, except that the temperature within the cloud is below freezing. Snow, however, is not frozen rain. At freezing temperatures water vapor forms into solid crystals of water which we call snow. Melting snow gives us water.

Different Forms of Precipitation. Five of the six pictures on these two pages show precipitation. Find the one which shows something else.

Rain drops passing through a freezing layer of air form into small pellets of ice and fall to the ground mixed with the rain which did not freeze. During the winter, rain sometimes freezes when it strikes the earth forming sheet ice. The weight of sheet ice often breaks down tree branches and telephone and electric wires. During sleet and sheet ice weather, many highway accidents occur. When these conditions exist, motorists are advised to be extra cautious.

Rain, snow, hail and sleet are called by one common name—*precipitation*.

Dew and Frost. Dew and frost differ from rain and snow in that they do not fall from the air. They are not included in the definition of the weather term precipitation.

Dew forms when warm moist air comes into contact with a colder surface. It may form on the ground, on blades of grass, on automobiles, or on anything at the earth's surface that is cold enough. Dew forms best on clear nights. Then there are no clouds which otherwise act as a blanket to prevent the cooling of the earth's surface.

Frost occurs when the water vapor in the air condenses on freezing surfaces to form ice crystals. Fruit crops are very sensitive to frosts. They are damaged when late spring frosts come after warm weather has caused the trees to bloom. Frost kills the open blossoms which would later form the fruit. In such cases, the trees produce little or no fruit during the year.

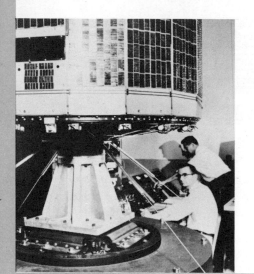

WEATHER INSTRUMENTS

Recent developments and improvements in the design of electronic devices, rockets, and calculators have all helped in the business of predicting the weather.

In the photograph above and to the left, a large ocean liner is making its way slowly through a dense fog. This was once highly dangerous. Now, thanks to radar and other new devices, accidents due to poor visibility are rare.

Above, right, the paths of weather elements, such as storms and fronts, are automatically tracked on a large map. To the left, final touches are put on our weather satellite, *Tiros*, before it was sent into orbit. Now it photographs cloud formations and relays the important information back to earth.

What Is Weather? Weather is the condition of the air at any given time and place. It refers to atmospheric conditions for short periods of time such as an hour, a day, or a week. Temperature, atmospheric pressure, moisture conditions, the amount and kinds of clouds, and winds are known as *weather elements*. Since the weather elements change from day to day and from hour to hour, it is hard to predict what the weather will be like for more than a few days ahead.

Each day after the sun rises, temperatures generally increase until about the middle of the afternoon. Later on, as night approaches, the temperature goes down until the following sunrise. As the temperature changes, all the other weather conditions change, too. The atmospheric pressure, the winds, and moisture conditions in the air change every time the temperature rises or falls. These changes bring about gradual or sometimes very sudden changes in weather.

The Weather Bureau. Our government has set up a bureau which gives weather service to all parts of our country. The Weather Bureau is part of the Department of Commerce and has its main office in Washington, D.C. It has many weather stations in all parts of the United States.

At these stations, complete observations are made every day at 1:30 A.M., 7:30 A.M., 1:30 P.M., and 7:30 P.M., Eastern Standard Time. The information is reported to Washington, D.C., as well as to other main offices. Additional weather information is also sent to these offices from neighboring countries, ships at sea, and airplanes in flight.

All the information gathered is recorded on a blank map of the United States. The finished map gives the weather conditions at each station. Numbers and other symbols are used to save space. This map is then used by the weathermen in making their predictions for the following day. It gives the most accurate weather information possible. Perhaps you have seen a weather map in your daily newspaper.

Airlines people use weather maps before clearing their flights. This information protects the lives of the pilot, crew members, and passengers, as well as millions of dollars worth of aircraft and cargo. Even the route the plane is to take will be based upon the available weather information. Frequent radio bulletins are sent out to fliers on long flights to insure their safety.

Everyone benefits in comfort and convenience from the work of the Weather Bureau. It tells us how warm to dress and whether or not to wear rubbers and raincoat, or carry an umbrella. Business people who ship perishable goods, fuel dealers, farmers, merchants, and many others depend upon information given out by the Weather Bureau.

HURRICANE HUNTERS

The strange, saucer-shaped object in the picture above is a radar set. It can detect large masses of violent air, such as hurricanes, as they develop far at sea.

The United States Weather Bureau, assisted by the Armed Forces, maintains radar and other devices to locate these damaging storms. Sometimes, daring pilots fly their planes right into one of these storms so they can record its course and speed.

Now, people living in the path of an approaching storm usually receive early enough warning so that they can protect their lives and property. Sometimes, however, scientific devices fail, and storms take a terrible toll in human suffering and property loss. In spite of his many wonderful achievements, man can never hope to control the world of nature completely.

THE UNITED STATES WEATHER BUREAU

For centuries, men have been able to look at various signs about them—in the sky, in the air, in the ocean waves—and come close to predicting the next day's weather. A farmer in one part of the country might know that an east wind and a certain type of cloud formation occurring together usually bring rain. A sailor might know that a "falling barometer"—a sharp drop in air pressure —usually brings strong winds.

It was not until the last fifty years or so, however, that serious attempts were made to predict weather, several days in advance, with scientific precision. Gradually, instruments were developed which went beyond the well-known thermometer and barometer.

A gauge was invented which would accurately measure the speed of the wind. Other devices soon appeared—to measure rainfall, moisture in the air, average daily temperatures and other conditions. Gradually, weather predicting became a science. It is known today as *meteorology*.

The United States Weather Bureau was started under the control of the Signal Corps of the Army in 1870. As the science of meteorology grew, so did the United States Weather Bureau. From its start as a small agency of the Army, it has grown to its present position as one of the most important bureaus of the Department of Commerce. It maintains branches and stations all over the

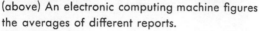

(above) An electronic computing machine figures the averages of different reports.

(opposite) From the flight tower of an airfield; statistics go to district centers

(top right) A meteorologist at the district center tapes his findings on a recorder.

(middle right) A business machine card is made out and punched to record statistics.

(lower right) Graphs which record hourly changes in weather must be checked often.

United States and in some foreign countries.

Today, weather observers from more than 800 stations report twice daily to their district centers. These are larger offices, placed in different sections of our country. The district centers study the various reports and from them make their predictions. They supply newspapers, radio and television stations, airlines, shipping lines, and other groups with the necessary information about the coming weather. In addition, automatic computing machines compare all the reports from the district centers and sort them. By this means, it is often possible for the Weather Bureau to predict weather for weeks, or even months, in advance.

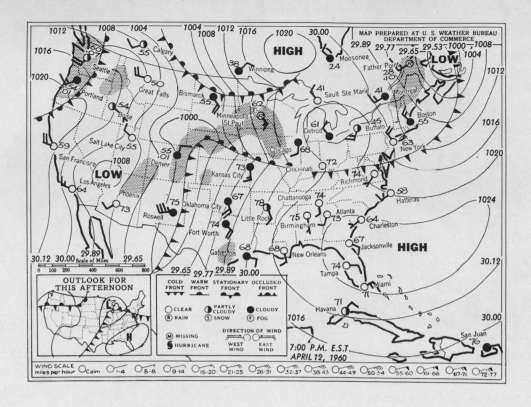

Weather Map of the United States. This special map is not so complicated as it looks. The various symbols help show the weather at a glance.

Charting the Weather. The earth's atmosphere is made up of large bodies of air called *air masses*. These air masses take on the temperatures and moisture condition of the surface areas over which they form. As air pressures change, due to unequal heating of the earth's atmosphere, these air masses move from the regions where they were formed.

Air masses moving in from the polar regions are cold, and those from the direction of tropical regions are warm. Air masses that develop over the land are dry and those that develop over the sea are moist. Each air mass always carries along with it the weather conditions of the region where it developed.

The boundary where two different air masses meet is called a *front*. The greatest changes in the weather always occur at or near the fronts because of the meeting of warmer and cooler air. By keeping track of the movements of air masses and fronts, the weatherman is better able to make his daily weather predictions. The weatherman can, with the help of his sensitive instruments, measure such things as changing temperature and pressure, wind direction and speed, relative humidity, kind and amount of precipitation, kind and amount of clouds, and other weather elements.

Weather experts study each new weather map together with several older ones before they venture a prediction. They know from a study of the maps the position of the different air masses and fronts and the direction and speed with which they are moving. By knowing the kind of weather taking place within the air masses shown on the map, as well as the changes of weather that occur at the fronts, predictions can be made with considerable accuracy.

Weather and Climate. Climate is not just another word for weather. Weather is the condition of the air on a given day or two. *Climate* means the kind of weather a region has year after year. Climate refers to how hot or cold it is from season to season, whether there is much or little rainfall, the kind and direction of the winds, and the amount of cloudiness.

Before describing the climate of a place, we must have on hand a record of its temperature and rainfall from month to month. We must also understand how its latitude, altitude, distance from the sea, prevailing winds, and position with respect to mountains affect the climate.

How Latitude Affects Climate. As you go from the equator toward the poles, it becomes generally colder. In the tropics or low latitudes, which enjoy vertical rays of the sun, we find high average temperatures and hot climate the year round. In the polar regions or high latitudes, where the rays of the sun are most slanting, we are likely to have low average temperatures and cold climate the year round. In the intermediate zone or middle latitudes average temperatures are neither too high or too low. However, there are great temperature differences between the summer and winter seasons especially in the interior of the continents.

The climate of a place cannot be determined from latitude alone. Places in the same latitude often have entirely different temperatures or may differ in the amount of rainfall. Local conditions can give a cooler climate to a tropical region, or a warmer climate to a polar region. In addition, as you have already learned, a place may move from one wind belt to another in the course of a year.

LATITUDE AND CLIMATE. The Eskimo of the Polar latitudes differs greatly as to food, clothing, and shelter from the dweller in tropical latitudes of South America, Indonesia, and other lands near the equator. Heavy fur clothing, snow huts or log-and-sod cabins, and meat and fish suit people in cold lands; light clothing, straw houses, fruit and vegetables suit the people of hot countries.

Low Altitude

High Altitude

Prevailing Winds and Climate. The Sahara Desert, in the picture below, is an example of lands in the Trade Winds Belt. The climate is the same all year—hot and very dry. (Right) the changeable climate in Prevailing Westerlies lands— mild summers and winters, four distinct seasons, rain and snow.

Altitude and Climate. Places located along the same degree of latitude do not always have the same climate. Differences in surface, closeness to bodies of water, and winds can bring about differences in climate. The lowland along China's east coast, for example, has a hot, moist climate; the high plateau of Tibet has a cold, dry climate. They are both at about 30° north latitude.

How Altitude Affects Climate. Let us consider two places having the same latitude. If one is lowland area at sea level, while the other is a mountain region several thousand feet above sea level, they will have distinctly different climates even though they are both in the same latitude, sometimes even though they are located close together. As an average, the temperature falls at the rate of about three degrees for every one thousand feet above sea level. Therefore, at an altitude of a mile above sea level, temperature would be about sixteen degrees lower than at sea level in the same latitude.

For example, Guayaquil, a coastal city in Ecuador, and Quito, the capital city of Ecuador, located high in the Andes Mountains, both lie approximately on the equator. Guayaquil is hot and humid throughout the year, while Quito has a mild climate.

Water Bodies and Climate. The interiors of continents in the middle latitudes have climates with hot summers and cold winters. The coldest place in the Northern Hemisphere is not at the North Pole, which is surrounded by water, but deep in the continental interior of northern Asia where winter temperatures sometimes go down to ninety degrees below zero. In this same region, temperatures may rise quite high during the summer. Places located inland at great distance from the sea are said to have a *continental interior climate*.

Lands in the middle latitudes located near large bodies of water, as well as islands in the ocean, are said to have *marine climates*. Winds that blow in from the oceans (which are cooler than the land in summer) keep the summer temperatures from becoming too high. In the winter when the ocean waters are warmer than

Prevailing Westerlies

the land, the winds that blow in from the oceans keep the winter temperatures from becoming too low. Cities located along the coast or on islands, therefore, have milder climates than inland cities.

Sometimes even in a continental interior a large lake or inland sea may make the climate of the surrounding region somewhat milder. For example, in the United States, cities on the Great Lakes have winters a little warmer and summers a little cooler than they would if the lakes were not there.

In most cases, places located near large bodies of water have milder climates than places located at greater distances from the water.

Winds and Climate. In many parts of the world, winds blow from the same direction much of the time. Such places have fairly even climates, and the temperature

conditions do not change greatly from season to season.

Places having marine climates owe their climate to the prevailing winds that blow in from the sea. The western coasts of North America and Europe have marine climates because the westerly winds blow toward them from over the Pacific and Atlantic oceans.

Places located in the interior of continents generally receive winds blowing from all different directions. Therefore, they have changeable weather and an unsettled climate.

Throughout most of the North and South intermediate Zones, the prevailing winds over the oceans blow from the west. For this reason, places along the west coasts in the belt of the prevailing westerly winds have even milder temperatures than places along east coasts. For example, the climate of the west coast of the United States is milder than that of the east coast.

Mountains and Climate. Where the windward side (side struck by the wind) of a mountain faces or is near the ocean, the rainfall is especially heavy. For example, the windward slopes of the Sierra Nevadas and the Cascade Mountains face the Pacific Ocean. The moisture-laden winds from the ocean bring this region the heaviest rainfall in the United States.

The leeward sides (side away from the winds) of the Sierra Nevadas and the Cascades have far less rainfall than the windward sides. Our American deserts are on the leeward side of these mountains.

Mountains sometimes protect places from cold winds. The Alps protect the Po Valley in northern Italy from the cold winds of the north. In our own country the Central Valley of California is protected from cold winds by the high surrounding mountains.

Storm Damage. This aerial photograph shows dramatic evidence of the damage storms can cause. A hurricane caused these floods, ruining homes.

Storms and Climate. The climate of a region may be greatly influenced by the movement of storms. In the middle latitudes the climate is characterized by very changeable weather. Areas of low pressure, called *cyclones,* or lows, form along the boundaries of the great warm and cold air masses. These lows or cyclonic storms move from west to east in the United States and other middle latitudes countries. They bring unsettled weather to places in their paths. Between the lows are areas of high pressure, called *anticyclones,* or highs, which usually bring clear weather. It is the succession of lows and highs which brings the daily changes of weather we find in most of the middle latitude lands.

Violent tropical storms called *hurricanes* occur in the Atlantic Ocean and the Gulf of Mexico near the West Indies. Most of these storms occur during the months of August, September, and October. They generally move toward Florida and the Gulf Coast, where they sometimes do tremendous damage with their violent winds. Hurricanes often move up the eastern coast of the United States causing considerable damage to coastal cities in their path. Similar storms occur in the Pacific near the Philippines and move toward Japan and the coast of China. In the Orient, these storms are called *typhoons,* a combination of Chinese words meaning "Big Wind."

Tornadoes, or twisters, are extremely violent storms which often move across wide, flat, land areas in the interior leaving death and wreckage behind them. In our country these storms are more numerous in the southern and central states. When such storms strike large towns and cities, millions of dollars' worth of damage is done.

Sometimes violent local storms occur. Thunderstorms are quite common in many parts of the world, especially during the summer season.

Climates of the World. No two places in the world have exactly the same climate. However, places in different parts of the world have climates that are similar in seasonal temperatures, amount of rainfall,

Weatherman's View of a Hurricane. On the viewing plate of his radar set, the weatherman sees this picture of the approach of a violent storm.

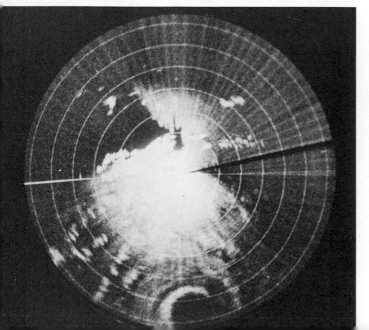

and other weather factors.

Not very long ago, geographers divided the world into exact zones. The boundaries of the zones were marked by the Tropics of Cancer and Capricorn and the Arctic and Antarctic Circles. Thus we had the Torrid, or hot, zone between the tropics; the Frigid, or cold, zones between the circles and the poles; the Temperate, or in-between, zones between the tropics and the circles. However, climates within each of the zones were so different that words like hot, cold, or in-between could not really be used to describe the climate within any zone. All places in the so-called Torrid Zone are not hot. All places in the so-called Frigid Zone are not the coldest places on the earth. Many places in the so-called Temperate Zone are not really temperate but have very hot summers and very cold winters.

Today geographers divide the world into climatic zones as shown on the map on this page.

The Approach of a Twister. This storm gives the appearance of a huge, black funnel. Its violent winds cut a path of disaster across the land.

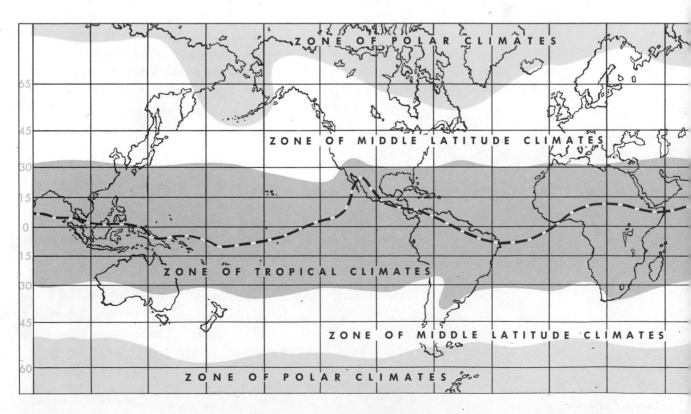

Adjusting to a Low Latitude Climate. In Africa, near the equator, the hot, rainy climate causes people to dress lightly and build special homes.

Tropical or Low Latitude Climates. Places at or near the equator are in the Doldrum Belt all year. They have a tropical rain forest, or jungle, climate. Among the tropical rain forest areas are the Amazon Valley of South America, the Congo Basin of Africa, and the islands of Indonesia. They have high temperatures and are rainy throughout the year. Afternoon thundershowers occur almost daily.

Moving north and south from the equatorial region we find areas that are not, as a rule, so hot nor so rainy. Because the wind and calm belts shift north and south during the year, these areas are in the Doldrum Belt for parts of the year and in the Trade Wind Belt for the other parts. Rainy and dry seasons alternate in these lands. With less rainfall, there is no jungle but dense grasslands instead. These trop-

Climate in the Trade Wind Belt. This is the beginning of the *llanos*, or grasslands, of Venezuela. There is a dry season and a rainy one.

ical grasslands are called *savannas*. We find such grasslands in Venezuela (llanos), Northern Brazil, India, Burma, South Africa (veldt), the Sudan, and Northern Australia.

North and south of the savannas are regions that are in the Trade Wind and Horse Latitude belts all year. They receive little rainfall throughout the year. Among them are the Sahara of North Africa, the Arabian Desert, the Great American Desert of the Southwestern United States and Northern Mexico, the Kalahari Desert of South Africa, the Atacama Desert of Peru and Chile, and the Great Sandy Desert of Australia.

Middle Latitude Climates. Most places in the Middle Latitudes lie entirely, or at least partly, in the Prevailing Westerlies Belt. These regions have changeable temperatures and irregular rainfall. The winter and summer seasons are much more noticeable because of greater temperature differences.

The lands of southern Europe and Northern Africa which border the Mediterranean Sea, as well as some lands on the western sides of continents, like southern California or Central Chile, have a dry sub-tropical, or "Mediterranean," climate. During the summer these areas are in either the Trade Wind or Horse Latitude belts. Their summer is warm to hot and almost rainless. During the winter they are in the belt of the Prevailing Westerlies. Their winter season is mild and rainy although the yearly rainfall is never great.

Places that lie in the same latitudes but are located on the eastern sides of continents have a wet sub-tropical climate. They have no really dry season and there is more rain in summer than in winter. The total yearly rainfall is greater than in lands with a Mediterranean climate. Most of the

Mediterranean Climate. This is Monaco, on the coast of the Mediterranean Sea. People here enjoy a climate which affords mostly pleasant weather.

rain comes in short, heavy showers, so there is plenty of sunshine. Regions with a wet sub-tropical climate are the southeastern United States along the Atlantic and Gulf coasts, southeastern China, and Japan.

Lands on the western side of continents that are in the belt of the Prevailing Westerlies throughout the year have marine west-coast climate. These areas are influenced most by winds which blow from over the ocean all year. They have mild winters and cool summers with no distinct dry season. Wherever there are mountains in such regions, more rain always falls on their windward side. Among the regions with a

marine west-coast climate are the north-western United States, southwestern Canada, northwestern Europe, southern Chile, Tasmania, and New Zealand.

By far the greatest parts of North America, Europe and Asia lie north of the subtropical areas and east of the marine west-coast areas. They have continental climate with great extremes of temperature, sudden weather changes, blizzards in winter, and thunderstorms in summer. Winters are cold and summers are hot and humid. The most extreme continental climate, with the greatest temperature difference between winter and summer, is found in the State of Alaska. Temperatures ranging from 75 degrees below zero to 93 degrees above zero have been recorded at Fort Yukon. Other great temperature ranges are found in northern Canada, northern Europe, and Siberia.

Marine West Coast Climate. This resort is located on the windward side of the Rockies. Winds from the nearby Pacific bring mild weather all year.

The Frozen Wastes of Antarctica. It never becomes warm enough in this polar climate to melt the ice. Men can just barely exist in such a climate.

Polar Climates. Most of the areas beyond the Arctic and Antarctic circle have polar climates where it never really becomes warm.

Extending from the Arctic Ocean some distance inland in northern North America, northern Europe, and northern Siberia, are regions with a *tundra* climate. During the bitter cold winter, nights are long and days short. In summer the days are long and the sun is warm enough to thaw the ground to a depth of several feet. The only kind of vegetation that can live on the tundra are mosses and lichens.

Most of Greenland and Antarctica are buried under a great blanket of snow and ice. Here on these great icecaps it never becomes warm enough to melt the ice as fast as it accumulates. The icecaps are uninhabited except for occasional explorers, weather observers, and scientists. These areas have a *polar* climate.

Man and Environment. With the intelligence God gives them, men adapt themselves to heat and cold, wet and dry climate, high and low altitudes. They make their homes and provide for their families in all climates where life can exist. Men are not at the mercy of the elements, but provide for themselves by storing up food, by building houses for shelter to keep them warm or cool, and by making clothing to protect themselves from sun, wind, insects, heat, and frost.

Men are the lords of creation, created so by God Himself. They tower above all the animals, whom they master. Although depending on God for their daily needs, men use the elements for their own purposes. The earth belongs first to God, then to man, God's children, to whom He gave it for a home. It is the duty of men to use the earth and its resources with respect, as God meant them to be used.

Facts *to remember*

1. Weather is the condition of the air at any given time with respect to temperature, pressure, moisture, and winds. Climate is the kind of weather a region has over the years.
2. The atmosphere, which extends to a height of several hundred miles above the earth's surface, is a mixture of gases. Among these gases are nitrogen, oxygen, carbon dioxide, and water vapor and a number of rare gases.
3. Energy from the sun reaches the earth's surface and heats it. This heat is transferred from the surface of the earth to the atmosphere.
4. Because of its weight, the atmosphere exerts pressure on the earth's surface. The pressure of the air changes because all parts of the atmosphere are not equally heated.
5. Winds move from places where the pressure is high to places where the pressure is low. In some places, the direction from which the wind blows is fairly constant. In other places, it varies greatly, or there may be very little wind at all.
6. Water enters the air by evaporation to become water vapor. The amount of water vapor that can remain in the air depends on temperature of the air. Water vapor leaves the air by condensation and becomes water.
7. Clouds, fog, rain, snow, hail, sleet, dew and frost may occur when condensation takes place in the atmosphere.
8. The Weather Bureau sends out complete weather information several times a day. This weather information appears on maps in the form of numbers and symbols.
9. Air masses are large bodies of air that have the same temperature and moisture conditions. By locating the different air masses and charting their movement weather can be predicted.
10. Great changes of weather take place along the boundaries of different air masses, or fronts.
11. The factors that control climate are: latitude, altitude, distance from the sea, position with respect to mountains and movement of storms.
12. The world can be divided into several different climatic belts. Each belt has its own set of temperatures, rainfall, and other weather conditions. They are: the tropical rain forests, the savannas, the low latitude deserts, the Mediterranean, the marine west coasts, the continental, the tundra, and the polar ice caps.

What *have I learned?*

I

Complete each of the following sentences, choosing the correct word or words in the parenthesis.

1. Of the following, the one that does not affect climate is (latitude, longitude, altitude).
2. A continental climate has summers that are (hot, cold, mild).
3. A destructive storm that sometimes moves north along the eastern coast of the United States is known as a (tornado, hurricane, typhoon).
4. On the windward sides of mountains near the sea the climate is likely to be (hot, cold, rainy).
5. Most of the world's great deserts are located in the belt of the (doldrums, trade winds, westerlies).
6. The most slanting rays of the sun strike the earth's surface in the (tropics, middle latitudes, polar regions).
7. A middle latitude city will have the least difference between summer and winter temperatures if it is located (near the coast, far inland, in the mountains).
8. Of the gases in the atmosphere, the most abundant is (oxygen, carbon dioxide, nitrogen).
9. Of the following, the best absorber of the sun's energy is (land, water, air).
10. The prevailing winds blowing from the horse latitudes toward the doldrum belt are the (westerlies, trades, easterlies).
11. Air can hold more moisture when its temperature (increases, decreases, remains the same).
12. A Mediterranean climate has summers that are (mild and rainy, hot and dry, cool and dry).
13. The doldrums are a belt of (heavy rains, low temperatures, steady winds).
14. The savannas are (deserts, grasslands, jungles).
15. The coldest temperatures in the Northern Hemisphere occur (at the North Pole, in the interior of Asia, on the western coast of Europe).

II

Answer each of the following in a complete sentence.

1. What name is given to the energy that reaches us from the sun?
2. What do we call an area of cool, heavy air?
3. What kind of climate do we find in those places in the middle latitudes which are located a great distance inland?
4. What is the name of the process by which a liquid or a solid changes into a gas?
5. What general name is given to moisture that leaves the air as rain, hail, sleet, and snow?

Facts *to understand*

Give a reason in a complete sentence for each of the following.

1. Air pressure becomes less and less, the higher we ascend into the atmosphere.
2. Winds blow from areas of high pressure to areas of low pressure.
3. Dew and frost are more likely to occur on clear nights.
4. Places near the coast have milder temperatures than places located farther inland.
5. Vertical rays of the sun have a greater heating effect than slanting rays.
6. The Northern Hemisphere has warmer summers than the Southern Hemisphere.
7. Temperature changes in the atmosphere cause changes in the pressure of the atmosphere.
8. It is possible for certain places to be located in one wind belt for part of the year, and in another wind belt for another part of the year.
9. The warmer the air, the greater the rate of evaporation of moisture into the air.
10. Dew and frost are not included in the weather term *precipitation*.

UNIT SIX REVIEW

Questions for Discussion and Review

1. Why is the time of creation as told in the Bible not really different from the explanations of the scientists? 2. How are the great distances in space measured? 3. What methods are used by scientists to figure out the length of time living things have existed on the earth? 4. What do scientists mean when they say they are "splitting the atom"? 5. How does the sun compare in size with other stars? 6. Explain what solar system means. 7. Name the planets in order of their distance from the sun. 8. Tell the difference between rotation of the earth and revolution of the earth. 9. Explain how the motions of the earth are used as the basis for keeping time. 10. Give the reasons why we have a change of seasons on the earth. 11. Explain what is meant by phases of the moon. 12.

What conditions produce an eclipse of the moon? the sun? **13.** Give one advantage and one disadvantage of a Mercator map. **14.** If two cities located on the same meridian are 10° of latitude apart, what is the distance between them? **15.** A city located in the standard time belt is crossed by the 75th meridian west. Another is near the 120th meridian west. What is the standard time difference between the two cities? **16.** Compare the Northern Hemisphere and the Southern Hemisphere with respect to land and water surfaces. **17.** Mention three movements of the sea and explain the cause of each. **18.** How do salt and other minerals get into the sea? **19.** Explain how the earth's atmosphere is heated by energy from the sun. **20.** What is the difference in meaning between weather and climate? **21.** How does the climate on windward sides of mountains differ from the climate on the leeward sides? **22.** Give some reasons why places having the same latitude may have a different climate. **23.** What are air masses? Why do they move over the earth's surface? **24.** How does a tornado differ from a hurricane?

Getting Information from Globes, Maps, and Charts

1. From the drawing on page 246, discover how Eratosthenes first measured the circumference of the earth.
2. Use a globe to demonstrate why a great circle route is the shortest distance between two points on the earth's surface.
3. Study the diagram showing the earth's revolutions on page 249. Where do the vertical rays strike the earth's surface on June 21? December 21? March 21? Sept. 23? Which season begins on each of those dates?
4. Study the diagram of the phases of the moon on page 254. How much of the moon is lighted by the sun at each phase? Why is the moon invisible at new moon?
5. Use the diagram on page 286 to explain the difference between neap and spring tides.
6. Study the cloud pictures on page 301. Make a list of the different clouds and write a one-sentence description of each.
7. Consult the weather map on page 308. Explain the numbers and symbols which are used to describe the weather at a particular city.

8. Collect newspaper weather maps for three consecutive days. Follow the progress of air masses and fronts on these maps and try to predict the weather for the fourth day.

Using Your Encyclopedia

Use reference books such as *Compton's Pictured Encyclopedia* for information on these topics. Prepare to give a report on one of them.

1. The World's Largest Telescopes
2. Origin of the Solar System
3. How the Most Distant Planet was Discovered
4. Sunspots and Their Effect on the Earth
5. Man-Made Satellites
6. The Surface Features of the Moon
7. The Midnight Sun
8. How the Sun and Stars Are Used to Find Latitude
9. Weather Instruments and Their Use
10. Rain-making
11. How a Radiosonde Works
12. History of the United States Weather Bureau

Using Geography Words

Write a sentence using each of the following to show you understand its geographic meaning.

light year	rotation	latitude
galaxy	revolution	longitude
fossil	star trails	parallel
sun spots	vertical ray	meridian
planet	solstice	standard time
planetoid	equinox	International Date Line
satellite	eclipse	isthmus
meteor	phase	continental
meteorite	sphere	shelf
		plain
comet	projection	plateau
oxygen	map scale	mountain
axis	map legend	sea level
inclination	degree	climate
weather	atmosphere	insolation
barometer	evaporation	condensation
relative humidity	precipitation	air mass
front	climate	marine
tundra	savanna	continental

Final Test

Choose from the parenthesis the correct word or words to complete each sentence. Write the sentence correctly on your answer paper.

1. A light year is a measure of (time, distance, space). **2.** The sun when compared in size to other stars is (small, large, average). **3.** The age of the earth is estimated to be several (thousand, million, billion) years. **4.** Of the following, (planets, satellites, stars) are not members of the solar system. **5.** The planet whose orbit is closest to the sun is (Mars, Mercury, Earth). **6.** Small iron and nickel bodies which drift about in space are called (comets, meteors, satellites). **7.** When it is summer in the Northern Hemisphere it is (spring, summer, winter) in the Southern Hemisphere. **8.** The vertical rays of the sun are at the equator on (Mar. 21, June 21, Dec. 21). **9.** The moon takes about (one week, two weeks, three weeks) to go from the new moon phase to full moon phase. **10.** An eclipse of the sun can occur only at (new moon, full moon, first quarter) phase. **11.** Of the following, the most accurate map is a (Mercator projection, Polar projection, globe). **12.** Black lines drawn on globes and meeting at the poles are called (parallels, meridians, circles). **13.** The instrument used to determine latitude is called a (sextant, chronometer, sun dial). **14.** If it is Wednesday just east of the International Date Line, it is (Tuesday, Wednesday, Thursday) just west of it. **15.** Of the following, (Asia, the Pacific Ocean, the Atlantic Ocean) has the greatest area. **16.** Of the following movements of the sea, the one not caused by wind is (tides, currents, waves). **17.** The gas of the atmosphere which varies most in amount from day to day is (oxygen, nitrogen, water vapor). **18.** The horse latitudes are belts of (little rainfall, heavy rainfall, moderate rainfall). **19.** The process by which water enters the air is called (insolation, evaporation, condensation). **20.** The type of climate with great differences in summer and winter temperature is known as (continental, marine, Mediterranean). **21.** The weather instrument which measures atmospheric pressure is the (thermometer, barometer, anemometer). **22.** Winds move over the earth's surface because of (unequal air pressure, rotation of the earth, gravity). **23.** The United States is located mostly in the belt of the (doldrums, trades, westerlies). **24.** The waters of the Gulf Stream compared to the temperature of surrounding waters of the Atlantic Ocean are (colder, warmer, about the same). **25.** The number of planets revolving about the sun is (five, seven, nine).

Applying Christian Principles

Choose the correct ending for each of the incomplete sentences below. Then copy the sentences on your answer paper.

1. The most important advantage of living in the space age is that it **a.** increases our possibility of trade with other nations, **b.** helps us to learn more about our neighbors overseas, **c.** makes it easier to wage war.

2. The orderly movement of bodies in the solar system is an example of **a.** the fact that scientists are never wrong, **b.** God's power and wisdom in the Creation, **c.** the theory of evolution.

3. The best use for scientific knowledge is to use it **a.** for making new discoveries, **b.** to help others, **c.** to make things more comfortable for ourselves.

4. God expects us to **a.** use everything He put on the earth for our needs, **b.** to conserve resources for future generations, **c.** use our resources to wage war.

5. Man is not at the mercy of storm, flood, and fire because **a.** God gave man intelligence, **b.** science always protects us, **c.** our clothing and shelter always prevent damage and harm.

6. In the Book of Genesis God makes clear to us **a.** that the work of Creation took exactly six days **b.** the fact of Creation in a way our limited minds can understand **c.** the entire meaning of the universe.

7. Further and more complete study of the seas and oceans of the world should result in **a.** bigger and faster steamships **b.** new ways to make use of many of the resources which God has provided for us **c.** a way to raise sunken treasures.

8. The great distances which exist between bodies in space should lead us to **a.** think of the universe as infinite **b.** marvel at the greatness and wisdom of God **c.** give up as hopeless any plans of mankind to travel in space.

9. Man is different from all the other creatures in nature because he **a.** is able to read and study **b.** has found a way to send rockets and satellites into space **c.** has an immortal soul which he has a duty to save.

Table 1

Area and Population

World Summary

	square miles	population
Africa	11,635,000	261,000,000
Antarctica	5,100,000	——
Asia	17,035,000	1,877,500,000
Australia	2,974,581	10,604,000
Europe	3,850,000	484,500,000
North America	9,028,716	273,000,000
South America	6,860,000	148,000,000

Europe

	square miles	population	Catholics
Albania	10,629	1,607,000	92,632
Austria	32,376	7,067,000	6,338,846
Belgium	11,775	9,153,000	8,800,000
Bulgaria	42,796	7,867,000	50,000
Czecho-Slovakia	49,381	13,742,000	8,600,000
Denmark	16,619	4,617,000	26,608
Estonia	17,413	1,196,000	?
Finland	130,165	4,497,000	2,340
France	212,659	46,200,000	38,399,000
Germany, East	41,645	17,241,000	1,858,770
Germany, West	95,931	56,172,000	26,618,935
Greece	51,843	8,389,000	55,000
Hungary	35,918	10,045,000	5,998,000
Iceland	39,758	179,000	806
Ireland	27,136	2,815,000	2,645,820
Italy	116,372	50,463,762	50,211,443
Latvia	24,695	2,094,000	500,000
Lithuania	26,173	2,713,000	?
Luxembourg	999	314,000	313,000
Netherlands	15,800	11,702,229	4,688,300
Norway	125,064	3,614,000	6,891
Poland	120,355	29,965,000	29,200,000
Portugal	35,466	9,146,000	8,300,000
Romania	91,584	18,567,000	1,700,000
Soviet Union	1,914,939	54,000,000	10,000,000*
Spain	195,504	30,559,000	30,293,000
Sweden	173,378	7,542,459	27,500
Switzerland	15,944	5,470,000	2,174,831
United Kingdom	94,511	52,675,094	4,941,415
Yugoslavia	98,766	18,538,150	5,894,032

Asia

	square miles	population	Catholics
Aden	112,000	660,000	300
Afghanistan	250,000	13,000,000	None
Bhutan	18,000	700,000	——
Burma	261,789	21,527,000	186,021
Cambodia	88,780	4,952,000	54,108
Ceylon	25,332	10,167,000	711,436
China	3,760,339	669,000,000	3,000,000
Hong Kong	391	3,178,000	177,279
India	1,221,880	440,316,000	6,148,627
Indonesia	735,865	95,189,000	1,271,095
Iran	628,060	20,678,000	28,893
Iraq	172,000	7,085,000	212,570
Israel	7,993	2,203,300	40,599
Japan	142,688	94,053,000	285,364
Jordan	37,500	1,690,000	46,449
Korea	85,285	32,970,000	486,127
Laos	91,000	1,850,000	24,831
Lebanon	4,000	1,822,000	689,000
Malaysia	130,407	10,019,000	189,941
Nepal	54,362	9,407,000	700
Pakistan	364,737	93,812,000	318,239
Philippines	115,758	28,727,000	21,639,181
Saudi Arabia	870,000	6,500,000	6,000
Soviet Union	6,735,201	163,500,000	10,000,000*
Syria	72,234	4,561,000	166,000
Thailand	200,148	27,181,000	111,893
Turkey	296,500	28,602,000	21,176
Vietnam	127,000	30,616,000	1,300,000
Yemen	75,000	5,000,000	——

Australia and New Zealand

	square miles	population	Catholics
Australia	2,974,581	10,603,936	2,137,373
New Zealand	103,736	2,414,984	346,531

Africa

	square miles	population	Catholics
Algeria	847,500	11,020,000	946,000
Burundi	10,744	2,500,000	1,384,582
Cameroun	166,880	4,500,000	761,727
Central Africa	238,000	1,180,000	144,424
Chad	495,000	2,571,000	75,616
Congo (Brazzaville)	139,000	790,000	266,042
Congo (Leopoldville)	904,757	14,150,000	4,996,354
Dahomey	44,290	2,050,000	240,784
Ethiopia (+Eritrea)	398,350	22,000,000	136,154
Gabon	102,290	410,000	190,899
Ghana	91,843	6,943,000	602,325
Guinea	96,865	3,000,000	22,027
Ivory Coast	127,520	3,300,000	231,529
Kenya	224,960	7,287,000	913,707
Liberia	43,000	2,500,000	12,769
Libya	679,000	1,216,000	37,858
Malagasy	228,000	5,200,000	1,104,486
Mali	450,000	4,100,000	19,197
Mauritania	418,810	1,000,000	2,000
Morocco	172,104	11,925,000	394,556
Niger	490,000	3,000,000	13,200
Nigeria	339,169	35,752,000	1,665,539
Rwanda	10,166	2,500,000	673,435
Senegal	76,000	2,260,000	155,591
Sierra Leone	27,925	2,500,000	22,557
Somali Republic	262,000	2,030,000	3,700
Republic of S. Africa	472,359	16,122,000	885,376
South-West Africa	317,887	534,000	62,999
Sudan	967,000	12,109,000	200,000
Tanganyika	362,688	9,404,000	1,487,705
Togo	20,400	1,480,000	228,821
Tunisia	58,000	4,168,000	70,000
Uganda	93,981	6,845,000	2,005,273
United Arab Republic	386,198	26.570.000	172,698

Area and Population—Continued

Africa—Continued

	square miles	population	Catholics
Upper Volta ..	105,900	4,467,000	137,257
British Territories ..	785,418	10,355,000	2,000,000
Portuguese Territories ..	793,030	11,969,855	1,906,747
Spanish Terrs. .	117,001	286,000	200,000
French Somaliland ..	8,880	81,000	5,080

North America

	square miles	population	Catholics
Bahamas	4,404	106,677	17,692
Bermuda	21	42,640	4,410
British Honduras	8,867	90,343	56,000
Canada	3,851,809	18,238,247	8,230,000
Costa Rica	23,421	1,225,000	1,089,192
Cuba	44,206	6,933,000	5,830,000
Dominican Rep.	19,333	3,098,000	3,036,791
El Salvador ...	8,259	2,501,000	2,454,780
Guatemala	42,042	3,868,000	3,486,390
Haiti	10,714	4,233,000	2,874,363
Honduras	44,482	1,883,000	1,876,205
Jamaica	4,411	1,638,000	600,000
Mexico	758,259	36,091,000	33,984,000
Nicaragua	57,145	1,477,000	1,476,120
Panama	28,576	1,084,000	796,836
Puerto Rico ...	3,435	2,349,000	2,100,000
Trinidad	1,864	859,000	120,000
United States ..	3,628,150	187,000,000	42,876,665

South America

	square miles	population	Catholics
Argentina	1,072,700	20,009,000	17,727,925
Bolivia	416,040	3,462,000	3,345,400
Brazil	3,286,270	70,799,000	64,171,400
British Guiana .	83,000	566,000	83,000
Chile	286,397	7,802,000	6,706,940
Colombia	439,520	14,447,000	14,673,300
Ecuador	116,270	4,455,000	4,105,187
French Guiana	35,135	31,000	27,129
Paraguay	157,000	1,812,000	1,703,238
Peru	514,059	10,365,000	9,800,000
Surinam	55,400	308,000	37,206
Uruguay	72,172	2,827,000	2,357,000
Venezuela	352,150	7,524,000	6,982,272

Table 2 Populations of Major Cities

A

City and Country	population
Aachen, *West Germany*	170,000
Aarhus, *Denmark*	118,493
Abadan, *Iran*	283,625
Aberdeen, *Scotland*	185,379
*Abidjan, *Ivory Coast*	125,700
*Accra, *Ghana*	388,231
Adana, *Turkey*	230,024
*Addis Ababa, *Ethiopia*	500,000
Adelaide, *Australia*	587,656
Agra, *India*	375,665
Aguascalientes, *Mexico*	126,222
Ahmedabad, *India*	788,333
Akron, *Ohio*	290,351
Albany, *New York*	129,726
Albuquerque, *New Mexico*	201,189
Aleppo, *Syria*	451,435
Alexandria, *Egypt*	1,600,000
*Algiers, *Algeria*	870,000
Allahabad, *India*	332,295
Allentown, *Pennsylvania*	108,347
Alma-Ata, *USSR*	455,000
Amagaski, *Japan*	405,955
Amarillo, *Texas*	137,969
*Amman, *Jordan*	280,000
Amritsar, *India*	325,747
Amoy, *China*	240,000
*Amsterdam, *Netherlands*	866,342
Anaheim, *California*	104,184
*Ankara, *Turkey*	646,151

City and Country	population
Anshan, *China*	400,000
Antwerp, *Belgium*	849,432
Arad, *Romania*	106,457
Arak, *Iran*	60,000
Archangel, *USSR*	256,000
Arequipa, *Peru*	124,334
Arnheim, *Netherlands*	124,818
Asmara, *Ethipoia*	132,000
Assiut, *Egypt*	400,000
Asunción, *Paraguay*	210,000
Astrakhan, *USSR*	294,000
*Athens, *Greece* 1,852,709
Atlanta, *Georgia*	487,455
Augsburg, *West Germany*	207,050
Auckland, *New Zealand*	448,365
Austin, *Texas*	186,545
Arellaneda, *Argentina*	380,000

B

City and Country	population
*Baghdad (Gr.), *Iraq*	552,047
Baku, *USSR*	968,000
Baltimore, *Maryland*	939,024
*Bamako, *Mali*	105,000
Bandung, *Republic of Indonesia* 1,046,089
Bangalore, *India*	778,977
*Bangkok, *Thailand* 2,318,000
Barcelona, *Spain* 1,800,000
Bari, *Italy*	311,268
Barnaul, *USSR*	320,000
Barquisimeto, *Venezuela*	203,000

(*denotes capital city)

Major World Cities—Continued

City and Country	population
Barranquila, *Colombia*	456,000
Basel, *Switzerland*	200,700
Basra, *Iraq*	206,000
Baton Rouge, *Lousiana*	152,419
*Beirut, *Lebanon*	500,000
Belem, *Brazil*	402,170
Belfast, *Northern Ireland*	440,100
*Belgrade, *Yugoslavia*	700,000
Belo Horizonte, *Brazil*	693,328
Benares, *India*	355,777
*Bengazi, *Libya*	70,533
Bergen, *Norway*	115,000
Berkeley, *California*	111,268
*Berlin, *East Germany*	1,084,010
Berlin, *West Germany*	2,202,200
*Berne, *Switzerland*	161,300
Bielefeld, *West Germany*	175,174
Bilbao, *Spain*	281,000
Birmingham, *Alabama*	340,887
Birmingham, *England*	1,105,651
Bloemfontein, *Rep. of South Africa*	163,000
Bochum, *West Germany*	366,383
*Bogotá, *Colombia*	1,200,000
Bologna, *Italy*	441,143
Bombay, *India*	4,146,191
*Bonn, *West Germany*	145,063
Boras, *Sweden*	67,016
Bordeaux, *France*	257,946
Boston (Gr.), *Massachusetts*	2,589,301
Bradford, *England*	295,768
Braila, *Romania*	102,491
*Brasilia, *Brazil*	141,742
Bratislava, *Czecho-Slovakia*	247,000
*Brazzaville, *Republic of the Congo*	105,200
Bremen, *West Germany*	564,979
Bremerhaven, *West Germany*	141,800
Bridgeport, *Connecticut*	156,748
Brisbane, *Australia*	620,121
Bristol, *England*	436,440
Brno, *Czecho-Slovakia*	306,371
Brunswick, *West Germany*	245,983
*Brussels (Gr.), *Belgium*	1,398,326
Bucaramanga, *Colombia*	200,000
Bucharest, *Romania*	1,236,905
*Budapest (Gr.), *Hungary*	1,850,000
Buenos Aires, *Argentina*	3,799,200
Buffalo, *New York*	532,759
Bursa, *Turkey*	153,190
Bydgoszcz, *Poland*	231,000

C

Cadiz, *Spain*	107,856
Cagliari, *Italy*	148,500
*Cairo, *Egypt*	3,100,000
Calcutta, *India*	2,926,498
Calgary, *Canada*	279,062
Cali, *Colombia*	600,000
Callao, *Peru*	131,305
Camaguey, *Cuba*	204,254
Cambridge, *Massachusetts*	107,716
Camden, *New Jersey*	117,159
*Canberra, *Australia*	56,430
Canton, *China*	1,650,000

City and Country	population
Canton, *Ohio*	113,631
Cap Haitien, *Haiti*	60,000
Cape Town, *Republic of South Africa*	731,484
*Caracas, *Venezuela*	1,371,875
Cardiff, *Wales*	251,270
Cartagena, *Colombia*	180,000
Casablanca, *Morocco*	960,812
Catania, *Italy*	361,466
Cebu, *Philippines*	259,194
Changchun, *China*	420,000
Changsha, *China*	700,000
Changteh, *China*	300,000
Charleroi, *Belgium*	469,259
Charlotte, *North Carolina*	201,564
Chattanooga, *Tennessee*	130,009
Chelyabinsk, *USSR*	688,000
Chemnitz, *East Germany*	286,226
Chengtu, *China*	440,000
Chenteh, *China*	510,000
Chicago, *Illinois*	3,550,404
Chihuahua, *Mexico*	149,437
Chinkiang, *China*	220,000
Chittagong, *Pakistan*	364,205
Christchurch, *New Zealand*	220,510
Chungking, *China*	1,620,000
Cincinnati, *Ohio*	502,550
Ciuj, *Romania*	154,752
Cleveland, *Ohio*	876,050
Cochabama, *Bolivia*	90,037
Cologne, *West Germany*	200,000
*Colombo, *Ceylon*	480,000
Columbus, *Ohio*	471,316
*Conakry, *Guinea*	100,000
Concepción, *Chile*	167,468
Constantine, *Algeria*	217,000
Constantsa, *Romania*	100,000
*Copenhagen, *Denmark*	960,913
Cordoba, *Argentina*	635,000
Cordoba, *Spain*	178,973
Corpus Christi, *Texas*	167,690
Coventry, *England*	305,060
Croyden, *England*	252,387
Curitiba, *Brazil*	361,309
Czestochowa, *Poland*	148,000

D

Dacca, *Pakistan*	556,712
Dairen, *China*	1,054,000
*Dakar, *Senegal*	234,500
Dallas, *Texas*	679,684
*Damascus, *Syria*	454,603
Davao, *Philippines*	231,833
Dayton, *Ohio*	262,332
Dearborn, *Michigan*	112,007
Debrecen, *Hungary*	130,000
Delhi, *India*	914,790
Denver, *Colorado*	493,887
Des Moines, *Iowa*	208,982
Detroit (Gr.) *Michigan*	1,670,144
Dniepropetrovsk, *USSR*	658,000
Donetsk, *USSR*	701,000
Dortmund, *West Germany*	635,199
Douala, *Cameroun*	125,000

(*denotes capital city)

Major World Cities—Continued

City and Country	population
Dresden, *East Germany*	493,515
*Dublin, *Ireland*	535,488
Duisberg, *West Germany*	503,851
Duluth, *Minnesota*	106,884
Dundee, *Scotland*	182,959
Dunedin, *New Zealand*	105,003
Durban, *Republic of South Africa*	655,000
Düsseldorf, *West Germany*	700,000

E

City and Country	population
*Edinburgh, *Scotland*	468,378
Edmonton, *Canada*	337,568
Eindhaven, *Netherlands*	168,858
Enschede, *Netherlands*	126,122
Elizabeth, *New Jersey*	107,698
Elizabethville, *Republic of the Congo*	182,638
El Paso, *Texas*	276,687
Erfurt, *East Germany*	186,000
Erie, *Pennsylavnia*	138,440
Erivan, *USSR*	509,000
Essen, *West Germany*	728,578
Evansville, *Indiana*	141,543

F

City and Country	population
Fatshan, *China*	450,000
Fez, *Morocco*	280,000
Flint, *Michigan*	196,940
Florence, *Italy*	438,138
Foochow, *China*	400,000
Fortaleza, *Brazil*	514,818
Fort Wayne, *Indiana*	161,776
Fort Worth, *Texas*	356,268
Frankfort, *West Germany*	671,624
Frederiksberg, *Denmark*	118,993
Freiburg, *West Germany*	139,000
Fresno, *California*	133,929
Fukuoka, *Japan*	647,122

G

City and Country	population
Galatz, *Romania*	102,232
Gary, *Indiana*	178,320
Gdansk (Danzig), *Poland*	286,000
Gelsenkirchen, *West Germany*	389,952
Genoa, *Italy*	775,106
General San Martin, *Argentina*	269,514
Geneva, *Switzerland*	168,900
Ghent, *Belgium*	455,022
Glasgow, *Scotland*	1,054,913
Glendale, *California*	119,442
Gorki, *USSR*	942,000
Gorlovka, *USSR*	293,000
Goteborg, *Sweden*	408,436
Granada, *Spain*	232,054
Grand Rapids, *Michigan*	201,487
Graz, *Austria*	237,041
Greensboro, *North Carolina*	119,574
Groningen, *Netherlands*	146,301
Guadalajara, *Mexico*	737,346

City and Country	population
*Guatemala City, *Guatemala*	385,000
Guayaquil, *Ecuador*	403,184

H

City and Country	population
Haarlem, *Netherlands*	169,497
Hagen, *West Germany*	197,036
(The) Hague, *Netherlands*	605,876
Haifa, *Israel*	174,000
Haiphong, *Vietnam*	367,000
Hakodate, *Japan*	243,183
Halifax, *Canada*	92,511
Halle, *East Germany*	278,700
Halsingborg, *Sweden*	77,006
Hamadan, *Iran*	100,000
Hamburg, *West Germany*	1,836,958
Hamilton, *Canada*	273,991
Hamma, *Syria*	173,000
Hammond, *Indiana*	111,698
Hangchow, *China*	600,000
Hankow, *China*	800,000
Hanoi, *Vietnam*	638,000
Hanover, *West Germany*	576,185
Harbin, *China*	760,000
Hartford, *Connecticut*	177,397
*Havana, *Cuba*	1,158,203
(Le) Havre, *France*	165,000
Heidelberg, *West Germany*	127,651
*Helsinki, *Finland*	464,100
Hiroshima, *Japan*	431,336
Hobart, *Australia*	115,887
Holguin, *Cuba*	226,644
Homs, *Syria*	293,500
Hong Kong (Br.), *China*	3,100,000
Honolulu, *Hawaii*	294,194
Houston, *Texas*	938,219
Howrah, *India*	433,630
Hue, *Vietnam*	104,500
Hyerabad, *India*	1,166,860

I

City and Country	population
Ibadan, *Nigeria*	600,000
Iloilo, *Philippines*	150,976
Inchon, *Korea*	402,000
Indianapolis, *Indiana*	476,258
Indore, *India*	310,859
Innsbruck, *Austria*	100,699
Irkutsk, *USSR*	365,000
Isfahan, *Iran*	255,000
Istanbul, *Turkey*	2,000,000
Ivanavo, *USSR*	332,000
Izmir, *Turkey*	370,923

J

City and Country	population
Jackson, *Mississippi*	144,422
Jacksonville, *Florida*	201,030
*Jakarta (Batavia), *Republic of Indonesia*	3,317,562
Jedda, *Saudi Arabia*	250,000

(*denotes capital city)

Major World Cities—Continued

City and Country	population
Jersey City, *New Jersey*	276,100
*Jerusalem, *Israel*	161,000
Jogjakarta, *Republic of Indonesia*	341,424
Johannesburg, *Republic of South Africa*	1,096,541

K

City and Country	population
*Kabul, *Afghanistan*	300,000
Kaliningrad *USSR*	202,000
Kanpur (Cawnpore), *India*	705,383
Kansas City, *Kansas*	121,901
Kansas City, *Missouri*	475,539
Kaohsiung, *Taiwan (Formosa)*	438,429
*Karachi, *Pakistan*	1,912,598
Karaganda, *USSR*	398,000
Karlsruhe, *West Germany*	244,000
Kassel, *West Germany*	209,792
*Katmandu, *Nepal*	175,000
Katowice, *Poland*	269,000
Kawasaki, *Japan*	632,975
Kazan, *USSR*	643,000
Keelung, *Taiwan (Formosa)*	286,373
Khabarovsk, *USSR*	322,000
Kharkov, *USSR*	930,000
*Khartoum, *Sudan*	93,103
Kiel, *West Germany*	272,000
Kiev, *USSR*	1,102,000
Kingston-upon-Hull, *England*	303,268
Knoxville, *Tennessee*	111,827
Kobe, *Japan*	1,113,977
Kowloon, *China*	675,000
Krasmoyarsk, *USSR*	409,000
Krasnodar, *USSR*	312,000
Krefeld, *West Germany*	210,519
Krivoy Rog, *USSR*	386,000
*Kuala Lumpur, *Malaysia*	316,230
Krakow, *Poland*	479,000
Kuibyshev, *USSR*	806,000
Kure, *Japan*	210,000
Kyoto, *Japan*	1,284,818

L

City and Country	population
*Lagos, *Nigeria*	379,000
Lahore, *Pakistan*	1,296,477
Lanchow, *China*	600,000
Lansing, *Michigan*	113,058
Lanus, *Argentina*	244,473
*La Paz, *Bolivia*	347,394
La Plata, *Argentina*	410,000
Lattakia, *Syria*	109,216
Lausanne, *Switzerland*	118,900
Leeds, *England*	510,597
Leicester, *England*	273,298
Leipzig, *East Germany*	592,821
Leningrad, *USSR*	3,300,000
Leon, *Mexico*	209,469
*Leopoldville, *Republic of the Congo*	389,547
Liege, *Belgium*	607,117
Lille, *France*	194,616

City and Country	population
*Lima, *Peru*	1,262,107
Lincoln, *Nebraska*	128,521
Linz, *Austria*	196,206
*Lisbon, *Portugal*	818,382
Little Rock, *Arkansas*	107,813
Liverpool, *England*	747,490
Ljubljana, *Yugoslavia*	155,000
Lodz, *Poland*	708,000
*Lome, *Togo*	70,000
London, *Canada*	169,564
*London (Gr.), *England*	8,171,902
Long Beach, *California*	344,168
Los Angeles, *California*	2,479,015
Louisville, *Kentucky*	390,639
*Luang Prabang, *Laos*	45,000
Lübeck, *West Germany*	233,320
Lucknow, *India*	496,861
Ludwigshafen, *West Germany*	167,440
Lugansk, *USSR*	274,000
*Luxembourg, *Luxembourg*	80,000
Lvov (Lwow), *USSR*	410,000
Lyons, *France*	553,039

M

City and Country	population
Macao (Port.), *China*	187,772
Macon, *Georgia*	122,876
Madison, *Wisconsin*	126,700
Madras, *India*	1,725,216
*Madrid, *Spain*	2,000,000
Madura, *India*	361,781
Magdeburg, *East Germany*	260,618
Magnitogorsk, *USSR*	311,000
Makassar, *Republic of Indonesia*	603,767
Makeyevka, *USSR*	358,000
Malaga, *Spain*	350,000
Malang, *Republic of Indonesia*	374,554
Malmo, *Sweden*	235,370
*Managua, *Nicaragua*	176,569
Manchester, *England*	661,041
Mandalay, *Burma*	186,000
Manila (Gr.), *Philippines*	3,006,627
Mannheim, *West Germany*	312,000
Mansura, *Egypt*	146,700
Maracaibo, *Venezuela*	456,000
Mar del Plata, *Argentina*	270,000
Marianao, *Cuba*	229,576
Marrakech, *Morocco*	241,900
Marseille, *France*	661,492
Mecca, *Saudi Arabia*	300,000
Medan, *Republic of Indonesia*	532,129
Medellin, *Colombia*	650,000
Meknes, *Morocco*	177,128
Melbourne (Gr.), *Australia*	1,907,366
Memphis, *Tennessee*	497,524
Merida, *Mexico*	170,513
Meshed, *Iran*	242,000
Messina, *Italy*	251,423
Mexicali, *Mexico*	171,648
Mexico City (Gr.), *Mexico*	4,829,402
Miami, *Florida*	291,688
Milan, *Italy*	1,580,978
Milwaukee, *Wisconsin*	741,324

(*denotes capital city)

City and Country	population
Minneapolis, *Minnesota*	482,782
Minsk, *USSR*	509,000
Miskole, *Hungary*	175,000
Mobile, *Alabama*	202,779
*Mogadishu, *Somali Republic*	86,643
Molotov (Perm), *USSR*	628,000
*Monrovia, *Liberia*	53,000
Monterrey, *Mexico*	596,993
*Montivideo, *Uruguay*	922,885
Montgomery, *Alabama*	134,393
Montreal, *Canada*	1,191,062
*Moscow, *USSR*	5,032,000
Mosul, *Iraq*	340,541
Moulmein, *Burma*	103,000
Mukden (Shenyang), *China*	2,290,000
Mülheim (Ruhr), *West Germany*	186,114
München-Gladbach, *West Germany*	153,543
Munich, *West Germany*	1,102,914
Murcia, *Spain*	243,000
Murmansk, *USSR*	226,000

N

Nagasaki, *Japan*	344,153
Nagoya, *Japan*	1,591,935
Nagpur, *India*	449,099
*Nairobi, *Kenya*	186,000
Nanking, *China*	1,113,972
Nantes, *France*	222,790
Naples, *Italy*	1,179,608
Nashville, *Tennessee*	170,874
Natal, *Brazil*	162,537
Newark, *New Jersey*	405,220
New Bedford, *Massachusetts*	102,477
Newcastle, *Australia*	208,905
Newcastle, *England*	269,389
*New Delhi, *India*	2,000,000
New Haven, *Connecticut*	152,048
New Orleans, *Louisiana*	627,525
New York City, *New York*	7,781,984
Niagara Falls, New York	102,394
Nice, *France*	244,360
*Nicosia, *Cyprus*	82,000
Nijmegen, *Netherlands*	131,593
Nikolayev, *USSR*	224,000
Ningpo, *China*	300,000
Niteroi, *Brazil*	245,467
Nizhni Tagil, *USSR*	338,000
Norfolk, *Virginia*	304,869
Nottingham, *England*	311,645
Novosibersk, *USSR*	887,000
Nuremburg, *West Germany*	461,319

O

Oakland, *California*	367,548
Oberhausen, *West Germany*	259,000
Odense, *Denmark*	105,915
Odessa, *USSR*	667,000
Ogomosho, *Nigeria*	139,000
Oklahoma City, *Oklahoma*	324,253

City and Country	population
Omaha, *Nebraska*	301,598
Omdurman, *Sudan*	132,619
Omsk, *USSR*	579,000
Oporto, *Portugal*	310,475
Oran, *Algeria*	430,000
Osaka (Gr.), *Japan*	3,011,563
Oshogobo, *Nigeria*	122,000
*Oslo, *Norway*	461,591
Ostrava, *Czecho-Slovakia*	199,902
*Ottawa, *Canada*	429,750
Oxford, *England*	106,124

P

Palembang, *Republic of Indonesia*	723,000
Palermo, *Italy*	587,063
Palma, *Spain*	140,000
*Panama City, *Panama*	200,000
*Paris (Gr.), *France*	2,850,189
Pasadena, *California*	116,407
Paterson, *New Jersey*	143,663
Patna, *India*	362,817
Patras, *Greece*	95,364
Pecs, *Hungary*	115,000
*Peiping, *China*	4,140,000
Penang, *Republic of Malaysia*	234,930
Penza, *USSR*	605,000
Peoria, *Ilinois*	103,162
Perth, *Australia*	419,755
Peshawar, *Pakistan*	218,691
Philadelphia, *Pennsylvania*	2,002,512
*Phnom-Penh, *Cambodia*	550,000
Phoenix, *Arizona*	439,170
Pilsen (Plzen), *Czecho-Slovakia*	134,273
Piovdiv, *Bulgaria*	162,518
Piraeus, *Greece*	183,877
Pittsburgh, *Pennsylvania*	604,332
Ploesti, *Romania*	114,560
Plymouth, *England*	204,279
Poona, *India*	480,982
Port Said, *Egypt*	240,000
*Port-au-Prince, *Haiti*	200,000
Portland, *Oregon*	372,676
Porto Alegre, *Brazil*	641,473
Portsmouth, *England*	215,198
Poznan, *Poland*	408,000
*Prague, *Czecho-Slovakia*	988,949
*Pretoria, *Republic of South Africa*	420,000
Providence, *Rhode Island*	207,498
Puebla, *Mexico*	287,952
Puntarenas, *Costa Rica*	49,870
Pusan, *Korea*	1,162,614
Pyongyang, *Korea*	285,965

Q

Quebec, *Canada*	357,568
*Quezon City, *Philippines*	394,374
*Quito, *Ecuador*	277,270

(*denotes capital city)

Major World Cities—Continued

R

City and Country	population
*Rabat, *Morocco*	224,901
Ramat Gan, *Israel*	82,000
*Rangoon, *Burma*	740,000
Rawalpindi, *Pakistan*	340,175
Reading, *Pennsylvania*	98,177
Recife, *Brazil*	797,234
Regina, *Canada*	112,141
Resht, *Iran*	109,491
*Reykjavik, *Iceland*	76,000
Richmond, *Virginia*	219,954
*Riga, *Latvia*	605,000
Rio de Janeiro, *Brazil*	3,307,613
*Riyadh, *Saudi Arabia*	280,000
Rochester, *New York*	318,611
Rockford, *Illinois*	128,075
*Rome, *Italy*	2,160,773
Rosario, *Argentina*	761,300
Rostock, *East Germany*	155,351
Rostov-on-Don, *USSR*	597,000
Rotterdam, *Netherlands*	729,744

S

City and Country	population
Sacramento, *California*	191,667
*Saigon, *Vietnam*	1,800,000
*Salisbury, *South Rhodesia*	260,800
Salonika (Thessaloniki), *Greece*	373,635
Salt Lake City, *Utah*	189,454
Salvador, *Brazil*	655,735
Salzburg, *Austria*	106,897
*Sana, *Yemen*	75,000
San Antonio, *Texas*	587,718
San Diego, *California*	573,224
San Francisco, *California*	740,316
San Jose, *California*	204,196
San Jose, *Costa Rica*	144,454
San Luis Potosi, *Mexico*	159,640
*San Salvador, *El Salvador*	203,000
Santa Ana, *El Salvador*	109,711
Santa Clara, *Cuba*	144,630
Santa Fe, *Argentina*	275,000
*Santiago, *Chile*	1,914,539
Santiago de Cuba, *Cuba*	166,565
Santo Domingo, *Dominican Republic*	367,053
Santos, *Brazil*	265,735
São Paulo, *Brazil*	3,850,000
Sapporo, *Japan*	523,829
Sarajevo, *Yugoslavia*	395,000
Saratov, *USSR*	581,000
Saskatoon, *Canada*	95,256
Savannah, *Georgia*	149,245
Scranton, *Pennsylvania*	111,443
Seattle, *Washington*	557,087
Semarang, *Republic of Indonesia*	520,565
Sendai, *Japan*	425,272
*Seoul, *Korea*	2,444,883
Seville, *Spain*	500,000
Sfax, *Tunisia*	65,635
Shanghai, *China*	7,100,000
Sheffield, *England*	493,954
Sherbrooke, *Canada*	66,554

City and Country	population
Shiraz, *Iran*	171,000
Shizouka, *Japan*	328,819
Shreveport, *Louisiana*	164,372
Sian, *China*	1,500,000
Siangtan, *China*	300,000
Singapore, *Republic of Malaysia*	1,665,400
Skopje, *Yugoslavia*	167,000
*Sofia, *Bulgaria*	725,756
Solingen, *West Germany*	177,175
Somerville, *Massachusetts*	94,697
Soochow, *China*	260,000
South Bend, *Indiana*	132,445
Spokane, *Washington*	181,608
Springfield, *Massachusetts*	174,463
Srinagar, *India*	207,787
Stalingrad, *USSR*	680,000
Stalino, *USSR*	1,050,000
Stalinsk, *USSR*	377,000
Stavanger, *Norway*	53,000
St. Etienne, *France*	181,730
St. John, *Canada*	95,563
St. Johns, *Canada*	90,838
St. Louis, *Missouri*	750,026
St. Paul, *Minnesota*	313,411
St. Petersburg, *Florida*	181,298
*Stockholm (Gr.), *Sweden*	1,125,000
Stoke-on-Trent, *England*	265,506
Strasbourg, *France*	200,921
Stuttgart, *West Germany*	648,639
Subotica, *Yugoslavia*	118,000
Sucre, *Bolivia*	60,092
Suez, *Egypt*	156,300
Surabaya, *Republic of Indonesia*	1,310,631
Surakarta, *Republic of Indonesia*	445,305
Sverdlovsk, *USSR*	777,000
Swansea, *Wales*	166,740
Sydney (Gr.), *Australia*	2,181,211
Syracuse, *New York*	216,038
Szczecin (Stettin), *Poland*	269,000
Szeged, *Hungary*	136,752

T

City and Country	population
Tabriz, *Iran*	290,000
Tacoma, *Washington*	147,979
Taegu, *Korea*	678,277
Taichung, *Taiwan (Formosa)*	286,058
Tainan, *Taiwan (Formosa)*	324,147
*Taipei, *Taiwan (Formosa)*	947,922
Taiyuan, *China*	500,000
Tallin, *Estonia*	280,000
Tampa, *Florida*	274,970
Tampere, *Finland*	127,300
Tampico, *Mexico*	122,197
*Tananarive, *Malagasy*	240,000
Tangier, *Morocco*	141,926
Tanta, *Egypt*	175,000
Tashkent, *USSR*	911,000
*Tegucigalpa, *Honduras*	125,000
*Tehran, *Iran*	2,000,000
Tel Aviv-Jaffa, *Israel*	383,000
Tetuan, *Morocco*	101,155
Three Rivers, *Canada*	53,477

(*denotes capital city)

City and Country	population
Tientsin, *China*	3,100,000
Tiflis, *USSR*	694,000
Tilburg, *Netherlands*	138,546
Timisoara, *Romania*	142,251
*Tirana, *Albania*	59,887
*Tokyo (Gr.), *Japan*	10,115,795
Toledo, *Ohio*	318,003
Tomsk, *USSR*	249,000
Topeka, *Kansas*	119,484
Toronto, *Canada*	1,824,481
Torreon, *Mexico*	179,955
Toulouse, *France*	268,863
Tourane, *Vietnam*	110,500
Trenton, *New Jersey*	114,167
Trieste, *Italy*	273,390
Tripoli, *Lebanon*	100,000
*Tripoli, *Libya*	170,000
Trondheim, *Norway*	59,000
Tsinan, *China*	472,279
Tsingtao, *China*	850,508
Tucson, *Arizona*	212,892
Tucuman, *Argentina*	251,000
Tula, *USSR*	345,000
Tulsa, *Oklahoma*	261,685
*Tunis, *Tunisia*	680,000
Turin, *Italy*	1,019,230
Turku, *Finland*	127,400

U

Ufa, *USSR*	546,000
*Ulan Bator, *Mongolian Republic*	150,000
Upsala, *Sweden*	79,292
Utica, *New York*	100,410
Utrecht, *Netherlands*	256,332

V

*Vaduz, *Liechtenstein*	3,300
Valencia, *Spain*	544,306
Valencia, *Venezuela*	161,443
Valparaiso, *Chile*	261,684
Vancouver, *Canada*	790,165
Varna, *Bulgaria*	119,769
Vasteras, *Sweden*	79,210
Venice, *Italy*	336,184
Veracruz, *Mexico*	144,232
Verdun, *Canada*	78,317
Verona, *Italy*	221,138
Vicente Lopez, *Argentina*	149,958

City and Country	population
Victoria, *Canada*	154,152
*Vientiane, *Laos*	138,000
*Vienna, *Austria*	1,670,000
Vilnyus, *Lithuania*	235,000
Vinh, *Vietnam*	150,000
Vladivostok, *USSR*	283,000
Volvograd, *USSR*	591,000
Voronezh, *USSR*	454,000

W

*Warsaw, *Poland*	1,136,000
*Washington, *District of Columbia*	763,956
Waterbury, *Connecticut*	107,130
*Wellington, *New Zealand*	249,138
Wenchow, *China*	631,276
Wichita, *Kansas*	254,698
Wichita Falls, *Texas*	101,724
Wiesbaden, *West Germany*	258,700
Wilmington, *Delaware*	95,827
Windsor, *Canada*	114,367
Winnipeg, *Canada*	475,989
Winston-Salem, *North Carolina*	111,135
Worcester, *Massachusetts*	186,587
Wroclaw, *Poland*	429,000
Wuhan, *China*	1,800,000
Wuppertal, *West Germany*	420,000

Y

Yanchow, *China*	250,000
*Yaoundé, *Cameroun*	60,000
Yarmouth, *England*	65,000
Yaroslavl, *USSR*	406,000
Yawata, *Japan*	332,163
Yokahama, *Japan*	1,375,710
Yokosuka, *Japan*	287,000
Yonkers, *New York*	109,634
Youngstown, *Ohio*	166,689

Z

Zagreb, *Yugoslavia*	470,000
Zahle, *Lebanon*	40,000
Zamboanga, *Philippines*	131,411
Zaporozhe, *USSR*	435,000
Zaragoza, *Spain*	301,000
Zhadanov, *USSR*	284,000
Zurich, *Switzerland*	428,000
Zwickau, *East Germany*	129,394

(*denotes capital city)

Table 3 Exports and Imports

EUROPE

CHIEF EXPORTS	← country →	CHIEF IMPORTS
Iron and steel products, textiles, coal, flax	Belgium	Wool, cotton, wheat, meats, metal goods
Tobacco, eggs, barley, corn, silk, attar of roses	Bulgaria	Textiles, machinery, metals, paper
Dairy products, pork, fish	Denmark	Textiles, mineral oils, coffee, oil cake, automobiles
Wood pulp, paper, timber, butter	Finland	Machinery, foods, cotton, textiles
Cotton, woolen, and silk textiles, wine, iron and steel products	France	Wool, cotton, wheat, pearls, precious stones, machinery, wines, coffee, meats, fruits
Iron and steel goods, machinery, chemicals, coal and coke, textiles, paper	Germany	Meats, wheat, cotton, wool, timber, iron ore, oilseeds
Tobacco, currants, wine, raisins	Greece	Wheat and other foods, textiles
Cereals, cattle, hogs, hides	Hungary	Foods, textiles, mineral oils, machinery
Cattle, pork, dairy products, eggs, horses	Irish Republic	Foods, coal, machinery, iron and steel products
Silk, textiles, rice, hemp, automobiles, chemicals, fruits	Italy	Cotton, wheat, coffee, wood, petroleum products, iron and steel products
Meats, dairy products, sugar, textiles, machinery	Netherlands	Timber, cereals, coffee, coal, mineral oils, chemicals
Fish, wood products, aluminum	Norway	Foods, automobiles, machinery
Wood products, coal, metals, meats, eggs	Poland	Cotton, chemicals, metals
Fish, wine, cork	Portugal	Fish, wheat, sugar, cotton, iron and steel
Corn, barley, wheat, petroleum products, timber	Romania	Textiles, metals, machinery
Wheat, wood products, petroleum products, furs	Russia (USSR)	Cotton, wool, machinery, tea, rubber
Fruits, olive oil, wines, cork, lead	Spain	Cotton, machinery, fertilizers, automobiles, corn
Wood products, meats, iron ore, metal goods	Sweden	Coal, iron and steel, copper, foods
Textiles, cheese, watches, clocks, machinery	Switzerland	Foods, silk, cotton, wool, iron and steel, coal
Textiles, iron and steel products, machinery, coal	United Kingdom	Foods, wool, cotton, rubber, petroleum products, metals, wood products
Livestock, eggs, fruits, wood	Yugoslavia	Textiles, coffee, rice, machinery

ASIA

CHIEF EXPORTS	← country →	CHIEF IMPORTS
Tea, rubber, copra, coconut oil	Ceylon	Rice, textiles, coal, petroleum products
Bean cake, beans, silk, coal, eggs, millet, tea, cotton	China	Sugar, rice, cotton, petroleum products, silver, coal, paper
Wheat, tea, rice, oilseeds, cotton, jute, gunny cloth	India	Cotton manufactures, machinery, sugar, iron and steel products
Rice, rubber, coal, zinc, fish	Indochina	Textiles, machinery, foods
Rubber, sugar, tobacco, petroleum products	Indonesia	Textiles, rice, iron and steel products
Dates, hides	Iraq	Textiles, iron and steel products
Raw silk, textiles, coal, glass, metals, tea, sugar, drugs	Japan	Cotton, wood, oil cake, wool, iron and steel products, mineral oils
Rubber, tin, rice, copra	Malaya	Rice, coal, foods, iron and steel goods
Oil, rugs, fruits, cotton	Iran	Textiles, sugar, tea, metals, automobiles
Fruits, nuts, silks, hides	Israel	Textiles, foods, machinery
Copra, sugar, tobacco, manila hemp	Philippine Islands	Textiles, machinery
Rice, tin, rubber, teak, tungsten	Thailand	Foods, textiles, metal products
Rugs, hides	Syria	Textiles, hardware
Fruits, tobacco, rugs	Turkey	Cotton, textiles, metals, coffee, tea, sugar

AFRICA

Wines, sheep, wheat, fruits, nuts, wool	Algeria	Textiles, sugar, coffee, petroleum products
Cobalt, gold, diamonds, uranium ore, rubber, palm nuts, ivory	Belgian Congo	Petroleum products, textiles, clothing, machinery
Cotton, cotton seeds, cottonseed cake, onions	Egypt	Tobacco, timber, flour, automobiles, coal
Hides, meat, gold, vanilla	Madagascar	Textiles, iron and steel goods
Wheat, barley, hides, skins	Morocco	Textiles, machinery, hardware, tea, sugar, candles, spirits
Olives, hides	Tunisia	Textiles, metal products
gold, diamonds, wool, hides and skins	Union of South Africa	Textiles, clothing, timber products, machinery

AUSTRALIA

Wool, wheat, flour, butter, meats, sugar, lead	Australia	Textiles, petroleum products, automobiles, machinery, iron and steel products
Dairy products, wool, meats	New Zealand	Textiles, iron and steel products, machinery

SOUTH AMERICA

CHIEF EXPORTS	← country →	CHIEF IMPORTS
Corn, wheat, linseed oil, wool, meats, hides, quebracho extract	Argentina	Oils and fats, textiles, iron and steel products, timber, machinery
Tin, silver, lead, copper, rubber	Bolivia	Wheat, textiles, petroleum products
Coffee, oranges, hides, rubber, yerba maté	Brazil	Machinery, petroleum products, automobiles
Copper, nitrate, iodine, wool, oats, barley, wheat	Chile	Machinery, petroleum products, automobiles, iron and steel goods
Coffee, bananas, hides, platinum, petroleum	Colombia	Foodstuffs, textiles, iron and steel products, automobiles
Coffee, cacao, bananas, rice, balsa wood	Ecuador	Foods, textiles, machinery
Oranges, yerba maté, timber, hides, tobacco, beef, quebracho extract	Paraguay	Textiles, machinery
Cotton, sugar, vanadium, petroleum, hides, copper	Peru	Foods, textiles, machinery
Meats, hides, wool, linseed oil	Uruguay	Textiles, machinery, lumber, petroleum products
Petroleum, coffee, cacao, iron ore, sugar, gold	Venezuela	Iron and steel products, foods, textiles

NORTH AMERICA

CHIEF EXPORTS	country	CHIEF IMPORTS
Wheat, wood pulp, paper, wood, manufactured products, fish, iron	Canada	Sugar, coffee, rubber, tea, cotton, mineral oils, machinery, textiles
Coffee, bananas, cacao	Costa Rica	Textiles, iron and steel products, foods
Sugar, tobacco, molasses	Cuba	Foodstuffs, machinery, various manufactured articles
Sugar, coffee, cacao, tobacco	Dominican Republic	Textiles, iron and steel goods, foods
Coffee, sugar, henequen	El Salvador	Textiles, machinery, iron and steel goods
Coffee, bananas	Guatemala	Textiles, iron and steel products, foods
Coffee, cotton, wood	Haiti	Textiles, iron and steel products
Bananas, sugar	Honduras	Iron and steel products, foods
Petroleum, silver, lead, zinc, coffee	Mexico	Machinery, textiles, iron and steel products
Bananas, mahogany, coffee, sugar	Nicaragua	Textiles, foodstuffs, machinery
Bananas, cacao, hides, cabinet woods	Panama	Foods, textiles, machinery
Cotton, mineral oils, wheat, iron and steel products, lumber, machinery	United States	Sugar, raw silk, wood, spices, tin, coffee, tea, rubber, wood pulp, paper

Table 4 # The Planets and the Solar System

Distance from Sun
(in miles)

Planet	Greatest	Least
Mercury	43,355,000	28,566,000
Venus	67,653,000	66,738,000
Earth	94,452,000	91,342,000
Mars	154,760,000	128,330,000
Jupiter	506,710,000	459,940,000
Saturn	935,570,000	836,700,000
Uranus	1,866,800,000	1,698,800,000
Neptune	2,817,400,000	2,769,600,000
Pluto	4,300,000,000	2,750,000,000

Distance from Earth
(millions of miles)

	Greatest	Least
Mercury	136	50
Venus	161	25
Earth	—	—
Mars	248	35
Jupiter	600	367
Saturn	1028	744
Uranus	1960	1606
Neptune	2910	2677
Pluto	3600	3200

Table 5 # Size and Time

World Dimensions

Population of the Earth	2,700,000,000 people
Diameter of the Earth	8,000 miles (approx.)
Circumference of the Earth	25,000 miles (approx.)
Area of the Earth	197,000,000 square miles
Land Area of the Earth	56,000,000 square miles U.S. 6% of land area
Water Area of the Earth	141,000,000 square miles
Highest Altitude of Land, Mt. Everest, Asia	29,002 feet
Lowest Altitude of Land, Dead Sea, Palestine	1,292 feet
Greatest Depth of Ocean, off Philippine Islands, Pacific Ocean	34,218 feet

Size and Time—Continued

Oceans and Areas

Arctic Ocean 5,541,000
Atlantic Ocean 31,529,000
Pacific Ocean 63,985,000
Indian Ocean 28,357,000

Mountains and Heights

Asia, Mt. Everest, Nepal-Tibet 29,002
South America, Mt. Aconcagua, Argentina 23,081
North America, Mt. McKinley, Alaska 20,269
Africa, Mt. Kilimanjaro, Tanganyika 19,565
Europe, Mt. Elborus, Caucasus 18,481
Antarctica, Mt. Markham 15,100
United States, Mt. Whitney, California 14,495
Australia, Mt. Kosciusko, New South Wales 7,328

Islands and Areas

Greenland, Arctic Region 837,000
Papua (New Guinea) East Indies 342,232
Madagascar, Indian Ocean 228,707
Borneo, East Indies 282,416
Baffin, Arctic Region 231,000

Rivers and Lengths

miles

Nile, Africa 4,000	Amur, Asia 2,900	Hwang, Asia 2,700
Amazon, South America 3,900	Lena, Asia 2,860	Mekong, Asia 2,600
Yangtze, Asia 3,100	Yenisei, Asia 2,800	Mackenzie, Canada 2,500
Congo, Africa 2,900	Missouri, United States . . . 2,723	Mississippi, United States . . . 2,470

Standard Time Differences

At 12 o'clock noon U.S. Eastern Standard Time (New York City), the standard time in foreign cities is as follows:

	Bogotá . . . . 12:00 NOON	Honolulu . . . . 7:00 A.M.*
	Bombay . . . . 10:30 P.M.	Hongkong . . . . 1:00 A.M.*
	Budapest . . . . 6:00 P.M.	London . . . . 5:00 P.M.
	Buenos Aires . . . . 2:00 P.M.	Mexico City . . . . 11:00 A.M.
	Calcutta . . . . 10:30 P.M.	Moscow . . . . 8:00 P.M.
	Capetown . . . . 7:00 P.M.	Paris . . . . 6:00 P.M.
Athens . . . . 7:00 P.M.	Caracas . . . . 12:30 P.M.	Rome . . . . 6:00 P.M.
Baghdad . . . . 8:00 P.M.	Geneva . . . . 6:00 P.M.	Tokyo . . . . 2:00 A.M.*
Belfast . . . . 5:00 P.M.	Halifax . . . . 1:00 P.M.	Warsaw . . . . 6:00 P.M.
Berlin . . . . 6:00 P.M.	Havana . . . . 12:00 NOON	Winnipeg . . . . 11:00 A.M.

*next day

Index and Pronunciation

KEY: This list of key sounds will help you to pronounce the words marked in the index:

āte	ănother	ēve	silĕnt	charĭty	hŏt	fŏŏt	ūnite	then
alwăys	ärm	hēre	makĕr	ōld	cŏntain	out	hŭt	thin
câre	ȧsk	ĕvent	īce	ōbey	sŏft	oil	circŭs	pictûre
hăt	Africȧ	ĕnd	ĭll	ôr	mōōn	ūse	fûr	menü

*denotes photo caption

Credits

The full color global relief photographs, reproduced on the pages listed below, were photographed for the exclusive use of WILLIAM H. SADLIER, INC., in their textbooks and related publications. The photographs are of the six-foot geo-physical relief globe, photographed by special arrangement with GEO-PHYSICAL MAPS, INC., copyright 1956, New York. The global photography was done by CARU STUDIOS.

Global relief photographs: cover, 2-3, 18-19, 54-55, 94-95, 130-131, 194-195, 226-227

The maps reproduced on the pages listed were made by the following *cartographers:*

GENERAL DRAFTING CO., INC., 6, 22, 44, 58, 78, 98-99, 107, 134-5, 152-3, 172-3, 179, 184, 198-199, 246, 247, (bottom), 256-257 (top), 259, 262, 263, 264, 266, 288-9

CARU STUDIOS: 4 (top), 5 (bottom), 7, 16, 20 (bottom), 56, 96 (bottom), 133, 136, 140, 143, 146-7, 178, 234, 236-237 (bottom), 238-9, 247 (top), 250, 251, 258, 259, 267, 268, 271, 274-5, 294, 295

HAGSTROM MAP CO., 249

NEW YORK TIMES, 308

VITALE STUDIOS, 313

The illustrations reproduced on the pages listed were made by the following *artists:*

CARU STUDIOS, 12 (top), 13 (bottom)

H. B. VESTAL, title, 17, 53 (top), 93, 129, 193, 225

VITALE STUDIOS, 8, 67, 86, 110 (top), 232, 241, 243 (bottom), 254 (top), 260-261, 269, 278-9, 280 (top), 284-5, 286, 293, 296-7, 298, 299, 300-301, 306

The *photographs* reproduced on the pages listed were obtained from the following sources:

AMERICAN MUSEUM OF NATURAL HISTORY, 230 (Hayden Planetarium), 231, 242 (Hayden Planetarium), 242 (bottom), 243 (top), Yerkes Observatory, Williams Bay, Wisconsin), 248, 253 (Lick Observatory University of Southern California), 254 (bottom), 257 (bottom), 276, 282-283 (bottom), 283 (top)

BLACK STAR PUBLISHING COMPANY, 126 (bottom left), 156, 159

CANADIAN PACIFIC RAILWAY, 316 (top)

CHARLES PHELPS CUSHING, 20 (top, Sawders), 24 (top, Sawders), 33 (Sawders), 38 (bottom), 41 (Sawders), 50 (Sawders), 75 (Sawders), 108 (top, Sawders), 115 (top Sawders), 120 (bottom, Sawders)

FREELANCE PHOTOGRAPHERS GUILD, 35, 66 (top), 76 (top), 85, 86, 97 (top, A. Miller), 115 (bottom), 122 (top), 125 (bottom), 126 (top), 137 (bottom), 138 (bottom, Gatti), 139 (top, Gatti), 155 (Weldon King), 161 (Weldon King), 163 (top, Gatti), 175 (top, Gatti), 175 (bottom, Weldon King), 180 (bottom left, Weldon King), 185 (bottom left, Weldon King)

FRENCH GOVERNMENT TOURIST AGENCY, 315

EWING GALLOWAY, 25, 28, 37, 73 (top, left), 73 (top, right), 73 (bottom), 84, 90 (top), 96 (top), 113 (top), 119 (left, top right, bottom right), 136 (bottom), 141, 148, 149, 150 (Lanks), 156 (bottom), 157, 166 (top), 169 (top), 174 (2), 176 (bottom), 178, 181 (bottom, right), 185 (top, right), 186 (bottom, B. Holmes), 228, 252, 270, 271 (2), 277 (top), 287 (2), 290 (bottom), 303 (left), 311 (top), 314

PHILIP GENDREAU, 39 (bottom), 48, 49 (top), 61 (top, right), 61 (bottom, left), 121, 125 (top), 142 (Delavarre), 144 (Insert), 189, 281, 292, 300-301, 302 (top, bottom), 303 (top, bottom, right), 309 (4), 311 (bottom), 312 (2), 313 (top), 314 (top)

GRACE LINES, 47

HOUSE OF PHOTOGRAPHY, 26 (Charles Perry Weimer), 32 (bottom, Charles Perry Weimer), 36 (Charles Perry Weimer), 42 (top, Charles Perry Weimer), 43 (Charles Perry Weimer), 57 (left, Charles Perry Weimer), 57 (right), 61 (bottom right), 62, 63 (bottom, Charles Perry Weimer), 105 (bottom, Charles Perry Weimer), 112, 113, 116-117 (Charles Perry Weimer), 158 (top), 162 (bottom, left), 162 (top), 162 (bottom, right), 170 (Wilcox), 183 (Dan Weiner)

LOOK MAGAZINE, 110 (bottom), 111 (3)

MARYKNOLL, 10 (right), 11 (left), 11 (right), 40, 188

F. A. PLATTNER, S.J., 8, 10

MONKMEYER PRESS PHOTO SERVICE, 4 (bottom, Mann), 5 (top), 13 (Silberstein), 25 (bottom), 29, 46 (Fujihira), 49 (Mann, bottom), 70 (bottom), 74 (bottom), 77 (Barna), 80, 100 (Shier), 108 (bottom), 114 (Fujihira, top), 120 (Watson, top), 143 (bottom), 144 (top), 145, 169 (bottom), 176 (top), 181 (left)

PAN AMERICAN COFFEE BUREAU, 103

PIX, INC., 277 (bottom, Ernest Reshovsky), 316 (bottom)

RAPHO-GUILLUMETTE, 42 (bottom, Silberstein), 72, 90 (bottom, Davis Pratt), 104 (Davis Pratt, top)

RELIGIOUS NEWS SERVICE, 167, 171 (left)

SHOSTAL PRESS AGENCY, 1, 14 (Charles Weimer, bottom), 30 (Robert Leahey), 31 (Joe Barnell), 46 (bottom, Joe Barnell), 50 (J. D. Winbray, top), 63, (top), 66 (bottom, John Oros), 70 (bottom, Art D'Arazien), 71 (Doris Jacoby), 79 (Art D'Arazien), 82 (Art D'Arazien), 83 (top), 83 (bottom), 87, 102 (top left, Barnell), 102 (bottom, Barnell), 106, 114 (bottom), 121, 122 (bottom), 137 (top, W. R. Donagho), 138 (top, Charles Erikson), 139 (bottom, H. Street), 146 (top, Thelma Johnson, bottom, Paul Hufner), 147 (bottom, Rupert Leach), 151 (Paul Hufner), 154 (top, Charles Erikson), 158 (bottom, J. D. Winbray), 159 (top, Maynard Williams), 163 (bottom, left, James Bishop), 170 (top, Albert Addy, bottom, D. O'Shea), 171 (bottom, right, Erich Kollmar), 182 (H. Street), 186 (top, H. Street), 187 (Ace Williams)

SOUTH AFRICAN TOURIST CORPORATION, 133 (bottom)

THREE LIONS, 14 (top, Pet.), 21 (Manning), 27 (Manning), 39 (Evans), 45 (Evans), 65 (top, bottom, Peterson), 68 (Evans), 74 (Evans), 88 (left), 89 (Evans), 124, 164 (Nerton), 165 (Nerton), 180 (top, left, Evans), 188

UAT FRENCH AIRLINES, 137, 137 (insert)

US WEATHER BUREAU, 305 (Raytheon), 306, 307

UNITED PRESS INTERNATIONAL, 60 (Acme), 64 (Acme), 101 (bottom), 245, 280 (bottom), 290 (top, Acme), 304 (3), 310 (bottom)

WIDE WORLD PHOTOS, INC., 32 (top), 36 (top), 38 (top), 69, 86 (left), 88 (top, bottom, right), 152, 163 (bottom, right), 180 (right), 181 (top, right), 185 (top, left)

WHITE FATHERS MISSIONS, 154 (bottom), 159 (bottom, left)

*Set in Linotype Times Roman by American Typesetting Corporation
and Primar Typographers, Inc.*

Typography design by William Nicoll

Format by F. Sadlier Dinger

Printed by Polygraphic Company of America, Incorporated

Bound by Van Rees Book Binding Corporation, and John F. Cuneo Company

Published by William H. Sadlier, Inc., New York and Chicago

World
ATLAS

The New Catholic Geography Series

ATLAS OF THE WORLD

The pages of maps in this atlas cover the entire world. They have been brought together so that you can turn to them whenever you need a good map. The detailed maps are here for reference and they should be used constantly for obtaining all kinds of geographic information.

The maps employ different colors to indicate different political sub-divisions such as states and countries. Other symbols are used to show such features as mountains, large bodies of water, rivers, capital cities, etc. The relative size and importance of cities are indicated by the size of the type used to name them. A scale of miles is given with many of the maps so that the distance between places can be accurately measured. Parallels and meridians are indicated to help you locate places with respect to the equator and the prime meridian.

Get into the habit of consulting your atlas frequently. It will help you gain a better understanding of the way geography influences people's lives in our country and in other lands. Use the maps to make comparisons and to help you solve geographic problems. The atlas should be used as a reference in just the same way as you use your dictionary or an encyclopedia.

PUBLISHED BY

W. H. Sadlier, Inc.

Printed in the United States of America

I-66 CS

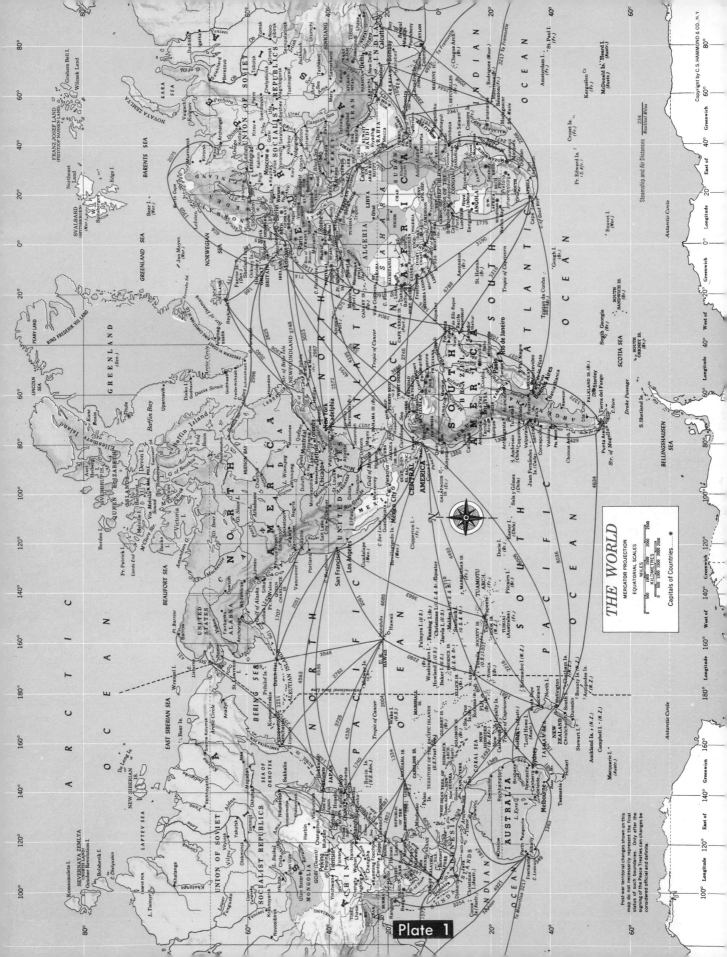

THE WORLD

MERCATOR PROJECTION

EQUATORIAL SCALES

MILES

KILOMETRES

Capitals of Countries......●

Post-war territorial changes shown on this map do not necessarily represent the final status of such boundaries. Only after the signing of the Peace Treaties can changes be considered official and definite.

Steamship and Air Distances

Plate 1

UNITED STATES

POLYCONIC PROJECTION

SCALE OF MILES

0 50 100 200 300 400

SCALE OF KILOMETRES

0 100 200 300 400

Capitals of Countries .... ☆
State Capitals .... △
International Boundaries .... —

Copyright by C.S. Hammond & Co., N.Y.

Plate 3

Plate 4

UNITED STATES
Northeastern Section

POLYCONIC PROJECTION

SCALE OF MILES

National Capitals .... ⊗
State and Provincial Capitals ...... ◉
International Boundaries ...... ·—·—·
State and Provincial Boundaries ...... ·····

Copyright by C. S. HAMMOND & CO., N. Y.

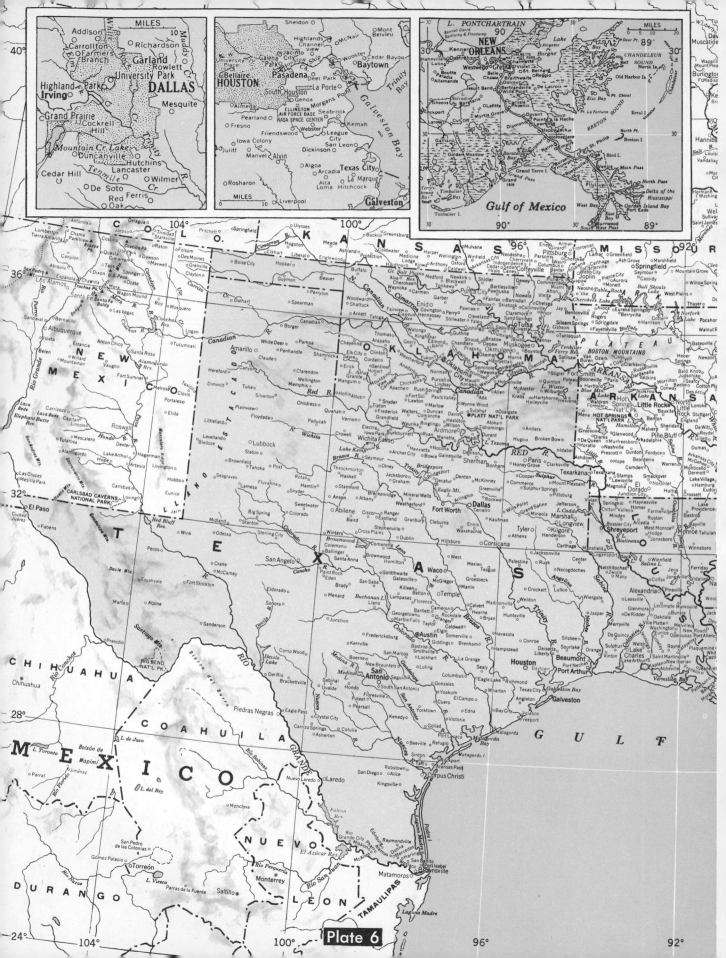

Plate 6

UNITED STATES
Southeastern and
South Central Section

POLYCONIC PROJECTION

SCALE OF MILES

0   50   100   150   200   250

National Capital .... ⊛
State and Provincial Capitals .... ⊙
International Boundaries ....
State and Provincial Boundaries .... — ⋅ —
Canals ....

Copyright by C. S. HAMMOND & Co., N.Y.

Plate 7

Plate 8

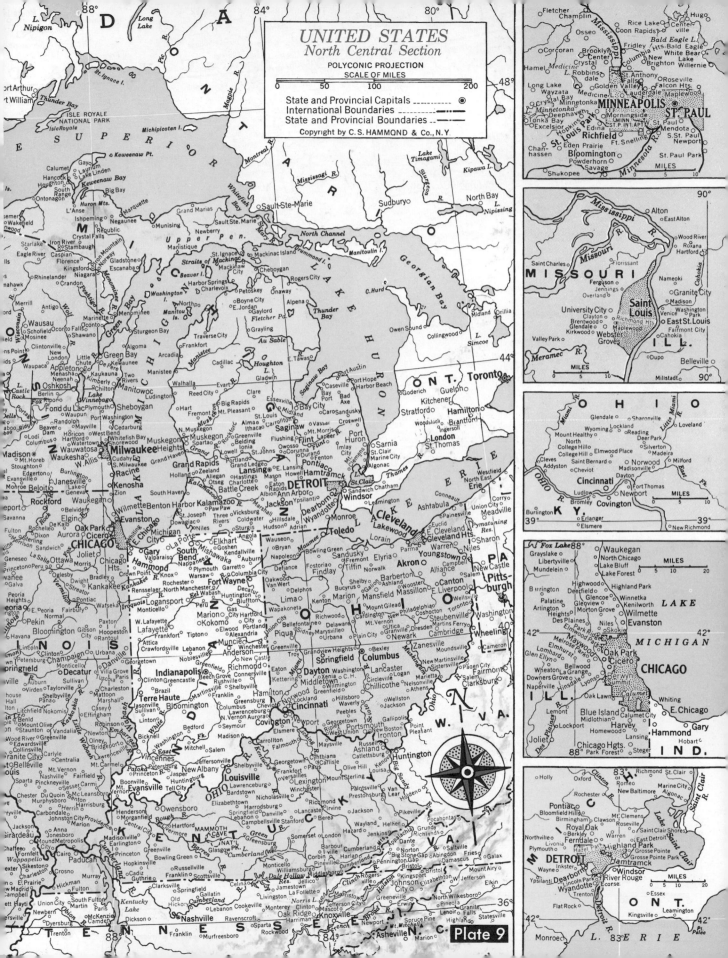

UNITED STATES
Western Section

POLYCONIC PROJECTION
SCALE OF MILES

0   50   100   200   300

State and Provincial Capitals
International Boundaries
State and Provincial Boundaries

Copyright by C.S. HAMMOND & Co., N.Y.

Plate 10

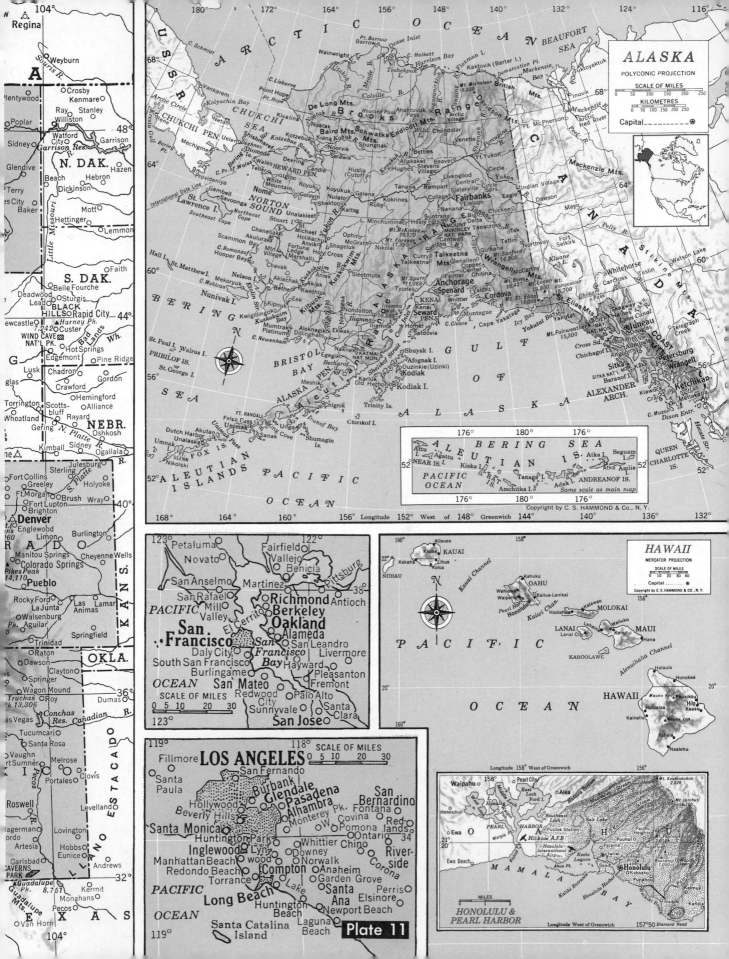

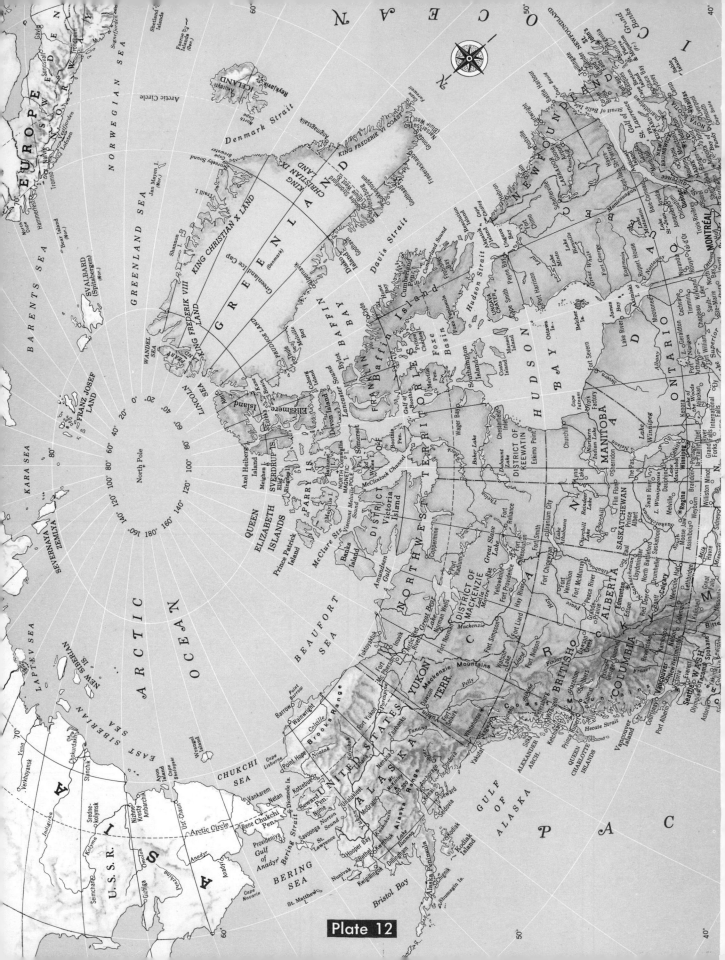

Plate 12

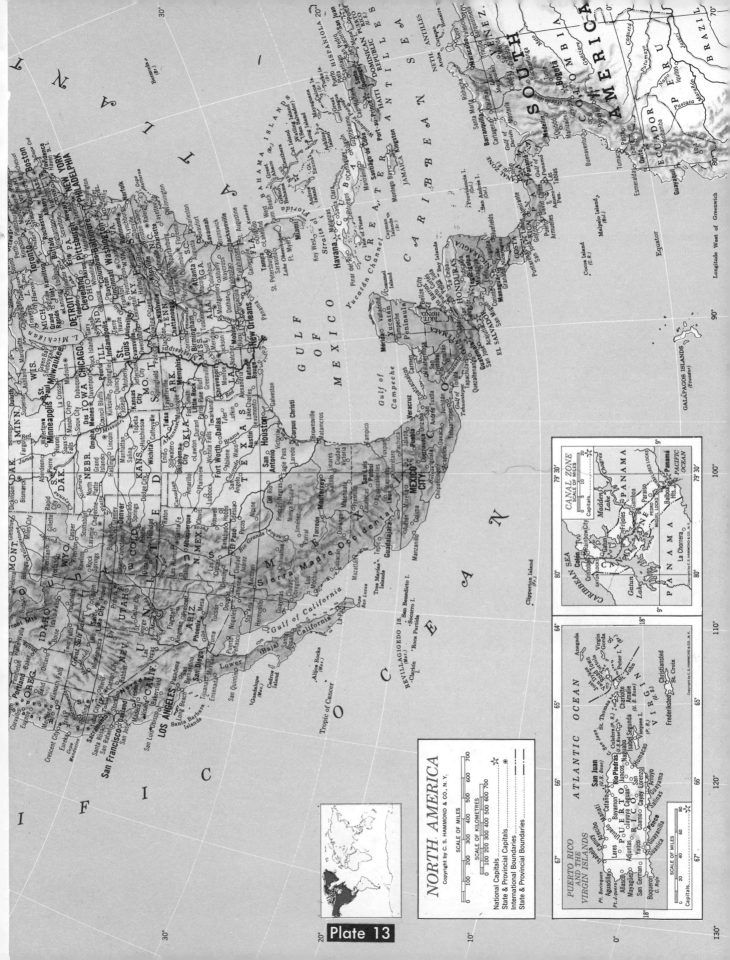

NORTH AMERICA

Copyright by C. S. HAMMOND & CO., N.Y.

SCALE OF MILES
100   200   300   400   500   600   700

SCALE OF KILOMETRES
100 200 300 400 500 600 700

National Capitals .... ★
State & Provincial Capitals .... ⊛
International Boundaries .... — · — · —
State & Provincial Boundaries .... — — —

CANAL ZONE

SCALE OF MILES
0   5   10   20

Capitals .... ★

CARIBBEAN SEA

PANAMA

PACIFIC OCEAN

Colón · Cristóbal · Gatún · Madden Lake · Gatún Lake · Frijoles · Gamboa · Balboa Hts. · Panamá · Paraíso · La Chorrera

Copyright by C. S. HAMMOND & CO., N.Y.

PUERTO RICO AND THE VIRGIN ISLANDS

SCALE OF MILES
20   40   60   80

Capitals .... ★

ATLANTIC OCEAN

San Juan · Río Piedras · PUERTO RICO · Ponce · Mayagüez

VIRGIN ISLANDS
St. Thomas · Charlotte Amalie · St. John · St. Croix · Christiansted · Frederiksted

Copyright by C. S. HAMMOND & CO., N.Y.

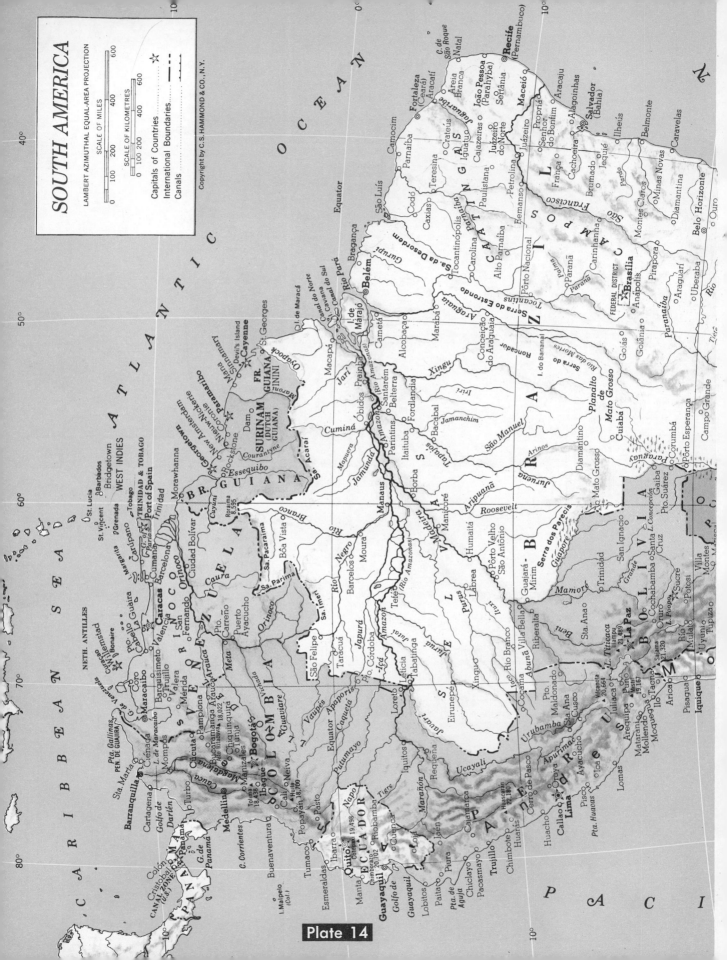

SOUTH AMERICA

LAMBERT AZIMUTHAL EQUAL-AREA PROJECTION

SCALE OF MILES

0 100 200 400 600

SCALE OF KILOMETRES

0 100 200 400 600

Capitals of Countries .... ⍟

International Boundaries .... —·—·—

Canals .... ⊨

Copyright by C. S. HAMMOND & CO., N.Y.

Plate 14

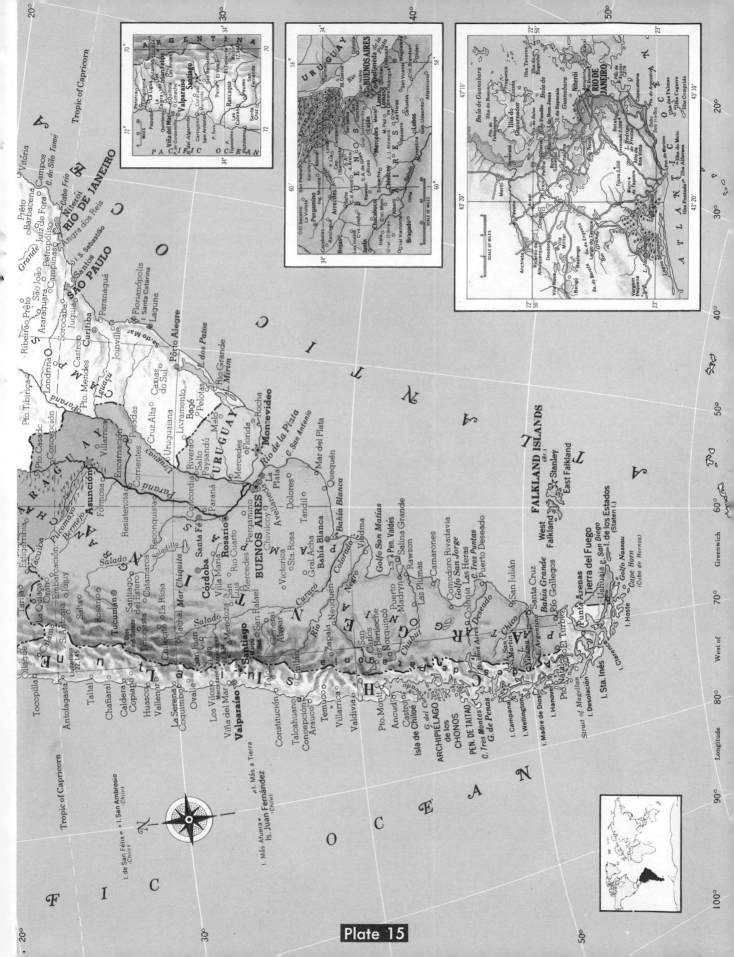

Plate 15

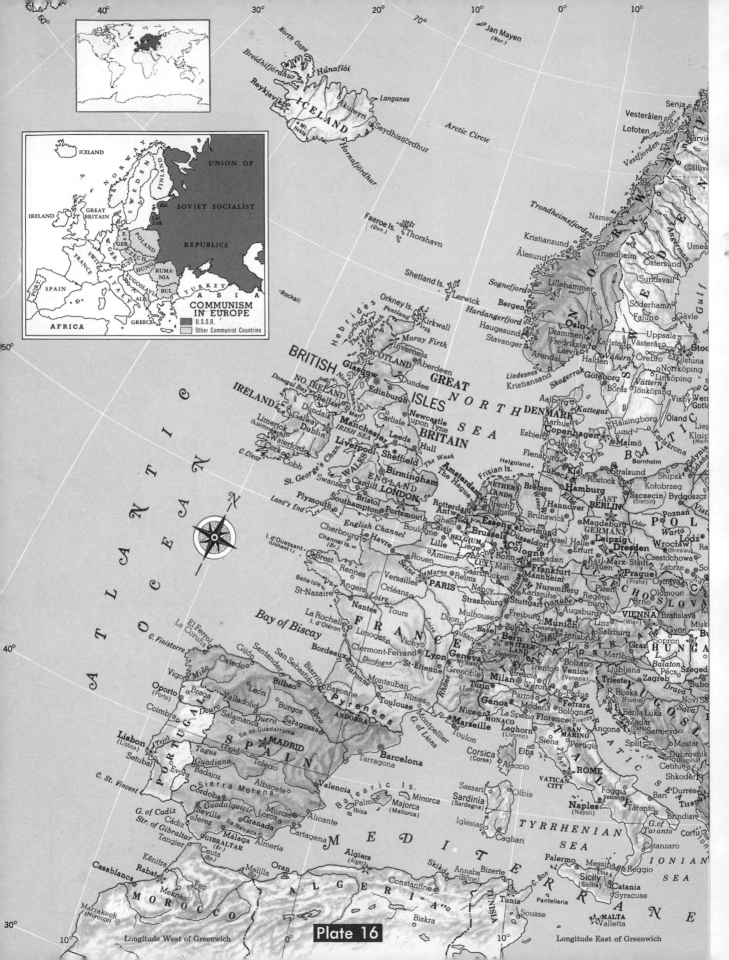

Plate 16

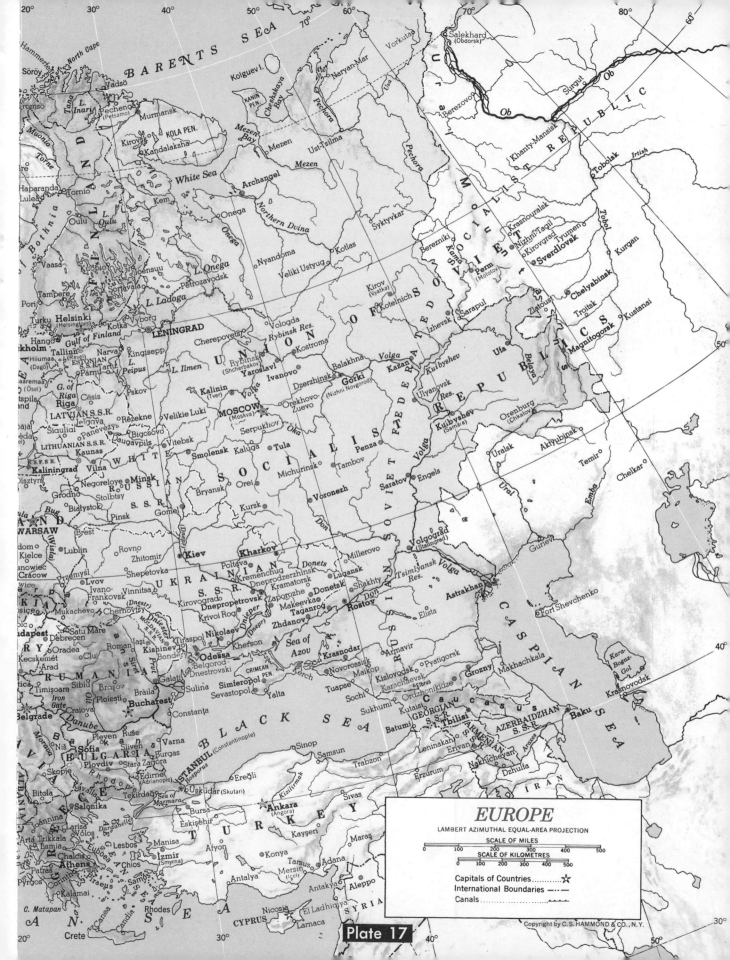

EUROPE
LAMBERT AZIMUTHAL EQUAL-AREA PROJECTION
SCALE OF MILES
0   100   200   300   400   500
SCALE OF KILOMETRES
0   100   200   300   400   500

Capitals of Countries............☆
International Boundaries.........-·-·-
Canals...................................

Copyright by C.S. HAMMOND & CO., N.Y.

Plate 17

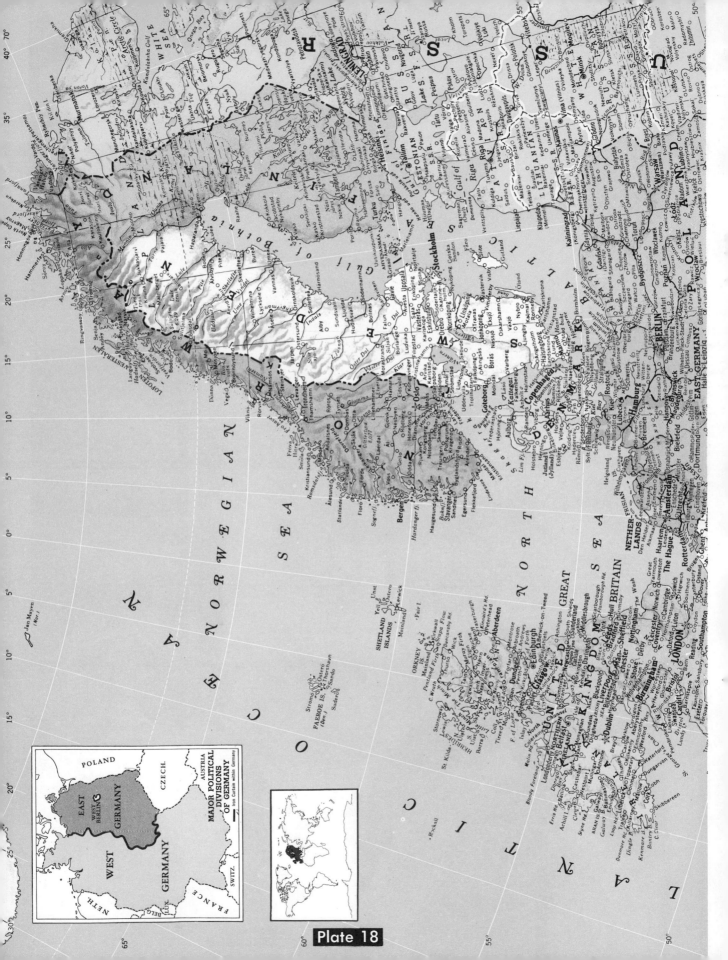

Plate 18

WESTERN and
CENTRAL EUROPE

CONIC PROJECTION

SCALE OF MILES

SCALE OF KILOMETRES

National Capitals
Administrative Centers
International Boundaries
Internal Boundaries
Canals

Copyright by C. S. HAMMOND & CO., N.Y.

Plate 19

BALKAN STATES

CONIC PROJECTION

SCALE OF MILES

0 25 50   100   150   200   250

SCALE OF KILOMETRES

0   60   120   180   240   300

Capitals of Countries _____⊛ Canals _____
International Boundaries _____

Plate 20

Copyright by C.S. HAMMOND & Co., N.Y.

16°   Longitude East of Greenwich   20°   24°   28°   2535

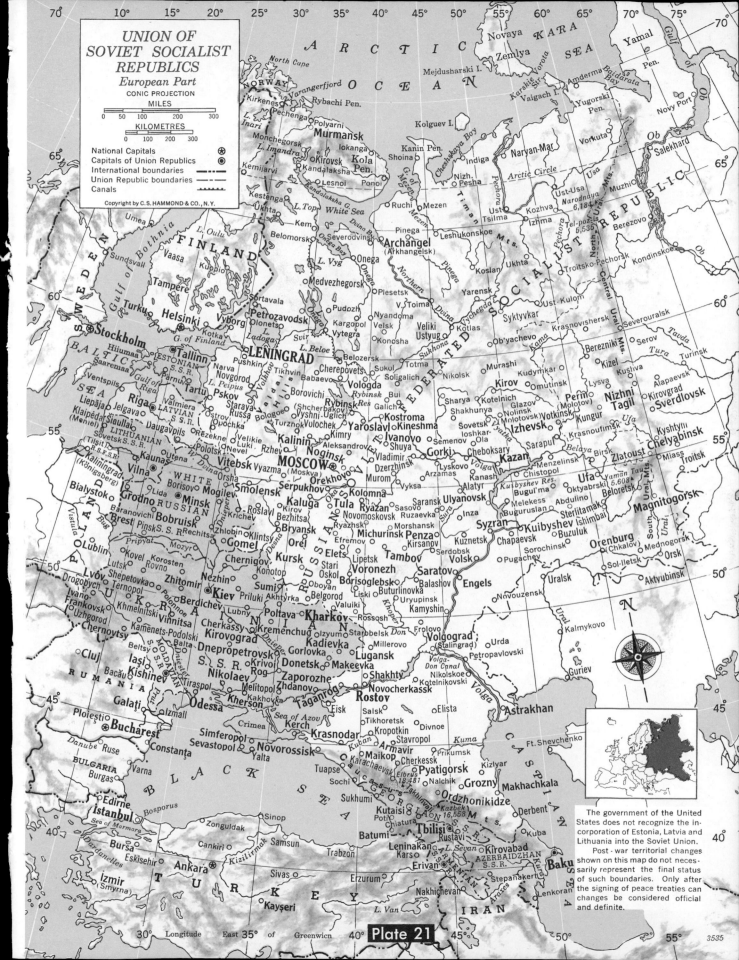

UNION OF SOVIET SOCIALIST REPUBLICS

European Part

CONIC PROJECTION

MILES

0 50 100 200 300

KILOMETRES

0 100 200 300

National Capitals ⊗
Capitals of Union Republics ◉
International boundaries —·—·—
Union Republic boundaries —·—·—
Canals ·······

Copyright by C.S. HAMMOND & CO., N.Y.

The government of the United States does not recognize the incorporation of Estonia, Latvia and Lithuania into the Soviet Union.

Post-war territorial changes shown on this map do not necessarily represent the final status of such boundaries. Only after the signing of peace treaties can changes be considered official and definite.

Plate 21

Longitude East 35° of Greenwich

3535

Plate 22

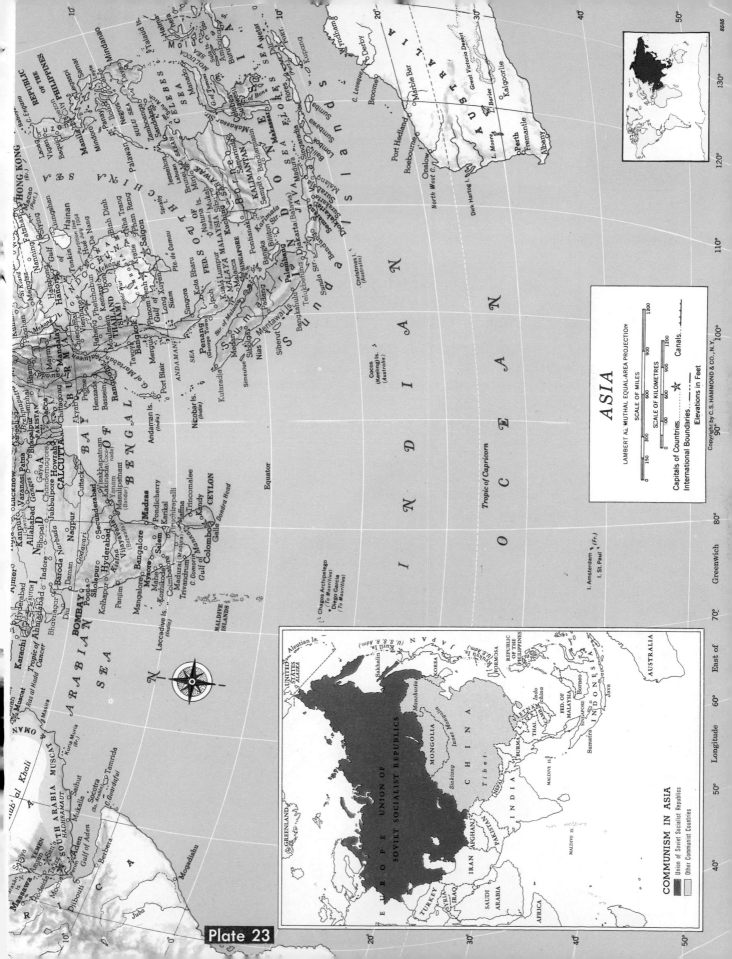

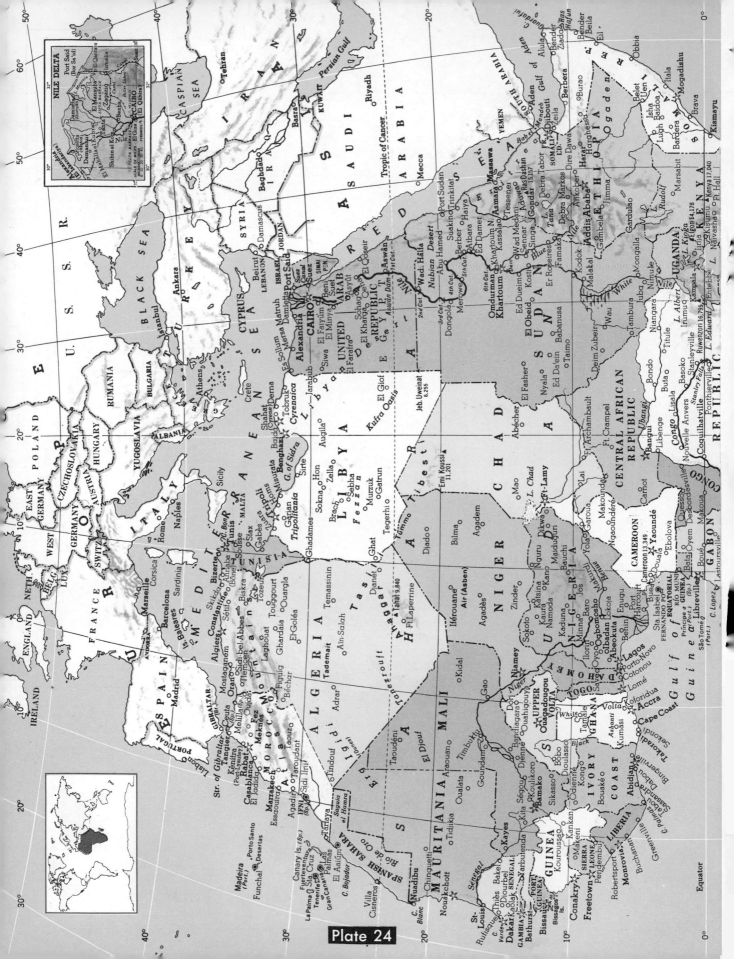

Plate 24

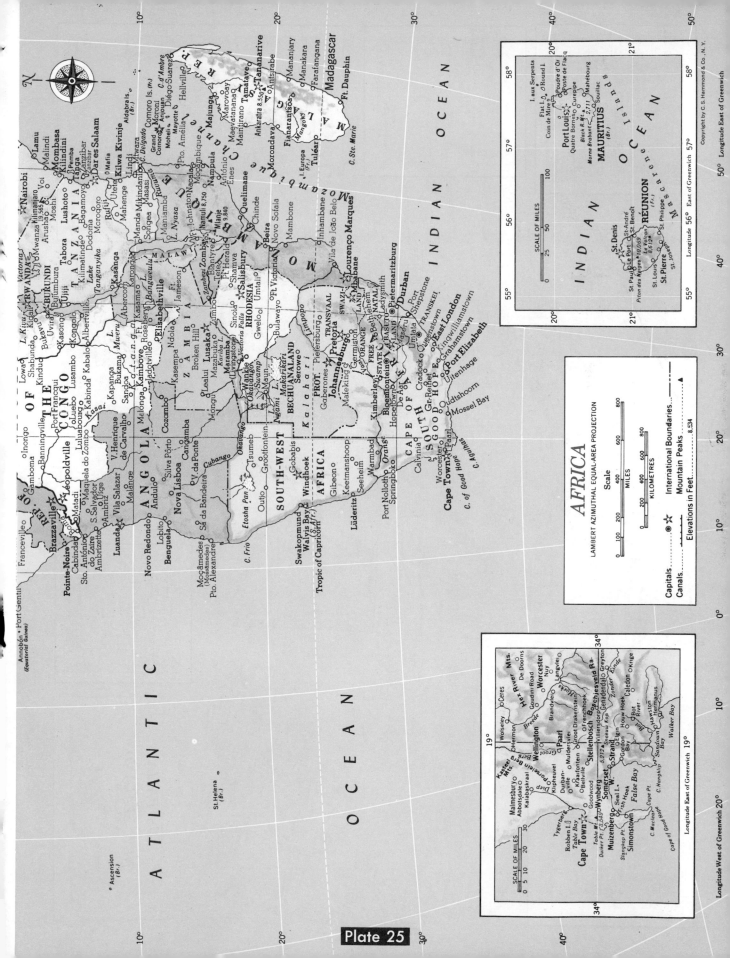

Plate 25

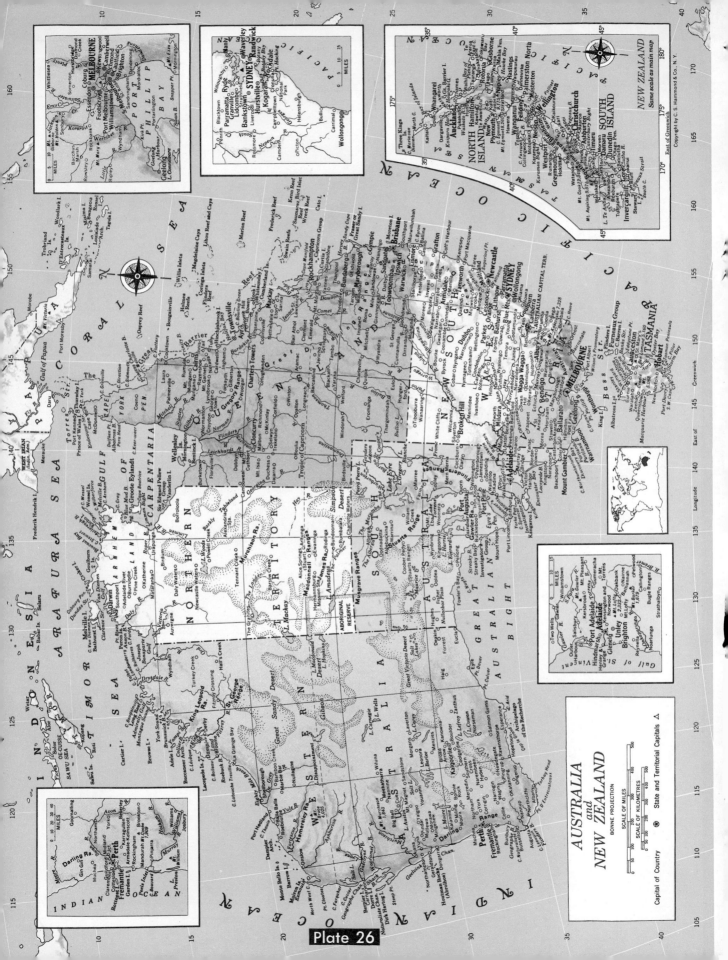

AUSTRALIA
and
NEW ZEALAND

BONNE PROJECTION

SCALE OF MILES

SCALE OF KILOMETRES

Capital of Country ⊛   State and Territorial Capitals ⩎

Plate 26

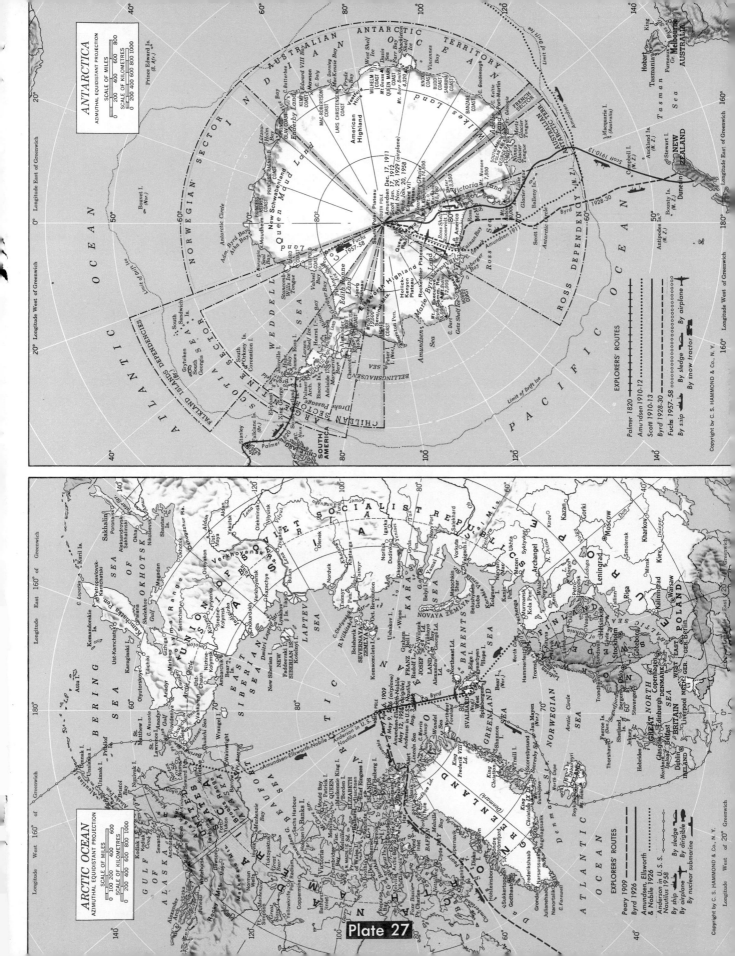

Plate 27

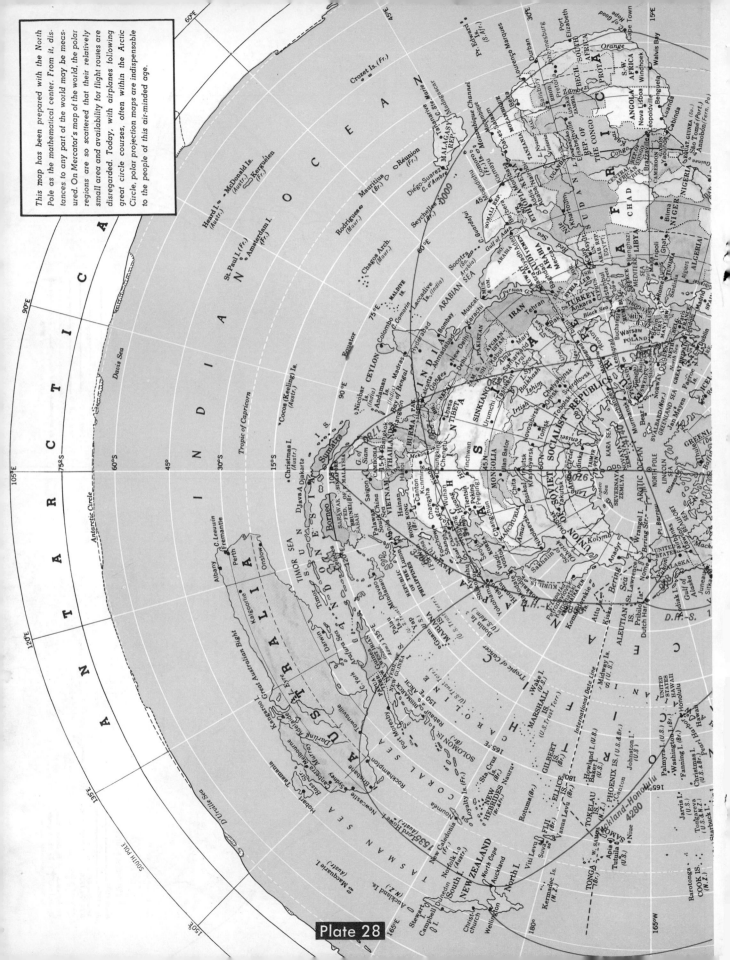

This map has been prepared with the North Pole as the mathematical center. From it, distances to any part of the world may be measured. On Mercator's map of the world, the polar regions are so scattered that their relatively small area and availability for flight routes are disregarded. Today, with airplanes following great circle courses, often within the Arctic Circle, polar projection maps are indispensable to the people of this air-minded age.

Plate 28

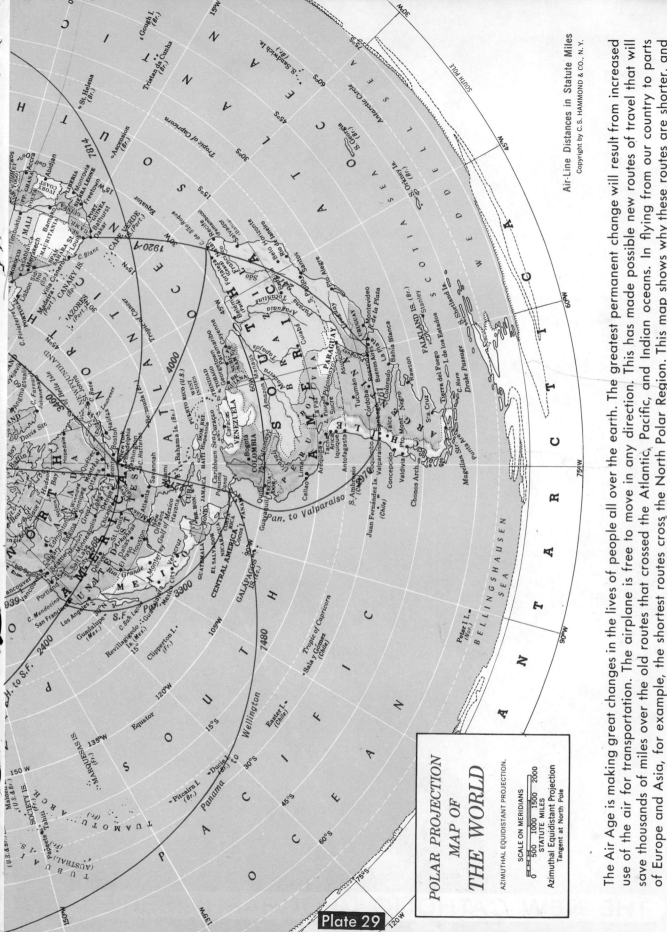

POLAR PROJECTION
MAP OF
THE WORLD

AZIMUTHAL EQUIDISTANT PROJECTION.

SCALE ON MERIDIANS
0   500   1000   1500   2000
STATUTE MILES
Azimuthal Equidistant Projection
Tangent at North Pole

Air-Line Distances in Statute Miles
Copyright by C.S. HAMMOND & CO., N.Y.

The Air Age is making great changes in the lives of people all over the earth. The greatest permanent change will result from increased use of the air for transportation. The airplane is free to move in any direction. This has made possible new routes of travel that will save thousands of miles over the old routes that crossed the Atlantic, Pacific, and Indian oceans. In flying from our country to parts of Europe and Asia, for example, the shortest routes cross the North Polar Region. This map shows why these routes are shorter, and so it is useful in mapping great circle routes. Any straight line drawn through the North Pole on this map projection represents a great circle route. A straight line drawn between two places on any other map projection would not indicate the shortest route.

Plate 29

THE NEW CATHOLIC GEOGRAPHY SERIES